Navigating the Internet with Your Macintosh®

Tamsin Douglas and Ned Snell

sams.net

201 West 103rd Street
Indianapolis, Indiana 46290

To Robert
—Tamsin Douglas

To Nancy, José, and Juan
—Ned Snell

FIRST EDITION

International Standard Book Number: 1-57521-043-6

Library of Congress Catalog Card Number: 95-07045

98 97 96 95 4 3 2 1

Interpretation of the printing code: the rightmost double-digit number is the year of the book's printing; the rightmost single-digit, the number of the book's printing. For example, a printing code of 95-1 shows that the first printing of the book occurred in 1995.

Composed in AGaramond and MCPdigital by Macmillan Computer Publishing

Printed in the United States of America

President, Sams Publishing *Richard K. Swadley*

Publisher, Sams.net Publishing *George Bond*

Managing Editor *Cindy Morrow*

Marketing Manager *John Pierce*

Publishing Manager
Mark Taber

Development Editors
Angelique Brittingham
Fran Hatton

Production Editors
James Grass
Alice Martina Smith

Technical Reviewers
Angela Allen
Joern Wettern, Ph.D

Editorial Coordinator
Bill Whitmer

Technical Edit Coordinator
Lynette Quinn

Formatter
Frank Sinclair

Editorial Assistant
Carol Ackerman

Cover Designer
Tim Amrhein

Book Designer
Alyssa Yesh

Production Team Supervisor
Brad Chinn

Page Layout
Mary Ann Abramson, Charlotte Clapp, Terrie Deemer, Louisa Klucznik, Ayanna Lacey, Steph Mineart, Casey Price, Andrew Stone, Tina Trettin, Susan Van Ness, Mark Walchle

Proofreading
Georgiana Briggs, Michael Brumitt, Donna Martin, Nancy C. Price, Brian-Kent Proffitt, SA Springer

Indexer
Greg Eldred

Overview

Contents

Acknowledgments

My deepest thanks to those who guided, corrected, nurtured, and otherwise uplifted this book:

Angela Allen

Angelique Brittingham

Fran Hatton

James Grass

Alice Martina Smith

Mark Taber

Joern Wettern

— *Ned Snell*

To Mark Taber, my editor at Sams, for being so professional, encouraging and promptly answering ALL my e-mail. Thanks.

And to Robert, my very best friend and husband, for all his moral support and for sharing his Macintosh know-how. And for stepping in and saving the MacTCP chapter and my sanity. Without you I couldn't have done it. Thanks Sweetie!

—*Tamsin Douglas*

About the Authors

Tamsin Douglas is an author and journalist who recently relocated with her husband, Robert Macfarlane, to Bermuda. Originally from Toronto, she graduated from Montreal's McGill University in 1988 with a degree in Anthropology. Before moving to Bermuda from Montreal, she co-authored a best-selling guide book, *The Guide to Ethnic Montreal*, and worked as a journalist—including a stint as a restaurant reviewer for the local cultural weekly paper, *The Mirror.* While at the paper, she was also the system administrator for the Mirror's online service, Babylon. She now works for Internet (Bermuda) Limited, the first Internet provider on the island, doing customer support, web authoring, and media relations.

Ned Snell is an award-winning computer journalist and author. Ten years ago, after a brief career as a teacher, Snell entered the software industry as a documentation and training specialist for several of the world's largest software companies. He then moved into the computer trade magazine business, where he served as staff writer and eventually as editor for several national publications.

Introduction

The goal of this book is simple: To show you how to use all of the Internet from a Macintosh running System 7 or above.

Realizing that goal involves not only navigating the ins and outs of "the Net" (as you are henceforth authorized to call it), but also revealing the ways Macintosh software supports that journey. As you move along, you'll see that the job is by no means a snap—if it were, why would there be so many books about it? You'll also see that a little time spent getting properly set up, a little more time learning your way around, and a little patience will return lifetime rewards in the form of the world's largest library, most current newspaper, and most stimulating conversations.

As a Macintosh-based user, you are set to take full advantage of the Internet using the Mac's superior graphical interface which makes navigating the Net that much easier. Pity the poor dino-DOS user who must crawl along the Info Highway, one typed-in command at a time (if they can remember them in the first place). With a Mac, you can easily click your way through cyberspace and you'll find it's not much more difficult than learning a new program.

The '70s—Incubation

In the early 1970s, the embryo of what we now call the Internet was little more than a national network of computers in government offices, defense companies, and a few universities. The network was designed not so much to share information as to test various cold-war scenarios for protecting defense computing in time of war. If the nation's strategic computing resources were spread around the country, the experiment posited, and linked by a wide-area network that could reroute itself around any computer that went dead, no single attack could bring down the whole defense network.

By the end of the '70s, this network had evolved into a valuable system for sharing information; it was eventually accepted into the fold of other computers and other networks in non-defense government offices, universities, and research institutions. Any computer system that could run the networking protocol called TCP/IP—the fundamental glue that holds the Internet together—was technically equipped to hook into the network. Many did and took advantage of the growing *internetwork* (a network of networks) to exchange e-mail with one another and conduct research by tapping into each other's databases.

During the same years, companies like Apple were already building the first real personal computers.

The '80s—An Active Childhood

By the early 1980s, the IBM PC had made its debut. Bill Gates was already getting rich off the royalties from DOS, the operating system his fledging company, Microsoft, had purchased from another company and licensed to IBM to provide the new PC with an easy-to-use operating system.

In 1984, Apple fired back with the first Macintosh. The Mac was designed from scratch to use a revolutionary graphical, point-and-click interface. It was hailed as a major innovation in computing, although most of the basic ideas were conceived by researchers at Xerox's PARC facility. Apple's innovation was to bring these ideas to the marketplace in the first cute Macintosh, containing a whopping 128KB of RAM (that's 1/8th of a megabyte.)

Macs started connecting to the Internet in 1987, when Apple introduced MacTCP. This little software widget provided two important additions to the Macintosh operating system: the ability to connect to IP networks, like the Internet, and a common interface for programmers to write Internet applications on the Macintosh. That meant that users could be assured that any Internet application would run on their Mac with MacTCP. In the IBM-compatible world, by contrast, there were several implementations of TCP/IP on DOS, and applications had to be written to one of the competing "standards." Applications were written to one of these competing interfaces, and would not run on the others. It was several years before an equivalent standard, WinSock, was introduced for Microsoft Windows 3.1.

Also in the '80s, the CompuServe online information service grew to more than 1 million users. By the close of the '80s, Prodigy debuted—the first online service successfully marketed to computer novices and home users (they sold it through *Sears*, for crying out loud). At the time, there was little public awareness of anything called "the Internet." But the potential of online communication—especially in the areas of e-mail, news retrieval, and file downloading—was beginning to enter the public consciousness, especially among personal computer users. The emergence of local area networks in corporate settings also contributed to personal computer users' awareness of online communication and its potential.

The emerging Internet continued to expand using gateways and links into other, preexisting networks in the U.S. and abroad. In the 1980s, much of that internetwork fell under the auspices of the U.S. government's National Science Foundation (NSF), which set acceptable use policies that still influence the Internet today. Even then, the complete internetwork was never controlled by any single organization or government. (It remains uncontrolled to this day.)

Already the largest internetwork in the world, the Internet remained the somewhat complicated province of engineers, scientists, professors, and the few "hackers" who found their way in. News stories about computer crime—and Clifford Stoll's best-selling book *The Cuckoo's Egg* (which detailed his discovery of a German spy who stole U.S. defense secrets through the Internet)—revealed to many that some sort of global computing network existed. But again, it was widely perceived as an expert's tool—regular folks fiddled around in Prodigy. After all, fooling around with the big network could lead to "global thermonuclear war," as the 1983 film *Wargames* suggested.

The '90s—Explosion!

In 1991, Gopher was developed at the University of Minnesota. Gopher enabled users to access many Internet resources from simple, consistent menus. They introduced a graphical Gopher client, TurboGopher for the Macintosh. This was a giant leap forward in making the Internet easier to navigate. By 1993, graphical software for browsing the World Wide Web had emerged, most notably Mosaic. (See Figure IN.1.) Internet users could at last point-and-click their way around the Internet (although not all of the Internet) using computing skills they already understood. Communications companies with their own dedicated Internet access began selling dial-up subscriptions through which individuals could operate their own software to access resources on the Internet—the popular "dial-up IP" Internet account.

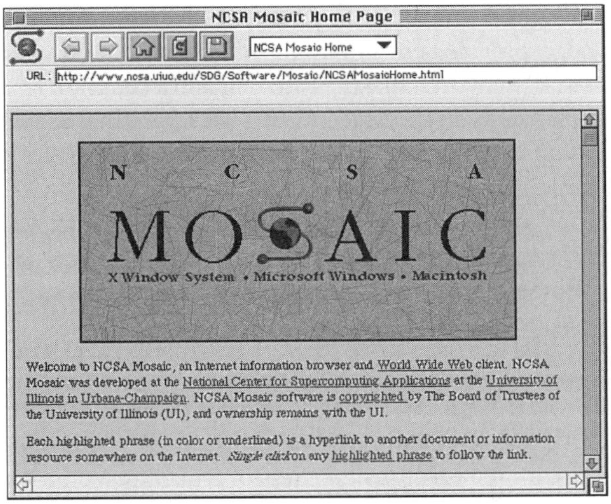

FIGURE IN.1.
Mosaic, the application that redefined the Internet's look, feel, and population.

Graphical Web browsers like Mosaic brought the look and feel of the Macintosh graphical-user-interface to the Internet.

The same logic brought about the introduction of America Online, which included (actually, required) a graphical interface (initially the GEOS interface, and later Mac or Windows) and made online communication graphical and friendly. A fast success, America Online prompted CompuServe to play catch-up by introducing its own, now popular, graphical front-end, CompuServe Information Manager. Online services such as America Online and CompuServe were designed primarily for Windows users first. It wasn't until 1994 that Mac users got their own piece of the online action with Apple's eWorld. Based on the same interface as America Online, Apple has smoothed out some of the wrinkles and turned it into an environment entirely comfortable for mouse-oriented Mac users.

Once the online world became friendlier toward graphic-based users, like those on a Macintosh, it spurred on a lot of people who had once demurred to get connected. Soon, the slick graphics and easy navigation offered by Web browsers caught the attention of the mass media, and a series of consumer-oriented print and TV stories about the wonders of the Internet began. That series continues unabated.

The emergence of solid Macintosh Internet software, plus the not-altogether-truthful marketing of the online services as gateways to the Internet (see Chapter 1, "The Basics: What's Involved in Setting Up and Going Online?"), finally cemented the Internet in the public consciousness.

Who this Book Is For

By design, this book is written for people who:

- Have at least some experience using a Macintosh computer
- Have little or no experience with the Internet—but want some
- Use System 7 or 7.5—or plan to

This book won't make you an "Internet guru"—If you're like most people, you don't need to be one. All most people need—or want, in fact—is sufficient information to set up for the Internet, connect to it, navigate all the way to the farthest corners of it, and look up new sites and sights. That's what this book offers. It contains more than you'll find in a typical "dummies" or "idiot's" title (these kinds of books get you started but leave you a little under-equipped for the full Internet). This book offers less information, however, than titles that teach you how to configure your own UNIX Internet servers, give you a blow-by-blow description of each event in the history of the Internet, and tell you the names, addresses, and hobbies of all the programmers behind what you see online.

This book provides detailed information about the Internet, about setting up a Mac for the Internet, and about using Macintosh-based Internet applications. If you're completely new to the Mac, you may want to learn a little about that environment before moving on to this book and the Internet beyond. If you already have some Internet experience, this book will show you the particulars of using Macintosh applications for Internet navigation.

Finally, this book concentrates on using an individual dial-up IP connection to the Internet (as described in Chapter 1) because dial-up IP connections offer the most complete and most powerful Internet access for Mac users today.

Except for some of the setup instructions, however, most of what you find in this book also applies to TCP/IP Internet connections made through a corporate local-area network (LAN). If your LAN administrator sets you up for such an account, you'll find that virtually everything in this book (except for portions of Chapter 3, "Configuring Your Macintosh for the Internet") works as described. As for Chapter 3, LAN users can benefit by reading it anyway, because it contains useful information about how the Macintosh and the Internet work together. But LAN users don't have to perform the configuration steps in Chapter 3; instead, ask your LAN administrator to set you up and supply you with instructions for connecting to the Internet. Then begin navigating with Chapter 4, "An Introduction to Internet Tools and Resources."

You can also access Internet resources through online services such as the eWorld or America Online. If you haven't decided how you plan to get to the Internet, this book will help you choose. In particular, Chapter 2, "One-Stop Shopping: Apple's eWorld," gives an overview of the Internet options offered through eWorld.

What If I'm Still Using System 6?

If you're not yet using System 7 or 7.5, you'll find that most of the information in this book still applies to you. But you will have to replace the newer versions of software supplied with this book with older versions.

Don't get your knickers in a twist quite yet. It's not all that difficult. We did supply you with a program, called Fetch, which is compatible with System 6.0.7. You can use Fetch to go out onto the Net and collect all the software you need. You can read how to do this in Chapter 12, "Collecting Files with FTP." In addition, Appendix B, "The Internet for System 6 Users," at the back of this book, tells you where to find the older versions of the software you'll need.

Chapter 3 covers setting up your Mac to access the Internet. MacTCP and MacPPP, the software that you use to connect to the Internet, both work fine with System 6.

You can use this book effectively to learn how to navigate the Internet with System 6.

How Is this Book Organized?

This book is divided into four parts:

- The chapters in Part I, "Getting Set Up," provide a complete overview of configuring your Mac to drive on the Information Highway, as well as the basics of setting up an Internet account, and the option of using Apple's online service eWorld as an Internet provider.
- The chapters in Part II, "Communicating and Getting Around," cover each type of Internet tool and resource in detail. Part II begins with three introductory chapters that provide an overview of Internet resources, instructions for selecting and acquiring Internet software (including free software and shareware provided with this book), and a tutorial in Internet customs and manners—all to get you off to a good start. The remaining eight chapters cover each of the major Internet tools in detail.
- The chapters in Part III, "Finding People, Places, and Other Resources," show various techniques for tracking down specific information on the Internet. You'll need these techniques when you try to locate information about a particular subject from among the vast, varied resources on the Internet.
- The chapters in Part IV, "Putting It Together," offer an overview of three important uses for your Internet navigation skills: office tasks, education, and fun. Each chapter concludes with a directory of valuable starting places and Internet sites to check out.

At the back of this book, you can find a complete Index for reference.

PART I

GETTING SET-UP

CHAPTER 1

THE BASICS: WHAT'S INVOLVED IN SETTING UP AND GOING ONLINE?

First Questions

Online Services Versus IP Accounts

Establishing an Account with an Online Service

Establishing an Account with an Internet Provider

Summary

For many *newbies*, as Internet novices are known, the hardest part about the Internet isn't getting around, it's *getting there*. Such basic questions as "What do I need?," "Where do I start?," and "How do I choose?" can freeze folks up before they even begin. By asking yourself these questions before you embark on choosing an Internet provider, you'll be better equipped to make an informed choice about what type of Internet access you want.

This chapter explains the basic ways people access the Internet; it also shows you what you need to support the access method you choose. Near the close of the chapter, you find out how to locate and sign up with an Internet access provider.

First Questions

By first considering how and why you plan to go online, you can make more informed choices about the type of Internet access you need and the software you require. This information can help you determine the type of Internet *account* (a subscription with a company that provides access to the Internet) you need, or whether you might do better by signing up with a commercial *online service*, such as America Online. Questions to ask yourself are covered in the following sections.

What Do I Want from the Internet?

What is inspiring you to become an Internet user in the first place? Is it because you need to exchange e-mail messages or perform research? Do you already know of a specific Internet resource you need, or are you simply interested in "surfing" the Net?

Following is a list of the basic types of resources available through the Internet. Each of these is described in Chapter 4, "An Introduction to Internet Tools and Resources," and detailed in subsequent chapters. Consider carefully which may be most valuable to you. Note that, in most cases, you'll need a special program, called a *client program*, to use each of these resources.

- **E-mail**—Exchange personal messages with others
- **Mailing lists**—Receive automatic deliveries of e-mail and news about a given topic from a wider range of people
- **Newsgroups**—Find and exchange messages and news about a given topic
- **The World Wide Web**—Jump dynamically among a wide array of Internet activities and information sources; most effective when used through a software program called a graphical *Web browser*
- **Telnet**—Connect to and use remote computer systems in universities, government offices, and corporations
- **FTP**—Copy to your Mac (download) files containing research information, software, and more
- **Gopher**—Find information easily through menus
- **Interactive communication**—Converse "live" with other users

Tip

If all you want is Internet e-mail, you don't need a full-fledged Internet account. You can send and receive Internet e-mail from the regular accounts provided by the online services such as eWorld (no special Internet options required). You can also subscribe to "e-mail only" accounts offered by many Internet access providers. These accounts offer Internet e-mail—and nothing else—for a very reasonable rate, typically $10 per month or less.

Is the Internet Enough?

Sounds like a silly question because popular wisdom holds that *everything* is on the Internet. But in truth, the commercial online services like America Online and eWorld do offer personal financial services, databases of magazine and newspaper articles, or other services that don't yet exist on the Net in any useful form. Finding and downloading files and performing other tasks may also be significantly easier than it is on the Net.

You owe it to yourself to investigate what the commercial online services offer—and don't offer—before assuming that a regular Internet account is for you. See "Online Services Versus Internet Accounts," later in this chapter.

How Much Time Will I Spend Online and How Much Money Do I *Want* To Spend?

This is a tricky one. Among the online services and the various Internet access providers, there are as many pricing plans as there are ways to cut a dollar. A realistic assessment of the time you expect to spend online, or the limits of your budget, can help you choose.

The most common pricing scenario is a basic, minimum monthly fee for which you get a certain number of hours online; additional hours are billed at a per-hour rate. For example, a typical dial-up Internet account may cost $20 a month, for which you get up to 100 hours online. Any hours in addition to 100 in the same month may be billed at $2 per hour. However, some providers may charge higher monthly rates for unlimited use; others may offer "startup" accounts at a low rate ($10 to $15) for 15 to 20 hours a month of online usage.

The online services have their own spin on this in that they may charge different rates for different services. For example, CompuServe has a selected group of activities included in its basic $9.95 monthly fee. But many of the more exciting features in CompuServe are called "extended" services and cost $4.80 per hour on top of the regular CompuServe rate. At this writing, some of the other major online services—America Online and Prodigy—charge extra, in one way or another, for access to Internet resources. (Note that eWorld does not charge extra for access to Internet services.) CompuServe offers three hours of Internet access free to those who pay $9.95 a month for a regular CompuServe account, and charges an extra $15 per month (in addition to the $9.95) for an account allowing up to 20 hours of Internet access per month.

Note

> If you're considering using the Internet through an online service, check with the services about their current Internet capabilities and pricing options. The services are changing rapidly at this writing, so options and prices may have changed by the time you read this.

Is There an Internet Provider in my Local Calling Area?

Whether you use an online service or a dial-up Internet provider, you are on the phone every minute you're online. The last thing you want to do is add long-distance phone charges to your regular online fees.

Unfortunately, not every local calling area in the U.S. is served by a dial-up Internet provider. At this writing, you're more likely to find a local number for accessing CompuServe, America Online, or eWorld than for an Internet provider—although, anywhere near a major city, you're likely to find local numbers for all three online services and a few Internet providers. Still, if your local calling area is served by online services alone, you may find that the combined cost of a regular Internet account and the long-distance charges make an online service preferable.

Some Internet providers have toll-free (800) numbers, but that's not a solution. They all charge extra for 800-number access.

Online Services Versus IP Accounts

So why not just use an online service as your "Internet gateway"? That used to be an easier question than it is today. Until very recently, the Internet access provided by the online services was severely limited, in comparison to a regular *IP account* (a type of Internet account that offers access to all types of Internet resources through a modem connection). Most significantly, the online services did not support graphical browsing of the World Wide Web, which today is the most exciting and most popular Internet resource of all. (See Chapter 10, "Browsing the World Wide Web.")

At this writing, Prodigy, America Online, CompuServe, and eWorld have all delivered their own graphical *Web browsers*, the software required for browsing the World Wide Web. All three browsers offered by the online services are derivatives of established, popular Web browsers; although they differ, any one of them will serve you well. By now, you should be able to use any Internet resource—including most of those listed at the beginning of this chapter—from any of the four major online services. But not yet.

So—other than cost, on what basis do you choose between online services and regular Internet accounts? Following are lists of the pros and cons of online services as Internet gateways.

Pros: Online Services...

- Are easier to set up and use than IP accounts. The service provider supplies a single software package that dials the online service and leads you through the process of supplying billing information, passwords, and so on. Once you sign up, most activities work the same as any other—and all work from the same interface (except for Web browsing). Users new to online communication always find the online services easier, at first, than straight-up Internet.
- Have many local access numbers all over the United States, Canada, and in other countries as well. Not only do online services improve your chances of finding a local access number, they also make using the service while traveling or after a move simpler—you simply look up the local access number for wherever you are. When I moved from Indiana to New Jersey, I had to find and sign up with a new Internet provider; my old provider had access numbers only in Indiana, so I had to sign up with a New Jersey-based Internet provider. I also have a CompuServe account. After I moved, I simply dialed one of CompuServe's New Jersey numbers to use the service, instead of the Indiana number I used to use.
- Are run by big, well-established companies and have millions of subscribers. Your local Internet access company may have only hundreds of subscribers and may have been founded last month. Although I'm never one to assume that it's better to do business with big companies than with small ones, consider the fact that small, local Internet providers come and go and may not have the resources to effectively deal with rising numbers of subscribers, equipment failures, and other problems without interrupting service. AOL, Prodigy, CompuServe, and eWorld are well-established.
- Offer good online or telephone support. Local Internet providers may also offer support but many don't have the experience of online services in dealing with the problems of newbies. Your chances of getting effective support, at first, are much better with a major online service. As you become more experienced, you may find the commercial services *less* helpful because your knowledge of the Internet may begin to exceed theirs.

Cons: Online Services...

- Are inflexible and don't let you choose the type of software you want to use. You have to access e-mail, newsgroups, and other Internet resources through *their* interface, and you have to use *their* Web browser. If you don't like it, tough. Dial-up IP accounts require you to choose and set up your own software, but then again, *you* get to choose and you can change if and when something better comes along.
- May have complex pricing structures. Dial-up accounts have very simple pricing structures; fees at the online services can be unfathomable—this much per month, this much extra for these services, an extra 30 cents for Internet e-mail messages, an extra fee for hours over the first five per month, a $2 surcharge during a full moon....

- May force you to wait for access to new kinds of services. When you have an IP account and a new Internet resource emerges that requires special client software, you can get the software and use the new service. When you are in the control of an online service, you must wait until the service offers support for the resource. The Internet is changing rapidly these days; it's nice to be able to stay on top of the wave.

It's important to note, however, that the accounts offered through online services work more like regular IP accounts every year. Within a few years, it's likely that there will be no functional difference between the two. When that happens, it will be time to reevaluate the situation.

Establishing an Account with an Online Service

Establishing an account with an online service provider is a simple matter of calling 'em up. They do the rest. They usually mail you a disk containing their software or give you instructions for dialing the service and downloading any necessary software. CompuServe, AOL, and eWorld also offer "free-trial" disks bundled with magazines, modems, and new Macs.

You don't even have to make a phone call to sign up for eWorld, if you just bought a new Macintosh. Its software ships with new Macs, and includes a pamphlet explaining how to install the software and access eWorld. For more about eWorld, see Chapter 2, "One-Stop Shopping: Apple's eWorld."

Establishing an Account with an Internet Provider

To establish an account with a dial-up Internet access provider, you must first know what type of account you want. The typical types of dial-up accounts offered are as follows:

- **E-mail only**—Cheap access to nothing but e-mail.
- **Shell accounts**—Text-only accounts for which most of the Internet software runs on the service provider's computer, not yours. These accounts are affordable but don't enable you to choose and run your own client software—and you can't use a graphical Web browser through them. That's a waste of a Macintosh.
- **IP accounts**—Available in two types (SLIP and PPP), these accounts offer a true Internet connection and the ability to install and use whatever client software you like. A dial-up IP account is required for using a graphical Web browser, which is one of the best ways to use the Internet today.

Because of their flexibility, ability to support Macintosh client software, and relative affordability, dial-up IP accounts are the best choice for navigating the Internet with your Mac. Most of the navigation techniques shown in this book—and all the software referred to and shown in the figures—require IP accounts.

Of the two IP account types—SLIP and PPP—PPP is preferable because it connects you to the Internet more quickly and because it's easier to set up, configure, and use. If the only account provider you can find supports just SLIP, that's okay. SLIP works with all the same client software as does PPP. SLIP, however, is a different can of worms than PPP when it comes to setting it up.

Locating an Access Provider for an IP Account

There are several ways to track down an access provider:

- Consult the list of Internet providers in the Appendix of this book.
- Ask the computer specialist at your company or university, if you have access. Many educational institutions and corporations offer net access to their students and employees.
- Look for an ad in a local computer newsletter.
- Watch for local newspaper stories about the Internet, or look up the last one at your local library. These articles often feature sidebars that list local providers.
- Stop at a local computer store and ask whether they know any providers.
- Check the Yellow Pages under *E-mail*, *Computers*, or *Communications*.

When comparing the providers in your local calling area, consider the following points:

- Pricing plans
- Software provided
- Support
- Whether PPP is offered or only SLIP

Finding a Net Provider On the Net

Of course, it's easier to find a provider if you're already on the Internet.

Just after I moved from Indiana to New Jersey, I dialed up my old Indiana Internet account (at night, when long-distance rates are low) and searched the World Wide Web (see Chapter 18, "Finding It on the Web") for the term *access providers*. That search led me to a Web page that enabled me to zero in on the names, numbers, and offerings of local providers from among a database of providers all over the world. Some providers have Web pages that enable you to sign up for an account straight from the Web.

If you're *really* stuck for a provider, consider signing up with an online service that supports Web browsing. Then you can do what I did. If you find a provider you like, quit the online service. If not, keep the online service until a good local provider shows up.

In fact, you may be able to conduct your Web search, find your access provider, and quit the service all within the free trial period most online services offer. (But *I* did not tell you that!)

Signing Up with an Access Provider

To sign up for your account, call the provider's sales line. (As a new Internet user, steer clear of providers who require you to use an online sign-up routine and won't sign you up over the telephone. These providers are obviously not equipped for helping newbies.)

The access provider usually mails you a floppy disk containing the required networking software for establishing a connection to the Internet, plus client software for most Internet resources. A good provider will preconfigure the software with necessary phone numbers, server addresses, and other information; others include instructions for configuring the software yourself. Note that you can use the software sent to you only to get started; after you gain some experience, you can easily replace the software with something you like better.

Be sure that the access provider gives you the following information. You need this information to configure your client software. (Don't worry about what all this means; you learn what to do with this information in Chapter 3, "Configuring Your Macintosh for the Internet.")

- Your username and password (you may be allowed to select these)
- Your complete e-mail address
- Your Internet IP address, unless the provider's server assigns IP addresses dynamically
- The domain name of the provider's Internet server
- The addresses of the provider's news server (NNTP) and mail (SMTP) server
- The address of the name server (DNS)
- The telephone number (or numbers) for dialing up the server and connecting to the Internet

Also make sure that you learn the telephone number (or numbers) and e-mail addresses for technical support.

After your account has been established by your provider, you must install TCP/IP and SLIP or PPP support on your Macintosh, as described in Chapter 3. Then you use configuration screens to install your client software and configure it by supplying basic account information (your e-mail address, your provider's server address, and so on). Although this may sound a little daunting, the whole process should take less than an hour. And when you're done, you're ready to rock and roll.

Summary

You have some choices to make before you can embark on an appropriate Internet strategy. Making the right choices from the start can save you headaches—and money—later on.

Before you move on to configuring your Macintosh Internet environment, check out Chapter 2 to learn what Apple's online service, eWorld, offers—and what it doesn't offer.

CHAPTER 2

ONE-STOP SHOPPING: APPLE'S eWORLD

What Is eWorld?

How Does eWorld Provide Internet Access?

Why Use eWorld for Internet Access?

Setting Up an eWorld Account

Using Newsgroups Through eWorld

Using Internet E-Mail Through eWorld

Using the World Wide Web, Gopher, and FTP Through eWorld

Summary

eWorld is Apple's first attempt to horn in on the rapidly expanding online market by providing Mac users with their very own network service. It is a great idea, that so far, hasn't quite taken off.

For all sorts of reasons—mismanagement, poor marketing, and bad press have all been blamed—Apple's eWorld has become, according to some critics, just a ghost town on the Info Highway. Only in full operation since 1994, it's still way too early to confirm whether eWorld will be a total flop for Apple.

Some of the criticism leveled at eWorld is probably justified, but in my opinion, eWorld has a lot going for it, too. For one, eWorld hasn't been plagued with incidents of sexual predation and abuse like other national online services. The reason is that eWorld system administrators learned from the mistakes of others and do not allow members to use false names—a measure aimed at getting users to behave responsibly online.

eWorld's graphic interface is both welcoming and a creative departure from most online services available today. Continuing Apple's intuitive user interface philosophy, eWorld's graphics enable users to easily navigate through the system with a simple click of the mouse. Despite the high graphic content, images on eWorld are also surprisingly quick to display on your screen—which can't be said of its competitors. The longer graphics take to draw on your screen, the more you have to pay in connect time charges.

eWorld is also the only place online where Mac users will find comprehensive information front and center (not just as an afterthought) about Apple products and Macintosh software. It's also a convenient online spot for Mac users to congregate, to find other Mac users and like-minded individuals. PC users are welcome, of course, but at this writing, eWorld does not support a PC client, so it is primarily a hang-out for Mac users.

As online services go, eWorld has much in its favor and is definitely worth a look-see. Note: To register as a new member on eWorld, you need a registration number and password, which are supplied with the software diskettes. The registration number and password are written on the software diskette labels. eWorld software is available with most new Macs or you can call eWorld at 1-800-775-4556 to request the software.

This chapter briefly describes what eWorld is and then describes some of eWorld's Internet access capabilities.

Note

> Throughout this chapter, you'll see references to various types of Internet resources, such as *newsgroups* or the *World Wide Web*. Don't worry if you don't yet know what these things are—you don't need to know what they are to understand this chapter.
>
> Each of the major types of Internet resources is introduced and described in Chapter 4, "An Introduction to Internet Tools and Resources," and explained in detail in Chapters 7, "Exchanging E-Mail" through 14, "Interacting in Real Time: Talk, Chat, and Games."

What Is eWorld?

eWorld is a commercial online information service, very much in the spirit of the popular America Online service. Although it looks different, eWorld's highly graphical interface is based on modified America Online software. (See Figure 2.1.) As such, much of what is written here about eWorld also applies to America Online; if you're familiar with America Online then you'll have no problem accessing eWorld and vice versa.

FIGURE 2.1.
The Welcome to eWorld screen, the starting point for most activities on eWorld.

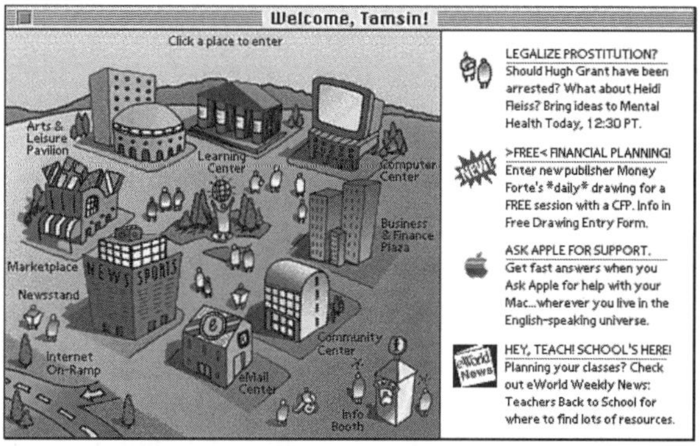

eWorld supports modem speeds up to 28.8KB/second (depending on the city from which you call). eWorld does not charge a premium for high-speed access, so you'll be able to get more out of your online time with a faster modem, especially when downloading files.

So far, eWorld is available only in the United States, Canada, the United Kingdom, Australia, and New Zealand. Apple designed eWorld as an international service, and plans to expand to non-English-speaking countries soon.

How Does eWorld Provide Internet Access?

If you have a dial-up Internet connection you can connect to eWorld using PPP and the eWorld software client version 1.1 or later. This is especially useful if you live in a place where there is no local access number for eWorld. On the other hand, if you connect to eWorld through your dial-up Internet connection, you'll be paying twice; first for your Internet connection and second for the time you spend on eWorld. If you live in an area with a local access number you're probably better off to connect to eWorld directly rather than through an Internet access provider. I say probably, because in some cases, the local access number only connects at a slow speed such as 2,400 bps, which means you may be paying more in connect time charges.

One of the advantages of using eWorld is that the pricing scheme is simple: There is no extra cost to access Internet services. The basic charge is for four hours connect time per month. Anything over the four hour limit is billed on an hourly basis.

Set up like a small community, eWorld's opening Welcome screen after you connect is the "Town Square" window featuring a landscape of buildings. (See Figure 2.1, shown previously.) If you click a building, you enter the main window or "lobby" of the building with icons for additional services or other sections within the building.

eWorld offers a wide range of services, including access to Internet e-mail and newsgroups. Some of the services eWorld offers include the following:

- **E-mail**—Using eWorld's e-mail client, you can exchange e-mail with other eWorld users and with Internet users as well.
- **Discussion Boards**—Users can post public messages or questions regarding a topic and read other users' questions, comments, and answers in eWorld's Discussion Boards. There are many different conferences, each centering around a given topic. Although these forums are similar to Internet newsgroups, they are not Internet newsgroups.
- **Internet newsgroups**—eWorld packages the various categories of Internet newsgroups into folders. (This is described in Chapter 9, "Browsing Newsgroups.") You can navigate to them, read messages, and post messages.
- **Conferences**—In conferences, eWorld users communicate "live" with one another in groups by typing their comments in a window that all participants can read. Although this facility is similar to Internet Relay Chat, it is not Internet Relay Chat. (Internet Relay Chat is described in Chapter 14.)
- **Software Libraries**—eWorld offers an extensive holding of files for downloading. The library is heavily slanted (for obvious reasons) toward Macintosh freeware, shareware, and demo versions of programs and files. In addition, software updates, stand-alone applications, fonts, sounds, graphics, utilities, QuickTime movies and information files are also abundantly available.
- **Apple Customer Center**—This forum features the latest information on Apple products, as well as a help desk where eWorld members can get quick answers to their technical support questions.
- **Information Services**—These are the usual online information services folks have come to expect from online services: news, sports, weather, stock quotes, and special interest services.

I have only hit on some of eWorld's most important services, but I think you'll find eWorld has a lot more to offer, as well as a few surprises, too.

eWorld's Internet services, apart from Internet e-mail and newsgroups, include access to the World Wide Web, Gopher, FTP file transfers, and mailing lists.

eWorld's Internet Access Is Not "Full" Internet Access

It's important to understand that eWorld's Internet services do not provide access to all the major Internet resources. There is no provision for the Internet live communications facilities: Internet Relay Chat, Talk, and MUDs or Gopher (as described in Chapters 13, "Navigating with Menus: Gopher," and 14).

More importantly, unlike regular dial-up IP Internet accounts, eWorld does not enable you to select and install your own choice of Internet client tools. You are required to use the eWorld interface for e-mail, newsgroups, the Web, and FTP.

These restrictions exist because eWorld is an online service, not a true Internet provider that offers dial-up IP accounts. (See Chapter 4.) eWorld's servers are connected to the Internet, but you're not—eWorld works the Internet on your behalf and shows you the results. All the software that actually negotiates the Internet is run on the server, not on your Mac. The eWorld software you run does the job of displaying the Internet information that the eWorld server collects for you.

With a dial-up IP account, you are truly on the Internet—the provider's server merely supplies the communications link. That's why you can access any Internet resource through an IP account and use whatever client software you prefer.

Why Use eWorld's Internet Services?

Although eWorld's Internet access is incomplete and restricted, there *are* reasons to use eWorld as your link to the Internet.

First of all, some folks need, or want, only Internet e-mail access and newsgroups. If you're in this category, an eWorld account can supply all the Internet functions you need—and at a cost that's probably favorable to most genuine Internet accounts. (Note that CompuServe and America Online also offer Internet e-mail and newsgroups, so shop around.)

For those who want more of the Internet, eWorld supplies its own Web browser, as well as easy FTP access. If you're connecting to eWorld through a local access number (not through a dial-up Internet connection) an eWorld account offers a very easy setup and configuration routine. You don't have to fiddle with TCP/IP, PPP, or SLIP on your Mac. All you have to do is properly install the eWorld software and it pretty much does the rest. Using eWorld is also an advantage if you use the Internet when you travel. When away from home, you can switch to another eWorld access number so that the connection is still a local call. With most regular IP accounts, you have to dial the same number you dial at home—and pay the long-distance charges.

Although eWorld's Internet services leave out live communications facilities, comparatively few Internet users visit these anyway. The most important Internet services—e-mail, Web access, FTP, Gopher, and newsgroups—are all available through eWorld's Internet access. Although you cannot select your own client software for accessing these resources, the tools eWorld supplies are fully capable, if not exceptional. Using eWorld also saves you the hassle of finding, choosing, and configuring your own client software.

Setting Up an eWorld Account for Use via the Internet

To access eWorld using your dial-up Internet account, you must install the eWorld client version 1.1 or later on your computer. Also, make sure that you have already installed and configured MacTCP and PPP. (See Chapter 3, "Configuring Your Macintosh for the Internet.") To access eWorld through a local access number, all you need is the eWorld software. You can find the local access number after launching eWorld, or call the support number to find the number in your area.

You install the eWorld client software by inserting eWorld disk 1 in your diskette drive. When you double-click the installer icon, further installation instructions display on your screen. eWorld installs several folders, the application and a readme file in one folder on your computer. After you have followed the installation instructions, restart your machine.

At this point the access instructions for dial-up Internet account users diverge from the steps for those connecting to eWorld through a local access number. If you are going through a local access number, simply launch the eWorld application. An electronic Access Assistant provides instructions on-screen to help you choose your modem settings, find the nearest local access phone number, and register as a new member. Be sure to have your credit card information ready.

Otherwise, if you are connecting to eWorld using your dial-up Internet account, you must do things differently. First, launch MacPPP to connect to your Internet provider. Before opening the eWorld client, locate the eWorld TCP connection file in the For MacTCP Users folder and drag it onto the eWorld Files folder.

Double-click the eWorld application icon in the eWorld folder to launch the client. A Connecting to eWorld screen is displayed as part of the sign-up process. Select the Over a network connection radio button in the Connecting to eWorld screen and click the Continue button. Next, a Network connection screen is displayed showing that eWorld TCP is selected. Click the Use the same network radio button under Second Attempt and click the Continue button.

Once you have completed configuring the eWorld client for TCP/IP access, the rest of the registration process is automated by an electronic Access Assistant which provides instructions on-screen. Have your credit card ready.

The installation and configuration process is a one-time thing. The next time you want to connect using your dial-up Internet connection, simply connect to the Internet as you would normally using Config PPP and then launch eWorld by double-clicking the eWorld application icon in your eWorld folder. Once the Connect to eWorld screen appears, type your password in the Password: field and click the Connect button.

If you're connecting to eWorld via a local access number, simply launch the eWorld application, enter your password in the Password: field when the Connect to eWorld screen appears. Then, click the Connect button to tell your modem to dial eWorld.

Tip

> Ok, I admit this one is silly. If you want to change your eWorld Town Square window (the Welcome screen) from daytime to night, just click on the sky in the upper-left corner. It may take a few clicks, but eventually you should hit the 'hot spot' that will transform the sunny sky into a starry night. See, I told you it was silly. Rumor has it, that there are other "hot spots" in the Town Square, but you'll have to find those for yourself.

Using Newsgroups Through eWorld

To access eWorld's Internet services, click the Internet On-Ramp icon at the bottom left corner of the Welcome window. A window of Internet choices is displayed. Clicking the Newsgroups icon takes you to the Newsgroups area—the Internet Message Boards window.

Your first task is to set up a list of newsgroups to which you'd like to subscribe. If you already know the name of a newsgroup, click the Find & Add button. In the Find & Add dialog box, type in the name of the newsgroup you want to find and click the Find button. The results of the search are displayed in the Find & Add window. Select the newsgroup you want to subscribe to and click the Add to Your Newsgroups button. A dialog box appears that says `You have been subscribed to the selected group(s)`. Click the Ok button. Close the Find & Add results window, and the Find & Add dialog box to return to the Internet Message Boards (Newsgroups) window.

To see a list of newsgroups available through eWorld, click once on the Browse & Add Newsgroups button. It will take awhile for all the groups to be listed; be patient. Once the list is displayed, you can browse for a newsgroup that interests you. If you find one you like, you can subscribe to it (so that you won't have to wade through the full list of newsgroups each time you want to refer to it) by clicking the Add to Your Newsgroups button. When you finish selecting the newsgroups you want, close all the windows.

To read messages in a newsgroup after you set up your newsgroups list, click the Read Your Newsgroups button. Double-click on a newsgroup in the list to open it and then double-click on a message to display it. (See Figure 2.2.)

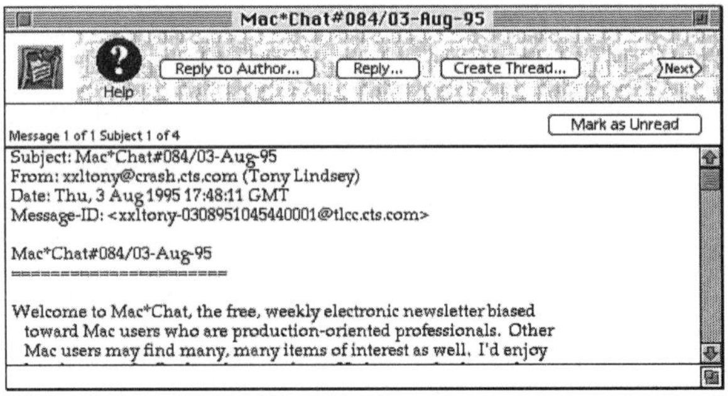

FIGURE 2.2.
A message displayed in an Internet newsgroup on eWorld.

From the screen shown in Figure 2.2, you can reply to the message (replying means that you post a new message with the same subject line as the one you're reading) or compose a new message to be posted to this newsgroup.

Note

> eWorld tries hard to mask some of the "techie" appearance of the newsgroup naming schemes. (This is described in Chapter 9.) On the Internet, newsgroups are loosely categorized by general type through a series of abbreviations separated by periods: `sci.` (science), `comp.` (computers), `soc.` (social issues), `alt.` ("alternative" groups covering a wide range of interests), and so on. Real newsgroup names look something like this:
>
> `alt.video.laserdiscs`
>
> `sci.language.translation`
>
> Once you get used to them, newsgroup names are no big deal; in fact, they're helpful. However, eWorld hides them in favor of gathering groups of a type together in a hierarchical folder structure. You'll find, for example, a `sci.` folder that holds other folders containing various subcategories. Within a particular newsgroup, eWorld also creates folders containing threads (messages that share the same subject line). Through this categorization, eWorld lets you point-and-click your way through newsgroups until you find what you want.

eWorld's method of hiding actual newsgroup names may frustrate experienced Internet users. Fortunately, few experienced users are likely to switch to eWorld for Internet activities. For new users, eWorld's approach makes newsgroup access a little less daunting, if more time consuming. Also, because eWorld masks newsgroup names, eWorld prevents users from acquiring the skills necessary to use newsgroups in any way other than through eWorld. Those who want to make heavy use of newsgroups and who are not especially interested in eWorld's other services should seriously consider a regular dial-up IP account and good newsreader software.

Sending Internet E-Mail Through eWorld

Using eWorld's mail client to send Internet e-mail is just the same as sending e-mail to other eWorld users. In other words, it's dead easy.

When you connect to eWorld, it's easy to find out if you have received any e-mail. A red mail truck parked next to the eMail center in the Town Square signals you have new mail. Clicking on the red mail truck takes you to a folder with your unopened e-mail. To read your e-mail, double-click on a message.

Sending eMail is just as simple whether you're mailing to an Internet address or to one on eWorld. Click on the eMail Center icon, choose Compose New Message, enter the e-mail address in the To: field and write your message in the text field. To send your message, click the Send Now button. (See Figure 2.3.)

FIGURE 2.3.
Sending e-mail on eWorld.

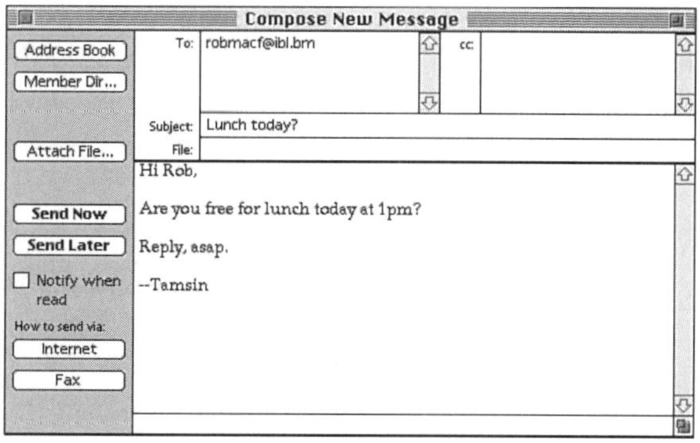

Tip

> To save money on connect time charges to eWorld, you can read and write e-mail offline. To write e-mail offline, launch eWorld, but do not connect. Choose Compose New Message from the eMail menu. When you are finished composing your message, click the Send Later button. Next time you connect to eWorld, choose Send Mail in Out Box from the eMail menu.
>
> To save a message on your hard drive to read later, open the message and click the Save on drive button. After you disconnect from eWorld (but do not quit the application), choose Saved Mail from the eMail menu to read your message.

Note

> For more about using e-mail, see Chapter 7.

Note

> If you want eWorld to automatically collect your e-mail for you, investigate the Automatic Courier located in the eMail menu. This handy feature enables you to schedule when you send mail, receive mail, and get files.

Using the World Wide Web, Gopher and FTP Through eWorld

eWorld's Web browser is as capable as any browser available today. It does not have all the high-end bells and whistles of popular browsers like Mosaic or Netscape Navigator, but it has the most important features (except for a built-in newsreader and send-only e-mail).

eWorld's feature set is comparable to other popular browsers— for example, it displays the text of a Web page before the graphics, and enables you to jump to another page before the graphics for the first page have finished appearing. Considering the time some graphics take to travel through the Web and appear on your desktop, this feature is a real time-saver. It supports Netscape extensions such as backgrounds and centered text. You can also Gopher and FTP to your heart's content with eWorld's browser just like Netscape or Mosaic.

eWorld's Web browser automatically stores on your Mac copies of the Web pages you visit. If you return to the same page twice, the browser doesn't have to download the entire page again—another significant time-saver which makes cruising the Web that much more efficient.

eWorld's Web browser works along the same lines as Netscape, MacWeb, or Mosaic. For more about the World Wide Web, see Chapter 10, "Browsing the World Wide Web."

Summary

Should you use eWorld for Internet access? I don't know. This chapter has shown what you get with eWorld, and what you give up. The rest is up to you.

In Chapter 3, you discover how to configure your Macintosh for the Internet.

CHAPTER 3

CONFIGURING YOUR MACINTOSH FOR THE INTERNET

What is TCP/IP?

What is PPP?

What You Need To Know Before You Start

An Overview of Configuration

Configuring MacTCP

Configuring MacPPP

Connecting to the Internet

Troubleshooting Your Internet Configuration

Summary

Those who find the Internet intimidating do so for two reasons:

- The resources available on the Internet are inconsistently accessed and operated and so require a range of skills and knowledge.
- Properly configuring your computer and software to access the Internet causes migraines and, in some cases, divorce.

Although most of this book addresses the first problem, this chapter is dedicated to alleviating the second problem. Fortunately, that's the lesser of the two problems; although configuring a Mac for the Internet can be frustrating, once you get it right, you rarely have to bother with it again. Navigation skills, on the other hand, you must learn and relearn over and over and over until your head explodes. Every time you think you know your way around, new resources bloom, others die, and still others relocate—navigation never ends.

This chapter leads you through the steps required to set up a Macintosh for access to an Internet provider through a dial-in PPP account. (See "What is PPP?" later in this chapter.) It also covers how to install MacTCP. (See "What is TCP/IP?" later in this chapter.) You need both MacTCP and MacPPP to access the Internet with your Macintosh.

If your Internet service provider supplies you with instructions on configuring MacTCP and MacPPP, follow them rather than the steps in this chapter.

What Is TCP/IP?

TCP/IP (Transmission Control Protocol/Internet Protocol) is the fundamental glue of the Internet, the one thing all networks and computers on the Internet have in common. Because versions of the TCP/IP communications program (more properly described as a protocol or protocol stack) are available for all types of computers, all types of computers can communicate with one another through the Internet. Two decades old, TCP/IP was developed by a defense agency but is now a public standard owned and controlled by no company or government. TCP/IP is enhanced and updated under the auspices of an independent standards organization.

What Is PPP?

The TCP/IP standard does not, by itself, support transmission through modems over telephone lines. To enable a modem-based TCP/IP connection, you need another protocol in addition to TCP/IP: Point-to-Point Protocol (PPP). This protocol enables TCP/IP to run through a serial communications medium, of which a modem connection is one type.

What You Need To Know Before You Start

When you configure your Mac for Internet access, you have to enter a variety of information about your Internet account. All this information is supplied to you by your access provider;

with the exception of Internet addresses, you don't really need to think about any of this stuff after you complete the configuration.

The next few pages briefly describe the various roles played by MacTCP and MacPPP which are required for configuring your Macintosh for the Internet.

Your Computer's Internet Address

Each and every computer on the Internet has a unique IP address, expressed in four sets of numbers separated by periods. A typical IP address looks like this:

```
198.41.0.6
```

This address enables any computer on the Net to find any other so that the two can communicate. Your service provider's computer has its own IP address. Whenever you are on the Internet, you have your own IP address as well. That address may be the same every time, or it may be different each time you log on. Some providers use a system which automatically assigns each user's computer a different IP address each time the user logs on.

Your computer's Internet address doesn't have anything to do with your own Internet electronic mail address—we'll discuss e-mail addresses later.

Name Servers

To communicate with another computer on the Internet, your computer needs to know the IP address of that other computer. Fortunately, the Internet domain name system can help you out by letting you specify a name (for example, `ftp.apple.com`), instead of an address (for example, `130.43.2.3`). These names are much easier to remember than numerical addresses.

A Domain Name Server (DNS) is a computer on the network that translates these names you specify into the numerical IP addresses your computer can use. When you configure your Mac for the Internet, you have to enter the IP address of a Domain Name Server. Your Internet provider should provide you with the IP addresses of their Domain Name Servers.

Subnet Mask and Gateways

You may have to supply two final pieces of information when configuring MacTCP:

- **Gateway**—A *gateway* is a network router (a specialized computer) required to properly direct your Internet traffic. The gateway computer has a numerical IP address just like other computers on the Internet. Depending on your service provider's setup, you may have to specify a numerical gateway address.
- **Subnet mask**—The *subnet mask*, sometimes described more briefly as the *netmask*, is a numerical IP address that identifies the network membership for your Mac. With MacTCP, depending on the value you enter for your IP address, the subnet mask defaults to one of three values. For manual configuration, your service provider must provide you with the subnet mask. For example, `255.255.255.0`.

A Login Name and Password

Your service provider must also provide you with a login name and password for the provider's dial-up server.

An Overview of Configuration

Before you can set up your Mac for dial-up access to a PPP Internet account, you need to do the following:

1. Install and configure a modem. A 14,400 bps modem or faster is ideal; a 9,600 bps modem may work in a pinch—temporarily. Modems running at 28,800 bps are great, but not all access providers support this speed yet. Still, 28,800 bps access is growing in popularity, so if you must buy a modem now, a 28,000 bps modem is a good investment, even if your provider supports only 14,400 bps. (Buy the faster modem and then shop for a faster provider!) Anything slower than 9,600 bps is unacceptable for a PPP account: even a 9,600 bps modem will do only one thing quickly—exhaust your patience.
2. Locate an Internet access provider and establish an account. (See Chapter 1, "The Basics: What's Involved in Setting Up and Going Online?.") Your configuration is determined not so much by the Internet as by your service provider's Internet servers. The settings you need depend entirely on how that server is set up—and server configurations vary widely, even among those that use PPP.

   Your access provider will tell you exactly which configuration settings you require. At the very least, the provider must tell you the following:

   - The telephone number your modem must dial to access the server
   - Your user ID and password (you can probably choose one or both of these yourself) for logging on to the network
   - Whether the server assigns you an IP address (and sometimes a subnet mask) automatically; if your provider does not assign IP addresses automatically, the provider will give you your unique IP address, subnet mask, and gateway address.
   - Your full Internet e-mail address
   - The DNS addresses
   - The e-mail (SMTP) server address
   - The news server (NNTP) address

Note

> You won't need the SMTP and NNTP server addresses for configuring MacTCP and MacPPP, but you will need them when configuring client software to use e-mail and newsgroups.

3. Configure MacTCP.
4. Configure MacPPP.

Configuring MacTCP

There are two methods for configuring MacTCP. If your Internet provider supplies you with an IP address for your own computer, then you need to proceed with "Manual MacTCP configuration." Otherwise, you can proceed with "Automatic MacTCP configuration."

Automatic MacTCP Configuration

1. Open Control Panels from your Apple menu.
2. Open the MacTCP control panel.
3. In the top part of the window, click the PPP icon. (See Figure 3.1.)

FIGURE 3.1.
The TCP control panel.

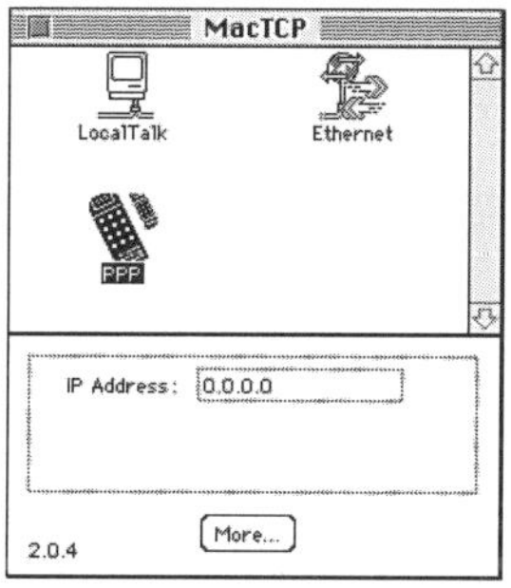

4. Click the More… button in the bottom section of the MacTCP window. This daunting dialog box (see Figure 3.2) is not as difficult to configure as it looks, since you'll be using the automatic configuration method.

FIGURE 3.2.
Setting up the TCP configuration dialog box ("automatic" configuration).

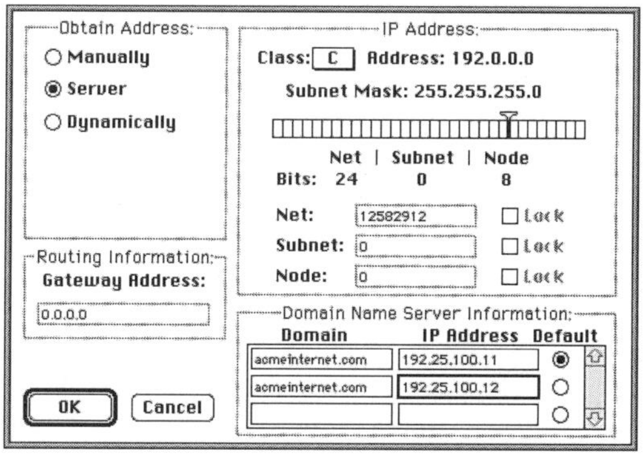

5. Click the Server radio button in the upper-left-hand corner.
6. Under the box, “Domain Name Server Information,” fill in the Domain and IP address for each Domain Name Server address that your service provider gave you. Click the radio button under the “Default” column for the first entry. Take another look at Figure 3.2 to see what your dialog box should look like.
7. Ignore the other settings and click OK.
8. Close the MacTCP window. MacTCP may warn you that changes will take effect after the next restart. If so, make sure you restart your computer before you try to connect to the Internet.
9. Proceed with “Configuring MacPPP,” later in this chapter.

Manual MacTCP Configuration

1. Open Control Panels from your Apple menu.
2. Open the MacTCP control panel.
3. In the top part of the window, click the PPP icon. (See Figure 3.1, shown previously.)
4. Click the More… button in the bottom section of the MacTCP window. Don’t worry! We’ll guide you through configuring this dialog box. (See Figure 3.3.)

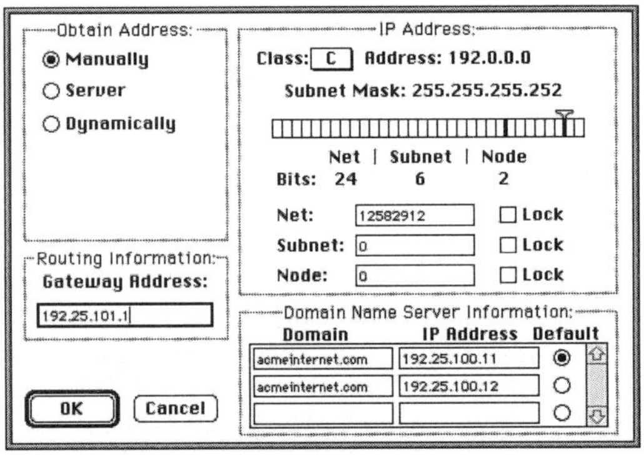

FIGURE 3.3.
Setting up the TCP configuration dialog box (“manual” configuration).

5. Click the Manually radio button in the upper-left-hand corner.
6. Under the box, “Domain Name Server Information,” fill in the Domain and IP address for each Domain Name Server address provided to you by your service provider. Click the radio button under the “Default” column for the first entry.
7. Under the Routing Information box, enter the numerical gateway address as specified by your Internet provider.
8. Under the “IP address” box, choose class A, B, or C from the pop-up menu, depending on the first number in your IP address:

First Three IP Digits	*Class*
1 through 126	A
127 through 191	B
192 through 223	C

9. If necessary, adjust the little sliding widgety thingy so that the subnet mask matches the one given to you by your Internet provider. Take another look at Figure 3.3 to see what your dialog box should look like.
10. Click OK.
11. Enter the IP address for your computer in the IP Address box in the lower part of the MacTCP window. (See Figure 3.4.) Close the MacTCP window.

FIGURE 3.4.
Entering your machine's IP address.

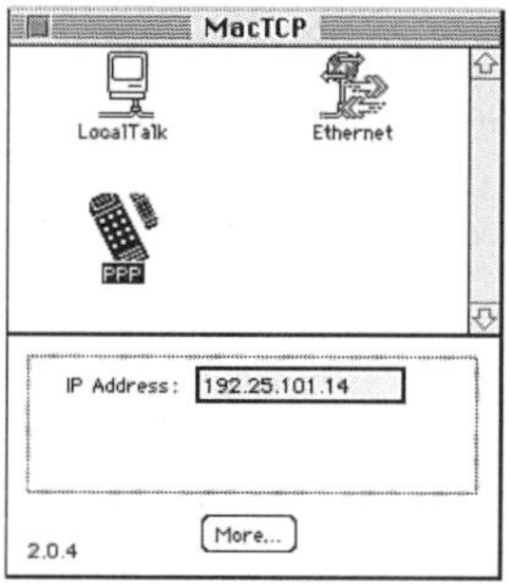

12. MacTCP may warn you that changes will take effect after the next restart. If so, make sure you restart your computer before you try to connect to the Internet.

Configuring MacPPP

1. Open Control Panels from your Apple menu.
2. Open the Config PPP control panel. (See Figure 3.5.)

FIGURE 3.5.
The Config PPP control panel.

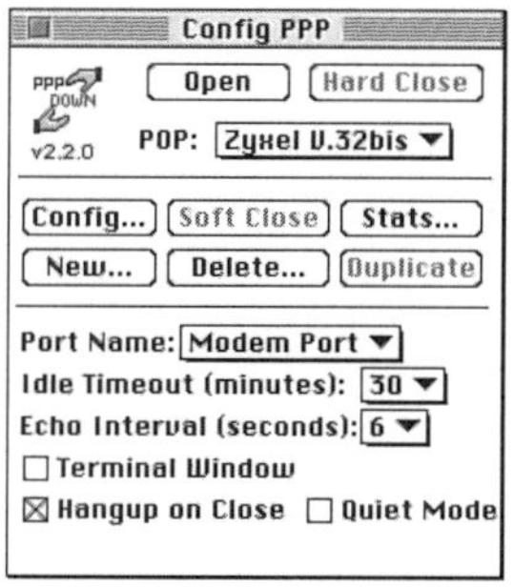

3. If your modem is connected to the Modem Port on your computer, leave Port Name: as Modem Port. If it's connected to the printer port, select Printer Port.

4. The Idle Timeout will make MacPPP hang up after a specified period of inactivity. This can be very helpful if you leave your computer connected and walk away from it. You can set a time between 5 and 120 minutes.
5. Leave Echo Interval set to Off.
6. Check the Hangup on Close check-box.
7. Choose a modem from the "PPP server" menu. If your modem is not listed, try Hayes-Compatible. If you don't know what type of modem you have, consult your modem manual.
8. Click the Config button, and the dialog box shown in Figure 3.6 appears.

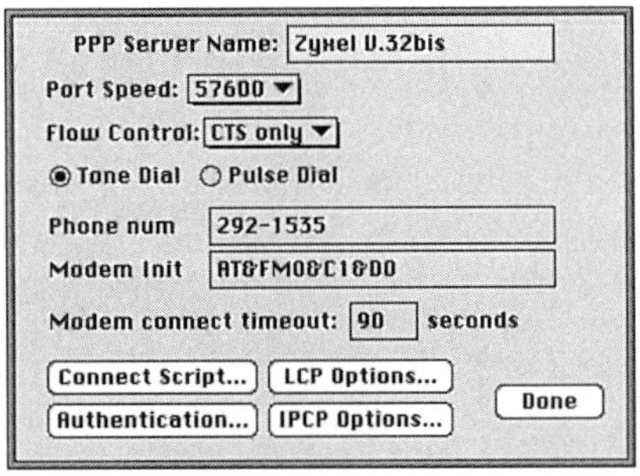

FIGURE 3.6.
The Config dialog box.

9. If your phone line can handle touch-tone dialing, click the Tone Dial radio button. If it can't handle touch-tone dialing, click the Pulse Dial radio button.
10. Fill in the telephone number supplied by your Internet provider in Phone Num.
11. Click the Connect Script button and you get the dialog box shown in Figure 3.7. (See the following Note.)

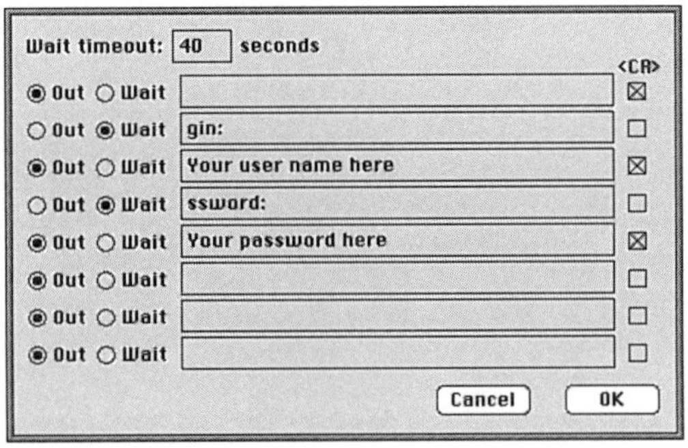

FIGURE 3.7.
The Connect Script dialog box.

12. In the third line, enter your user name as given by your Internet provider.
13. In the fifth line, enter your password as given by your Internet provider.
14. Click the OK button.

15. Now, click the Done button. To exit MacPPP, close the Config PPP window. (See Figure 3.5, shown previously.) Whew! You're finished configuring MacPPP (and MacTCP) and you're ready to connect to the Internet.

> **Note**
>
> The set-up described in steps 11 to 14 only applies to "scripted" PPP connections. Most service providers support this type of connection. If your service provider requires PAP (Password Authentication Protocol) then you need to contact your provider for instructions on setting up.

Connecting to the Internet

To connect to the Internet, first switch on your modem if necessary and then open Control Panels in the Apple menu. Double-click the Config PPP icon and click the Open button. (See Figure 3.8.) A progress dialog box will appear indicating that your modem is connecting to your Internet provider's server.

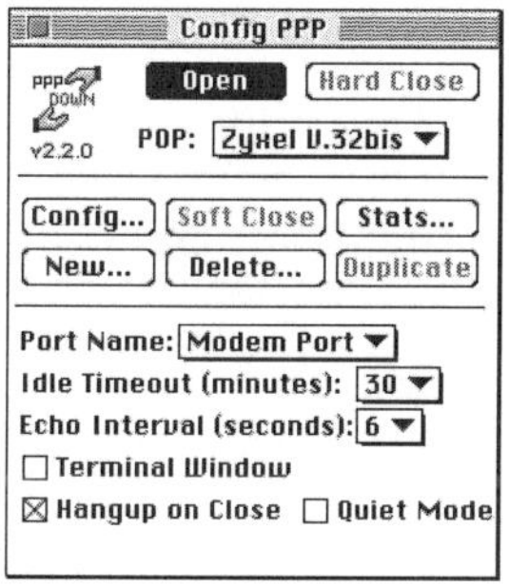

FIGURE 3.8.
The Config PPP control panel, ready to connect to the Internet.

Once you're connected you can launch an Internet tool, such as your e-mail program. (See Chapter 5, "Choosing Client Software for Internet Services.") For more information on e-mail addresses, see "Your E-Mail Address," later in this chapter.

Disconnecting from the Internet

To disconnect from the Internet, return to the Config PPP control panel and click the Hard Close button. This will disconnect your modem from your Internet provider's server.

> **Warning**
>
> When you disconnect, you should also be sure to quit all your Internet client applications. If you leave them running, they may request PPP to reopen your Internet connection, wasting valuable connect time.

Your E-Mail Address

Now that you have configured your Mac to jump onto the Info Highway, you need to know your Internet e-mail address so you can get busy sending and receiving Internet mail.

My Internet e-mail address looks like this:

```
tamsin@ibl.bm
```

A user's Internet address is made up of three parts:

- A username (`tamsin`)
- The "at" symbol (`@`)
- A domain name, which identifies the computer through which the user is connected to the Net (`ibl.bm` is the domain name of my service provider's computer).

The Internet at large can't really work with these word-based Internet addresses—it needs the numerical IP addresses to locate computers. A program called a *name server* automatically translates word-based Internet addresses into numerical IP addresses and vice versa. Domain names are a system unto themselves for identifying computers. They can be as simple as the two-word `apple.com`, or they can be much longer. The words in a domain name are separated by periods. Keep an eye on the rightmost word; it often identifies the type of institution or the country the computer is in. This rightmost word is called the *top-level domain.* Top-level domains for computers in the U.S. use three-letter abbreviations that identify the type of institution:

Top-Level Domain	*Institution Type*
`.com`	A *com*mercial enterprise or business
`.edu`	An *edu*cational institution
`.gov`	A non-military *gov*ernment office, department, or agency
`.mil`	A *mil*itary government office, department, or agency
`.net`	A *net*work, typically made up of different types of institutions
`.org`	An institution that doesn't fit any of the preceding categories, usually a non-profit outfit

For computers residing outside the U.S., you'll see a two-letter abbreviation identifying the country. For example:

Domain Abbreviation	*Country*
`.au`	Australia
`.at`	Austria
`.bm`	Bermuda
`.ca`	Canada
`.dk`	Denmark

`.fr`	France
`.de`	Germany (*De*utschland)
`.it`	Italy
`.jp`	Japan
`.no`	Norway

For example, `apple.com` is a U.S. commercial site; `mit.edu` is a U.S. academic site (Massachusetts Institute of Technology, in this example).

Typically, you use full Internet addresses (*`name@domain`*) to address e-mail and to identify yourself to others on the Internet. When using some types of Internet resources, such as FTP, Telnet, and Gopher, you're not accessing a person but a computer. To use these resources, you have to know just the domain name of the computer that holds the resource you want.

> **Tip**
>
> If you acquire your Internet account through a commercial access provider, your Internet address is most likely made up of the name you use to log on to the provider's server plus the server's domain name. In my address (`tamsin@ibl.bm`), `tamsin` is not just my Internet username, it is also the name I use to log on to the server, `ibl.bm`. The only other thing I need to complete the logon procedure is my password, and I ain't tellin'.

Troubleshooting Your Internet Configuration

Your Internet access provider should supply you with complete and accurate configuration information. If you've followed the instructions in this chapter and entered exactly the information your provider has given you, you should connect to the Internet through the provider.

If you experience problems, your first step should be to double-check your configuration, making sure that all your settings match the provider's instructions.

If you don't find a mistake, describe your problem to your access provider's technical support department. Often, access providers make changes to their own server configurations that require making changes in each user's configuration. Sometimes, the providers neglect to properly inform users of changes or they distribute out-of-date instructions to new users. If you can't get help from your provider, try the following:

- Get a new provider with better technical support.
- Make sure your modem has a Hardware Handshake cable which enables your computer to tell the service provider's modem when it is ready to receive more data. Without this cable, you may see problems such as poor performance or random disconnecting when operating at high speeds. If you bought a 14.4 Kbps modem packaged for the Macintosh, it should include this cable. If your modem doesn't have the Hardware Handshake cable, you can buy one cheaply from a computer store. The Hardware Handshake cable obviously does not apply to internal modems.

- The modem initialization string is the number one cause of connection problems. It is also, perhaps, the single-most difficult aspect of Config PPP to configure. The modem initialization string should turn on Hardware Handshaking on your modem. If you're in doubt, consult your modem manual or contact the modem's manufacturer and ask them what initialization string you should use for MacPPP. They should be happy to help you out.
- Another common trouble-maker is the connect script (see steps 12 to 13 in the "Configuring MacPPP" section, earlier in this chapter). If you can't connect, double-check with your provider that you have entered the connect script accurately.

Summary

Properly configuring your Macintosh for Internet access can be tricky, but if you pay close attention to any information supplied by your service provider, and carefully follow the steps outlined in this chapter, the world is your reward. Once you're set up, you rarely have to change your configuration—unless you change service providers, move, or install a different modem.

This chapter concludes Part I of this book. In Part II, "Communicating and Getting Around," you discover the Internet resources themselves. You also learn the techniques for navigating among the resources—and for making the most of them.

PART II

COMMUNICATING AND GETTING AROUND

CHAPTER 4

AN INTRODUCTION TO INTERNET TOOLS AND RESOURCES

Electronic Mail (E-Mail)

Mailing Lists

Newsgroups

The World Wide Web

Telnet

FTP

Gopher

Talk, Chat, and Games

Summary

"Tools and resources" may not be the best way to put it. I've seen "activities" tried, and I've run across mentions of Internet "segments" and "areas." I think I once heard about Internet "branches" (technology redefined as nature—that's the spirit!). All these poor metaphors attempt to address the fact that the Internet is not, in practice, one environment.

The Internet is a grab bag of different "tools" (for lack of a better word), each of which is used to retrieve and use a different type of resource. For example, electronic mail (e-mail) is a *tool*; the messages sent and received through it are *resources*. Each type of tool and its accompanying resources has its own unique purpose and mode of operation (and its own chapter in this part of the book). E-mail is different from newsgroups, the World Wide Web is different from FTP, Talk is different from Chat. They're all part of the Internet in that they are accessed through the Net and they observe some standard policies such as TCP/IP and domain/name conventions for Internet addresses. Beyond that, however, they're all very different, and you must learn to use each as a separate entity—or rather, *tool*.

It helps to think of the Internet as a shopping mall (a metaphor not lost on those who've set up shops there), as opposed to a department store. Unlike a mall, a department store exists in a single structure, often one big room. Although there are departments, each is used by shoppers in the same way: each has the same return policy, accepts the same methods of payment, participates in the big sale, and so on. Once you buy something in one part of a department store, you know how to work the whole joint; you're a K-mart pro.

A mall, on the other hand, is a collection of independently operated shops held together by a giant corridor (or *backbone*). Each has its own way of doing things; each may have different policies for payment and returns, each is organized differently, and each requires a different type of knowledge on the part of the buyer. The shops share one access medium—the mall—but beyond that, they can be very different. You have to learn how to work each shop individually in a mall. The same is true of the resources on the Internet, as suggested by the diagram in Figure 4.1.

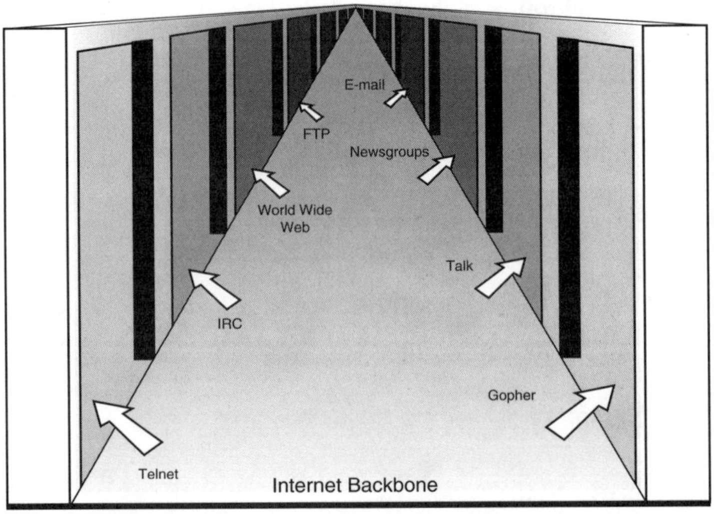

FIGURE 4.1.
The Internet is a corridor to various types of resources available along it, each of which is accessed through a different tool.

This inconsistency is the main reason new users are overwhelmed by the Internet. No individual tool is all that difficult to master, but facing them all in a big ugly heap can be terrifying, like eyeing the basement while thinking about cleaning it. Of course, the secret to a healthy Internet experience is to learn one thing at a time, starting with what's most important to you and moving on to other resources only when you've gained the confidence to do so. It also helps to keep in mind that the only people who use all the types of Internet tools and resources on a regular basis are people who write books about the Internet. Real human beings may dabble in many areas, but they generally frequent only two or three regularly—which makes perfect sense. When was the last time you visited every store in the mall?

The Unified Internet?

The World Wide Web, introduced later in this chapter and described in detail in Chapter 10, "Browsing the World Wide Web," attempts in various ways to smooth out some of the inconsistencies on the Internet. It does this in two ways:

1. Those who want to make information and activities available on the Web are required to follow certain rules for how they present information on their Web "pages" and for how users operate those pages. As a result, the Web offers a level of consistency that's rare elsewhere on the Net.
2. Other types of resources, such as newsgroups, Gopher and FTP file transfers, can be operated from within a Web page, which often simplifies their operation. In some cases, you may be able to perform a file transfer "behind the scenes" simply by clicking on a friendly Web page. This kind of arrangement insulates you from having to know how to operate an FTP file transfer.

Because the Web is fast becoming the most popular Internet resource, many Internet watchers (me included) believe it may soon become the sole tool for many Internet users. As the Web's ability to exploit other types of resources improves, much of the traditional Internet inconsistency will disappear—at least, from the user's point of view.

The inconsistency among Internet resources is exacerbated by the fact that each resource is often used through a different software *client*—each type of Internet tool demands its own software application on your Mac. Although the best software makes its associated resource easier to use, the new Internet user is still faced not only with learning about how each type of resource is used but also with learning how to operate the client software that operates the Internet tool that accesses the resource. This is yet another reason users are running in droves to the Web. On the Web, people can use one client program, their Web browser, for most Internet activities.

Chapter 5, "Choosing Client Software for Internet Services," covers the world of Internet software clients. The remainder of this chapter provides an overview of each of the principal Internet tool types.

Electronic Mail (E-Mail)

The most important and most widely used Internet resource is electronic mail, most often known as *e-mail* and often known simply as *mail*. With e-mail, anybody on the Internet can transmit a text message to anybody else on the Internet. The Internet's system of domain names (DNS) ensures that every user has a unique address, duplicated by none of the other 25 million Internet users. That enables you to type a message on your Mac, enter a single address line, and know that your message will be sent to the intended recipient, in Taiwan or Texas. Your recipient can read your message on his or her computer, print it, or even pass it on—electronically—to someone else.

Is E-Mail Private?

E-mail is relatively secure because most users' mailboxes are password protected. E-mail is not, however, snoop proof. Unscrupulous system administrators and others with the know-how can actually intercept e-mail on its way across the Internet. They may also be able to read it from the recipient's mailbox if they know how to defeat the passwords. Of course, for all intents and purposes, e-mail is as secure as paper mail, which can be lost, stolen, or opened and read along its way (perhaps not so surreptitiously as e-mail, however: tattered envelopes are a giveaway).

E-mail is also not spoof-proof. Some newsreader clients and Web browsers enable users to send messages made to appear as if they were coming from someone other than the actual sender. This causes no end of harm to the real owner of the e-mail address since in many cases forged messages contain offensive and slanderous material. There is no way to protect yourself from forged messages—other than not giving out your e-mail address to every Tom, Dick, and Mary on the street.

For more about Internet security, see Chapter 20, "Using the Internet in the Office."

To a great extent, what you can do with e-mail is governed by the capabilities of your e-mail software. You can use any e-mail program to compose and send messages and to receive and read messages sent to you. Many programs also provide *multiple recipients* and cc: support, two ways to send the same message to multiple recipients in one step. Other common features of e-mail programs are *forwarding*, which enables you to conveniently forward a received message to another user, and *reply*, which enables you to compose and send a message in reply to one you've received, without typing the address line.

In addition to ordinary text messages, Internet e-mail can send data files containing anything—photos, video clips, sound clips, program files, and so on—even though the facility is technically capable of carrying only text. The trick is that these items must be translated into regular text characters before they're sent; they must then be translated back into their proper binary data form on the recipient's computer before they can be used. Any good e-mail software package can do this.

Although e-mail is described as instantaneous, it's hardly so. Internet e-mail relies on *store and forward* technology, meaning that messages are held and stored on one or more computers along their journey and forwarded at regular intervals or when the network traffic allows.

Keep in mind that a straight path rarely exists between any two computers on the Internet. Although your messages travel at roughly the speed of light from one point to the next, they may pass through dozens of computers, networks, routers, gateways, and other Internet intersections en route, and they may be temporarily held up at any stop along the way. Given that, Internet e-mail is astoundingly reliable and still pretty fast—many messages reach their destinations within minutes, and few (even those traveling overseas) take more than a few hours. Federal Express can't touch it.

For more about e-mail, see Chapter 7, "Exchanging E-Mail."

Mailing Lists

Mailing lists exploit e-mail's broadcast capabilities to send copies of important messages to all the Internet users who want the messages. Sometimes known as *conferences, discussion groups,* or even simply as *lists,* mailing lists maintain lists of subscribers interested in news or comments related to a certain topic. The topics can be as serious as African politics or as trivial as Grunge music. All subscribers automatically receive e-mail containing news and comments about the topic of the list. Subscribing to a mailing list is usually a simple matter of sending an e-mail message to the list manager and requesting a subscription.

Mailing lists work like this: Subscribers e-mail to a single address their news, questions, or reactions (and arguments) to other messages. All the messages received at the list address are broadcast, using e-mail, to all subscribers, usually on a daily basis or more often. Subscribers check their e-mail mailboxes regularly for messages from the list; an especially active list can clog a subscriber's mailbox with hundreds of messages a day—a disadvantage that steers many users to an alternative type of discussion group: the newsgroup.

Because of the manual effort involved in broadcasting hundreds of messages a day and keeping up with an ever-changing list of subscribers, many mailing lists are operated by a computer program. Although these automated lists are still overseen by human beings, the day-to-day work of managing the list and broadcasting the messages is handled by software. There are many programs that manage mailing lists, but the most common type is called a *Listserv.*

Like most computer programs, Listservs and other mailing list programs are a little anal about how you interact with them. When you subscribe to an automated mailing list, you have to follow specific rules (such as phrasing your subscription request properly). Once you're in, however, you're in, and the list dutifully keeps you informed. Mailing list programs, sometimes also called *list processors,* offer other advantages. You can control, in some respects, how mail is forwarded to you and even temporarily shut off deliveries. You do this by sending the list program e-mail messages containing commands that the list processor understands.

> **Note**
>
> Just as e-mail can carry files containing graphics, video, and programs, so can folks post these for the collective benefit of all mailing list subscribers. However, such postings are often discouraged (or forbidden) because they result in very large messages that bog down the broadcast and annoy subscribers.

For more about mailing lists, see Chapter 8, "Subscribing to Mailing Lists."

Newsgroups

Newsgroups are similar to mailing lists in that they provide a forum for the exchange of news, comments, and other information (or misinformation, as happens in any public forum) among any and all interested Internet users. They differ from mailing lists in that newsgroups don't require e-mail for the message exchange (although messages can be posted to a newsgroup using e-mail). Subscribers must use a program called a *newsreader* to access the newsgroup, display a list of current messages, read selected messages, and post new messages with comments, questions, or replies to other messages. The messages themselves reside on computers called *news servers.*

At the time of this writing, there are literally thousands of newsgroups on the Internet. They address every topic imaginable, from various scientific disciplines, to activism, to fandom, to any of several popular sexual fetishes. Most newsgroups fall under the auspices of Usenet, a very loose affiliation of sites that use the same software and standards to manage their newsgroups. Properly configured news servers enable users to access all Usenet newsgroups from a single list, as if they were all stored on the same machine. The actual messages are, however, stored here and there around the Net. In addition to Usenet groups, there are other newsgroups available, often covering local topics, that typically follow Usenet conventions.

The disadvantages of newsgroups, when compared with mailing lists, are that you have to have a newsreader (and access to a news server) to use them. You also have to navigate to the newsgroup to check for news—with a mailing list, you simply check your e-mail. These requirements, however, are easily met by Macintosh users with IP accounts and any of the Mac-based newsreaders, most of which are shareware. Also, most client software for accessing the World Wide Web (see "The World Wide Web," later in this chapter) can interact with news servers and so function as a news reader.

As for the advantages of newsgroups, you display and read only what interests you and ignore what doesn't interest you. With a mailing list, although you don't have to read every message you receive, you do have to take the time to look over all the messages and delete the ones you don't care about. Newsgroups also don't pile up messages in your mailbox; you can shut down your Mac for a week to go spelunking and not worry that your mailbox will reach critical mass while you're gone.

Fantastic FAQs

Frequently Asked Questions files, or FAQs (pronounced *faks*, mainly so that computer journalists can recycle their hackneyed *fax/facts* puns in their Internet writing*), are text files of common questions and answers provided to bring new users of a given resource up to speed. They appear all over the Internet but are especially common in newsgroups. New subscribers can retrieve and read the newsgroup's FAQ before jumping in and posting questions other subscribers have already read—and answered—a zillion times. The presence of a FAQ not only orients new users, it also helps keep the message traffic in a newsgroup fresh and interesting for regular subscribers.

* Sams publishes a very useful, well-written, and popular book unfortunately titled *Your Internet Consultant: The FAQs of Life Online*. I rest my case.

Much more often than with mailing lists and particularly in groups for this activity, newsgroup postings feature data files containing programs, graphics, and more. Subscribers can selectively transfer these files to their Macs (*download* them) under the control of their newsreaders, which handle the necessary conversion of the files from the text format required for posting into usable binary files.

Newsgroups (and mailing lists) can be *moderated*, meaning that some human somewhere reviews each posting for appropriate and relevant content before allowing it to be posted or rejecting it. Moderated newsgroups always leave me wondering what's been cut—how do I know the moderator doesn't have his or her own agenda? Many newsgroups, however, are not moderated, resulting in a wonderfully open, unexpurgated exchange of information—with a staggering amount of digression, repetition, irrelevancy, and stupidity mixed in with the good stuff. You can decide which type of exchange you prefer and choose your newsgroups accordingly. Personally, I'd rather wade through the junk than wonder whether somebody's censoring stuff I may want to read.

Tip

Just to make sure that nobody misses anything, many newsgroups and mailing lists that cover the same topic are connected by automatic *gateways*. The gateways allow everything posted in the newsgroup to be funneled to the mailing lists, and everything posted to the mailing list to be posted on the newsgroup.

The World Wide Web

Simply put, the World Wide Web is where it's at. Known also as WWW or *the Web*, the World Wide Web is a subset of the Internet. It's a growing group of Internet sites that have created their own Web documents, or *pages*, to be presented to Internet users running a *browser*, the required client program for using the Web.

Web pages feature *hypertext links*, or highlighted keywords, that lead to other pages when the user selects them (Mac users just click the links). The neat thing about hypertext links is that they can lead anywhere: to another page of expanded information at the same Web site, to a page at another Web site, or even to other Internet resources, such as newsgroups. The use of more-or-less standardized pages makes the Web easy to learn and work with. The use of hypertext makes browsing the Web, for Macintosh users, a matter of clicking around through the links.

When viewed through a sophisticated graphical browser like Netscape Navigator or Mosaic (see Figure 4.2), a Web page can display color graphics and photos, and can access other applications to play sound, animation, and video clips (sort of). This facility for audio-visual stimuli has not only made the Web beloved among new Internet users, it's also made the Web the Internet hot spot for advertising, sales, and promotion—even MTV has a page on the Web. However, Web pages are not the exclusive province of large Internet sites and Big Business; anybody can create his or her own page and put it on the Web.

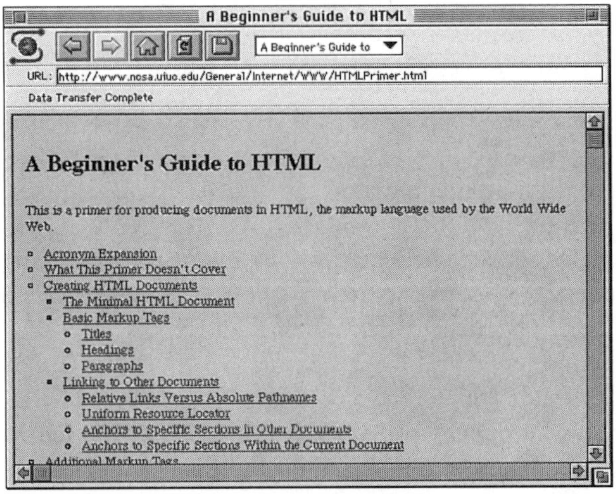

FIGURE 4.2.
A page on the World Wide Web, seen through the Mosaic browser.

Through the Web, users can access a variety of sophisticated search tools for generating lists of Web pages and other Internet resources related to a search topic. The lists are presented as hypertext links: clicking on any item in the list takes you to the information. As mentioned earlier in this chapter, Web pages can act as "front ends" to other Internet resources—including FTP file transfers, newsgroups and more. In many cases, the Web makes using these resources simpler and also affords users the luxury of performing many different Internet activities from within a single software program: the beautiful browser.

All this makes the Web not only relatively easy, but friendly and fun, too. In fact, most of the mass-media buzz about the Internet in recent years is a direct result of the Web and the sexy facade the browsers put there. When that happened, the perception of the Internet instantly changed from an unfathomable hacker's toolbox to the new middle-class illustrated encyclopedia, from nerd-tool to Nintendo.

There is a downside to the Web, however. The graphical information the Web carries and other architectural aspects of the Web weigh heavy on the Net. To use the Web, users must pack mighty modems—14.4 Kbps is a typical minimum for reasonable use of a graphical browser, and 28.8 Kbps is better. Even with a fast modem, the Web can be slow, as can be the browser software itself. Fortunately, browsers are employing neat tricks to make Web surfing less taxing, such as enabling users to scroll pages or activate links without waiting for all of a page's graphics to be displayed, or caching Web pages in memory or on disk for fast retrieval.

For more about using the World Wide Web and creating Web pages, see Chapter 10.

Telnet

Telnet is a charming throwback to old-fashioned hacking—one that's slowly disappearing as Telnet sites are displaced by, or upgraded to, Web sites or Gophers. In essence, you can use Telnet to dial into another computer system so that you can use the remote computer as if you were there, running programs and accessing information stored on that system. Telnet can be used to reach thousands of college library and public library card catalogs; federal, state and local government offices; interactive games (MUDs, described later in this chapter), and more. Like other Internet tools, Telnet requires client software. Originally developed for the scientific community, public domain NCSA Telnet is by far and away the most popular Telnet client for Macintosh users. (NCSA, by the way, stands for National Center for Supercomputing Applications, but you'll find out more on that in Chapter 11, "Tapping into Remote Systems with Telnet.")

Of course, remote computer systems available through Telnet don't enable just any Internet user to log on and go wild. Telnet systems have ways of keeping Internet visitors from accessing sensitive or costly resources. Usually, Internet visitors must log on with a generic username, such as `guest`, which signals the local security system to restrict access to some resources. Still, some computer systems—particularly government and university systems—are quite welcoming to Telnet visitors, even to the point of supplying help menus.

In general, Telnet is the most difficult of the principle Internet resources to learn. That's because you only really operate Telnet itself to *get to* the remote computer. After that, you have to figure out how to use the remote computer with no help at all from Telnet. Most of the time, that's not too hard. Most computers available through Telnet have menu-driven interfaces, so you can poke around simply by typing the number of a menu item you see on the screen and pressing Return. All it takes to use Telnet is comfort with computers, a little experience, and a little courage.

Still, every Telnet site is different and requires different login and operational steps. And why not? These computer systems were designed for the benefit of their regular users. Internet folks are allowed to visit, but it's their responsibility to find their way around, not the site's job to make things easy. When in Rome....

For more about Telnet, see Chapter 11.

FTP

File Transfer Protocol (FTP) is the standard Internet protocol for copying files from one computer to another across the Internet. FTP is actually used behind the scenes in many file transfer activities, including those performed by Web links. There is a world of *FTP sites*—computers on the Internet configured as FTP servers to enable users to download the files stored there. Using FTP requires special client software; a simple point-and-click FTP client for the Mac is the shareware, Anarchie.

What's out there? You name it. Software and hardware companies—Apple included—operate FTP sites so that users can download updated drivers, bug patches, new product information, and so on. Tons of shareware and public domain software (see Chapter 5) is available through FTP, including FTP client software. Books—including the Bible, the complete Shakespeare, and too much government information to think about—are available in text files through FTP. Virtually anything that can be stored in a computer file is out there somewhere on an FTP server.

Note

> Sams' parent company, Macmillan Computer Publishing, operates its own FTP server from which you can download the best Internet software tools available. (See Chapter 5.)

Some FTP servers are password protected so that their files can be downloaded only by authorized users. Many sites, however, are set up as "anonymous" FTP sites that require no passwords; anybody who knows the Internet address of the site can connect to it and download files. FTP sites can display lists of the files and directories, which are typically organized in a hierarchical fashion of directories, subdirectories, and files.

For more about FTP, see Chapter 12, "Collecting Files with FTP."

FTP = "Finding Things Painful"

The tangled trees of directories, files, and subdirectories at FTP sites can make finding a particular file tough; so can cryptic filenames that do little to tell you what's inside. Well-run FTP sites place an index file somewhere near the top of the tree (the entry point when you connect), so that you can download and read the index first, then go straight to what you want. Still, be aware that FTP works best when you know exactly what you're looking for and where to find it.

But if you don't know exactly what you're looking for, there is help. Built into Anarchie is a tool called Archie which you can use to search through databases of FTP files and sites. Based on a given search term, Archie can generate a list of directions to FTP files, including the location of the site, the exact filename, and its directory location.

For more about Archie, see Chapter 16, "Finding Files and Directories with Archie and Veronica."

Gopher

In the course of the evolution of the Internet's ease of use, somewhere between Telnet and the Web, Gopher happened. The brainchild of enterprising folks at the University of Minnesota, Gopher is a three-way metaphor: It's a pun for the ability to "go for" data; it suggests the animal's ability to burrow (for data); and it pays homage to the University of Minnesota's furry little mascot, a rat that lives in the country. (I often wonder how many people would feel warm and fuzzy about an easy-to-use Internet facility called *Rat*?)

In effect, the Gopher system places standardized, easy-to-use menus over Internet sites and their available resources. (See Figure 4.3.) From the user's perspective, Gopher makes navigating sites and checking out their contents simpler, because everything works the same way and navigating is a point-and-click proposition. Under the covers, Gopher is a *distributed client/server system.* Hundreds of Gopher servers distributed throughout the world each contain menus for their local resources. These servers are linked to other servers so that users running Gopher client software can attach to one server and have access to all of "Gopherspace," the complete set of Gopher sites (often simply called *Gophers*) and menus.

FIGURE 4.3.
A Gopher menu.

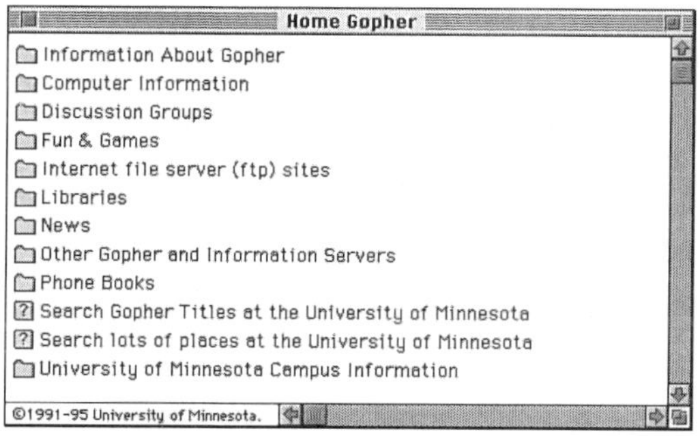

Only a portion of Internet resources is available through Gopher, but that portion includes a robust collection of universities, government offices, and other institutions. Gopher has a companion search tool, Veronica, that generates lists of Gopher menus that supply access to information on a given search term. The list is itself a Gopher menu, so you can click any item in the list to navigate to the resource Veronica dug up. All of Gopherspace (and Veronica) is also available through the World Wide Web, so many Mac users forego a Gopher client and do their burrowing from a Web browser.

For more about Gopher, see Chapter 13, "Navigating with Menus: Gopher."

Talk, Chat, and Games

The last and, probably, the least used of the principal Internet facilities are the interactive communications tools. These enable Internet users to communicate with other users in "real time," zinging messages across the Net and receiving a reply almost as fast as a reply can be typed, so that a sort of online conversation is achieved. These facilities—all of which require client software or access to a server running client software—are used for heady purposes like scientific consultation and diplomatic communications. They're also used for fun and socialization.

One interactive tool is Talk, which sets up a one-to-one conversation between two Internet users. Each user's screen is split in two: everything typed by User A appears in one half, and everything typed by User B appears in the other half. In this way, the two users can carry on a typed conversation and can even "talk over" one another by typing at the same time. The split screen keeps the conversation from getting garbled. Talk supports only parties of two.

Internet Relay Chat (IRC, sometimes also known as *Chat*) lets two or more users participate in a given conversation, carried out in a virtual room called a *channel.* Each channel has a designated topic of conversation, although some are designated as "open" channels in which any topic is fair game. Any number of Internet users can join in the conversation, which is displayed, line by line, in one big listing that scrolls along on all participants' screens. Each user chooses (or is assigned) a unique username that appears next to his or her statements, so that everyone knows who's speaking.

The core IRC technology is used not only for conversation and conferences but for interactive games run under various names, including MUDs, MUSEs, and MOOs. In these games, users enter a virtual room set up for the game and governed by the game's rules. The traditional type of game is an offshoot of Dungeons and Dragons, a role-playing game in which players interact with each other within a fantasy environment. In recent years, the games have broadened into many different styles and permutations, and even to non-recreational, scientific role-playing exercises and experiments.

For more about Internet interactive communications, see Chapter 14, "Interacting in Real Time: Talk, Chat, and Games."

Summary

Logging on to the Internet doesn't really get you anywhere—it simply dumps you in a great big hallway from which you can open any of several doors. Each door is a tool, and behind it is a discrete type of Internet resource. To open the door and use what's behind it, you need the right client software and the right know-how.

Chapters 7 through 14 cover the doors and rooms in detail, one by one. Before you get there, however, you need to learn about the software you need (see Chapter 5) and about the customs and manners you are expected to observe when you arrive. (See Chapter 6, "Netiquette and First Tips").

CHAPTER 5

CHOOSING CLIENT SOFTWARE FOR INTERNET SERVICES

You know from Chapter 3, "Configuring Your Macintosh for the Internet," that you must install MacTCP and MacPPP to connect to the Internet. By themselves, TCP and PPP will get you onto the Net, but not around on it. For that, you then need client software to navigate the Internet's resources. (See Chapter 4, "An Introduction to Internet Tools and Resources.") This is where things start to get exciting. Using client software to mine the rich resources available on the Internet is the fun part.

Fortunately, all the software you need to get started on your Internet voyage is included with this book.

This chapter describes how client software works with your Macintosh and provides guidelines for finding and selecting your personalized Internet toolkit.

Software from Sams

The public domain, commercial and shareware programs described in this chapter are included with this book. Since Internet software is constantly changing and evolving, you'll also find out later in this chapter where to find out if you have the latest client versions. Don't forget, though, to pay your fees for the shareware you use with this book or for any new shareware you acquire.

How Client Software Works with Your Macintosh

Most Internet resources are accessed through a mechanism called client/server processing. Although a networking expert would beat me up for oversimplifying the definition, client/server processing is a way of controlling the exchange of information between two computers. One, called the client, sends commands (called queries) to the server, requesting an action. The server does what it's told and returns the results to the client computer. To make this work, the client must issue commands that the server understands. That's why you need newsreader client software to read the information on news servers and why you need FTP client software for commanding FTP servers to send files to your computer.

One of the beauties of Internet client software is that you can mix and match different programs to suit your tastes. You can pick which clients you want to use for each Internet resource. That enables you to select the individual client programs that best fit your needs. We chose the software included with this book because we thought it was the best of the bunch. But, you may find that another tool is better suited to your needs. For example, this book supplies you with shareware Eudora Light, but you may find that you prefer to use the commercial Eudora Pro or InterCon's mail program. It's up to you.

Client Configuration

Although most client programs need no special configuration to interface with MacTCP, they require some minor setup and configuration steps after installation. For example, to operate properly, some client software must know your e-mail address or the name of your provider's server. Newsreader clients (see Chapter 9, "Browsing Newsgroups") for working with newsgroups must know the address of a news server; e-mail software has to know the address of the provider's mail server.

To configure most Mac client software, you typically choose a preferences or settings or configuration menu item and fill in a simple dialog box, as shown in Figure 5.1.

FIGURE 5.1.
Configuring an e-mail client.

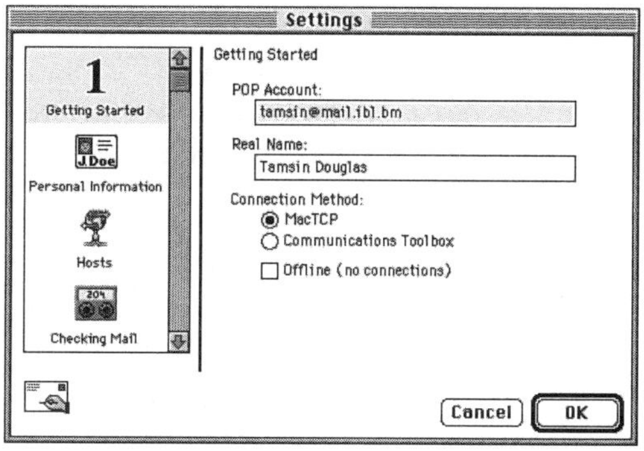

The specifics and type of configuration necessary for each particular type of client software is described, when necessary, in Chapters 7, "Exchanging E-Mail" through 14, "Interacting in Real Time: Talk, Chat, and Games" of this book.

Where *Is* the Software?

Like any software, Internet software is available in four basic forms:

- **Commercial**—Software you buy, like Eudora Pro (the commercial version of the Eudora Light e-mail program).
- **Demo**—A special version of a commercial software product that's crippled in some way (for example, it may be unable to save files) or designed to "expire" after you use it for awhile. Demos are designed to demonstrate a commercial product so that you'll pay to get the full-featured version or one that doesn't expire. Note that some people use demos that don't expire for years, putting up with their functional inadequacies as the price of the software.
- **Shareware**—Shareware is distributed free, on the honor system. You can try it for free, but if you intend to actually use it beyond the trial period, you are expected to send a nominal license fee (typically $10 to $50) to the programmer. Don't assume that everyone else is going to pay for the shareware program you're using. If you don't pay the developer, than he or she can't continue to make improvements in the software. Some of the best Macintosh Internet software (Anarchie comes to mind) is produced by independent shareware developers who rely on shareware payments.

They deserve to be paid for their efforts and have greatly contributed to the lowering of prices for commercial software. So support 'em—pay for your shareware.

- **Public domain**—Sometimes known as *freeware*, public domain software is distributed free of charge, usually by universities which produce software or out of the goodness of an independent programmer's heart. Technically, freeware is copyrighted software to which the owner grants licenses for free; public domain software is uncopyrighted, free software.

All these types of software can be acquired online. Shareware, demo, and public domain software can be downloaded from FTP sites (see Chapter 12, "Collecting Files with FTP"); commercial software can be ordered online from software vendors in online shops found on the World Wide Web. (See Chapter 18, "Finding It on the Web.")

In general, for the Mac user, shareware and public domain programs offer the greatest value. Also, acquiring and managing your own suite of Internet client software is not too difficult; doing so puts you in complete control. Once you assemble your own Internet toolkit, you'll have the expertise to upgrade or replace any piece of it as your needs change or as new, exciting programs hit the wires.

Figure 5.2 shows the contents of my Internet folder, which I keep on my desktop for easy access. All the programs shown are shareware or freeware (except for Netscape). Note that I keep a program called Stuffit Expander in the group, which I use for decompressing files received through FTP. For more about decompressing files, see Chapter 12.

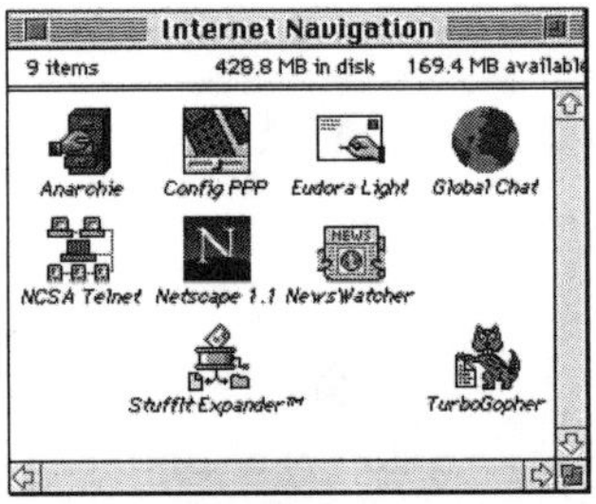

FIGURE 5.2.
A desktop folder holding the author's Internet toolkit.

Note that many Internet access providers supply a start-up disk for new users, supposedly featuring "free" software. These free disks almost always include a mixture of public domain and shareware programs. Although the software is free as far as the provider is concerned, you are expected to pay for the shareware eventually—the provider has not purchased a license on your behalf. For example, many providers supply new Mac-based subscribers with a copy of Anarchie; you are expected to pay for if you continue to use it.

Tip

When evaluating any Internet software, be sure to consider freedom of choice: One trend in packaged Internet software, particularly in all-in-one commercial packages, is to bundle all the software you need, preconfigured for connecting to one or more commercial Internet access providers. When you start up one of these packages, the software may lead you through the sign-up process for a particular Internet access provider with whom the software maker has cut a deal. You may or may not be able to easily reconfigure the software for any provider. Make sure that any Internet software package you purchase enables you to choose your own access provider.

Software from Sams

Sams Publishing has put together a collection of hand-picked freeware, shareware, and demo programs that you will find especially useful, including a Gopher client (see Chapter 13, "Navigating with Menus: Gopher"), a newsreader (see Chapter 9), and an easy-to-use FTP client. (See Chapter 12.) This software is included with the book. See Chapters 7 through 14 for guidelines on configuring specific types of Internet client software. System 6 users should also take a peak at Appendix B, "The Internet for System 6 Users," at the back of this book.

Note

You are responsible for properly licensing any shareware you acquire from Sams. Please note that Sams does not provide technical support for these programs or warrant their operation. Direct all questions to the developers of the respective programs.

Finding Updated Software, and Much More

There are numerous software archives on the Internet containing great freeware and shareware Internet clients for the Macintosh. Listed in this section are some URLs to get you started. For details on how to access a site using an URL, see chapters 10 and 12.

The Internet software section of the Web-accessible Info-Mac archive:

```
ftp://uiarchive.cso.uiuc.edu/pub/systems/mac/info-mac/_Communication/_MacTCP/
```

The communications directory in the University of Michigan Macintosh archive:

```
ftp://mirror.archive.umich.edu/mac/util/comm/
```

You can also use the bookmarks in Anarchie to find other sites with Macintosh software. See Chapter 12 for details.

Summary

If the Internet is indeed a highway, the vehicles people use to travel that highway are as much a matter of personal taste as any other vehicle. Whether you drive a Yugo or a Subaru or a Lincoln down that road is up to you. Familiarize yourself with the options and take a spin. If you don't like the feel of your vehicle, trade it in and try something else. Just make sure that whatever you choose is street-legal, affordable, and mechanically sound. Beyond that, suit your own tastes.

Speaking of rules of the road, Chapter 6, "Netiquette and First Tips," offers the final step in your preparation for online access: a rundown on Internet manners. Familiarize yourself with these customs to keep within the speed limit and on the correct side of the road. More importantly, "netiquette" will save you from horn-honks and filthy gestures from those with whom you share the highway.

CHAPTER 6

NETIQUETTE AND FIRST TIPS

The Internet is more than a place; it's a culture. Like the United States, it's a large and variable culture, cobbled together from many other cultures and fragmented into subcultures.

Also like the United States, the Internet harbors some who believe they have a special, manifest right to control the Internet and its culture and that everyone else should conform to their ways or stay offline. Surely new users, like guests in a foreign country, should be allowed some leeway when it comes to the rules; there's no excuse for Internet bigotry or for abusing the "newbies," which Net jocks have been known to do. On the other hand, a new immigrant to the Internet has an obligation to try to observe the local customs as much as possible.

This chapter provides an overview of the Internet manners you need to make a smooth transition onto the Internet, understand the behavior and vocabulary of those you encounter there, avoid insulting anybody, and avoid incurring angry "flame" messages sometimes blasted at users who run afoul of local customs. These manners and customs are generally bundled under the term *Netiquette* (*Net* + *etiquette*).

As the Internet becomes easier to use and more popular, its user base is becoming broader. No longer the exclusive workplace of the technological elite, the Internet is increasingly populated by people from many walks of life. Its culture and customs are evolving—and loosening up—as a result of its growth. So why not just tear up the rule book and start over? Because many of the traditional Internet customs make a lot of sense. The rules came about in response to certain problems, and they have served the Internet and its citizens well. Until the culture redefines itself, smart users play by the existing rules—which are really quite simple to learn and follow and are based on common sense more than anything else.

Who Defines Internet Etiquette?

"If nobody owns the Internet and it's unregulated," you ask, "who makes the rules?" Fair question. Answer: Nobody. Netiquette has its origins in the policies of the large internetworks that formed the Internet's backbone—in particular, NSFnet. But these rules, or rather, guidelines, have never been enforced and don't even really apply to general Internet users. Other customs have simply evolved; the ones that worked stuck around as tradition. As you review them, notice that most of the rules center around two goals:

- **Efficiency**—making sure that communication avoids unnecessary elaboration and repetition, and making sure that messages are properly addressed and return-addressed (to avoid excessive network traffic that could slow everybody down). Efficient communication also speeds up the process of reading and responding to messages on the Net.
- **Decorum**—making sure that the interaction stays friendly (or at least respectful), clean (within reason), and easy to read and understand.

You may not be surprised to learn that the efficiency rules are more closely observed than the decorum rules. Internet communication—especially in unmoderated newsgroups—can become childish, petty, peevish, vulgar, obscene, rude, and mean. You'll see it, but you can stay above it—or avoid it altogether—if you choose.

Note

In addition to the points of Netiquette described in this chapter, some experts may advise that it's also polite to use the Internet in ways that minimize your drain on network resources, sometimes informally (and inaccurately) described as *bandwidth*. This politeness takes two forms:

- When communicating with a special-purpose server, such as an FTP or Archie server, try to choose one geographically close to you.
- Avoid using resources during times of heavy load. For example, don't access a company's FTP server or Web page during that firm's normal business hours because that's when the company needs its computer resources for its own, internal operations.
- Avoid using real-time interactive resources (IRC and Talk) when slower communication methods (e-mail or newsgroups) would be just as effective. E-mail and newsgroups do not send data until there is a lull in traffic, but IRCX and Talk are not as "nice" to the network as a whole.

These tips are designed to prevent your Internet activity from further degrading overall network performance when the Internet may be overtaxed. In principle, observing these rules can't hurt. However, your efforts at being a network-thrifty Internet consumer may not pay off.

First, just because a server is geographically close to you doesn't mean that your connection to it is short and direct. Because the route between any two computers on the Internet usually passes through many other computers, your connection to a nearby server (unless it's your access provider's server) may actually loop far away and then back to the server—which means that a connection to a nearby server may exact the same toll as a connection to a distant one. Other factors, including the capabilities of the communications lines between computers along a route, may actually make using a distant server a more thrifty choice than using a nearby one. As a user, you have no real way of determining which route or server is the least costly to the network.

Second, it's very difficult to determine when the "peak," or busiest, hours are for any Internet resource. Some company's computers are actually more busy when the office is closed, and a company's Web server or FTP server may in fact be leased from another firm—in which case the company's own computer needs are unaffected by Internet activity.

If you notice, during certain hours, that a given resource or server is difficult to access or performs especially poorly, take that as a sign of peak activity and try to avoid using it during those hours. Otherwise, do what you want, when you want.

Basic Netiquette

The tips in the following sections cover the basics of Netiquette for messaging activities (e-mail, mailing lists, newsgroups, Talk, and IRC). Whenever you type, keep these guidelines in mind.

Watch Your Language

Remember that you're writing, not speaking. Sarcasm, facetiousness, comic hyperbole, and other colorful techniques of spoken expression depend heavily on speech inflection. They often fail to achieve their desired effect when written—except, of course, when written in a clever Internet book, where sarcasm and hyperbole are the rule.

If you try to be clever online, your message may backfire. The most common example occurs when one person writes something silly or exaggerated in fun, and someone else reads it completely seriously—and takes offense. Write what you mean, clearly and directly. Save the color for those with whom you've established a strong rapport—or for your own Internet book.

Making Your Meaning Clear

Internet shorthand abbreviations and emoticons (both covered later in this chapter) can help make your meaning clear and prevent misunderstandings. For example, if you make a facetious statement, you can follow it with the "smiley" emoticon:

:-)

Tilt your head to the left—it looks like a smiling face. That tells your reader you're kidding.

Avoid "Capital" Offenses

Some folks like to use ALL CAPITALS for emphasis or to point out that YOUR LAST MESSAGE WAS TOTALLY OFF-BASE, YOU MORON. A few of these folks are holdovers from the old mainframe computing days when all program code was written in uppercase—and e-mail was also typed in uppercase, from habit. (Some folks just left the Caps Lock key on all the time.) Most modern Internet users, however, type in uppercase letters TO SHOW THAT THEY'RE SHOUTING. It annoys readers. Don't do it. Make your point with strong, well-chosen words and persuasive logic, not tall letters.

Curb Quoting

The Reply or Respond features in many e-mail programs and in newsreaders may automatically "quote" the complete text of the message you're responding to by inserting it in your response. Quoting helps you show exactly what you're responding to; you can cut the copied message down to its relevant passages and respond to those passages directly. (During an argument, haven't you ever wanted the ability to show the other person *exactly* what he or she said?)

Unfortunately, some people use this feature lazily and leave the entire text of the copied message in every response. In the course of an ongoing e-mail, newsgroup, or list exchange, such messages grow like fungi because each new volley carries the entire history of the conversation within it. The mushrooming exchange lays unnecessary storage and transmission burdens on the Internet—and wastes the time of readers who must wade through old news to get to the new stuff. Cut quotes down to what matters; cut them completely when they're unnecessary.

Be Discreet

Newsgroup postings, mailing list messages, and statements made in a Chat session are public—anybody can read them. E-mail and Talk are supposed to be private, but really aren't. (They're designed to be private, and usually are, but they're not inaccessible to skilled computer snoops; see Chapter 20, "Using the Internet in the Office.") Remember also that your e-mail recipient can copy your message and forward it to others, without your knowledge. The laws regarding electronic communication are evolving, but in general, an e-mail message is the property of its recipient, not its sender. You may have no legal protection against the copying and distribution of what you write to others. More importantly, under current laws, business owners have the legal right to examine all e-mail stored on company-owned computers—without employees' consent or knowledge.

The moral? Phrase everything you say on the Internet as if you were talking to Geraldo Rivera. If you don't want the world to know about it, send a letter by U.S. post, make a phone call, or arrange a meeting in a dark alley—keep it off the Internet. Don't make the mistake of thinking your newsgroup and mailing list postings are read only by strangers around the world. You never know when your boss, co-worker, neighbor, spouse, or personal banker may come across one of your postings. E-mail is safer, but not air-tight. So be careful out there.

It should be noted that profanity is tolerated on the Internet, although it may get your message rejected in some moderated newsgroups and lists. Personally, I find the occasional strong word an effective tool. But if you're concerned about being thought a boor by those more prudish than you, or if you think kids shouldn't see what you're tempted to write, keep it clean.

Keep Cool

"Flaming" is the Internet word for sending an irate message. Flames may be appropriate in response to some events, but—as with all violent acts—flames have a way of igniting counter-flames and escalating into "flame wars," in which the offense that ignited the first flame is lost in the mêlée and never resolved. Flames also tend to make the writer look like a nutburger.

The nature of the Internet naturally enables people to lose their heads more freely—after all, if you flame at Phil in Tokyo, you don't worry about running into him later at the gas station and getting your face bashed in. Still, hot flashes on the Internet rarely accomplish anything. So stay cool. Make your points with reason. If somebody posts something stupid, tell him or her so—calmly. And remember: For all you know, Phil in Tokyo has a meeting with your boss next week.

Communicate Efficiently

Avoid sending unnecessary words, or unnecessary messages. You don't have to truncate your sentences down to telegrams ("Have read yr msg...Think you wrong...will send u 2nd msg to xplain...stop), but try to be concise. Consider using shorthand (see "Internet Shorthand," later in this chapter), where appropriate, to save space and time.

Many Internet users craft "signature blocks" (see Chapter 7, "Exchanging E-Mail") in their messages to identify themselves and feature some favorite quote or witticism. Signature blocks are a nice way of revealing the personality of the writer, but when they exceed a few lines—and they often do—they're wasteful and annoying. There's a guy who uses an entire dialog scene from the film *When Harry Met Sally* as his signature. Nobody welcomes his messages, and some people *really* hate him.

Internet users expect messages to be polite, but they don't expect entire messages to be sent solely for the sake of politeness. If someone answers your question in a newsgroup or list, don't post (or even e-mail) a thank you, unless you can work it into a message that has something else to say. Not posting thanks isn't considered rude; posting messages with no new information is.

Post No Bills

As explained in Chapter 20, commercial activity—including advertising and selling—was once restricted on the Internet, was recently tolerated, and is now encouraged. Still, such activities should be reserved to appropriate commercial zones, such as Web pages. Sending unsolicited e-mail ads, or posting ads on newsgroups and lists, is almost certain to ignite flames.

The exception is private sales among subscribers within a group. For example, I frequent a video laserdisc newsgroup; folks there often sell or trade their used laserdiscs with other subscribers. If you're in business, however, and want to sell your product or service on the Net, restrict your selling to Internet tools where it's appropriate. An easy way to find out whether commercial activity is tolerated in a given Internet tool is to hang out there awhile (*lurk* there), watching for any commercial activity and the responses to it. Lurking should tell you not only whether commercial activity is tolerated, but what type of activity is well received. In any case, make sure your ad relates to the topic of the newsgroup.

Tip

One type of commercial activity tolerated nowhere on the Net is chain letters. These are sometimes posted on newsgroups and mailing lists and sometimes broadcast with e-mail. Like paper-based chain letters, Internet chain letters are sometimes just games but are often money-making scams.

Newsgroup and mailing list moderators and the system administrators of local servers do their best to weed out chain letters; they may even be able to revoke the posting/mailing privileges of chain-letter senders. Also, the Internet community does a pretty good job of either ignoring chain letters or flaming offenders into submission.

Internet Shorthand

Over the years, a system of abbreviations has emerged for frequently used phrases. These "shorthand" abbreviations help writers keep messages concise. They're most useful in Talk or IRC sessions, when it's important to type quickly, but they're also used in other types of Internet messaging. Shorthand isn't Netiquette (nobody expects you to use it), but it's there if you need it. At the very least, you should be familiar with shorthand so that you can understand the messages of others who use it.

Following are the basic shorthand abbreviations. Despite the Netiquette discouragement of using ALL CAPS, (see "Avoid 'Capital' Offenses," earlier in this chapter), shorthand is always typed in caps, as any letter abbreviation should be.

Abbreviation	*Meaning*	*Example*
BTW	By the way	BTW, where's a good FTP site for downloading a picture of Kevin Costner?
IMHO	In my humble opinion	Kevin Costner has the dramatic range of a carrot, IMHO.
IMO	In my opinion (without the sarcastic/humorous tone added by *humble*)	Costner is a competent actor, no more, IMO.
LOL	Laughing out loud (tags a joke or a statement that's patently ludicrous)	*Wyatt Earp* represents the best in contemporary American cinema (LOL).
OTF	On the floor (laughing, presumably; same as LOL, only stronger)	Costner was believable as a 12th-century Englishman in *Robin Hood* (OTF).
OTOH	On the other hand	OTOH, he was pretty good in *Field of Dreams* and *JFK.*
ROTFL	Rolling on the floor laughing (same as LOL, but much stronger)	Costner is a modern-day Chaplin. (ROTFL)
YMMV	Your mileage may vary (functions as a disclaimer to evaluations or experiences, telling the reader not to expect the same results you describe)	I cried buckets at *Dances With Wolves,* YMMV.

Proper Use for Shorthand and Emoticons

Shorthand and emoticons (described next) are considered informal techniques and really aren't appropriate in formal communications such as e-mail business letters. They can also be overused, leading to messages that seem to be written in some bizarre, secret code. Use them selectively and sparingly. Avoid using both in the same message.

More importantly, observe whether they're used by those you correspond with, or by others in newsgroups or lists you frequent. If not, your readers may not even understand shorthand and emoticons, in which case you'd best stick to words.

Emoticons

Emoticons are little sideways faces formed out of two or more text characters. (The term derives from "emotion icons.") To see the face, you have to tilt your head to the left or lay your monitor on its right side (head tilting is better). Table 6.1 shows the most common emoticons.

Sometimes also called *smileys* after the most common example, emoticons are used to give the reader a sense of your emotional tone. For example, if you write, "I want to have your babies," but you're only kidding, you can make your intention clear by following your statement with a smile `:-)` or a wink `;-)` . You may also use emoticons to express an emotion outright—a smiley often follows the word *Thanks!*

Some emoticons attempt not to express an emotion, but rather to give the reader a sense of the writer's appearance—or rather, the appearance of the writer's Internet alter-ego. If you get mail from someone using the emoticon for the Pope `+-(:-)` be polite to this person, but keep your confession to yourself.

Table 6.1. Emoticons (tilt your head left to see the faces).

Emoticon	*Means You Are...*
`:-)`	Smiling
`:-(`	Frowning
`(:-(`	Frowning severely
`;-)`	Winking
`:-o`	Surprised
`8-0`	Shocked
`:-S`	Confused
`:-\`	Skeptical
`:-)'`	Drooling
`:-)8`	Well-dressed (see the bow tie?)

Emoticon	*Means You Are...*
`8-)`	Wearing glasses
`*<¦:-)`	Santa Claus (see the hat?)
`=:-)=`	Punk rocker with a goatee

Tip

In addition to emoticons and shorthand, you'll see messages annotated and embellished one more way. Some people surround action words with right and left carats (< >), and use them in the same way shorthand is used. The words are physical actions, but they're used to describe facial expressions or body language that indicates emotion, tone, or inflection. Here are some examples:

```
<grin>
<shrug>
<wink>
<sigh>
```

Sometimes, these are boiled down to a letter or two:

`<g>`	(a grin)
`<l>`	(a laugh)
`<s>`	(a sigh)
`<jk>`	(just kidding)

Last, and maybe least, comes a shorthand that many readers mistake for a typo:

`< >`	(no comment)

Summary

The Internet has room for everybody. You shouldn't approach it as a closed society in which you must stringently observe every little tradition. Still, like most traditions, the key points of Netiquette serve a useful purpose: they keep the information flow efficient, civil, and comprehensible. Familiarity with these guidelines can smooth your transition onto the Net and make you more productive there.

In Chapter 7, you begin your nuts-and-bolts exploration of Internet tools and resources with the most widely used one: e-mail.

CHAPTER 7

EXCHANGING E-MAIL

How E-Mail Works

Configuring Eudora Light

The Anatomy of an E-Mail Message

E-Mail Options

Using Eudora for E-Mail

Sending Mail to Online Services

Sending Internet Mail from Online Services to the Net

Summary

Known as *e-mail* or sometimes just *mail*, Internet electronic mail is the most-used Internet resource and also one of the simplest. Although there are other options, sending e-mail involves little more than typing your recipient's e-mail address, typing a message, and sending the mail on its way. Getting e-mail from others entails checking your mailbox and choosing a message to read from a list of those you have received. It's all pretty straightforward.

E-mail is made easy by one other fact: Eudora Light (the shareware version of Eudora included on diskette with this book) is simple to set up and use.

This chapter explains e-mail in detail, including how to configure the e-mail program Eudora Light.

How E-Mail Works

Transmitting a text message from any specific computer on the Internet to any other is made possible by two *protocols* (computer communications languages): Simple Mail Transfer Protocol (SMTP) for sending e-mail and Post Office Protocol 3 (POP3) for receiving e-mail. The Internet being the Internet, other mail protocols come into the stream at some points, but these are the principle vehicles.

SMTP is the mail standard in the Internet protocol suite. Each server on the Net that can receive mail has SMTP. The SMTP server of the sender contacts the SMTP server of the recipient before sending e-mail, making sure that the receiver's mail server is ready. If the receiving server is ready, the e-mail is transferred between the servers. If not, the sending server waits and tries again later. This is all part of the Internet's "store and forward" approach to e-mail: messages wait at various points along their journey and are forwarded when the traffic allows. This approach slows e-mail down but greatly increases the chances that your messages will make it through to their intended audience.

To send mail from a typical dial-up Internet account, your Mac communicates via POP3 with your mail server, then your mail server communicates with the recpient's mail sever via SMTP. Then, your recipient's mail server uses POP3 to pull the messages from their mail server.

Configuring Eudora Light

Before you can receive e-mail you need to configure your e-mail client. In this chapter, we'll be using Eudora Light. Your Internet provider should supply you with your e-mail account information when you subscribe to its service. Before you can configure Eudora Light, make sure you have the following information ready:

POP3 Account—The POP3 account consists of your username followed by the `@` symbol and the name of the POP server. For example, `tamsin@mail.ibl.bm`.

Note

> Depending on your Internet provider's set-up, your POP3 account username may be the same as your PPP login name, but usually they are different. Keep in mind, too, that your POP3 account name is not the same as your e-mail address, though they may look similar.

E-mail Address—This is the address other Internet users use to send you e-mail. For example, `tamsin@ibl.bm`.

SMTP Server Name—This is the name of the computer which processes your outgoing mail. For example, `mail.ibl.bm`. In most cases, the SMTP server name is the same as the name of the POP server.

To configure Eudora Light, follow these steps:

1. Launch Eudora Light. (See Figure 7.1.)

FIGURE 7.1.
The Eudora Light application inside the Navigation folder.

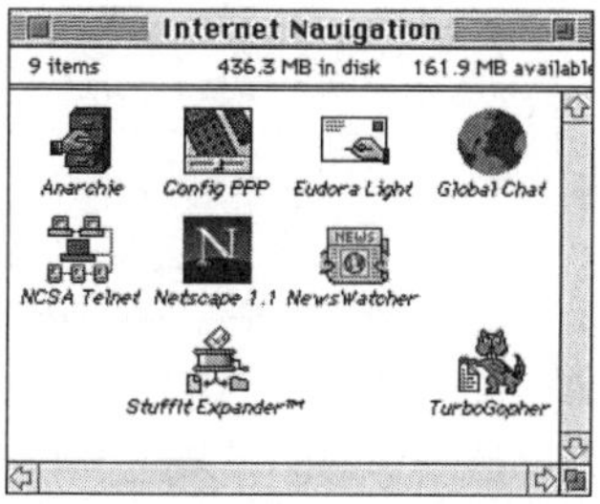

2. The first time you open Eudora Light, the Settings dialog box will appear with default settings already filled in. You must enter your e-mail account information in the Settings dialog box to use Eudora Light.
3. In the POP Account: field, type the POP (Post Office Protocol) account information, as supplied by your Internet provider. (See Figure 7.2.)

FIGURE 7.2.
The Getting Started settings.

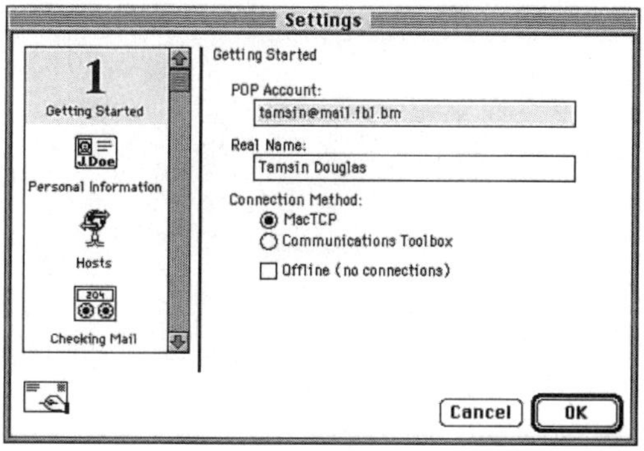

4. In the Real Name: field, type your name. Your real name will be attached to all of your outgoing mail messages.

Tip

For detailed explanations of the fields you encounter in Eudora's Settings dialog box, choose Show Balloons from the Balloon Help menu. When you move the mouse pointer to a Eudora menu selection or item on the screen, a brief description of that item is displayed.(See Figure 7.3.) To turn off Balloon Help, choose Hide Balloons from the Balloon menu.

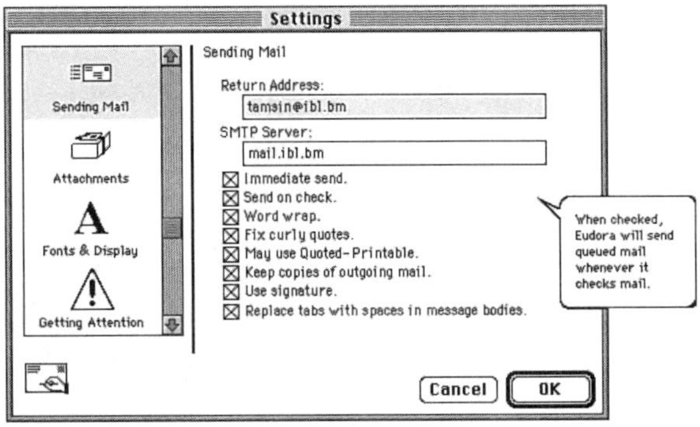

FIGURE 7.3.
An example of Balloon Help in Eudora Light.

5. When you are finished filling in this information, click on Personal Information.
6. In the Return Address: field, type your e-mail address. (See Figure 7.4.)

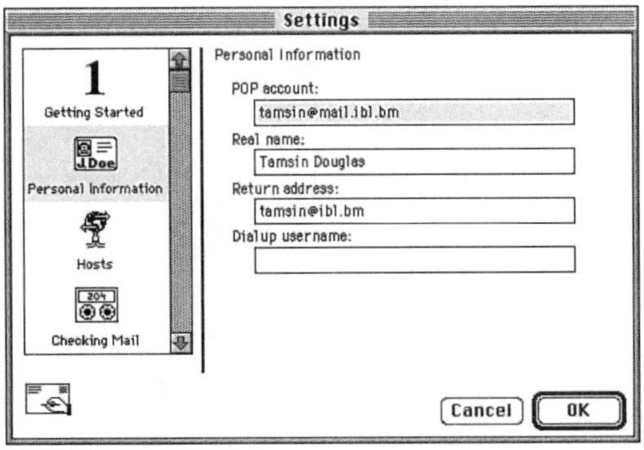

FIGURE 7.4.
The Personal Information settings.

7. Now click on Hosts.
8. In the SMTP: field, type the name of the SMTP server used by your Internet provider. (See Figure 7.5.)

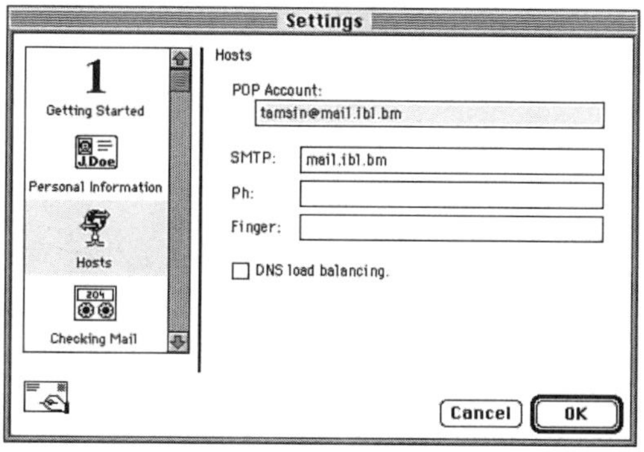

FIGURE 7.5.
The Hosts settings.

9. Now click on Checking Mail.
10. You may either use the default Checking Mail settings or configure it separately. (See Figure 7.6.)

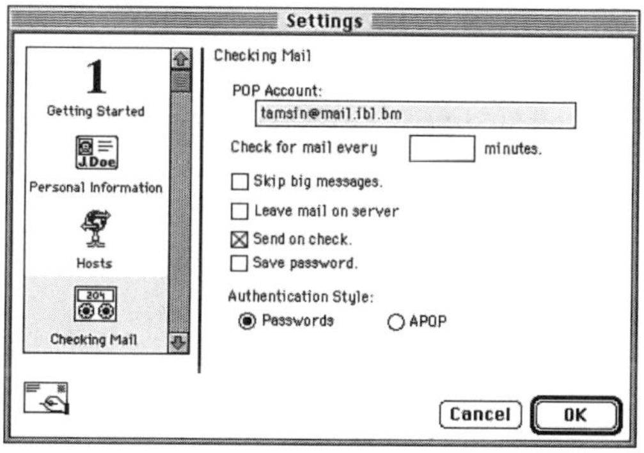

FIGURE 7.6.
The Checking Mail settings.

Warning

When you enter a value in the Check for mail field, Eudora will check for mail at the interval specified. If Eudora is open when you aren't connected to the Internet, you will get an error when Eudora tries to check for mail. Eudora may even activate Config PPP, squandering valuable Internet connect time. On the other hand, if you really need to know every 10 minutes whether someone has sent you mail, then you should enter 10 in this box.

11. If you want to retain copies of all the outgoing messages you send, check the Keep Copies of Outgoing Mail option. (See Figure 7.7.)
12. When you are done configuring Eudora, click the OK button to save your changes.

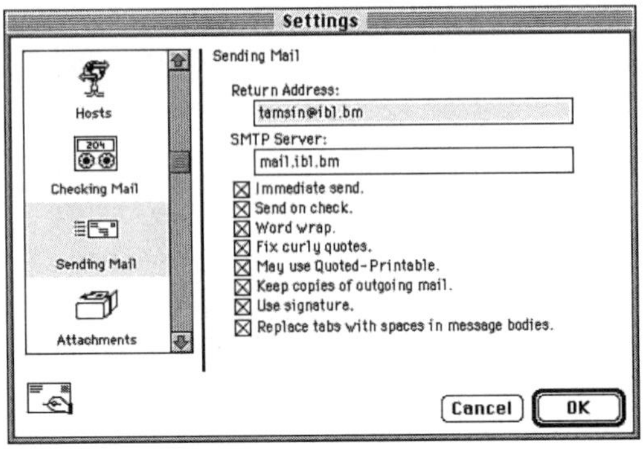

FIGURE 7.7.
Sending Mail settings.

Tip

For quick access to Eudora, you can make an alias of your Eudora settings and park it on your Desktop. Quit Eudora and return to the Finder. Select the Eudora Light program icon, choose Make Alias from the File menu and move the new alias on to your Desktop.

At this point, you are finished configuring Eudora Light and you're ready to send and receive e-mail (see "Using Eudora Light for E-Mail," later in this chapter). The following sections discuss the different parts that make up an e-mail message.

Tip

Many Internet Access Providers allow customers to hold more than one e-mail user code. This is particularly useful if you share your account with someone else, for example family members or co-workers. You can set up Eudora Light to handle multiple e-mail codes by creating separate settings for each user.

To make a new Settings file, follow these steps:

1. Open the System Folder and rename the Eudora folder (for example, to Tom's Eudora folder).
2. Launch Eudora. A new Settings dialog box is displayed. Configure the Settings for the new user following the same procedure as described in "Configuring Eudora Light," earlier in this chapter. When you have finished configuring the Settings, Eudora creates a new "Eudora Folder" containing the new Settings. Then Quit Eudora.
3. Click on the "Eudora Settings" in Tom's Eudora folder and make an alias (by choosing Make Alias from the Edit menu in the Finder) of the file. Drag the alias to the Desktop and rename it Tom's Mail.
4. Now, make an alias of the file "Eudora Settings" in the new Eudora folder and drag the alias to the Desktop. Rename it to My Mail.

5. From now on, launch Eudora by double-clicking on one of the aliases you have just created (not on the program icon itself) to open the appropriate mailbox. Clicking on the alias will open the appropriate mailbox for that user.

The Anatomy of an E-Mail Message

All outgoing e-mail, like all paper mail, requires only three basic parts: the name and address of the recipient, the subject of the message, and the message itself (on the Internet, of course, the name and address are combined into one item: an e-mail address). In an e-mail message, all the address information is contained in a block of lines called a *header*; the message is called the *body*. An optional block of lines at the bottom of the message, used to further identify the sender, is called a *signature*. Figure 7.8 shows an e-mail message with a header and body.

FIGURE 7.8.

An e-mail with a header and body.

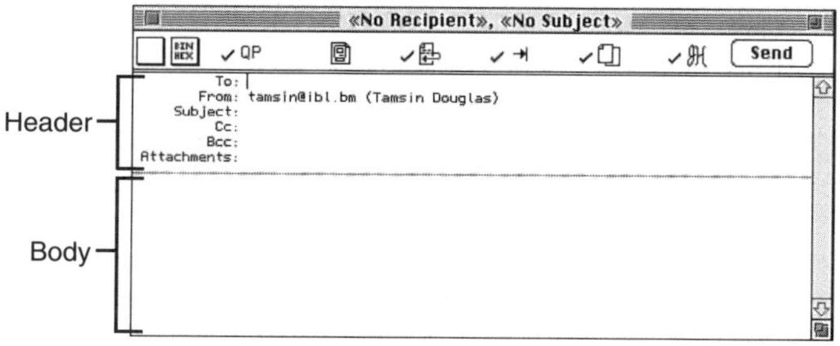

The Header

The header of an outgoing message is made up of several lines (the exact number, order, and labels vary by program). All headers of outgoing messages include a line for the following topics:

- `To:` The Internet address of the addressee.
- `Subject:` The subject of the message. This line is optional and may sometimes be labeled `Re:` as in a memo.
- `Cc:` (Carbon copy) Just as with paper correspondence, you can also copy your message to a third party. This is optional. See "Multiple Recipients" later in this chapter.
- `Bcc:` (Blind carbon copy) Works like `Cc:` only the names of the other recipients aren't included in the message header. See the "Multiple Recipients" section later in this chapter.
- `Attachments:` You can attach binary files to your e-mail messages. See "Attaching Files" later in this chapter.

You never have to deal with every line in a header because some are always filled in automatically by your e-mail program and some you can ignore. The Date and Time: line and the Message ID: line, for example, are generated automatically, as is your Internet address (in the From: line in messages you send).

- `From:` The Internet address of the sender.
- `Message ID:` An identification number automatically assigned to the message.
- `Date and Time:` The date and time at which the message was sent.

E-mail software, such as Eudora Light, tries to make messages look friendlier by hiding most of the header in the main message window. Rest assured, however, that the message always includes all the header information.

Typically, you only have to fill in the `To:` line to fully address an outgoing message. The Subject line is optional, but courteous users always supply one. Your Subject line appears in the list of messages your recipients see when they check their mailboxes. If you enter no subject, your recipients have to read your message to know what it's about. Nobody likes that. Worse, some busy e-mail users routinely delete messages that lack a subject line, assuming that such messages are unimportant.

The header of an incoming message is made up of several lines (the exact number, order, and labels vary by program). As a recepient of e-mail, the only header lines you need to worry about are `From:`, `To:`, `Date and Time:`, `Subject:` and sometimes `Cc:` and `Attachments:`.

Other lines may appear in the header of an incoming message, depending on the mail program used and the history of the message. For example, if the message is a reply to another message, a `Reply To:` line may appear, showing the address to which you should reply. (Replies can be noted in other ways; see "Reply," later in this chapter.)

Because headers sometimes report extra information, such as a listing of all the machines the message passed through on its way to you, headers can be intimidating. You really needn't pay much attention to them, however; most of the time, all you really need to know is who you're sending the message to and who the message is from. Consider the rest an electronic postmark.

The Body

The body of an e-mail message is simple text. As a rule, you can use any uppercase or lowercase character on your keyboard in the body, but you can't use any character formatting—fonts, bold, italic, and so on. Remember that your recipient may be using any type of computer, perhaps one that wouldn't know a font from a frosty milk shake. The use of bare, unadorned text ensures legible e-mail across the Net, regardless of the differences between the sender's and recipient's computers and software.

Copy and Paste E-Mail

You can copy text from any word processing application into an e-mail message. Simply highlight the text, choose Copy from your word processor's Edit menu, switch to your e-mail program, open a new message, click to position the insertion point in the space for the message body, and choose Paste from your mail program's Edit menu.

Copy and paste are handy for copying all or part of a letter composed in a word processor into an e-mail message. You may want to check the results, however. Your text should arrive unformatted in your e-mail program, even if it was rich with fonts and other attributes in the original application. Depending on how your word processor codes are formatting, unusual characters or codes may wind up in your e-mail message. In particular, quotation marks (" ") and apostrophes (') have a way of getting screwed up between a word processor and a raw text application. So check your pasted message carefully, and correct any glitches before sending it.

The Signature

A signature (not shown in Figure 7.8) is an optional bit of text used to close a message. It can be as simple as a traditional letter signature (Hugs'n Bugs, Tamsin). On the Internet, however, people like to use a few lines of text that tell the reader something about them or their personality. Businesspeople may use the signature like a letterhead or logo, listing the company's voice and fax numbers, regular mail address, slogan, and type of business. Others use their favorite quote, joke, or slogan. It's all very personal. E-mail software packages can be configured to supply your signature automatically at the end of all your messages.

Be aware that signatures are optional, and they can be a liability. What seems cute or clever to you may irritate others. Especially long signatures (those over four lines) are seen as wasting precious Internet resources and may annoy your correspondents who pay for each line of the e-mail they receive.

E-Mail Options

Sending an e-mail message requires entering an Internet address in the To: line, typing a message, and choosing Send from a button or menu. That's it. Optional capabilities are available, however, to make e-mailing more powerful or more convenient.

Reply

When reading a message you've received, you may want to compose your reply right away. Reply or Respond options in e-mail software open a window for a new message and pre-address it to the author of the message you've just been reading. Reply and Respond options may also do the following:

- Add an `In-Reply-To:` line to the header, showing the exact Message ID of the original message.
- Copy the original message's subject line as the new subject line, preceded by `Re:` (regarding). For example, if the original message's subject was `What's up at Sams?`, the Subject line in your reply might read, `Re: What's up at Sams?`. Although this saves you the trouble of typing a Subject line, you usually have the option to edit or replace this line when it's supplied automatically.
- Quote the text of the original message in your reply. You can delete the entire quote or cut it down to the passages to which you are responding to remind the sender of what he or she wrote. You can even break it up and insert your responses between passages. E-mail identifies quotes by marking in in some way. For example, your Eudora Light places greater-than signs (>) before each line of quoted text. In other programs, it may be a note at the beginning of the text such as "Tamsin wrote on September 11..."

The goal of Reply and Respond options is to save you the trouble of typing header information or quotes from the original message. Most of the time, you need only click the Reply button, type the message body, and click Send.

Tip

When using Reply, always check the header to make sure that your e-mail client has inserted the address you want. E-mail can come to you through various pipelines; choosing Reply does not necessarily address the reply directly to the message's originator.

For example, when you receive a message from a mailing list (see Chapter 8, "Subscribing to Mailing Lists"), the header sometimes shows the mailing list address as the sender of the message, not the address of the person who originally wrote the message and sent it to the list. Using Reply with such a message addresses your reply to the mailing list, not to the message's originator. Similarly, using Reply to answer a message that was forwarded to you (see "Forwarding," later in this chapter) addresses the reply not to the original composer of the message but back to the person who forwarded it to you.

If you find that Reply does not supply the address you want, scan the message header and the signature block of the original message for the correct address. With Macintosh e-mail clients, you can use copy and paste to copy the address from where you find it to the `To:` field.

Multiple Recipients

With most e-mail packages, you can address a single message to multiple recipients. In fancier software, you enter as many e-mail addresses as you want in a dialog box, or copy multiple addresses from an Address Book. (See "Address Books," later in this chapter.) All these addresses wind up in the `To:` portion of the header, separated by commas (,). Low-end e-mail clients may simply enable you to enter multiple recipients in the `To:` field and enter the intervening commas yourself. In either case, everyone in the `To:` list gets a copy of the same message, addressed to him or her personally (although the recipient can usually see the other recipients listed in the `To:` portion of the header).

Cc: and *Bcc:*

In addition to the multiple recipients capability of most e-mail clients (described in the preceding section), you have two other ways to send the same message to more than one person: cc: and bcc:. You use both of these features exactly as you use the multiple recipients capability: enter a list of e-mail addresses in a `Cc:` (or `Bcc:`) dialog box or type addresses in a `Cc:` or `Bcc:` line in the message header, separating addresses with commas.

These options differ from multiple recipients in that they're used to send copies of messages to people who are not the principal recipients. `Cc:` (carbon copy) duplicates the effect of `Cc:` copies of letters and memos. The message is actually addressed to, and intended for, the person or persons in the `To:` line. The `Cc:` recipients are others who should be made aware of the message. For example, when addressing a complaint to a mail-order company, you can `Cc:` your attorney, just to keep her informed. When you use `Cc:`, the addresses of the `Cc:` recipients appear in the message header (in a line labeled `Cc:`) so that all recipients can easily see who else received the same message.

`Bcc:` (blind carbon copy, sometimes labeled `bc:` for *blind copy*), works the same as `Cc:` except that the names of the recipients are not added to the header. When you read a blind copy, you do not know who else received the same message; when you read a `Cc:` message, you know who else got the message by looking at the list added to the header. `Bcc:` copies are useful when you want to keep a third party abreast of an exchange but without letting the other person know that the third party knows. If you want your lawyer to know about your communications with the mail-order company, but you don't want the mail-order company to know your lawyer is involved yet, you should put the company's address in the `To:` line and your lawyer's address in the `Bcc:` line.

Forwarding

Forwarding simply copies a message you've received and sends it along to another user. In most programs, you select Forward from the Message menu and supply the Internet address of the new recipient. When your recipient's message arrives, it usually includes all the header information from the original message, plus a note added to the header indicating that you forwarded the message. That way, the reader knows not only who sent the message to them, but also who was the original sender/recipient.

Most e-mail programs enable you to add your own comments to a forwarded message; these comments are clearly separated from the actual message so that the recipient isn't confused. Adding your own comments to a message before forwarding it is the Internet equivalent of sticking a sticky note on a paper you pass to a colleague.

Address Books

Address books are a feature of most e-mail packages, including Eudora Light (see "Nicknames," later in this chapter). You use an address book to keep a list of names and Internet addresses of people with whom you communicate often. That way, you needn't memorize anyone's Internet address. Some address books enable you to include other useful information in the database as well, such as the voice and fax numbers of each person. Some e-mail programs automatically create a new address book entry every time you exchange e-mail with someone new; in others you add the entry manually.

Tip

Some address books support *aliasing* (also known as *nicknames*), the ability to automatically supply the Internet address when you supply the recipient's full name (or even a nickname you can make up yourself).

To use an alias, simply type the name (or nickname) of the addressee in the `To:` line in the header. The address book automatically retrieves the appropriate Internet address from its database and enters it in the header. (Some e-mail programs, such as Eudora, show you only the nickname in the address line but still address the message properly when sending it.)

Encryption

Encryption is a method of translating an e-mail message into secret code so that it can't be read except by the intended recipient, who *decrypts* (decodes) the message before reading it. However, an encrypted message can be decrypted by anyone with the right software; better protection is afforded by *key encryption*, which requires the reader to know a secret password before the message is decrypted.

To use encryption, you must have an e-mail package that encrypts; your recipient must have an e-mail package capable of decrypting the particular encryption method used. There are several encryption methods. To use key encryption, you must also be able to inform your recipient of the correct password. A popular key encryption tool that works in conjunction with Eudora is PGP (Pretty Good Privacy) for Mac. Note that, at this writing, encryption/decryption is not supported by most e-mail clients.

At the moment, encryption is at the center of several big legal/political controversies. The main issue is whether Internet users should be permitted to encrypt messages in a way that prevents the Federal Government from reading them. The government says No, claiming it needs to conduct Internet surveillance to catch high-tech drug pushers, computer crooks, and tax cheats. Many users say Yes, claiming freedom of speech and privacy rights. Stay tuned.

For more about encryption and security, see Chapter 20, "Using the Internet in the Office."

Delayed Sending (Out Box)

Dial-up users may appreciate *out box features*, which provide the ability to create and address messages offline and queue them for later sending. An out box lets you compose your e-mail messages offline and then log on and send messages when it's most convenient. Usually, you can send all the messages waiting in your Out box with a single click. If you sign on regularly to check your e-mail and retrieve messages to your in box, it's convenient to save messages in your out box until you check for new e-mail. You can then retrieve incoming mail and dispatch outgoing mail in one online session.

> A good way to save valuable online time is to get in the habit of reading and composing mail offline. After you are finished transferring new messages to your In box, disconnect from the Internet to read them. You can write your replies while offline and send them the next time you connect to the Internet.

Tip

Attaching Files

Binary files such as programs, graphics, and any other computer files can be "attached" to e-mail messages and sent along to the recipient. To ride on the text-only Internet e-mail system, these binary files must be converted into text form before they are sent. The recipient must translate them back into their binary forms before using them.

A number of methods are available for doing this; the most common for Macintosh is BinHex. A newer, more powerful approach, called Multipurpose Internet Mail Extensions (MIME), is gaining favor. MIME is showing up in a growing number of e-mail programs, including Eudora Light.

The important point to remember about attaching files is that your recipient must be able to decode and use what you send. If you use BinHex to prepare and attach a binary file to an e-mail message, the recipient must have BinHex to use the files. If you use MIME, the recipient must also use MIME. And of course, the user must have the right computer and software to use the files once they're decoded. There's no point in sending a Macintosh program file to a mainframe computer user.

Using Eudora Light for E-Mail

You may already be familiar with many of Eudora Light's useful features, but do you know how this application came by its unique name? The program designer, Steve Dorner, named his e-mail client after one of his favorite American authors, Eudora Welty.

Eudora Light's overall reliability and functionality has earned it an excellent reputation as a popular freeware e-mail client among Macintosh users. As good a freeware product as it is,

Eudora Light lacks some of the more sophisticated features of the commercial version, Eudora Pro. Among other things, Eudora Pro enables you to filter messages into separate folders—very handy if you subscribe to mailing lists. (See Chapter 8.)

Sending Internet E-Mail with Eudora Light

To send an e-mail message using Eudora Light, follow these steps:

1. Open Eudora.
2. Choose New Message from the File Menu. A screen appears like the one shown in Figure 7.9.

FIGURE 7.9.
A new message in Eudora Light.

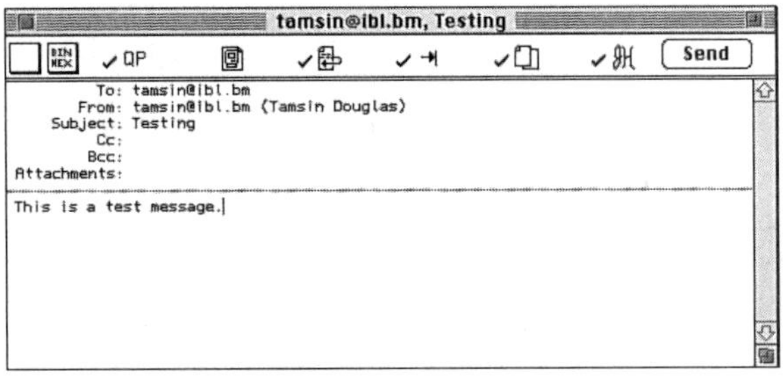

3. In the `To:` line, type your recipient's e-mail address. For example, you can type in your own e-mail address (a good way to experiment with Eudora Light is to send a message to yourself). Note that the `From:` line has been automatically filled in with your return e-mail address.
4. Point and click the mouse or press the Tab key to move the cursor to the `Subject:` line. Type a brief line of text indicating what your message is about; although you can leave the Subject line blank, it's impolite to do so.
5. Move the cursor below the dotted line to the lower portion of the message window and type in the text of your message. The scroll bar at the right of this region enables you to make your message as long or as short as you wish.
6. When you finish entering your message, do one of the following:
   - ◆ To send the message, click the Send button in the upper-right-hand corner of the message window or choose Send Message Now from the Message menu. If you are connected to the Internet, Eudora sends the message. A progress window is momentarily displayed, indicating that the message is being transferred to the network.
   - ◆ To save the message to edit and/or send later, choose Close from the File menu. A dialog box appears asking if you want to Save the message or Discard it. Click Save. The message is stored in your Out mailbox, ready for you to edit later or send the next time you connect to the Internet. You can open it later to make changes by choosing Out in the Mailbox menu and double-clicking on the

message which is stored in your Out mailbox and then send it as described in the preceding paragraph.

Using Nicknames in Eudora Light

Nicknames in Eudora Light function much like the Address Book feature discussed earlier in this chapter. A nickname (also known as an alias) is a short form of a full Internet address. For example, if your recipient's Internet address is `mary-anne_meeds@ixnews7.ix.netnex.com`, use an easy-to-remember nickname like Mary. When you type `Mary` in the `To:` line, Eudora supplies the address for you. Nicknames are especially useful for people with whom you correspond regularly, especially those with long or hard to remember e-mail addresses.

Creating a Nickname

1. Select the Nicknames option from the Window menu in Eudora Light. A window appears like the one shown in Figure 7.10.

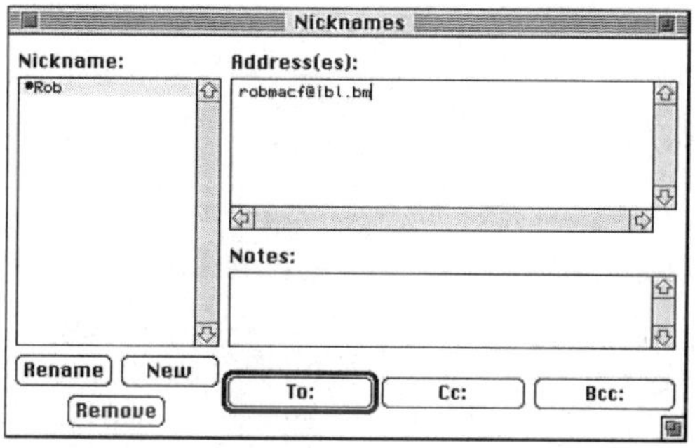

FIGURE 7.10.
The Nickname window is divided into three main fields: Nickname:, Address(es):, and Notes:.

2. To add a nickname, click the New button at the bottom of the Nickname: field. A nickname dialog box appears. (See Figure 7.11.) Type the nickname you'd like to assign. The checkbox in the dialog box enables you to add a nickname to the Quick Recipient List. (For more details, see "Using the Quick Recipient List," later in this chapter.) Click the OK button to save the nickname.

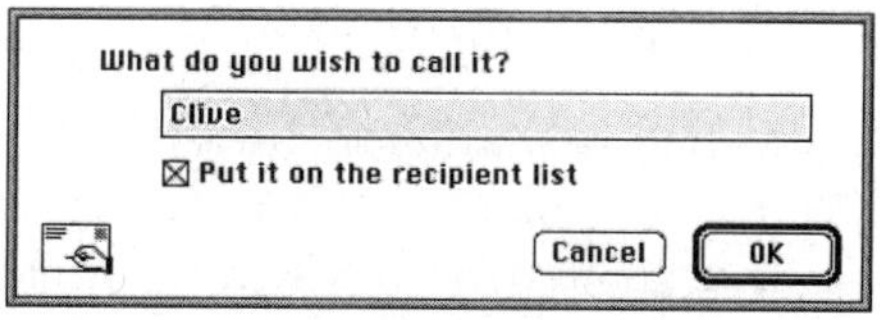

FIGURE 7.11.
The Nickname dialog box.

3. The new nickname appears in the Nickname List. In the Address(es): field, type the full e-mail address of the person to whom you gave a nickname. In the Notes: field you can add other information associated with the nickname such as a full name, phone and fax number and street address.

4. To add another nickname, repeat steps two and three. When you're finished modifying the Nicknames, save the changes (select Save from the File menu) and close the window.

Addressing E-Mail using Nicknames

When addressing a message, type the nickname of your recipient in the `To:` line. Eudora displays only the nickname in the address line but still addresses the message properly when sending it.

Using the Quick Recipient List in Eudora Light

The Quick Recipient List is a convenient way to automatically address a message to someone on your Nickname list. There are two methods of accessing the Quick Recipient List.

- You can open a new message and select Insert Recipient from the Edit menu and then choose a nickname from the pop-up list; the name is entered automatically in the `To:` field of your message.
- Or you can select New Message To from the Message menu and choose a name from the pop-up List. A new message appears with the nickname already entered in the `To:` line.

Checking for and Receiving E-Mail with Eudora Light

Your incoming mail waits for you on your Internet provider's server until you pick it up. When you have a new message, the server doesn't notify you it's there until you check for it. One way to receive incoming mail is to configure the Checking Mail setting. To configure Checking Mail, open Settings from the Special menu. Click on the Checking Mail settings to open it and type in a value (for example, `5` will set it to check every five minutes) in the Check for mail every field. Whenever Eudora is running, it will automatically check for mail at the interval you set.

The alternative is to check for mail manually. Anytime you are connected to the Net, select Check Mail from the File menu. You can check for mail manually as often as you like during a session. When you check for mail (either automatically or manually), Eudora retrieves any mail waiting for you on your Internet provider's server and delivers it to your In mailbox.

There are four ways Eudora notifies you that new mail has arrived in your In mailbox: an alert dialog box, a "New Mail" sound, a flashing mail icon in the Finder menu and the automatic opening of your In mailbox. You can turn on or off any or all of these options by choosing Getting Attention in the Settings dialog box (under the Special menu).

Each time you launch Eudora, you will be asked to enter your password (your password is case-sensitive and must be typed correctly to access your e-mail account) before Eudora will check for mail.

When mail is found, a progress window displays the number of new messages being transferred to your In mailbox.

Any messages retrieved are stored automatically in your In mailbox. To see new messages, double-click an unread message in your In mailbox. (See Figure 7.12.)

FIGURE 7.12.
The In mailbox displays unread messages (indicated by a bullet at the left of the message summary).

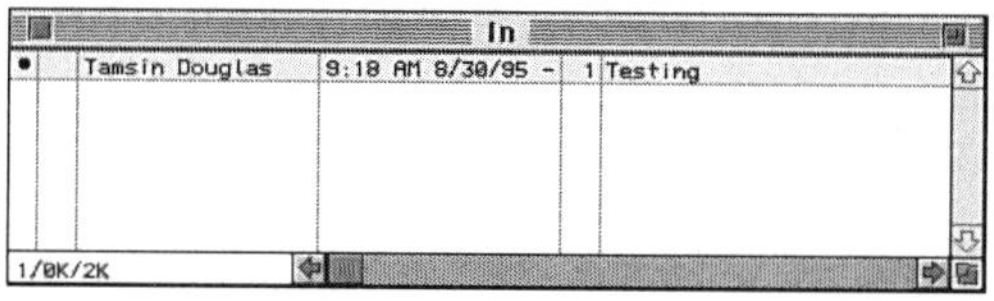

While viewing a message, you can choose either of two Reply options. Both options open a New Message window with the `To:` and Subject lines filled in and the original message quoted (>) in the message box.

- The Reply option in the Message menu addresses the reply only to the name listed in the message header as the sender—the `From:` address.
- The Reply to All option (hold down the Option key when you select Reply from the Message menu) addresses the reply to everyone whose name appears in the header: the sender, all cc: recipients, and anyone who forwarded the message.

Warning

> Watch out when using the Reply to All option. You don't want to flood mailboxes with unnecessary messages. Always check the recipient list and make sure that everyone listed there really needs to see the message.

A Forward option also appears in the Message menu. This option opens a message window showing the complete text of the original message and leaves the `To:` line blank for the forwarding address. The header of the forwarded message shows that you were the original recipient and that you forwarded the message.

Sending Attachments with Eudora Light

With many e-mail clients, including Eudora Light, you can attach files to e-mail messages. The attached file can be of any type: a simple text file or a program, or a binary file containing a graphic, a word processing document, or anything else. When the recipient receives the e-mail message, he or she automatically receives the attached file, as well; the file is stored on the recipient's hard disk in a file separate from the e-mail message itself.

Because Internet e-mail is technically capable of carrying only text, binary files must be converted into a text-character format by the sending e-mail program; the files must be converted back to their original forms by the recipient's e-mail program. One way to convert Macintosh files is with a method called BINHEX. Increasingly, however, e-mail programs use Multipurpose Internet Mail Extensions (MIME), a more sophisticated method of adding binary information to e-mail messages. When you attach a file through MIME, your recipient must also have a MIME-compliant e-mail program to decode the file back to its binary form.

Prior to sending an attachment, find out if your recipient can read attachments and whether he or she have software that can covert the file you're sending. Before attaching a file to a message in Eudora, first type in the header and subject of the message and then select what format you will need to encode attachments sent with outgoing messages. Choose the format from the Attachment Type pop-up menu located on the icon bar of the outgoing message. (See Figure 7.13.) There are three different formats to choose from in Eudora Light: AppleDouble, AppleSingle and BinHex. Use AppleDouble for recipients who are using a MIME-compliant e-mail client; AppleSingle only if requested by the recipient; and BinHex for files destined for recipients with older Macintosh e-mail programs such as previous versions of Eudora.

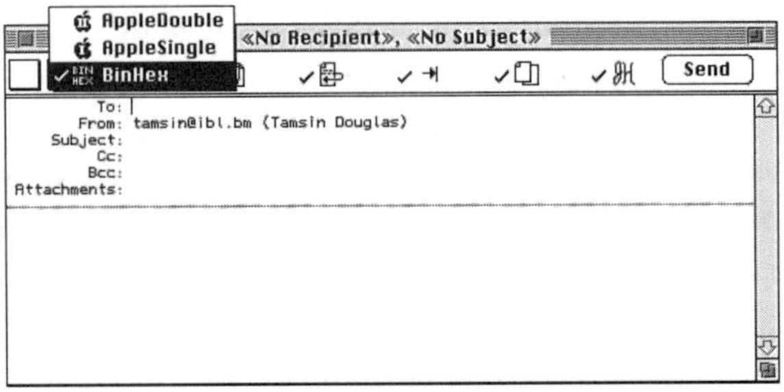

FIGURE 7.13.
The Attachment Type pop-up menu on the icon bar of a new message.

After determining how you will encode the attachment, choose the Attach Document option in the Message menu. A standard file dialog box is displayed. Select the desired file and click the Open button to attach the document to the message. The file name and the disk from which it was copied is displayed in the Attachments: field of the message header, as shown in Figure 7.14.

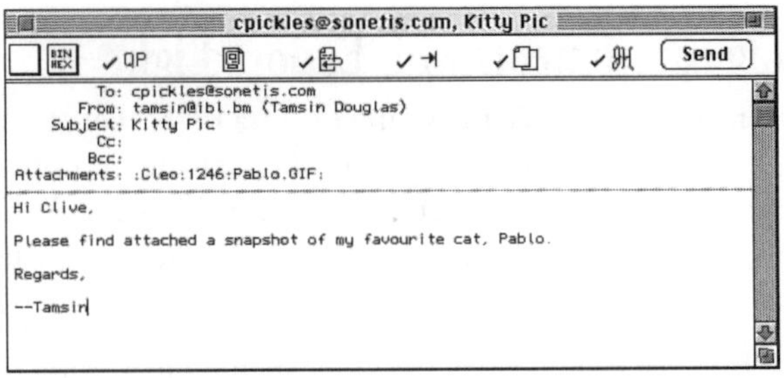

FIGURE 7.14.
An outgoing message with an attached document.

Note

> Your recipient must have the necessary application for opening any file you send as an attachment. For example, to open a Microsoft Word file you have attached to an e-mail message, your recipient must have Microsoft Word (or another word processor that can convert and open Word documents).

Sending Mail *to* Online Services

Just because your aunt Shirley isn't on the Internet doesn't mean you can't send her Internet mail. You can send mail through the Internet to users of any of the commercial online services, including eWorld, America Online, CompuServe, and others. This is madc possible by Internet gateways set up by each online service. Note that users of these services can send you e-mail from the services, as well (the exact steps and costs vary by service).

All the steps for sending e-mail from the Internet to an online service are the same as for any other Internet mail message; the only thing that changes is the address format. Each online service requires a slightly different approach. Your job is to rewrite the user's online service ID as an Internet address.

eWorld and America Online—Add the letters `@eworld.com` to the end of the user's eWorld username (ditto for America Online, except you add the letters `@aol.com` to the end of the username). For example, if the username is `fredo`, address Internet e-mail like this:

```
fredo@eworld.com
```

```
fredo@aol.com
```

CompuServe—Add the letters `@compuserve.com` to the end of the user's CompuServe ID number and change the comma that appears in the middle of this CompuServe address into a period. For example, if the user's ID number is `72727,3322`, address Internet e-mail this way:

```
72727.3322@compuserve.com
```

Sending Internet Mail *from* Online Services to the Net

At this writing, eWorld, America Online and CompuServe offer access to most Internet services. Still, even their most complete Internet accounts still require you to use their regular e-mail facilities, even for Internet mail. If you use CompuServe as your Internet access provider (see Chapter 2, "One-Stop Shopping: Apple's eWorld," and Chapter 3, "Configuring Your Macintosh for the Internet"), you have to do things a little differently to send mail to Internet users.

From CompuServe—Add `INTERNET:` before the Internet address. To send Ned (`nsnell@carroll.com`) Internet mail from CompuServe, address it as follows:

```
INTERNET:nsnell@carroll.com
```

Summary

E-mail provides the best of both worlds: simplicity (when you want it) and powerful flexibility (when you need it). As your experience on the Internet expands, you'll wonder how you ever lived this long without e-mail.

In the next chapter, you discover a great offshoot of e-mail: mailing lists. These "discussion groups" send you a steady stream of e-mail covering your favorite subject. Cool.

CHAPTER 8

SUBSCRIBING TO MAILING LISTS

How Mailing Lists Work

Where To Find Lists

Subscribing to a List

Using Your Subscription

Summary

One of the strange consequences of working at home is that the delivery of the day's mail becomes a major event. Despite the fact that I hardly ever get any interesting mail, I wait expectantly for it. Maybe I'll get a great letter or a cool catalog. Maybe my last book suddenly sold 5,000 copies in Canada and an extravagant check is coming. Maybe my ship came in.

This anticipation, coupled with the daily reality of bills and junk mail, means I'm depressed every afternoon by 3:30 (or by noon when my mail carrier takes a day off and is replaced by someone fully ambulatory). An Internet mailing list—a tool that automatically delivers e-mail about a given subject to anyone who wants it—guarantees that I get something interesting in my e-mail on a regular basis. It keeps me going.

> **Note:** Subscribing to a mailing list and retrieving deliveries means that you have to be able to send and receive Internet e-mail. Understanding the information in this chapter requires an understanding of e-mail, which you can acquire by reading Chapter 7, "Exchanging E-Mail."

How Mailing Lists Work

The principle of mailing lists, sometimes also known as *discussion groups*, is simple: Someone sets up an Internet account as a central repository for the list (a "post office") and puts out the word that this is the address for a discussion list covering, say, botany. A separate account is set up for the administration of the list; botanists and botany buffs send subscription requests to the administration account so that they can be added to the list.

Subscribers send e-mail containing news, comments, questions, answers, and any other botany-related information to the list address. (The folks who run the list, its *owners*, typically also collect and supply information to the list.) All e-mail received by the list account is forwarded by e-mail to every person on the list.

The timing of the forwarding varies. Some lists forward each message to everyone immediately after the message arrives at the list account; others forward messages in batches at regular intervals. All lists forward messages at least once a day, unless there's nothing to forward.

This is all accomplished in one of two ways: manually (some poor soul maintains the list of subscribers and performs the forwarding) or automatically, through one of several programs that can accept subscriptions and do the forwarding with little or no human involvement. Several such programs are available, but by far the most common is a family of programs called Listservs. In fact, you're more likely to encounter a Listserv list today than any other type.

> **Note:** A single mailing list program, or list processor, can manage several different lists. Although the lists may be on different computers, they are still managed by the one program reached through one e-mail address. When subscribing to an automated list,

you must indicate in your subscription request the name of the list you want. You learn how to do this later in this chapter.

When you use an automated mailing list, you control a computer program through e-mail remote control. The program not only enables you to subscribe to, and unsubscribe from, a mailing list, it also enables you to control how and when mail is delivered to you in several important ways. Of course, being a computer program, the list processor can understand your subscription requests and other commands only if you phrase them properly, using the required commands and nothing else (see "Subscribing to a Listserv List," later in this chapter). The steps for subscribing to a manual mailing list and for making changes to your subscription aren't terribly formal—because a human being reads your requests, as long as you make your meaning clear, it doesn't matter how you phrase your requests.

Beyond subscribing and maintaining your subscription, the processes for using manual and automated lists is identical. You send news in e-mail messages to the list address, and you receive the latest messages each time you retrieve your e-mail.

Keep Your Addresses Straight

The most common mistake made by mailing list newbies is failing to remember the distinction between the *subscription* address and the *list* address.

The *subscription address* is the one to which you send your subscription requests and any other mail related to the maintenance of your subscription. For automated lists, the subscription address is often informally called by the name of the list processor. For example, you may be instructed to send subscription requests "to the Listserv."

The *list address* is only for postings of information, questions, or comments intended for all subscribers.

If you send news to the subscription address, it won't reach the other subscribers. Worse, if you send a message about your subscription to the list address, the message will probably wind up in the mailbox of every subscriber (unless it is helpfully intercepted by a moderator). The inevitable result: at least embarrassment, at worst a torrent of flames from annoyed subscribers who learn your e-mail address from the header on your message.

Remember that most mailing lists live up to the nickname *discussion group.* In addition to messages about important topical news and events, you find ongoing conversations among subscribers. One person posts a question or comment, another responds, another responds to the response, and so on. As with any conversation, the result can be an illuminating exchange of insight and information, an endless series of ill-informed thrusts and parries, or a complete digression away from the original question to another subject—maybe a relevant one, maybe not.

The List Police

As with newsgroups (described in Chapter 9, "Browsing Newsgroups"), some mailing lists are *moderated.* In a moderated mailing list, an appointed person or persons reviews each message for appropriate and relevant content before allowing it to be forwarded to other subscribers.

Moderated lists are less prone to babbling digressions among subscribers and pointless repetition of the same points. However, some users worry that moderators may—deliberately or otherwise—censor information that seems inappropriate to them but may not seem so to others. In any case, there are many more unmoderated lists than moderated ones.

In rare cases, a list may be restricted to people with certain qualifications or may be limited to a maximum number of subscribers (usually because of the limitations of the computer used to manage the list). Such restrictions are typically reported in responses to subscription requests.

Where To Find Lists

A good way to find a list is through colleagues or friends with similar interests. Failing that, there are ways to locate lists through the Internet itself.

A master index of Internet mailing lists, which includes all types of lists—manual lists, Listserv lists, and lists maintained by other programs—is available. Each entry in the alphabetical list includes the list's name, a complete description of the list, and instructions for subscribing. The index is stored in a group of text files; a good way to find a list is to open each file in a word processing application and do a text search for words related to your interests.

You can acquire this master index in three ways:

- The list is posted in the newsgroup `news.lists`. (See Chapter 9.)
- Using anonymous FTP (see Chapter 12, "Collecting Files with FTP") at address `rtfm.mit.edu`. Download the group of files stored in the directory /pub/usenet-by-group/news.answers/mail/mailing-`lists`.
- On the World Wide Web (see Chapter 10, "Browsing the World Wide Web," and Figure 8.1) at `http://www.neosoft.com/internet/paml`. When you access the list through the Web, you can search for mailing lists by name or subject.

In fact, a range of search tools is available on the Web to hunt down all types of Internet resources related to a topic. Although they run on the Web, many of these tools can find the names and addresses of mailing lists related to a topic as well. For more about Web searching, see Chapter 18, "Finding It on the Web."

FIGURE 8.1.
A master index of mailing lists accessible on the World Wide Web.

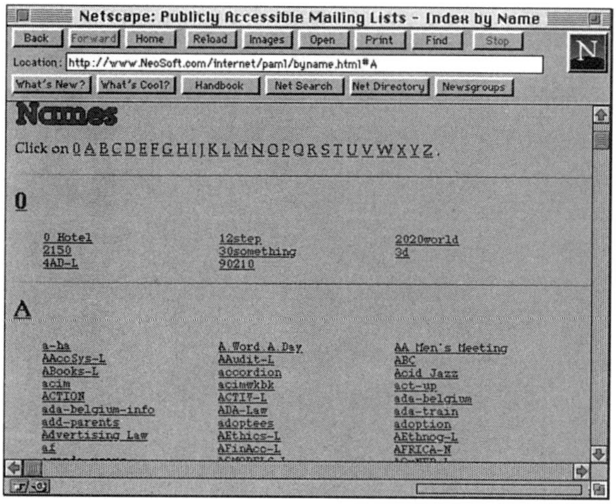

> **Tip**
>
> There is a Listserv that will send you a good directory of mailing lists. Send an e-mail message to this address:
>
> `listproc@listproc.listproc.net`
>
> Use no subject line, and use only the following as the body of the message:
>
> `list global`
>
> You will receive a list of e-mail lists by return e-mail.

You can also find tips and other information about lists in various newsgroups. (See Chapter 9.) Often, you can find the subscription address for a mailing list on a given topic by locating a newsgroup about the same topic (which is easier to do than locating a mailing list by topic) and posting a message asking other users for suggestions—although you may decide that the newsgroup itself supplies all the information you'd hoped to glean from a mailing list.

Here are a few useful newsgroups for new mailing list users:

- `news.lists`
- `news.announce.newusers`
- `news.newusers.questions`

There are thousands of mailing lists. Table 8.1 offers a taste of what's available. (Don't worry about the subscription commands; these are described later in this chapter.)

Table 8.1. A sampling of mailing lists.

Listname	*Subscription Address*	*Subscription Command*	*Description*
Babylon 5 Reviews	`Listproc@cornell.edu`	`SUBSCRIBE B5-REVIEW-L` *`firstname lastname`*	Commentary on *Babylon 5* TV show
biodiv-l	`listserv@bdt.ftpt.ansp.br`	`subscribe biodiv-l` *`firstname lastname institution`*	Biodiversity discussion
buffalo-bills	`dkvalent@netcom.com`	`subscribe`	Discussion of the Buffalo Bills football team
diabetic	`listserv@lehigh.edu`	`subscribe diabetic` *`firstname lastname`*	Information exchange among diabetics
Forensic Linguistics	`mailbase@mailbase.ac.uk`	`JOIN FORENSIC-LINGUISTICS` *`firstname lastname`*	Discussion and newspaper reports about forensic linguistics
net-lawyers	`listproc@lawlib.wuacc.edu`	`ssubscribe net-lawyers`	Discussion of Internet use among lawyers
SDOMINGO	`listserv@enlace.bitnet`	`subscribe sdomingo` *`firstname lastname`*	Discussion of culture and events in the Dominican Republic
Sunset Boulevard	`majordomo@world.std.com`	`subscribe sunset-blvd`	Discussion of the hit Andrew Lloyd Webber musical

Subscribing to a List

As you can tell from Table 8.1, the exact steps required to subscribe to mailing lists vary. Subscribing to a manual list is different from subscribing to a Listserv list—and even Listservs vary a little. Three facts mean this isn't such a big problem:

- When you locate the name and address of a list, you almost always find subscription information mentioned along with it.
- Most lists today are controlled by a Listserv and accept the standard Listserv subscription commands. The lists automated by other list processors usually accept Listserv subscription commands (or minor variations thereof).
- As long as you send your subscription request to the correct address, if you send an incorrectly phrased request, you usually get a return message detailing the proper phrasing. Try to get it right the first time, but rest assured that you'll probably receive a little coaching if you mess up.

The important thing to remember is that any mailing list really needs only three pieces of information, no matter how it's administered: your e-mail address, your name, and the name of the list to which you want to subscribe. Subscribing is the simple process of providing this information to the list owner in the proper format.

Determining the Type of List

Because most lists are automated, it's simplest to first identify the lists that *are definitely* automated. Any list whose subscription address begins with or includes the words `listserv`, `majordomo`, or `listproc` is an automated list and requires specific commands for subscribing. When an address does not contain these words, it still may be automated, but it may not be. If the subscription instructions accompanying a list description tell you to subscribe using the word `SUB`, it's probably a Listserv list or one of its cousins.

Subscribing to a Manual List

Because manual mailing lists are managed by people who can read letters, all you have to do is send a cordial letter to the subscription address (*not* the list address!), requesting a subscription and including your full name and e-mail address. See Figure 8.2 for a sample request message.

Of course, if you receive any specific instructions, follow them to the letter. Note that there are many variations; some lists actually want you to insert your subscription request in the subject line, not the message body.

Subscribing to a Listserv List

To show how to subscribe to an automated list, this section describes the usual steps for subscribing to a Listserv list because Listservs are the most common type. Be aware, however, that different list processors require different commands.

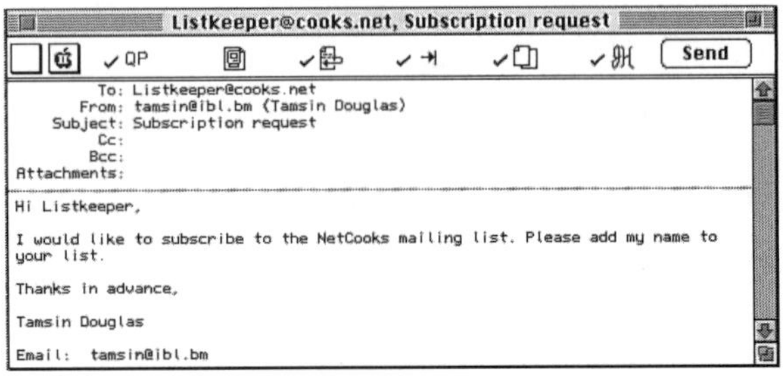

FIGURE 8.2.
Subscribing to a manually maintained list.

When you send e-mail to a Listserv, you're running a computer program by remote control. As with any computer program, you must phrase and format your commands the way the program wants you to. When you send an e-mail message to a Listserv, it reads the body of the message for valid commands and ignores anything else it finds.

The most important command a Listserv understands is `SUB`, the command to subscribe. The command has this syntax:

SUB *listname firstname lastname*

For example, to subscribe to a Listserv list about Internet tools for Macintosh users (called Apple-Internet-Users), I sent this command to the e-mail address of the Listserv (`listproc@abs.apple.com`), as shown in Figure 8.3:

```
SUBSCRIBE apple-internet-users Tamsin Douglas
```

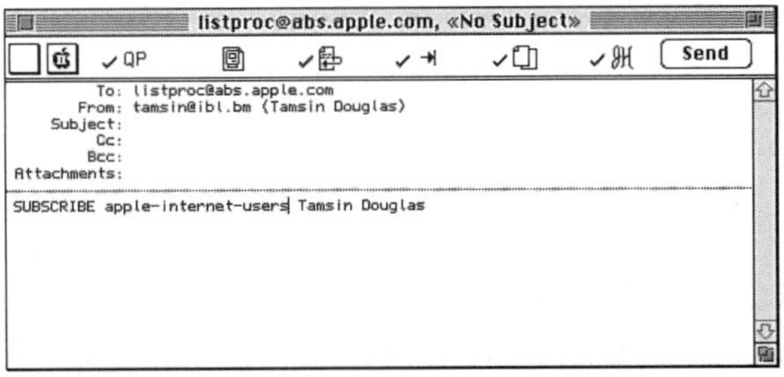

FIGURE 8.3.
Subscribing to a Listserv list.

If you know the address of the Listserv, but not the name of the list, use the `LIST` command (described later in this chapter) to find the names of all lists served by a given Listserv.

Tip

> The instructions for subscribing to a Listserv list sometimes show the command `SUB`; at other times, the command is `SUBSCRIBE`. Even if you see `SUBSCRIBE`, `SUB` will probably work. Nevertheless, because there are variations among list programs and among versions of Listserv, always follow any subscription instructions to the letter.

Observe that you don't have to include your e-mail address in the `SUB` command; Listserv gets that automatically from the header of your message. Listserv programs pretty much scan the header for your e-mail address, the body for commands, and ignore everything else. Instructions for subscribing to Listserv lists often tell you to leave the Subject line blank, but it really doesn't matter. At worst, typing a subject line causes the Listserv to spit back an error message, but it won't prevent your subscription from going through.

Confirming Your Subscription

After you send your subscription request, check your e-mail from time to time for a response. How long it takes to get a response depends on the list; most Listserv lists respond within hours (sometimes minutes); manual lists may take days to get back to you.

When a response arrives, it will contain one of the following:

- A notice that your subscription has been accepted, followed by your first batch of messages. Often, the acceptance notice includes important information, such as any special rules of etiquette, addresses of related mailing lists, important list administration addresses, and instructions for canceling your subscription. You may want to delete old messages from time to time, but hold onto the confirmation message for future reference.
- A request to confirm your subscription. When issued by a Listserv, confirmation requests instruct you to follow specific steps to confirm. Typically, you're asked to reply to the confirmation message, using the words `OK` or `CONFIRM` as the body of the message. Shortly after you confirm, you receive your subscription notice and your first messages. Confirmation messages ensure that the subscription request is authentic.
- A notice that your request was improperly phrased or did not include all the required information. These error messages usually contain instructions for resubmitting your request correctly. If the list is limited, you may also receive a message denying your subscription, usually with an explanation. Denials are rare, especially on Listserv lists.

Tip

> The first message or two you receive from a mailing list—especially your subscription confirmation—usually contain valuable information, such as commands for subscription maintenance, codes of conduct, and instructions for canceling your subscriptions.
>
> Make sure that you save such messages. Don't clean them out when you clean out old e-mail messages. You will need this information later. You may also receive other administrative messages from time to time, informing you of changes to the list address or other important information. Keep these messages as well. They can save you headaches later on.

Using Your Subscription

Once you sign up, there's nothing to do except check your e-mail regularly to collect the latest messages. Well-equipped e-mail programs come in handy with mailing lists: they may offer ways to sort your messages by date submitted or by subject and to conveniently discard the messages that don't interest you.

Sorting features in e-mail programs are more important than you may realize. Some lists support very heavy traffic. For example, within two days of subscribing to the Apple-Internet-Users list mentioned earlier in this chapter, I received more than 25 messages. (See Figure 8.4.)

FIGURE 8.4.
A mailing list can pile up messages fast.

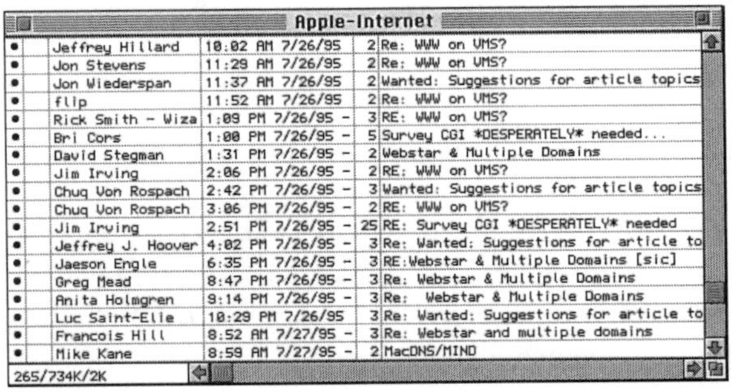

> **Special Etiquette for Mailing Lists**
>
> Before posting any questions or comments on a mailing list, spend some time reading current messages or archives (described later in this chapter). "Lurking," as reading without posting any messages of your own is called on the Net, can help you become familiar with the basic vocabulary and expertise level of the other subscribers. Lurk for a while so that you don't ask what others consider "stupid" questions or report information that everybody else already knows.
>
> If, after lurking, you feel that your expertise level is not right for the group, lurk a while longer until you come up to speed, or look for another list that's a better match.

Posting a Message

To post news or a message for everyone on the list, simply send e-mail to the list address. Again, be sure to send it to the *list* address, not to the address you used to subscribe—the list administration and the list itself are handled in separate accounts. If you forget the list address, look for a line called `Originator` or `Sender` in the header of any message received from the list. The list address appears there. Post only news, questions, and comments intended for all subscribers to the list address. Any questions about, or changes to, your subscription must be sent to the subscription address, sometimes also called the administration address.

If you want to use the Reply function of your e-mail program, check the `To:` address of your reply message; your e-mail program automatically addresses the message for you. For many mailing lists, a reply will be addressed to the original poster of the message or to the list administrator rather than the list. The `Reply-To` line in the header of the original message tells your e-mail program how to address the reply.

Most Reply functions copy the Subject line (and precede it with `Re:`—see the messages in Figure 8.4) from the first message and quote the first message's text in the body. The `Re:` subject line helps subscribers follow the *thread*. By reading all messages with the same subject in order, subscribers can follow the thread of the conversation. These subject lines also help those who have posted a question easily find answers posted by others. When replying to a message in a thread, it's good netiquette to quote some of the text from the preceding post to ground your comment in context.

If you use Reply to automatically address your mail, but you're sending something new instead of responding to another message, be sure to write a new subject line and delete the quotes to avoid confusing other subscribers.

Tip

> Sometimes, an ongoing conversation through a list may lead to the need to communicate directly with another subscriber—*outside* the list. For example, you may want to ask a question that falls outside the boundaries of the list's topic, but one which you suspect a certain subscriber can answer. Or perhaps you want to send a private question or comment to a particular user.
>
> To communicate privately with another subscriber, use the address in the From: line of the header on a message from that person.

Commands

In addition to `SUB` (or `SUBSCRIBE`), there are other Listserv commands you can use to maintain a Listserv subscription.

To use these commands, address e-mail to the Listserv (the address you use to subscribe, *not* the list address), and type the command as the body of the message. In general, you can include multiple commands in one message, using a separate line for each command. Do not include anything in the body *except* commands.

The commands described in Table 8.2 work with most Listservs you will encounter. Remember that there are variations and that some commands may require different phrasing on some systems.

Tip

> To learn the proper command syntax and other useful information about a particular Listserv, send an e-mail message to the Listserv address with the word `HELP` as the body of the message. You should receive a reply message containing general instructions for using that Listserv.

Table 8.2. Some common Listserv commands.

Command Syntax	*Effect*
`LIST`	Returns an e-mail message that lists the names of all lists served by this Listserv.
`INDEX` *`listname`*	Returns an e-mail message that lists all files (see "Reading Back Issues," later in this chapter) available from the list.
`INFO ?` or `Info listname`	Returns an e-mail message that lists all help files related to the list, such as FAQs or general instructions.
`REVIEW`	Returns an e-mail message that lists all subscribers to the list (including their e-mail addresses), except for those who have used the CONCEAL option (described later in this table).
`QUERY listname`	Returns an e-mail message listing all your current subscription options, any of which you can change with the `SET` command.
`SET listname option`	Sets options for your subscription. Replace *option* with one of the following keywords:
	`REPRO` All messages you send to the list are forwarded to you along with everybody else.
	`NOREPRO` Messages you send are forwarded to everyone on the list except you.
	`ACK` Acknowledgment notices are sent to you when the list receives your postings.
	`NOACK` No acknowledgments are sent.
	`CONCEAL` Hides your e-mail address in the message produced by `REVIEW` so that other subscribers won't know your e-mail address. *Note:* If you post any messages to the list, your e-mail address appears in the header, even if you use the `CONCEAL` option. The only way to remain anonymous is to use `CONCEAL` *and* post no messages.

Command Syntax	*Effect*	
	NOCONCEAL (default)	Your e-mail address appears in the message produced by REVIEW.
	MAIL (default)	All messages are sent to you when they are sent to others.
	NOMAIL	Puts your mail on hold. No messages are forwarded to you until you send the command MAIL. This option is useful if you plan not to use e-mail for a while and don't want messages to pile up in your mailbox.
	FILES (default)	Files attached to messages are sent along with the files.
	NOFILES	Only messages are sent, saving the extra account space any attached files require. (If you read a message containing a file you want, note the filename and filetype and use the GET command to retrieve them, as described in "Reading Back Issues," later in this chapter.)

Reading Back Issues

As a new subscriber to a list that's been around awhile, you may want to read messages older than the current postings. Most Listservs store all past messages and files in archive files you can retrieve and read on your Mac.

To request a list of archives and other files available from a Listserv, send the INDEX command to the Listserv address. As with all Listserv commands, send the command in the body of an e-mail message to the address you use to subscribe, *not* the list address.

For example, to see the files available from the Apple-Internet-Users list, I sent this command to the Listserv; shortly after that, I received the message shown in Figure 8.5:

```
INDEX apple-internet-users
```

Observe that each file has a filename and a filetype. These elements are required for retrieving files. The filetypes are helpful for identifying the contents: FAQ files contain frequently asked questions. You may also see binary files containing programs, graphics, and so on. These may have expected extensions such as GIF (a graphic), but often have an extension of .SIT, which indicates a compressed file or set of files that must be decompressed before they can be used. (See Chapter 12.)

FIGURE 8.5.
A list of files available from a Listserv, retrieved with the `INDEX` *command.*

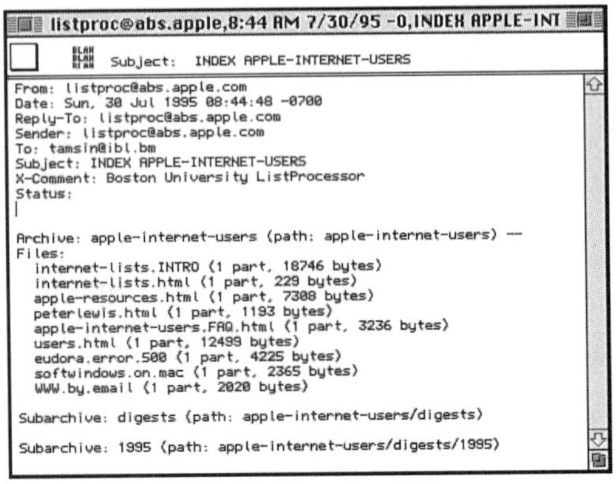

To retrieve a file, use the `GET` command:

```
GET filename filetype
```

Unsubscribing

When you no longer want or need a list, unsubscribe from it. You should receive complete instructions for unsubscribing in the acknowledgment message you receive when you subscribe (another reason to save that message). Typically, you send `UNSUB` (simple, *n'est pas*?). For a one-list Listserv, send this message:

```
UNSUB listname
```

Cleaning Out Your Subscriptions

Once they start signing up, folks begin to lose track of their subscriptions. After a while, it's easy to forget what your subscriptions are; it's even easier to forget the Listserv address for administration. In such cases, it's often a good idea to simply wipe the slate clean and unsubscribe from *all* your Listserv lists. You should also unsubscribe from all lists before changing your e-mail address (for example, if you change access providers). You can always resubscribe to lists you want to keep.

You can unsubscribe all lists with the command:

```
SIGNOFF * ( NETWIDE
```

Send this command to one Listserv; it will be forwarded automatically to all other Listservs known to the first one. In most cases, this command cancels all your Listserv subscriptions.

Summary

Mailing lists are a great way to stay informed about a topic and to engage in stimulating conversations with others. They're also easy to use and require only the most basic Internet access and software—an e-mail account and an e-mail client program.

Still, they're not for everybody. The Net offers yet another way you can enjoy the same kind of information—in many cases, the exact same information—you can get from a mailing list. You discover the other kind of Net discussion list—newsgroups—in Chapter 9.

CHAPTER 9

BROWSING NEWSGROUPS

Off the Internet, when you want to keep abreast of a subject, you can subscribe to dozens of newsletters, magazines, and journals, and enjoy regular deliveries of the latest news and views. Or, if you want to keep the postal service out of the equation, you can just stroll down to the local library's reading room whenever the mood strikes you. It's all a matter of personal preference.

On the Internet, mailing lists (see Chapter 8, "Subscribing to Mailing Lists") offer the first approach; *newsgroups* offer the second. When you use a newsgroup, the news doesn't come to you—*you* go to the news. A newsgroup is a topic-centered forum where users can post public questions, answers, news, and comments, or read the postings left by others. Newsgroups require a program called a *newsreader* that interacts with a *news server* to supply you with a list of available newsgroups, a list of *articles* (messages) within each newsgroup, and the complete text of any article you select.

For many years, newsgroups have comprised the most popular source of information on the Internet. This is changing, as the World Wide Web gains popularity (see Chapter 10, "Browsing the World Wide Web"). Because you can access newsgroups *through* most Web browsers (which can often double as newsreaders and communicate with news servers), newsgroups still represent the richest, most open trove of news, information, and conversation anywhere on the Net.

Macintosh users can use a Web browser to access newsgroups or a newsreader program like Newswatcher (see Chapter 5, "Choosing Client Software for Internet Services," for more details on Newswatcher).

How Newsgroups Work

You access newsgroups through a *newsreader*, a client application on your Mac that interacts with a *news server*, which typically runs on your access provider's network. News servers circulate newsgroup messages among themselves through Internet e-mail, using special headers that identify files as newsgroup *articles*.

Although users don't access newsgroups through e-mail, the reliance on e-mail for newsgroup transport across the Internet means that newsgroup articles face the same limitations as e-mail messages (such as the requirement that all messages feature text and nothing else; refer to Chapter 7, "Exchanging E-Mail"). Binary files (such as computer programs, graphics, and video clips) must be encoded in text form to be posted on a newsgroup, and an article posted to a newsgroup can take hours, even a day, to show up in the listings because of the natural delays in e-mail traffic and the time required for each news server to download the latest articles.

From the user's perspective, all newsgroups and their articles appear to be in the same place. And, in a way, they are—they're all stored on the news server. But they don't start out there. The original databases containing all current articles for a given newsgroup are stored on different news servers across the Internet. On a regular schedule, each news server receives copies of the group databases stored on the other news servers. That's why an article posted to a newsgroup may take a day or more to show up in the article list; it doesn't go on the list until the servers have been updated. Most servers are updated once a day; some are updated more frequently. Note that not all news servers accept all newsgroups; see "Non-Usenet Newsgroups," later in this chapter.

Usenet Groups

Most universally available newsgroups are known as *Usenet newsgroups* because they are distributed through the services of a software program originally developed to enable newsgroups. The group of computers that uses the software is known as *Usenet*, but despite the implications of the name, they are linked only in that they use Usenet software for creating, managing, and distributing newsgroups. The Usenet computers have no other affiliations and do not fall under any kind of centralized management or administration. The one exception is that, through mutual agreement, all the news servers observe a set procedure for the establishment of new newsgroups. All proposals for new Usenet newsgroups must be made through a procedure that involves announcing the proposal and getting feedback from the network community. Only if a proposed new group is determined to be necessary or popular is it allowed to join the Usenet team.

Also, through cooperation rather than imposed authority, Usenet has had the effect of establishing traditions for how newsgroups work. These traditions (except for the newsgroup-creation procedure) have carried over to most non-Usenet newsgroups, making the steps required to use a newsgroup highly consistent, regardless of which newsgroup you are using. As a rule, you use all newsgroups the same way, through the same newsreader, regardless of their source.

Usenet newsgroups are named under a system of categories and subcategories. A newsgroup name is made up of a series of words or abbreviations separated by periods. The first word indicates the broad subject area of the newsgroup; each word to the right more specifically defines the topic. Consider the names of these groups:

```
comp.sys.mac.games.action
comp.sys.mac.games.adventure
comp.sys.mac.games.announce
comp.sys.mac.games.marketplace
```

All fall under the same main category (`comp`) and three levels of subcategories (`sys.mac.games`); each defines its specific topic in the final word.

Many Usenet groups fall under one of the following major headings (although there are many more subject headings, as well). Sometimes, these headings indicate the subject area; other times, they indicate the type or style of information to be found there. Note that, for some topics, two groups have been set up; one is for the posting of news, the other is for discussion.

`biz`—Business Topics

Examples:

```
biz.general
biz.marketplace.computers.discussion
```

```
biz.marketplace.services.computers
biz.marketplace.services.discussion
```

`comp`—Computer Subjects, Both Recreational and Professional

Examples:

```
comp.edu.languages.natural
comp.home.automation
comp.infosystems.www.advocacy
comp.internet.net-happenings
comp.lang.c.moderated
comp.lang.cobol
comp.os.netware.connectivity
```

`sci`—Science Topics

Examples:

```
sci.aeronautics
sci.agriculture
sci.agriculture.beekeeping
sci.anthropology
sci.astro.research
sci.bio
sci.bio.ecology
sci.cryonics
sci.life-extension
sci.med.nutrition
sci.space.shuttle
```

`soc`—Social Issues: Culture, Politics, Environmentalism, and So On

Examples:

```
soc.couples.intercultural
soc.culture.caribbean
soc.culture.french
soc.culture.malaysia
soc.feminism
soc.genealogy.surnames
soc.history.war.vietnam
soc.men
soc.religion.christian.youth-work
soc.singles
soc.support.fat-acceptance
```

`talk`—Groups on Any Subject but Especially Devoted to Online Debate

Examples:

```
talk.abortion
talk.bizarre
talk.environment
talk.philosophy.humanism
talk.politics.guns
talk.religion.buddhism
talk.rumors
```

`news`—Information about Usenet and Newsgroups in General

Examples:

```
news.admin.net-abuse.announce
news.admin.policy
news.announce.newgroups
news.answers
news.groups.questions
news.groups.reviews
news.software.nntp
news.software.readers
```

`rec`—Recreational Subjects: Hobbies, Sports, the Arts, and So On

Examples:

```
rec.antiques.marketplace
rec.arts.books.tolkien
rec.arts.comics.marvel.universe
rec.arts.erotica
rec.arts.startrek.fandom
rec.boats.racing
rec.crafts.brewing
rec.food.recipes
rec.games.backgammon
rec.models.railroad
rec.music.beatles
rec.music.funky
rec.sport.boxing
rec.sport.football.college
rec.toys.lego
```

`misc`—Subjects Difficult To Categorize (*Potpourri* as They Say on *Jeopardy*)

Examples:

```
misc.activism.progressive
misc.business.facilitators
misc.education.home-school.misc
misc.education.medical
misc.fitness
misc.immigration.canada
misc.invest.funds
misc.jobs.offered
misc.kids.pregnancy
misc.news.southasia
misc.wanted
```

Note: `misc.kids.pregnancy` is not about pregnant kids, rather it's a group focusing on issues surrounding childbirth.

Non-Usenet Groups

Usenet's software accepts feeds from other sources, as long as the other sources observe the basic Usenet conventions for message headers and formatting. Once those feeds are accepted by a

Usenet server, their articles can be distributed along with all other newsgroups. This policy has led to the emergence of newsgroups that walk like Usenet groups and quack like Usenet groups, but aren't Usenet groups—they've been copied onto a Usenet server from some other source.

Many of these newsgroups are groups whose potential audience is so small, so trivial, or so weird that the group would probably not survive the formal Usenet acceptance procedure. For example, there are newsgroups designed primarily for local interest; I can access several groups about things to do here in New Jersey. You may find a huge listing of groups, all beginning with `ba`, about happenings and issues in greater San Francisco (also known as the *B*ay *A*rea).

In addition to some Usenet groups, there are other non-Usenet (but certainly not trivial or weird) groups that cover events and issues of international concern outside the United States. There are entire sets of groups devoted to Israel, Germany, China, and other countries. These newsgroups are frequented by residents of those countries, citizens of those countries residing elsewhere (and wanting news from home), and others interested in foreign lands. Note that many of the articles in these groups are written in the official language of the country covered.

Some such groups are distributed only locally, but some find their way into the whole Usenet distribution chain. (Those who create a non-Usenet newsgroup can control the breadth of its distribution: from locally to regionally to universally.) Even when these groups are distributed everywhere, the system administrators of specific news servers can "filter out" specified newsgroups so that local-interest newsgroups are often not seen beyond their local borders.

Note

> In addition to filtering out newsgroups devoted to distant cities, the administrators of some new servers, particularly those in corporate and university settings, may filter out other Usenet and non-Usenet groups according to a local policy. For example, some sites filter out any newsgroup with the word `sex` or `erotica` in its name; some filter out all the `alt` (alternative) newsgroups, described next.

The other major type of non-Usenet newsgroup is the alternative newsgroup, designed to support more off-the-wall topics and a loose, freeform style of exchange. The names of many of these begin with `alt`, though some `alt` newsgroups are legitimate Usenet groups.

Actually, although they have a reputation for raunchiness, the `alt` groups have among them many interesting, thoughtful groups that cover books, politics, and much more. The `alt` groups are also the principle carriers of porno writing and binary sex photos, nutball conspiracy theories, and hate-mongering. Virtually all `alt` groups are unmoderated (see "Moderated and Unmoderated Newsgroups," later in this chapter), which means that anything goes. Here are some examples of `alt` newsgroups:

```
alt.acme.exploding.newsgroup
alt.airline.class.action.lawsuit
alt.books.beatgeneration
alt.fan.bob-dole
alt.fan.fabio
alt.food.waffle-house
alt.internet.talk.bizarre
```

```
alt.personals.aliens
alt.pets.hamsters
alt.sports.baseball.bos-redsox
alt.support.househusbands
alt.tv.twilight.zone
```

Still other alternative newsgroups are non-Usenet groups formed to serve a very narrow field of interest—sometimes even an audience of one. Some jokers with too much time on their hands set up their own newsgroups with names like the following (these are real—I did not make them up):

```
alt.colin-ferguson.guiltier.than.even.oj
alt.conspiracy.usenet-cabal
alt.kill.the.whales
alt.music.yanni.aural-enema
```

If you visit such groups, you're likely to find few articles, if any. (This, by the way, is exactly the kind of thing Usenet's requirements for new groups were designed to prevent.) On occasion, however, groups with goofy names can be surprisingly active and useful.

Plumbing the depths of alternative newsgroups has its risks; it is not for the squeamish or easily offended. But if you're selective about which `alt` newsgroups you check out, you may find a gem among the rubble.

Moderated and Unmoderated Newsgroups

Moderated newsgroups are patrolled by one or more *moderators*, gatekeepers of sorts who read every article before it is posted, judging the message on its relevance, appropriateness, newsworthiness, or other criteria. Articles deemed inappropriate (or, in some groups, profane) are not posted. Moderated groups are relatively uncommon; even so, most of the moderating is not zealous—a message often has to be *way* off base to be rejected.

Moderated groups have advantages and disadvantages. Visit an `alt` group someday—virtually all of which are unmoderated—and you'll see what I mean. Mixed in with the useful information and reasonable questions and answers are discussions veering completely out of the jurisdiction of the group. These tangents usually begin as appropriate discussions, but when folks get sidetracked, there's no one to put a stop to it. In unmoderated newsgroups, you'll also find much more repetition, petty squabbling, profanity, shouting, and flaming. (See Chapter 6, "Netiquette and First Tips.")

On the other hand, some newsgroup users fear that moderation is equivalent to censorship. It's unlikely that any moderator sets out to be a censor, but when cast as a judge, anybody can subconsciously base choices on personal bias. Advocates of unmoderated newsgroups believe it's better to post everything, and let users decide whether or not it's appropriate.

Newsgroup users themselves can effectively keep the discussion on track by bringing peer pressure to bear—in the form of instructive and corrective messages—on users who post inappropriate material. Of course, that approach favors mob rule over censorship, which does not necessarily result in a more open flow of information (the biases of the moderator are simply replaced by the biases of the majority).

Such issues remind us that the Internet is, in effect, a global community. The culture will evolve, but there will always be controversy and disagreement—which is just as it should be.

Which Way To Go: Mailing List or Newsgroup?

The easy answer is that you needn't choose between mailing lists or newsgroups. You can use whichever type of discussion group suits your needs for a given subject or whichever one supplies the best information. Or, you can cover your bases and subscribe to both.

There is a great deal of overlap between newsgroups and mailing lists. For any important subject, you're likely to find both a newsgroup and a mailing list—or several of each. Also, many newsgroups and mailing lists are linked by *gateways* that automatically post every mailing list message on the newsgroup, and send every newsgroup message to the mailing list. When a gateway exists, mailing list subscribers and newsgroup subscribers both have access to all the same messages.

You may have technical reasons to favor one over the other, however. Some users have restrictions placed on the amount of e-mail they can receive (caused by severe storage limitations imposed by their access providers), so they may favor newsgroups. Users whose accounts include e-mail but no access to a news server have the decision made for them. Users who pay per-minute charges on their Internet accounts may appreciate the ability to log on, collect e-mail, and log off quickly, as opposed to spending time online browsing a newsgroup. (You can dramatically cut the online time required for using newsgroups by using a newsreader that supports offline operation. See "Working Offline," later in this chapter.)

If you have equal access to newsgroups and mailing lists, you may want to use newsgroups for high-traffic subjects and mailing lists for low-traffic subjects. High-traffic subjects clog your mailbox fast; sorting through (and ignoring) large numbers of messages is easier on a newsgroup. On the other hand, it's frustrating to open your newsreader, navigate to a low-traffic newsgroup, and retrieve the article list only to find there's nothing new; if you use a mailing list for low-traffic subjects, you know that when there's no mail, there's no news.

Using a Newsreader

Many different newsreaders are available for Macintosh users, in commercial, shareware, and free forms. (See Chapter 5 for tips on acquiring newsreader software.) Most World Wide Web browsers can also serve as newsreaders; see "Accessing Newsgroups with the Web," later in this chapter.

One of the most popular newsreaders is Newswatcher, a public-domain Macintosh program for Macs running System 7.0 or later. It was developed by Northwestern University and includes a comprehensive electronic manual detailing its many useful features. The examples in this chapter are based on NewsWatcher 2.0.

Sams was not able to license NewsWatcher, but you can download it using FTP from:

`ftp://mirrors.aol.com//pub/mac/util/comm/usenet/newswatcher2.0.sit.hqx`

For more details on FTP, see Chapter 12, "Collecting files with FTP."

Configuring the Newsreader

Newsreaders differ, but they all require one piece of information to operate: the host name or IP address of your news server. In addition, NewsWatcher also requires the name of your access provider's SMTP (mail) server. Your access provider should supply you with this information when you sign up. If your provider offers a startup software package, the news server address may be preconfigured in the newsreader software supplied.

To configure NewsWatcher, first connect to the Internet and then launch NewsWatcher. The first time you open NewsWatcher, the Welcome to NewsWatcher dialog box appears, as shown in Figure 9.1. If more than one person will be using NewsWatcher, click the Shared button.

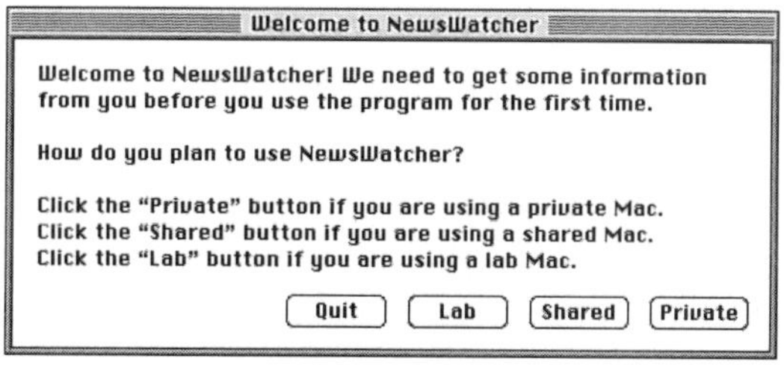

FIGURE 9.1.
The Welcome to NewsWatcher dialog box.

Note

If you choose the Shared option in the Welcome to NewsWatcher dialog box, NewsWatcher asks you to create a folder on your hard disk to be used as your personal NewsWatcher folder. Each individual who uses NewsWatcher has their own personal folder containing the list of newsgroups to which they subscribe. (*Note:* The Lab option is normally for those using a computer lab, as in an educational institution.)

After you have configured the Welcome to NewsWatcher dialog box, the Server Addresses dialog box appears. (See Figure 9.2.) Like many newsreaders, NewsWatcher provides a place to enter your e-mail (SMTP) server address so that you can send replies by e-mail (as described later in this chapter). In the News Server: field, enter the name or IP address of your news server. In the Mail Server: field, type the name of your SMTP (mail) server and then click the OK button.

Next, NewsWatcher asks you to fill out the Personal Information dialog box. (See Figure 9.3.) Your e-mail address is mandatory and you must use the Internet address convention (for example, `tamsin@ibl.bm`). You may, if you wish, leave the options for your full name and organization blank. When you are finished configuring the Personal Information dialog box, click the OK button. Now, NewsWatcher retrieves a full list of the available newsgroups on your access provider's news server.

FIGURE 9.2.
The Server Addresses dialog box in NewsWatcher.

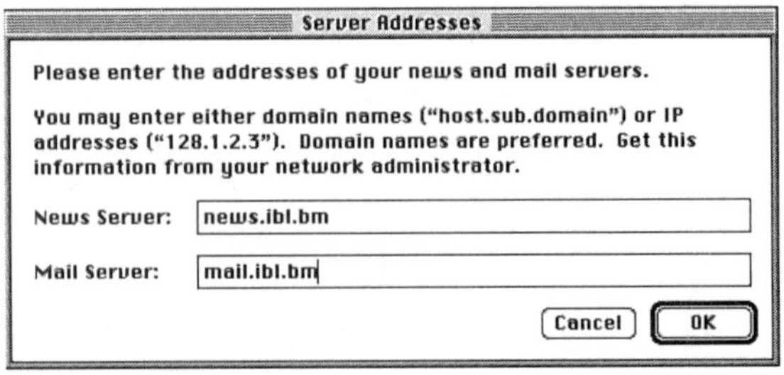

FIGURE 9.3.
The NewsWatcher Personal Information dialog box.

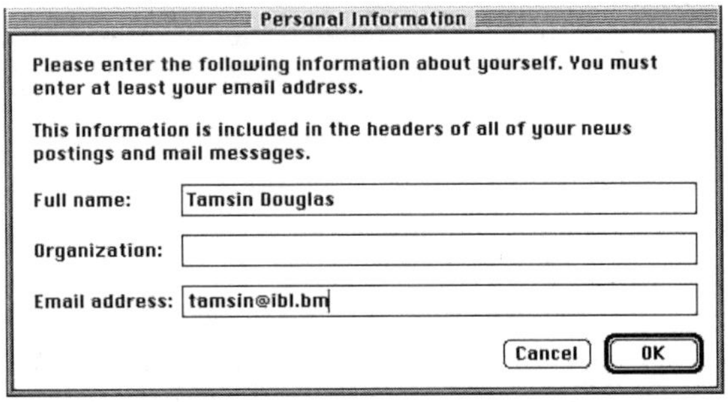

Note

News servers and newsreaders intercommunicate through a protocol called NNTP (network news transfer protocol). Sometimes, a configuration screen prompts you for a "TCP port" or "server type." For a news server, this entry should be `NNTP`.

Downloading the Group List

News servers maintain a master list that contains the names of all newsgroups they distribute, arranged alphabetically by name. This list typically includes all Usenet groups, many of the non-Usenet groups, and some local newsgroups. The list may even include a newsgroup or two exclusively for users of that news server; for example, some access providers set up a local newsgroup that accepts comments and suggestions for improving the service. Downloading the list can take several minutes or even longer. After all, there are—at this writing—more than 11,000 newsgroups.

When NewsWatcher finishes retrieving the list of available groups, it displays two windows: the Full Groups List window contains all the available news groups on your access provider's news server and the Untitled window is where you store the groups to which you want to subscribe.

Because the list changes as new newsgroups are added and old ones are cast off, you should download the list again from time to time. Most newsreaders offer a simple menu item for downloading the list. To update the list in NewsWatcher, choose Rebuild Full Group List from the Special menu.

Finding a Newsgroup

Once the group list is on your Mac, you can search for newsgroups covering topics that interest you. Most Macintosh newsreaders feature a simple text-search capability you can use to locate newsgroup names containing a particular word. In NewsWatcher, use the Find command in the Edit menu. For example, use the search term Internet to find newsgroups about the Internet. This search revealed the following groups, shown here to help you get started. (Remember that newsgroups come and go. By the time you read this, there may be new Internet newsgroups, and some of those listed may be dead and gone.)

```
alt.bbs.internet
alt.best.of.internet
alt.culture.internet
alt.destroy.the.internet
alt.horror.shub-internet
alt.internet.access.wanted
alt.internet.media-coverage
alt.internet.services
alt.internet.talk-radio
ba.internet
comp.internet.library
comp.internet.net-happenings
info.big-internet
```

Subscribing to a Newsgroup

The whole notion of "subscribing" is a little loose with regard to newsgroups. With a mailing list, you must formally subscribe before you can receive any messages at all. With a newsgroup, there's no requirement that you actually subscribe before you can read or post articles there. Unlike mailing lists, newsgroups maintain no list of members; an unsubscribed visitor to a group is no different from a subscriber as far as the newsgroup is concerned.

Subscribing simply tells your newsreader that you intend to visit a particular newsgroup regularly. The newsreader places the names of groups to which you have subscribed in a special menu or some other place so that you can choose among them quickly and conveniently without wading through the whole newsgroup list.

In NewsWatcher, the Untitled window you see the first time you run NewsWatcher is called the User Group List. This is where you store the newsgroups to which you want to subscribe. To subscribe to a newsgroup using NewsWatcher, select it in the Full Group List window and drag it into the Untitled window. NewsWatcher copies subscribed groups to the Untitled window and displays them as shown in Figure 9.4. When you are finished subscribing to the newsgroups you want, choose Save from the File menu to save your User Group List on your computer. Name the new file My News, for example. The next time you want to access these newsgroups, double-click this file. NewsWatcher launches, opens your list, and automatically checks for new articles posted to the newsgroups to which you have subscribed.

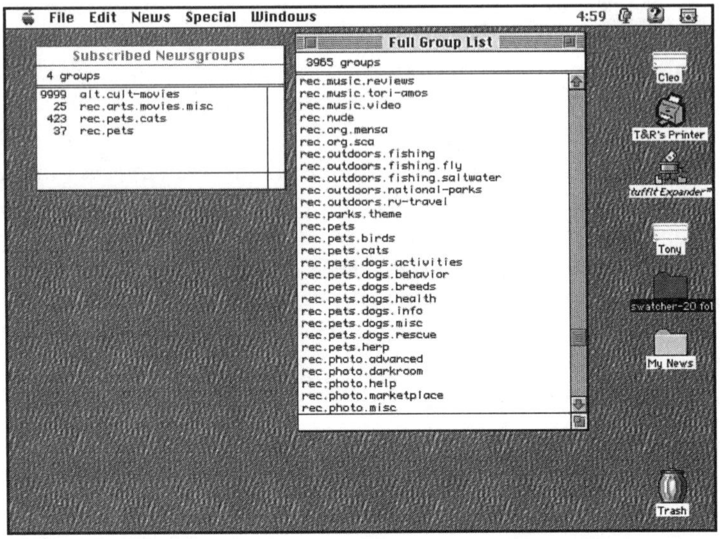

FIGURE 9.4.
NewsWatcher shows subscribed groups in a separate window.

Tip

> If you share a Mac, save your User Group List in the same folder that contains your NewsWatcher Prefs file. Always open NewsWatcher from this folder to access your personal list of subscribed newsgroups.

Pointing to a Newsgroup

Instructing your newsreader to visit a particular newsgroup is called *pointing* to the group. In most Macintosh newsreaders, pointing is a matter of double-clicking the newsgroup name in the newsgroup list, or highlighting it and clicking a button. (Of course, you must connect to the Internet and open your newsreader first.) Pointing to a newsgroup tells your newsreader to query the server and retrieve files for that newsgroup.

What happens after you point to a newsgroup depends on your newsreader. A very few download the entire text of all current articles in that newsgroup; others download only the headers at first. In either case, the result is a scrollable list of articles, including the names of senders and subjects, as shown in Figure 9.5.

The headers-only approach produces this list more quickly, but then requires a few moments to download the text of any article you choose to read. The header-only approach is valuable if you tend to read only a small proportion of the articles—why wait for all of them to be downloaded? Newsreaders that download the complete text of all articles, on the other hand, take longer to produce the article list but can display the text of any article instantly because the article is already stored on your Mac. The entire-text approach also enables you to work offline (see "Working Offline," later in this chapter) because you can log on, collect articles, and log off quickly. Working offline is valuable if you pay per-minute charges for Internet access.

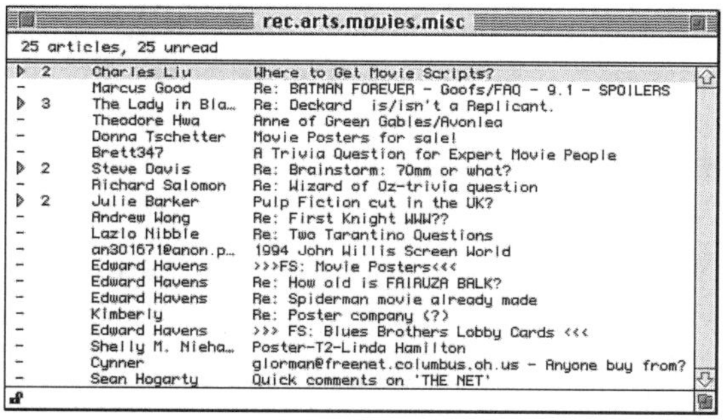

FIGURE 9.5.
A list of current articles in a movie newsgroup.

Tip

> Some newsreaders—NewsWatcher included—enable you to download only some of the articles (or article headers) when you point to a newsgroup. Some newsgroups have hundreds of current articles, which makes retrieval slow and wading through articles tedious.
>
> Figure 9.6 shows the dialog box in Preferences (under the File menu) you can use to specify a maximum number of articles NewsWatcher will retrieve. The default is 15000.

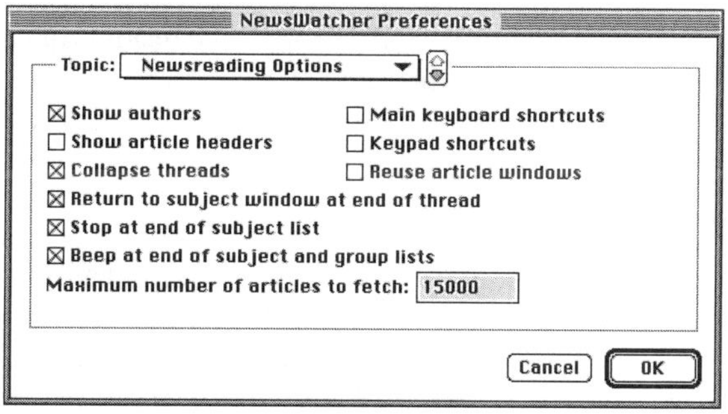

FIGURE 9.6.
Setting the maximum number of articles.

Sorting Articles

After the article list appears, some Macintosh newsreaders enable you to change the order of articles as they appear in the list. You may find it useful to sort your articles by date or by subject.

Especially valuable is the ability to sort articles by threads. A *thread* is an ongoing conversation, one article followed by all the responses to it, and the responses to the responses. Responses are indicated by placing `Re:` in the subject line, in front of the subject of the original article (refer to Figure 9.5, shown previously). Note that a `Re:` subject line does not by itself make an article a part of a thread. The header must show that the article is actually a reply to another message in the thread.

When articles are sorted by date or *article number* (a number automatically assigned to each article by the server that originally receives it), the threads are broken up by other articles listed between them and are sometimes rearranged so that they're out of order. Sorting by threads pulls all the articles in each thread together and arranges them in order so that you can read through them and follow the thread of the conversation.

In NewsWatcher, articles are presorted into threads when you open a newsgroup. A triangle control, like the one shown in Figure 9.7, indicates articles that have been grouped together or collapsed into a thread. By clicking on the triangle control, the thread expands to reveal all the articles in a thread.

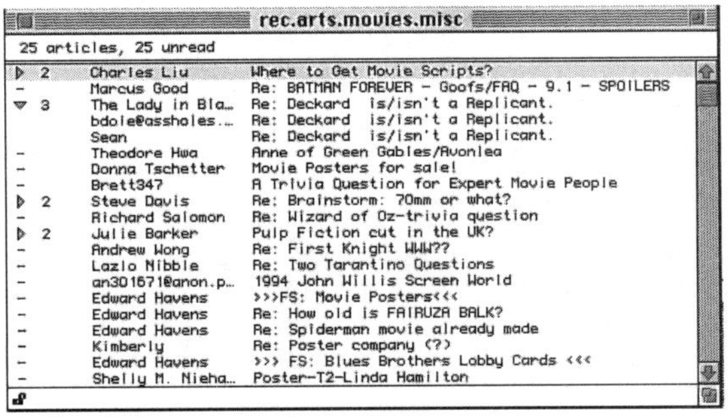

FIGURE 9.7.
Articles arranged in a thread.

Many newsreaders can also search through the headers of current articles for a given text string. Such a search capability enables you to quickly locate in the current list articles from a certain user or about a certain subject.

Reading an Article

Reading an article from within a Mac newsreader is almost always a matter of double-clicking the article's entry in the list. Standard Macintosh elements such as scroll bars are applied to move around within the article. When you're finished, click the Close box in the upper-right corner of the window or choose Close from the File menu.

When reading articles, you'll encounter the elements described in the following sections.

Quotes

Quotes are not the original words of the author of the article you're reading; they are excerpts from another article or articles to which this article is a response. Each line of text in a quote is preceded by a special character, usually a greater-than sign (>). Because the newsreader's ability to accurately sense the quotes varies, it's still useful to look for preceding characters and indentation as indications of quoting. The actual new text of the article appears in normal text, with no greater-than signs.

As shown in Figure 9.8, the quotes are usually preceded by a line that tells the source of the quotes. The quotes may show the entire text of the original article, or only the parts to which the writer is responding. Sometimes, responders indicate where they've cut the quotes by inserting a line that says `[snip]` or `[cuts]`.

FIGURE 9.8.
Reading an article.

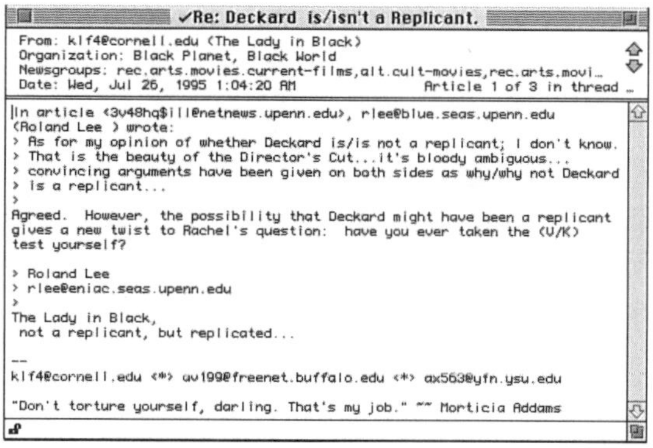

In an ongoing thread, an article may contain quotes within quotes within quotes—in responses that are responses to responses (*ad infinitum*). Each level of quoting is indented further than the one that precedes it and has more greater-than signs in front of it; in other words, the newer the quote, the less indented it is and the fewer greater-than signs precede each line. The multiple quotes are organized "middle out": Each response surrounds its quotes, and is surrounded by the response that quotes it. The actual new text in an article usually appears at the bottom, after all the quotes (which makes sense). Sometimes, the new text appears at the top of the message, above the quotes, so it's easy to find. Other times, the new text appears between the quotes, responding to each part of a quote separately. Most newsreaders enable you to insert your new text anywhere within the article; other newsreaders may force all new text to appear above or below the quotes.

Shorthand and Emoticons

Shorthand is a family of Internet abbreviations for common expressions—for example, BTW means *by the way. Emoticons* are little faces made out of text characters, used to indicate emotions or the intended tone of a statement. For more about shorthand and emoticons, see Chapter 6.

Files

Binary files, such as programs and graphics, can be posted on a newsgroup and selectively downloaded by subscribers. See "Working with Files," later in this chapter.

Responding to an Article

So you're browsing through a newsgroup devoted to Paul Simon (`alt.music.paul-simon` or something) and you come across an article that describes Art Garfunkel as the "co-writer" of *Mrs. Robinson.* Knowing that Paul Simon wrote both the words and music, you're burning to set the record straight (politely, of course—no flaming, no SHOUTING).

You simply select the follow-up feature in your newsreader (sometimes also called "respond" or something else—the terminology used in newsreaders varies), which works in exactly the same way that Reply features work in e-mail programs (see Chapter 7), except that the reply is automatically posted to the newsgroup and not e-mailed to the sender of the misinformation.

The Role of E-Mail in Newsgroups

Some newsreaders have a send-only e-mail capability through which you can "reply" to a newsgroup article. The steps for composing and sending an e-mail reply are the same as those for posting a follow-up, but a reply is not posted to the newsgroup—instead, it's sent by e-mail only to the original sender of the article to which you are responding. This is a useful capability when you have something to say to that person, but your response is not necessarily appropriate for, or relevant to, the newsgroup at large.

You must configure e-mail-capable newsreaders with the same information you supply to an e-mail program: your e-mail address and SMTP server address. (See Figures 9.2 and 9.3, shown previously.) Note that the send-e-mail capability does not make the newsreader a full-fledged e-mail program (because it still lacks the POP3 client capability to *receive* e-mail).

When properly configured, these newsreaders give you the option of sending a new article or a response in the following ways:

- As a posting to the newsgroup
- As e-mail to the sender of an article to which you're replying
- As both at once

Some articles reach the newsgroup through e-mail from users who may not be able to access articles there (these users identify themselves as such in their articles and request replies to be sent using e-mail). You may want to post your reply to the newsgroup for the benefit of other readers, and also send e-mail to make sure that the reply reaches the originator.

In other cases, you may choose to reply by e-mail for other reasons. For example, on a *Star Trek*-related group, a musicologist had posted an analysis of the opening theme music to the *Star Trek: Voyager* TV series. After reading his posting, I wanted to ask him a question about film music—a question that had nothing to do with *Star Trek*, and therefore was not appropriate for the newsgroup. So I sent him an e-mail reply, to which he also replied by e-mail. Over the next few weeks, we enjoyed a rewarding exchange of e-mail about film music.

Another time, I noticed what I felt was an unacceptable level of racism embedded in an article posted in a group that had nothing to do with race issues. So I made my point discretely and privately through e-mail.

When you select Reply or Follow-up, a window opens for a new article. The window contains the complete text of the original article, quoted in the body, and uses the same the Subject line as the original article. The letters `Re:` (for *regarding*) are automatically added to the beginning of the Subject line, unless the original message was itself a response—there's no need to create `Re:Re:Re:` subject lines. When displaying threads, some newsreaders progressively indent the vertical bars used to indicate repeating subject lines. Each level of indentation indicates another level of `Re:`.

Cut the quote down to exactly what you're responding to and enter your comments below it. Be concise and direct, and be polite. Avoid sending "me too" posts in which you add nothing to the subject under discussion; they're annoying and a waste of space. When finished, check your writing carefully and then post your article. The exact steps required for posting vary by newsreader; in NewsWatcher, you click the Send button in the icon tool bar at the top of the Reply message window.

Jumping into the Conversation at the Right Point

The tendency for threads to get broken up causes certain problems in newsgroups. For example, when a reader comes across a question, he or she sometimes posts an answer to it without first following the thread to the end to see whether the question has already been answered. Also, some users accidentally jump into the middle of a thread to post a comment. That makes the thread impossible to follow in a logical order.

Of course, these problems occur not simply because of disarranged threads, but also because of the time it takes for a new article to reach the group. Although it may appear that no one has responded to a question, the response may in fact be somewhere out on the Net, working its way to the newsgroup.

Still, it's always good practice to sort messages by thread before posting a response. That way, you can review all the points that have already been made and add your two cents worth at the end of the thread—where it belongs.

Posting a New Article

Posting a new article to a newsgroup is just like responding, except that you begin from the article list (instead of with an article open in front of you). You open a New Message window and enter a new subject line. Compose your message carefully, observing the rules of etiquette (refer to Chapter 6). Make sure that your message supplies information or insight that other people on the newsgroup will find useful, or poses a question that hasn't already been asked (and answered) a billion times on the newsgroup. When your article is ready, post it (in NewsWatcher, click the Send button in the icon tool bar at the top of the new message window).

Newsgroup Niceties

Before posting one word on a newsgroup, lurk for a while to soak up the culture and evaluate the vocabulary and expertise level of the other subscribers. Scroll through the article list to find any reference to a Frequently Asked Questions (FAQ) file (a text file of questions and answers designed to bring new subscribers up to speed). If you can't find a FAQ mentioned, nobody will mind if you post a brief message asking where it can be found. If a FAQ is available, someone will post it on the newsgroup again for you to pick up (see "Working with Files," later in this chapter) or will tell you how to get it with FTP (see Chapter 12, "Collecting Files with FTP"). Lurking and reading the FAQ can help you avoid posting information that's old news to everybody else, or asking a question that everybody's tired of answering.

For example, in the laserdisc newsgroup I frequent, subscribers analyzed the *Forrest Gump* laserdisc in great detail, commenting on—and arguing about—the quality of the video transfer, the value of the bonus documentary, and every other aspect of the disc. For a few weeks, *Gump* was the subject of about half the messages posted—at least a few dozen a day. After this had gone on for a couple months, somebody posted the question, "Anybody heard if *Forrest Gump* is coming out on laserdisc?" Luckily, nobody flamed the offender—but nobody answered him, either.

Don't expect your message to appear instantly in the article list. It can take hours—even a day or more—for a new posting to arrive. If your message inspires responses, you'll see them in the article list within a day or two. Sometimes, people respond with e-mail as well, because they can get your e-mail address from the headers on your newsgroup postings.

Working Offline

Browsing newsgroups can rack up the hours online fast. If you pay per-minute charges for your Internet access, or if you use the Internet at home and your significant other wants to pick up the phone without being blasted by a modem screech, you'll want to find ways to trim your time online.

Note

Nearly all newsreaders let you save the complete text of any article on your Mac's hard disk. When you open an especially long article, save it to disk and move on—you can read it later in Simple Text or another word processor. If you know what you intend to write before you go online, compose your articles offline and then dial up and send them. Some newsreaders support offline composing; for those that don't, like NewsWatcher, you can always compose your message offline in a word processor and then highlight the text you want to copy and select Copy from the Edit menu. Launch

NewsWatcher and choose New Message from the News menu. Click in the body area of the New Message, paste in the selected text (Paste from the Edit menu) and post the article.

Tip

In NewsWatcher, if you are running system 7.5, you can select an article in a newsgroup window and drag it out to the Desktop.

To *really* trim your time online, consider these tips:

- Use a newsreader that automatically downloads complete articles so that you can read them all offline. One newsreader to consider is NewsHopper, an inexpensive commercial newsreader from SW15 Software Ltd. You can find out more about NewsHopper on the Web at `http://www.demon.co.uk:80/sw15/`. (See Chapter 10.)
- Instead of using a newsgroup, subscribe to a mailing list that covers the same subject. Ideally, you want a mailing list that is gatewayed to the same subject's newsgroup so that all the newsgroup postings automatically go to the mailing list, and all mailing list entries are posted to the newsgroup. To find a mailing list gatewayed to a particular newsgroup, search the mailing list master list using the newsgroup name (or subject) as a search term. Chapter 8 explains how to find and search mailing list master lists. You may also find the companion mailing list named in the FAQ file for a newsgroup.

Accessing Newsgroups with a Web Browser

As mentioned earlier in this chapter, World Wide Web browsers can point to your access provider's news server. (See Figure 9.9.) Once you're connected to the server, using the Web browser is much like using any other newsreader: you point to a group, review a list of articles, read articles, post replies, and so on.

Note

In Figure 9.9, note that some newsgroup names appear to be partial names, ending in asterisks. Most newsreader clients simply show you the complete newsgroup listing, in alphabetical order (refer to Figure 9.4, shown previously). But Netscape Navigator attempts to make newsgroup access easier by gathering groups together into categories. If you click one of the incomplete group names, a list of the groups beginning with that name appears.

The little icons next to the category listings represent stacks of newspapers (multiple newsgroups); individual newsgroups have an icon that looks like a single newspaper.

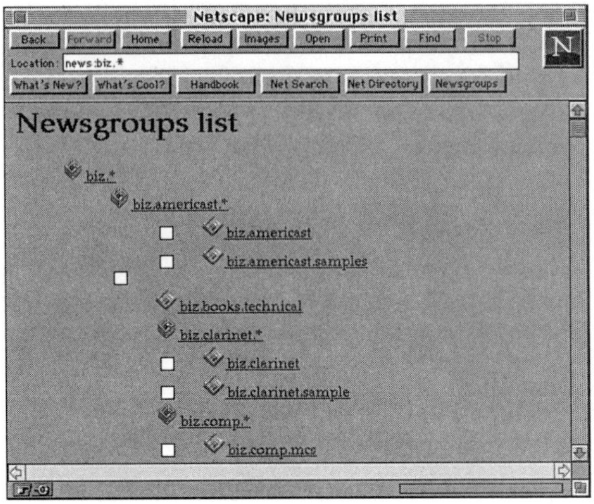

FIGURE 9.9.
Newsgroups seen through the World Wide Web.

The great thing about using a Web browser for newsgroup access is that the Web search tools (described in Chapter 18, "Finding It on the Web") often locate not only Web pages related to a search term, but newsgroups as well. These Web-based search engines ferret out a newsgroup more effectively than the search tools built into some newsgroups. Newsgroup search tools simply locate a character string within a newsgroup name, but Web searchers check databases and links that may lead to a newsgroup with the desired content, even if the search term doesn't appear in the group's name.

Web browsers may also do a more efficient job of indicating threads. Notice how the browser shown in Figure 9.10 groups messages under subject lines shown in heavy type; also notice how successive thread levels are indented.

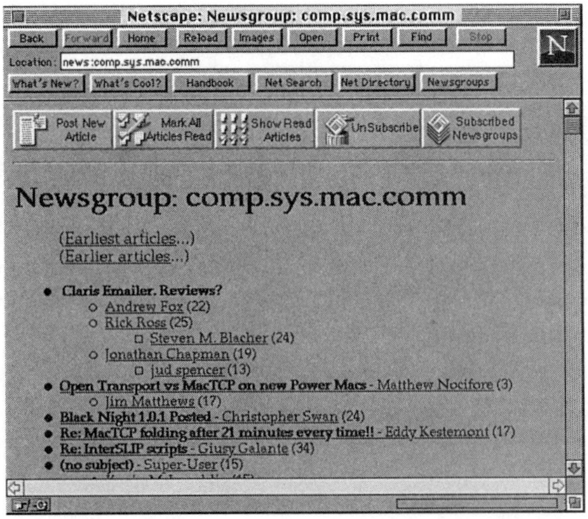

FIGURE 9.10.
A list of newsgroup articles, seen through the World Wide Web.

Like any newsreader, a Web browser must be configured with your news server address and e-mail address to provide newsgroup access. For example, to use the Netscape Navigator Web browser as a newsreader, choose Preferences from the Options menu to open the Preferences dialog box. Select the Mail and News option from the Preferences pop-up menu. (See Figure 9.11.) Fill in your mail server address in the Mail (SMTP) Server: field and enter your e-mail address in the Your email: field. This enables Netscape's send-only e-mail capabilities (which you can use to send e-mail replies to newsgroup articles or to send regular e-mail messages). You must also supply Netscape with your news server address in the News (NNTP) Server: field.

FIGURE 9.11.
Configuring Netscape to access newsgroups.

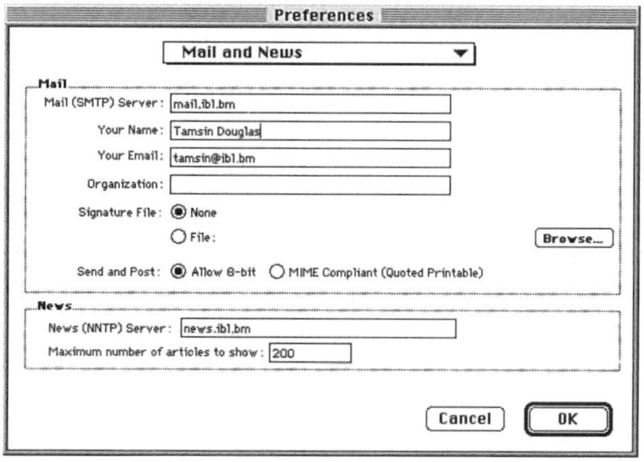

For more about using a Web browser to access newsgroups, see Chapter 10.

Working with Files

Newsgroups can be great places to pick up binary files containing Macintosh programs, graphics, and more. For example, fans of a given movie or music star often post scanned photos of the star on newsgroups where other fans congregate. Sound files featuring clips of popular recordings are also becoming popular. Be aware, however, that much of this stuff violates copyrights. Most of what's posted, such as fan photos, was created for publicity anyway, so many copyright owners aren't terribly concerned. Some are, however, and as awareness of the Internet grows, copyright protection is sure to become one of the major battlegrounds.

> **Tip**
>
> Each type of file downloaded from the Internet requires the right software to use it. Mac programs require Macs; sound and video clips require a player; graphics files require a viewing program; and so on.
>
> To learn about working with different types of files, see Chapter 12.

As is true with e-mail, binary files available over newsgroups must be encoded into a text-only form before they can be posted. They must be decoded on your computer before you can use them. Your newsreader takes care of encoding files before posting them and decoding files you receive. Encoding and decoding are usually accomplished by selecting a menu item. (Note that not all newsreaders have encoding/decoding capabilities.)

Files are easy to spot in a newsgroup; they're typically the longest articles (hundreds of lines) and the Subject lines (or the first few lines of the articles themselves) usually indicate what they are. You can actually open an article containing a file just as you can any other article. Once the article is open, you can choose your newsreader's decode function to decode the article and store the binary file on your hard disk. You may find it more convenient to save the encoded file on your hard disk first (see "Working Offline," earlier in this chapter) and decode it offline—even though decoding usually takes only a few moments.

Tip

> In NewsWatcher, binary files attached to an article are indicated by a small file icon at the top right-hand corner of the icon tool bar, as shown in Figure 9.12. NewsWatcher does not display the encoded text in a binary file. To extract the binary file in an article, click the icon, or choose Extract Binaries from the Special menu, or, if you are running System 7.5 drag the file icon out to the Desktop.

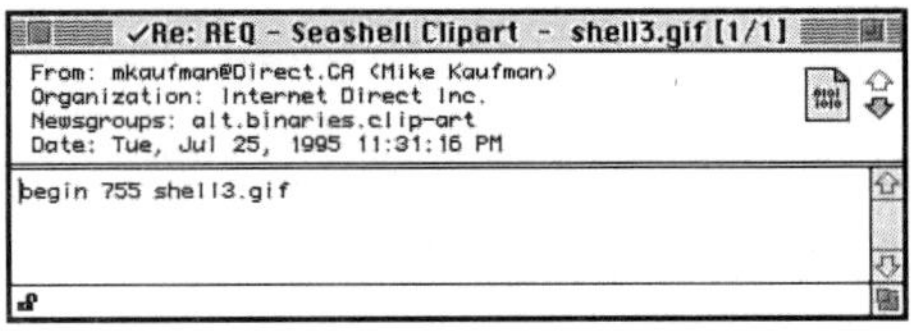

FIGURE 9.12.
NewsWatcher's binary file icon displayed in an article.

Summary

Newsgroups are a great source of information and can be great fun as well. They're an excellent way for new Internet users to break in their online skills, and a great way to meet folks from whom you can gain valuable advice.

In fact, after you try them out, you may consider newsgroups the coolest place on the Net...until you hit the World Wide Web, the hands-down coolest Internet resource. You discover the Web in the next chapter.

CHAPTER 10

BROWSING THE WORLD WIDE WEB

About the World Wide Web

Navigating the Web

Popular Web Browsers

Creating Your Own Web Page

Summary

The experts say roughly 25 million people inhabit the Internet. About 2 million use the World Wide Web, a small (but growing) part of the Internet. So how come you hear about the Web more than other, more well-traveled Internet resources?

Put simply, the Web—when seen through a software client called a *graphical browser*—is as close as you can get to making the Internet easy to use, good-looking, and fun. It's no coincidence that the explosion in mass-media interest in the Internet began with the appearance of Mosaic, the first graphical Web browser. Web-heavy reporting about the Internet has, in fact, led many to believe that the Web is the Internet, which it certainly is not. The appeal of Web browsers has also been the major factor in the rise of individual Internet accounts, and probably explains to some extent Apple's belief that Internet support was a "must-have" selling feature for eWorld. In other words, the Internet is fascinating, but the Web is *cool*. In mass-market America, *cool* gets you farther than *fascinating*.

Mea Culpa—I'm Web-Whipped!

I must admit that the popular appeal of the Web—and its legitimate usefulness—have strongly influenced my recommendations in this book. I advocate subscribing to dial-up IP accounts, despite their relative complexity and high cost compared to some alternatives, principally because graphical Web browsers require them. Although the Web is in its awkward adolescence, there's little doubt that it will become the focal point of Internet activity in the next few years.

The Web and its browsers have the effect of making the Internet a more dynamic, colorful, spontaneous, and warm and fuzzy place to hang out. The Web has also become the Internet medium of choice for doing business online (see Chapter 20, "Using the Internet in the Office"). The better browsers double as clients for other Internet resources, such as Gopher, newsgroups, and even e-mail. These multipurpose browsers don't really unify the Internet under one, easy-to-use interface, but they are as close as you can get. The Web also enhances the Internet by supplying a surprising range of tools and techniques for finding any type of information within the Web's grasp. (See Chapter 18, "Finding It on the Web.")

This chapter shows you what the Web is, how you can use browsers to navigate the Web and other resources, and how you go about creating your own place on the Web.

Note

Tips on using the Web's search engines to find information on (and off) the Web appear in Chapter 18.

About the World Wide Web

The Web was invented in 1990 at CERN, the European Particle Physics Laboratory in Switzerland. Today, an independent organization (of which CERN remains a part—as does M.I.T. and others), the World Wide Web Consortium oversees and nurtures the Web's growth. The Web Consortium is good to know about because its home page, shown in Figure 10.1, is a great place to learn about Web goings-on.

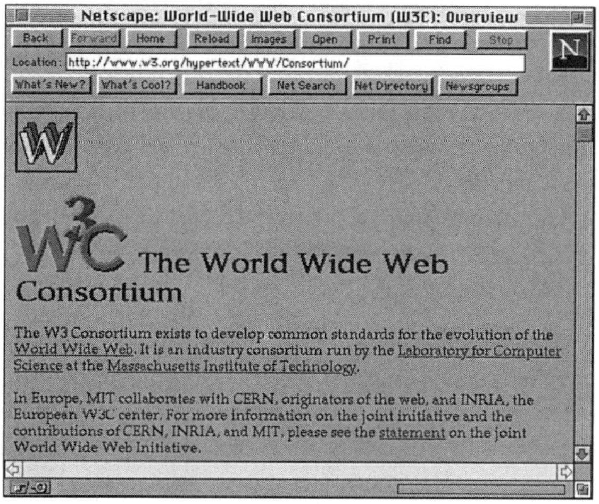

FIGURE 10.1.
The World Wide Web Consortium's home page.

Actually, Toto, There Are Several Places Like Home

An important concept for understanding the Web is *home.* A *home page* can be either of two things:

- The top page, or entry point, for all the Web documents and activities within a given Web site is the home page for that site. For example, the home page for Netscape is a popular starting point from which the majority of users (since Netscape Navigator is the current browser of choice among Web users) navigate through links down to more specific information about Netscape products and services and elsewhere.
- Your Web browser is configured with a home page, sometimes called a *startup page,* to which it navigates automatically whenever you start it up. Most browsers come with the browser software company's home page preconfigured as your home page, which isn't such a bad thing. The developers often pack their home pages with a good selection of links to search tools, cool new Web services, and other useful or interesting items—plus, of course, announcements about software updates and other products. Some Internet service providers send out browser software preconfigured with the service provider's Web page as home. If your

> provider is a local company, the Web page can be a good place to learn about local events. Providers sometimes also sell local advertising space on their Web pages, so don't be surprised to learn about the special at Eddie's Pizza from a provider's home page.
>
> You can use your browser's configuration dialog boxes to designate any page on the Web as your home page.

The Web Consortium has defined a set of standards and concepts for adding servers to the Web and for constructing the screens of information that appear to Web surfers. These screens, also known as Web *documents* or simply *pages*, are created within a special formatting language, *HyperText Markup Language* (HTML). A Web browser, by the way, is simply a program capable of interpreting the formatting of HTML documents and the navigation instructions they contain. The browser and the server communicate through another published standard, the *HyperText Transfer Protocol* (HTTP).

By publishing the specifications for HTML and HTTP, the Web Consortium has made it possible for anyone on the Internet to easily create Web documents and publish them. Making Web publishing easy and open has encouraged the growth of resources and activities. The terrific collection of Web documents available today, and the incredible network of links, has been created not by any Web-advocacy organization, but by the Internet public.

Hypertext and Hypermedia

The essential feature of HTML documents is *hypertext*. Hypertext is a method of embedding in one document links to other documents. These links show up in Macintosh Web browsers as highlighted words within a document, usually displayed in a bright color that's different from the color of the surrounding text. Click a link, and a different document appears, containing its own set of highlighted links for going elsewhere. Links are sometimes also called *hotlinks* or *hyperlinks*.

Often, the links within a document lead to expanded information about a subject. For example, observe the screen in Figure 10.2, from a document about the 1995 Cannes Film Festival. Notice the underlined words and phrases; each of these is a hypertext link to something else, or somewhere else. For example, if you click the hypertext phrase `The Competition`, the screen shown in Figure 10.3 shows you expanded information.

FIGURE 10.2.
The home page of a document about the Cannes Film Festival.

FIGURE 10.3.
The page that appears when a user clicks the link `The Competition`*, shown in Figure 10.2.*

Notice that the screen shown in Figure 10.3 has links of its own. You can continue browsing through these links or use your browser's "back" feature (usually it's a Back button) to jump back to the document shown in Figure 10.2.

> **Tip**
>
> Although it's impossible to show in a black-and-white figure, be aware that your Web browser may show you where you've been by changing the color of links you've used. (Both Netscape Navigator and Mosaic do this.) If you use the back arrow to jump back from the screen shown in Figure 10.3 to the screen in Figure 10.2, you'd see that the link `The Competition` has changed color. This feature is handy when you're browsing because it prevents you from checking out the same link twice by accident.

The beauty of links is that they can lead to anything on the Web—not just to expanded information about a document but to an entirely different document stored on a different Web server a continent away. Using this feature, Web document developers create documents with a certain amount of information of their own, peppered with links to other sites and other documents containing related information.

Hypertext is what makes true "browsing" possible. You can navigate to a Web document containing information about a topic you're interested in. Once there, you can use the links to jump around to other documents.

This nonlinear, dynamic browsing can result in very productive, exciting research sessions. It's much less structured than Gopher's system of hierarchical menus, which, although well organized, do not conform to the way people tend to think. Machines process information in an orderly fashion; humans jump from idea to idea, the way the Web enables them to. We can free-associate our way around the Web.

Web browsers contain a number of tools to keep you from getting lost. For example, you can click a back-arrow to move backward through all the documents you've visited, backing out to a place from which you can steer your search in a different direction.

Although links appear within the text of documents that also supply some information or descriptive text of their own (see Figure 10.2), some Web documents themselves are just lists of links. These Web "directories" are invaluable resources because they offer a jumping-off point for finding information all over the Web. Figure 10.4 shows a directory for fun stuff on the Web, compiled by Netscape and offered through Netscape's home page. Every line in this document (below the title) is a link to somewhere else.

FIGURE 10.4.

Best of the Net, courtesy of Netscape.

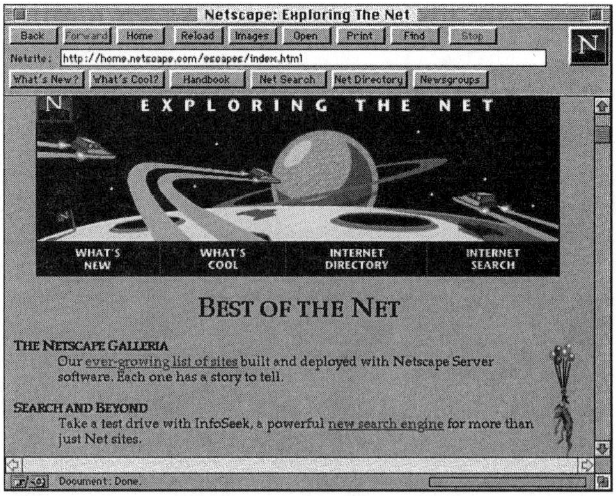

Web search engines (described in Chapter 18) build custom directories based on a search term you supply. From the directory generated by the search engine, you can jump to any of the related documents the engine has found. (See Chapter 19, "Finding Stuff Other Ways," for more about searching.)

Tip

> Links not only take you to another Web site or document, they can take you to a specific spot within a document. This capability, called *anchoring*, is especially useful for linking to specific, relevant passages in a long document. A link in a long document can even be used to jump to an anchor link somewhere else within the same document. This capability is used to create documents with a table of contents built from links that take you straight to a particular part of the document.

With the advent of graphical Web browsers in 1993, the concept of hypertext was expanded to deal with elements other than text. This enhanced way of working with hypertext, sometimes called *hypermedia*, expands Web browsing in two terrific ways that involve graphics and multimedia. (Technically, what we call *hypermedia* is still accomplished, under the covers, through hypertext. Although experts quibble over the terminology, from the user's point of view, *hypermedia* is an accurate descriptor.)

In the first application of hypermedia, on-screen graphics can themselves be links. Graphical links make browsing intuitive and fun—see a picture of something interesting, click it to see where it leads. Often, picture links lead to other documents, although they sometimes lead to a larger version of the same graphic. The smaller versions that serve as links are called *thumbnails*.

For example, Figure 10.5 shows a page from an online art gallery, including thumbnail links to artwork. Clicking the thumbnail of the painting of Mme Matisse activates a link that displays a larger version of the image. (See Figure 10.6.)

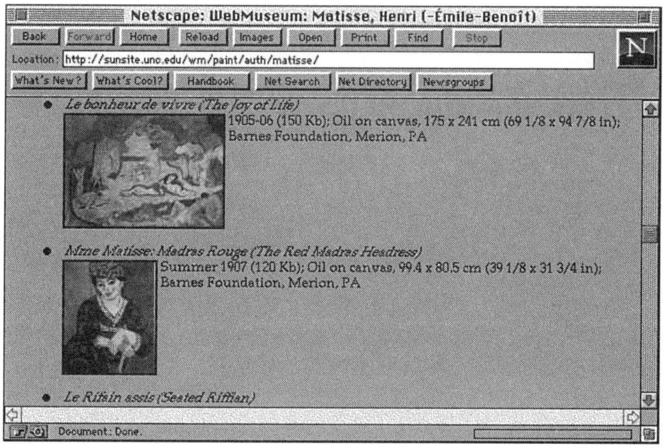

FIGURE 10.5.
An online gallery, with thumbnails of pictures that are also links.

FIGURE 10.6.
The enlarged version of the Matisse picture, which appears when you activate the thumbnail link in the screen shown in Figure 10.5.

Note

Some text-only Web browsers can access all the same documents as graphical Web browsers but they don't display the pictures. Such text-based browsers are typically used by people on text-only computer systems or dial-up terminal (as opposed to IP) Internet connections.

To be compatible with both graphical and nongraphical browsers, Web pages featuring picture links typically include a set of identical text links somewhere else on the page, for the text-only crowd.

In the second application of hypermedia, Web links can open a program and display or play a file within it. For example, a link may be designed to play a sound clip. Double-click the link, and your browser opens an application that plays sound clips, accesses a sound clip file on the Web as directed by the link, and plays it. Hypermedia on the Web supports full-color graphics, sound, animation, and video.

File Viewers (Helper Applications)

It's important to realize that Web browsers themselves don't have the capability to do much more than display text, fonts, and some types of color graphics files. For some other types of multimedia information accessed through the Web, the browser must open another program on your Mac that is capable of displaying or playing the file. These programs are called viewers or *helper applications.*

Good graphical Web browsers typically include some viewers of their own and may come preconfigured to access Macintosh programs that can act as viewers as well. For example, a browser may come preconfigured to open Apple's Movie Player for playing QuickTime video clips. You can encounter hundreds of types of files on the Web, and you may come across a type for which your browser has no viewer. When that happens, your browser typically gives you the option to download the file to your Mac's hard disk so that you can figure out how to play the file later, offline.

To add support for a file type, you have to locate your browser's viewers dialog box and enter a program filename for a program capable of opening the file type. Figure 10.7 shows Netscape Navigator's configuration facility, the Helper Applications screen which you reach by choosing Preferences in the Options menu and then choosing Helper Applications from the pop-up menu. The purpose of this dialog box is to instruct Netscape to use a particular Macintosh application for viewing a certain type of file (QuickTime movies, sounds, or images) from the Web. Certain helper applications are already preconfigured in Netscape. For example, Netscape launches Stuffit Expander when you click a link that points to a Stuffit archive file.

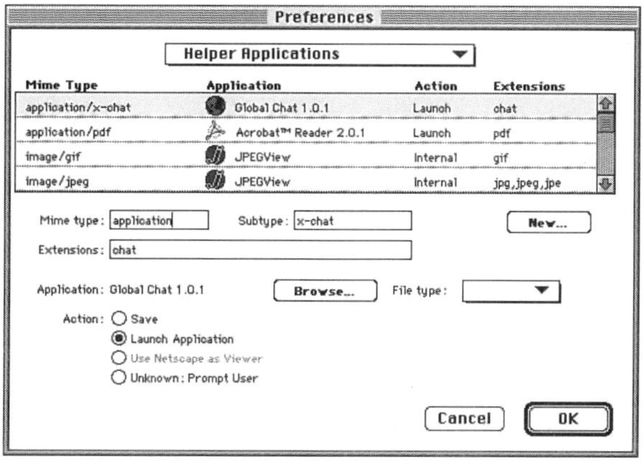

FIGURE 10.7.
Configuring viewers in Netscape through the Helper Applications screen in Preferences.

Tip

> When viewing a document containing information you'd like to keep, you can choose Save As from your browser's File menu. Most browsers enable you to save a Web document two ways:
>
> - As an HTML file. Saving information this way preserves the formatting and graphics on the page. But you can view it again only through your browser or through an HTML editor (see "Creating Your Own Web Page," later in this chapter).
> - As a plain text file. Saving information this way discards graphics and formatting, but preserves all the text in an editable text file you can view and edit through SimpleText, Microsoft Word, or any word processor or text editor.

Links to Other Resources

Finally, Web browsers can be used as front-ends to other Internet resources, including the following:

- FTP file transfers (see Chapter 12, "Collecting Files with FTP")
- Gopher menus and files (see Chapter 13, "Navigating with Menus: Gopher")
- Newsgroups (see Chapter 9, "Browsing Newsgroups")
- E-mail (see Chapter 7, "Exchanging E-Mail")
- Telnet sessions (see Chapter 11, "Tapping into Remote Systems with Telnet")

Web browsers can become front ends to other Internet resources in two ways. First, Web navigation is accomplished through Uniform Resource Locators, or URLs (see "Navigating the Web," later in this chapter). URL is pronounced *earl* or *you-are-ell*, depending on whether you believe in acronyms or abbreviations. URLs are a standard way of formatting server addresses and the locations of documents or resources within those locations, regardless of the type of Internet server or resource. URLs can point to Web servers and the HTML documents on them, FTP servers, specific files on FTP servers, Gopher menus, specific newsgroup messages, and so on.

You can type URLs yourself to navigate the Web. But the main thing links do is supply URLs to your browser, to tell it where to go. Because of the universal nature of URLs, links in Web documents can point to other types of resources. For example, a link may start an FTP session to download a file or display a Gopher menu. This approach is a great way to make resources available through the Web, and it can make certain types of activities—particularly file downloading—much easier.

The downside of this approach is that, to reach a particular resource, a link must be provided to it, or you must know how to phrase an URL correctly to reach what you want. Obviously, the Web has not yet accumulated links to every piece of information on all Internet resources. The Web does not, by itself, make client software for other Internet resources unnecessary.

More importantly, even when a link points to a resource, you can only do there what the link programs for you. If a link points to an FTP file, you can download that file with a click. But you can't check out other files on the same FTP site or perform other FTP activities there unless Web links are specifically provided for those activities. Finally, most Web links have to be updated manually; even those that are updated automatically do not instantly change when an item changes its location or name. When that happens, an old link is at a loss to find the item even though you may have little trouble finding it with the proper client software.

The other way Web browsers link to non-Web resources is by supplying their own, built-in versions of client software. For example, the Netscape Navigator features a built-in newsreader client and a send-only e-mail client. NCSA Mosaic and MacWeb support send-only e-mail and while you can read newsgroups, you can't reply to messages. (The technology has not been developed to enable browsers to *retrieve* e-mail.) Netscape has built-in FTP and Gopher clients. When you use these facilities, you are not really using the non-Web resources *through* the Web because a Web server may not be involved in the transaction. You are simply using a Web browser that mimics other types of clients to create the illusion of one-point access to all the Internet.

Where Is the Web?

Nearly all the HTML documents that appear as Web pages are stored on dedicated Web servers. *Web servers* are computers on the Internet especially configured to use the HTTP protocol. HTTP allows browsers and Web servers to communicate with one another and to interpret links. To the extent that Web browsers also reach into FTP servers, news servers, and other Internet computers, it can be said that the Web, in function if not in actuality, reaches into all corners of the Internet. But technically, the documents comprising the Web proper are on Web servers; the other stuff is ancillary to the Web, not part of it.

Anyone who wants to create and publish a Web page must set up a Web server or acquire space on someone else's Web server. Some Internet access providers lease space on their Web servers to anyone who wants to publish a document.

Navigating the Web

Navigating the Web is more than a matter of hyperlinking around. There are three basic tools for Web navigation that are essential for effective and convenient Web travel: URLs, bookmarks, and toolbar tools.

URLs

Uniform Resource Locators (URLs) are a way of standardizing the descriptions for Internet resources so that the description always includes the information your browser needs for accessing a particular item.

Tip

Look just below the toolbar in any of the screen images shown in this chapter. The URL of the Web page shown appears in a text box there. That spot is also where you can type a different URL to navigate to a particular Web site. When you activate a link, the URL shown in the text box changes to show you the URL where the link takes you.

To navigate across the Internet, your Web browser needs to know the following:

- Type of Internet resource (`scheme`)—Web, FTP, Gopher, Newsgroup, and so on. Common schemes include `http` (HyperText Transfer Protocol, used to access a Web server), `ftp` (File Transfer Protocol, used to access an FTP server) and `gopher` (Gopher protocol used to access a Gopher server). In a URL, the scheme is followed by the characters `://`. One exception are newsgroups, which begin with the characters `news:` and omit the double slashes. For example, the URL for the newsgroup `rec.arts.theatre` is `news:rec.arts.theatre`. Note that any Web browser supports FTP and Gopher, but not all support newsgroups.

- Server address (`host`)—The name of the server holding the resource.
- Port (`port`)—Sometimes (not always), a port number may be required by some servers for some resources.
- Path (`path`)—The location (usually a directory/subdirectory path and filename) of the resource on the server. Like the port, a path isn't always required.

In a URL, this information is formatted in a standard order:

```
scheme://host:port/path
```

For example, the URL `http://www.apple.com` points to a Web server (`http`) whose domain is `www.apple.com`. If you enter this URL in your Web browser, you'll visit Apple's Web site.

The URL `http://qtvr.quicktime.apple.com/toys/MacOS/QTVRPlayer.hqx` downloads the Quick Time VR program QTVRPlayer.hqx from the directory toys/MacOS on Apple's HTTP server (`qtvr.quicktime.apple.com`).

Note

> As a rule, servers on the Web are case-sensitive, which means that you must enter your URLs in the exact combination of uppercase and lowercase letters required. For example, if you see a reference to the URL `ftp://ftp.bigcorp.com/System7.5/Internet.doc`, and you enter it in all lowercase letters (without capitalizing System and Internet), you probably won't get through. Always follow the exact capitalization of any URL you enter.

Although URLs aren't all that tricky, most Web users don't spend much time fooling with them. After all, that's a link's job: to supply your browser with the URL of a Web page or other resource. For any resource you use often, whether you've first used a link to get there or not, you can create a *bookmark* (see "Bookmarks," later in this chapter) so that you can get there again without typing the URL. In general practice, you type URLs only when you have a written reference (not a link) to a resource, like the URLs accompanying descriptions of interesting Web pages in this book.

Toolbar Tools

On the toolbar of every graphical Web browser (and in their menus, as well), you can find an assortment of useful tools that differs from browser to browser. But you'll always find these four tools somewhere on the toolbar:

- Back—A left-pointing arrow. Click this to jump to the page you were looking at before the one you're on. Clicking Back multiple times takes you back farther, until you ultimately arrive at your home page.
- Forward—A right-pointing arrow. Click this to jump to the page that follows the one you're on. Forward works only after you've used Back. After you've gone back one or

more steps, Forward can take you ahead again. If you haven't gone back at all, there's no way for Forward to determine where you want to go—in other words, there is no "forward" until you first go back.

- Stop—Usually a stop sign. Sometimes, you can click a link or initiate another activity and suddenly realize that's not what you want to do. If it takes a browser a while to locate and transfer the document, you needn't wait until the operation is complete before starting over. Click Stop during any operation to cancel it.
- Home—A little house. Home takes you directly to the Web page configured as "home" in your browser. Home is handy when you browse too far into the forest and get lost, cold, or hungry. One click takes you home and reorients you so that you can start off in another direction.

Caching Is Faster

Some Web browsers achieve their Back and Forward capabilities by storing, or *caching*, Web pages on your computer. The number of pages stored varies, but anytime the browser can retrieve a page from memory instead of retransferring it through the Net, the page appears more rapidly and your impact on network resources is reduced. Sometimes, pages are cached in memory and on disk only for the duration of a session; other times, they're saved on disk for rapid retrieval in later sessions (this approach is called *persistent cache*).

Because of the savings caching makes for network resources, it's always better to use the browser's Back, Forward, or Home features to move to a page instead of using a bookmark or reentering the URL—when you have the choice. These toolbar tools typically retrieve cached pages when the pages are available; a bookmark or new URL entry forces the browser to retransfer the document, even if it's already cached.

Netscape takes persistent caching one step further. During a Web session, Netscape stores pages and keeps them on disk even after the session is over.

Bookmarks

Also used in Gopher clients, *bookmarks*—also known as *favorite places* and *hotlists*—are the URLs of resources you plan to use often. When you're somewhere you like and you want to be able to get back there easily, select your browser's Add Bookmark feature, which stores the URL of the current page and adds its title to a menu. (See Figure 10.8.) The next time you want to visit that resource, simply pick it from your bookmark list. The browser reads the URL from your bookmark file and takes you directly to the desired spot.

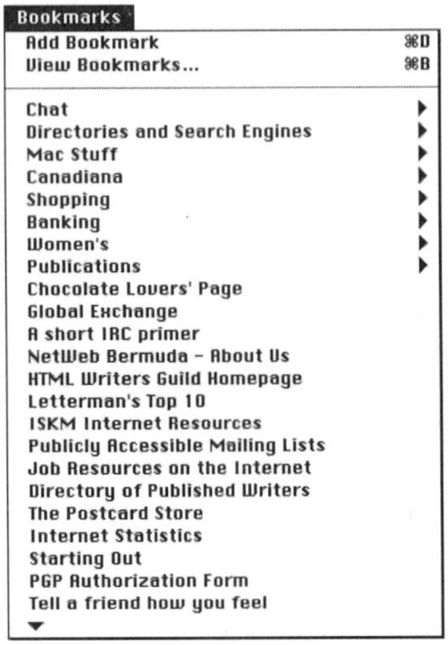

FIGURE 10.8.
A bookmark list in Netscape Navigator.

Bookmarks are especially handy if you've had to do a lot of linking and jumping to arrive at a given page and you don't want to repeat that navigation pattern to get there next time. (Yes, I could simply write down the URL but…my kid swiped all my pens.)

Tip

> During a Web session, better browsers build a history list containing the URLs of all the pages you've visited that session. You can access this list from a History menu and select a page to jump back to somewhere you've already been. You can do the same by clicking the Back toolbar button, but if the page you want was visited many links ago, selecting it from the History menu is much faster than clicking Back over and over. Most browsers discard the history list at the end of each online session.

Popular Web Browsers

The following pages describe three popular Web browsers for the Macintosh: Netscape Navigator, Mosaic, and MacWeb.

In addition to the three browsers described here, many other Web browsers are available. Because a dial-up Internet account enables you to choose any Web browser you like, it's a good idea to keep up with magazine reviews of developments in the browser arena. The browser market is very competitive right now; new, exciting browser capabilities debut monthly.

If you have not yet signed up for your Internet account and are considering using one of the online services as your Internet provider, you should be aware that eWorld, America Online, and Prodigy all supply Macintosh-based graphical Web browsers. These Web browsers are accessed only through the online service, not through a dial-up Internet account.

Netscape Navigator

Mosaic was the first graphical browser, but at this writing, Netscape Navigator (also called simply *Netscape*) is the most popular. Netscape's popularity is a result of its simplicity (just the right features, not too many, in big, friendly buttons) and its performance, which has always been sprightly thanks to its use of progressive rendering. Figure 10.9 shows the Netscape home page. Netscape Navigator is available free of charge to users in educational institutions, or to anyone for a trial period (without tech support or documentation). After the trial period, a $39 registration gets you support and a manual.

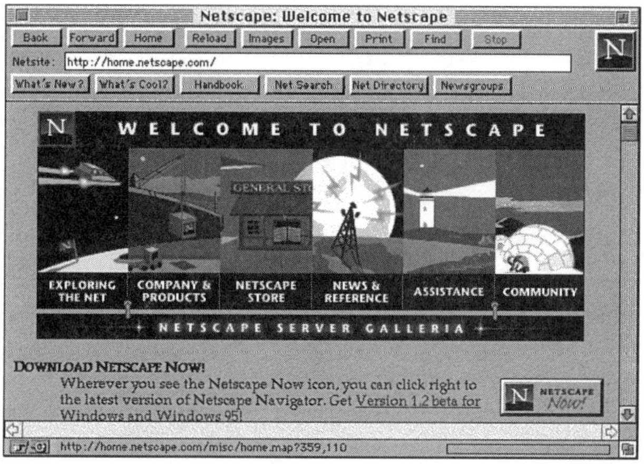

FIGURE 10.9.
Netscape Navigator at Netscape's home page.

Here are the basics for using Netscape Navigator:

- **Entering URLs.** You can manually enter and edit URLs in the Location box under the toolbar, or by choosing Open Location from the File menu to open a dialog box in which you can type a URL. A third way is through the Open button located on the Toolbar.
- **Toolbar tools.** The essentials—Home, Back, Forward, and Stop—are provided in clean, easy-to-see buttons.
- **Home page.** The home page is preconfigured to Netscape's home page (`http://home.netscape.com`) but can be changed through the Preferences dialog box (choose Preferences from the Options menu and select the Window and Link Styles screen from the pop-up menu).
- **Bookmarks.** To add a bookmark for the current page, choose Add Bookmark from the Bookmarks menu.
- **History.** Pages or URLs stored as history can be recalled by choosing the name of the page from the list under the Go Menu or by selecting View History from the Go menu.

- **Helper applications.** Choose Preferences from the Options menu and then select the Helper Applications screen from the pop-up menu.
- **FTP and Gopher.** FTP and Gopher resources are reached through available Web links. You can also enter URL's beginning with FTP or Gopher to access a specific site.
- **Newsreaders.** Netscape Navigator has a built-in, full-function newsreader client (see Chapter 9), which can be accessed by clicking the Newsgroups button under the Location URL text box. You must configure Netscape with the address of your news server by choosing Preferences from the Options menu and then filling in the Mail and News screen.
- **E-mail.** Netscape Navigator has a built-in, send-only e-mail client that can be accessed by selecting Mail Document from the File menu. The dialog box for composing an e-mail message doubles as the dialog box for creating a newsgroup posting. You must configure Navigator with the address of your mail server by choosing Preferences from the Options menu and then filling in the Mail and News screen.
- **Other useful features.** Netscape features a set of buttons, just below the Location URL text box, that activate links to useful pages including a search engine (Net Search), a Web directory organized by subject headings (Net Directory), and the latest fun places to visit (What's New! and What's Cool!). The Directory menu also supplies some helpful starting points. At this writing, Netscape is the only browser enabled to support credit-card security procedures for online shopping. (See Chapter 20.)

Netscape can be downloaded using FTP from this site:

```
ftp.mcom.com
```

If you have another browser, you can learn more about Netscape from its home page at this address:

```
http://home.netscape.com
```

Tip

> How can you identify a secure server? There are two simple ways for spotting a secure server: First, if the URL begins with `https://` (instead of `http://`) this indicates that a document is generated from a secure server. Secondly, a doorkey icon on a blue background at the bottom left corner of a Netscape window indicates a secure document. A broken doorkey indicates an insecure document.

Mosaic 2.0

Mosaic is an important application because, more than anything else, it is responsible for the Internet's recent popularity. Mosaic demonstrated to new users that the Internet can be friendly and fun. Mosaic has always been a freeware application, developed and distributed by the National Center for Supercomputing Applications (NCSA) at the University of Illinois at Urbana-Champaign. The NCSA Mosaic home page is shown in Figure 10.10.

FIGURE 10.10.
NCSA Mosaic 2.0 at the NCSA Mosaic home page.

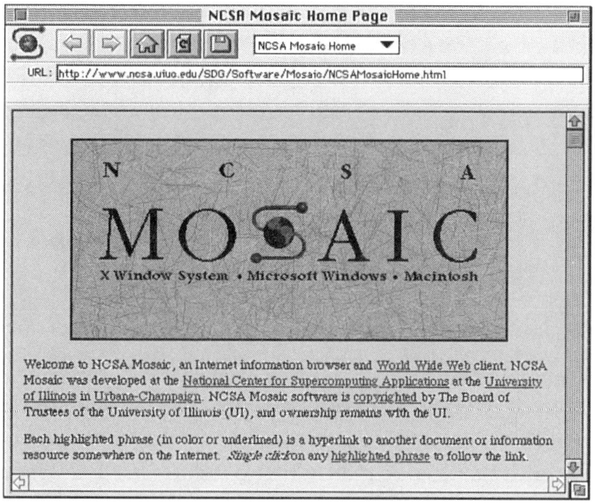

A graphical Web browser, Mosaic performs well, though it's not as slick as Netscape Navigator.

At this writing, Mosaic does not speed Web browsing by performing progressive rendering of on-screen graphics—something Navigator does. Instead, it first loads text and displays little placeholders in place of the graphics as it downloads the graphics in the background. You can go ahead and jump to another page before the graphics appear, but you have no idea what the graphics are going to be until they finish downloading. Progressive rendering displays the graphics in stages, so you can get an idea of what they'll look like before they actually finish appearing.

Here are the basics for using Mosaic:

- **Entering URLs.** You can enter and edit URLs manually in the URL field below the toolbar.
- **Toolbar tools**. Back, Forward, Home, Reload, and Save to Disk. You stop an activity by clicking the big globe, which spins whenever Mosaic is actively communicating with a server.
- **Home page.** Mosaic's home page is preconfigured to NCSA's Mosaic page (`http://www.ncsa.uiuc.edu/SDG/Software/Mosaic/NCSAMosaicHome.html`) but can be changed through the Preferences dialog box (see "Other useful features," later in this list).
- **Bookmarks (Hotlist).** To add a bookmark (a hotlist entry) for the current page, choose Add This Document from the **N**avigate menu.
- **History.** Pages or URLs stored as history can be recalled from the History List pop-up menu next to the Toolbar. By clicking on the History list a pop-up menu of previously visited documents appears.
- **Helper Applications.** Choose Preferences from the Options menu and click the Apps icon to configure helper applications.

- **FTP and Gopher.** FTP and Gopher resources are reached through available Web links. Links to popular Gopher servers appear in Mosaic's Network Starting Points in the Navigate menu. No built-in client functions are provided.
- **Newsreaders.** Mosaic does not boast a built-in, full-function newsreader client for using newsgroups (see Chapter 9), but you can access newsgroups by choosing Open URL from the File menu and entering the name of the newsgroup in the URL format. You must configure Mosaic with the address of your news server by choosing Preferences from the Options menu and then click the Gates icon. Enter the name of your news server in the Newshost: field. Then, select Open URL from the File menu, type the URL of a newsgroup (for example, `news:comp.sys.mac.misc`) in the Open URL dialog box and click Open.
- **E-mail.** Mosaic has a built-in, send-only e-mail client that you can access by choosing Mail Developers through the Balloon Help menu. You must configure Mosaic with the address of your mail server by choosing Preferences from the Options menu. Then, select the Gates icon and fill in the the name of your mail server in the Mail Server: field. Click the Misc icon in Preferences to fill in your e-mail address in the Email Address: field. As of this writing, this feature (version 2.0b12) doesn't function properly.
- **Other useful features.** The Starting Points menu is prebuilt with a helpful list of great places to start, including an extensive list of valuable home pages, a selection of Gopher servers, and an Archie gateway for locating FTP files. (Note, however, that these Starting Points links cannot be updated, and so tend to fall out-of-date over time.) Also, all Mosaic configuration and customization is performed through the Preferences dialog box (accessed by selecting Preferences from the Options menu).

Mosaic can be downloaded with FTP from the following site:

`ftp.ncsa.uiuc.edu`

If you have another browser, you can learn more about Mosaic from its home page at this address:

`http://www.ncsa.uiuc.edu/SDG/Software/Mosaic/NCSAMosaicHome.html`

Tip

At times you may find that a download or document transfer takes too much time to perform because the document is large or the link is slow. If you want to cancel a connection in progress or a download while using Mosaic, simply click the Mosaic logo icon in the toolbar.

MacWeb

MacWeb is a sparse, no-thrills browser without any of the deluxe navigating features you find in Netscape or even Mosaic. That's not necessarily a bad thing if you're looking for a plain, functional browser that is simple to use and won't eat up much memory. EINet, who developed MacWeb, is an Internet services company based in Texas that recently changed its name to TradeWave. Apart from their Web client, Tradewave is also known for their searchable Internet directory, the TradeWave Galaxy, which can be accessed through the MacWeb homepage listed later. Updated releases of MacWeb are few and far between, so keep checking TradeWave's MacWeb home page (`http://galaxy.einet.net/EINet/MacWeb/MacWebHome.html`) for news on the latest versions, as shown in Figure 10.11.

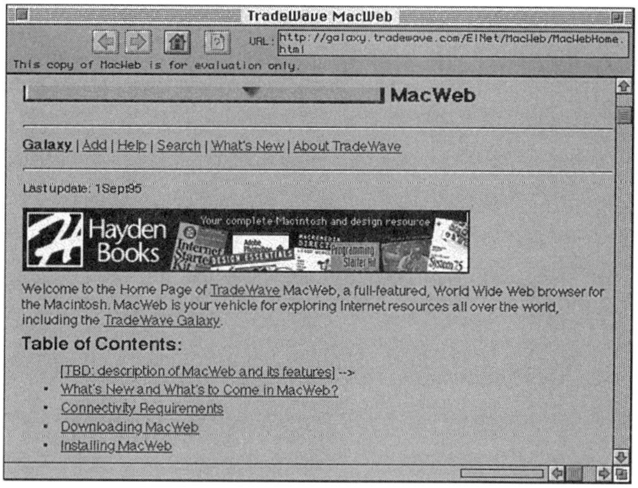

FIGURE 10.11.
MacWeb at TradeWave's home page.

Here are the basics for using MacWeb:

- **Entering URLs.** You can enter and edit URLs manually by typing an URL in the URL: field next to the toolbar or by choosing Open URL from the File menu.
- **Toolbar tools.** Back, Forward, Home, and Web Search. The Search tool enables you to search Web sites.
- **Home page.** MacWeb's home page is preconfigured to TradeWave's Galaxy MacWeb page (`http://galaxy.einet.net/galaxy.html`) but can be changed through the Preferences in the File menu.
- **Bookmarks (Hotlist).** To add a bookmark (a hotlist entry) for the current page, choose Add This Document from the Hotlist menu.
- **History.** Pages or URLs stored as history can be recalled from the History menu under the Navigate menu.
- **Helper Applications.** Choose Helpers from the Edit menu to configure helper applications.
- **FTP and Gopher.** FTP and Gopher resources are reached through available Web links. Links to popular Gopher servers appear in Tradewave's Galaxy Internet directory under the heading Interent and Networking in the Reference and Interdisplinary Information category. No built-in client functions are provided.

- **Newsreaders.** MacWeb does not have a built-in, full-function newsreader client for using newsgroups (see Chapter 9), but you can access newsgroups by entering a newsgroup URL in the URL: field next to the toolbar. You must configure MacWeb with the address of your news server by choosing Preferences from the File menu and entering the name of your news server in the News Host: field. Then, type the URL of a newsgroup (for example, `news:comp.sys.mac.misc`) in the URL: field and press Return. Alternatively, you can access newsgroups from Tradewave's Galaxy directory by choosing Internet and Networking from the Interdisciplinary Information category. Then, look for the Usenet Newsgroup Hierarchy under Collections.
- **E-mail.** Mosaic has a built-in, send-only e-mail client that you can access by choosing Mail Developers through the File menu. You must configure Mosaic with the address of your mail server by choosing Preferences from the Options menu and filling in the Email Address: field.
- **Other useful features.** The TradeWave Galaxy Internet directory is a great place to find a variety of information and Web resources. Galaxy's search tool enables you to scan Gopher servers, Web pages, and Telnet sites. MacWeb can be downloaded with FTP from the following site:

  `ftp://ftp.einet.net/einet/mac/macweb/macweb.latest.sea.hqx`

  If you have another browser, you can learn more about Galaxy and MacWeb from TradeWave at this address:

  `http://galaxy.tradewave.com/galaxy.html`

Creating Your Own Web Page

Creating a Web page is not difficult. Many folks do it for fun, which is why you come across "personal" pages on the Web that are clearly the pet projects of clever individuals. Sometimes, these pages are useful—especially when they're built with links to other resources. Sometimes, they're entertaining. And of course, sometimes they're self-indulgent wastes of disk space. But that's the Internet.

You may have some terrific reasons for creating a Web page. The most prevalent reasons today are for advertising, selling, or providing customer service for a business. (See Chapter 20.) People also create Web pages simply because they see the need for something that's not already on the Web, such as a page of links to resources related to a certain field.

Creating a Web page is three-step job:

1. First, you have to learn HTML (HyperText Markup Language) to produce a Web page using a Word Processor (such as Microsoft Word or ClarisWorks). The Web itself is a great source for learning all about HTML and the creation of Web documents. Start by checking out this handy guide, The HTML Primer, located at:

   `http://www.ncsa.uiuc.edu/General/Internet/WWW/HTML Primer.html`

Or go to Netcape's site where you'll find several pointers to excellent HTML reference works including information on HTML Extensions (tables, backgrounds, and so forth). Point your browser to:

`http://home.netscape.com/assist/net_sites/index.html`

2. When the document is complete, save it as an HTML document. An HTML document is really just a text file coded with special tags that identify links, headings, and the names and locations of graphics files to insert. ClarisWorks 4.0 offers a utility you can use to save ClarisWorks documents as HTML documents. There are also a number of HTML text editors available that make using HTML tags and saving documents as HTML files easier. Check out this list of HTML editors at:

   `http://www.yahoo.com/Computers/World_Wide_Web/HTML_Editors/Macintosh/`

3. Your finished HTML file must be published on a Web server. Because a Web server requires a dedicated high-speed communications line, small businesses and individuals typically rent space on a Web server from another company. Increasingly, Internet access providers rent space on their servers to individuals who want to publish a Web page.

Of course, this is the procedure for creating a very simple, beginner's Web page. A growing field of Internet consultants charge thousands of dollars to help businesses custom-design and publish eye-catching, state-of-the-art Web pages.

Summary

The Web is where it's at. You may well find that you spend more time on the Web than anywhere else on the Net. That's not a bad thing—because the Web is poised to become the real Grand Central Station of Internet activity. The more skilled you become on the Web, the better equipped you are for the future.

From the hippest, newest Internet resource, this book now takes you to the oldest, most unhip resource—which still has its uses. Chapter 11 introduces you to Telnet.

CHAPTER 11

TAPPING INTO REMOTE SYSTEMS WITH TELNET

Once upon a time, Telnet *was* the Internet. In the days before the World Wide Web, Gopher, and other sexy cyberstuff, Telnet was an amazing facility that let you connect to distant computer systems and run the programs residing there. It was the ultimate hacker's hammer, the key to every door. Telnet was also considered extremely easy to use—but so was DOS in those days.

Times change. Today, many Internet users never touch Telnet. Why? Well, much of what was once accessible only through Telnet is now available through Gopher menus (see Chapter 13, "Navigating with Menus: Gopher"), through Web pages, or through links into Telnet sessions initiated from Gopher menus and Web pages. In the abstract, Gopher and the Web don't necessarily make the computer easier to use, but they do make everything work the same way, and consistency has a way of making things easier. And when Gopher menus or Web pages are used to start a Telnet session, they can provide required login information automatically—logging in can be the most difficult part of using Telnet without these tools.

Tip

It's important to understand right up front that Gopher and the Web provide access to Telnet resources in two different ways:

- A Gopher menu or Web page may provide access to the same information previously offered only through the Telnet site—in effect, replacing a Telnet resource with a friendlier Gopher or Web resource.
- A Gopher menu or Web page can offer a menu item or link that, when activated, instructs your Gopher or Web client to open the Telnet session for you, using your own Telnet client as a "helper" application. This second scenario offers little advantage over plain-vanilla Telnet, except that Gopher and the Web may make the Telnet resource easier to find and, in many cases, easier to sign on to.

Telnet's Achilles' heel is that every computer system is different, and Telnet does nothing to make differing computers work more consistently. Telnet simply gets you connected to a remote computer—figuring out how to use it is your problem.

So why use Telnet? Frankly, you use Telnet to get to stuff you can't get to any other way. As the Web grows, that list is getting shorter. But there are some very useful facilities available through Telnet—in particular, public libraries. Even when Gopher or the Web act as your door into a Telnet session, you'll want to know something about Telnet so that you can work productively in the session once it begins. As a fully equipped Internet user, you'll benefit by learning how simple Telnet—and the systems it hooks you to—can be, especially when paired with tools that make Telnet easier or smarter.

About Telnet

The Telnet protocol is a client/server component of the TCP/IP suite, the family of protocols that make the Internet work. Known as the "terminal handler" in the suite, Telnet allows one computer to perform a *remote login* to another.

When a Telnet client is set up on your Mac, and the remote computer is configured as a Telnet server, you can connect to the remote and send it commands and menu selections. The remote, in turn, sends its screen output across the Internet to your Mac, so that you see on your screen exactly what you would see if you were using a terminal directly connected to that computer.

That screen display is usually *very* simple—text only, no colors, and no fancy fonts. (See Figure 11.1.) It's the simplicity of the display parameters used that helps ensure that any type of computer can communicate with any other—as long as TCP/IP and Telnet run the show. Fancy formatting can cause incompatibilities.

FIGURE 11.1.
A Telnet session.

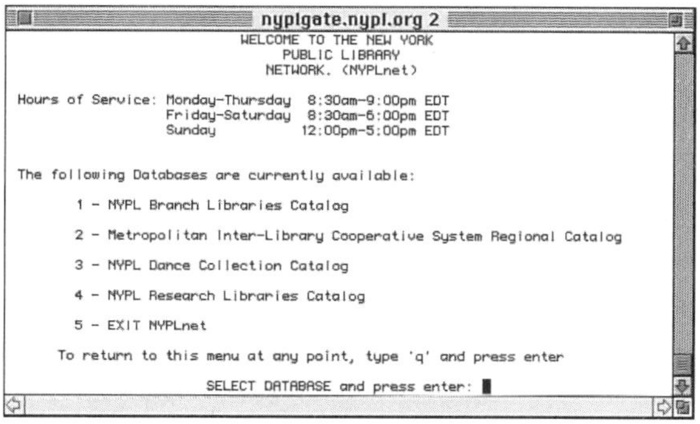

Through a Telnet connection, you can run programs that reside on the remote computer and access data files there. Best of all, you don't have to worry what type of computer the remote is; it can be an IBM mainframe, a supercomputer, a VAX, a Data General, or an obsolete Sperry chugging away in a basement on Long Island. The Telnet protocol and TCP/IP ensure that your Mac and the remote play nicely together.

To establish a Telnet connection, all you need to know is the address of the remote computer, a port number, and, in some cases, specific login information such as a username and password. Using a numeric IP address (described in Chapter 3, "Configuring Your Macintosh for the Internet,") works in almost all cases; in most cases, using a hostname also works.

Where Can Telnet Take You?

The most common use of Telnet is to search large databases available on corporate, government, and university computers. Telnet isn't valuable simply because the database resides on the remote computer, however. The powerful software required to effectively search the database, and the computer resources required to support a sophisticated search program, are at your fingertips through Telnet. From your Macintosh, you may be harnessing the processing horsepower of a corporate mainframe.

Tip

Telnet has a companion client tool, called Hytelnet, that makes locating and using Telnet sites easier. For more about Hytelnet, see Chapter 19, "Finding Stuff Other Ways."

The search tools on the World Wide Web can also reveal (and access) Telnet sites (see Chapter 18, "Finding It on the Web").

Among the more useful Telnet sites are these:

- **The Internet Network Information Center** (Telnet `is.internic.net`): Funded by grants from the National Science Foundation and managed cooperatively by three corporations, InterNIC (its NICkname) offers a range of information services about the Internet, including a sort of Internet "white pages and yellow pages" for finding people and organizations on the Net (see Chapter 17, "Finding People").
- **The New York Public Library**'s card catalog system (Telnet `nyplgate.nypl.org` and log in with username `nypl`): The complete, searchable catalog of the world's greatest public library.
- **Library of Congress Information System** (Telnet `locis.loc.gov`): Most of the card catalog of the U.S. Library of Congress is included in the LOCIS database. Public librarians and others can search the database to find information on any of the millions of titles listed. *Note:* LOCIS is unavailable most days after around 9:00 p.m. Eastern time. Try to use it during normal business hours.

Note

LOCIS is a perfect example of how Telnet has persevered under the shadow of the Web. At the Web page for the Library of Congress (`http://www.loc.gov`) you can quickly find lots of great information about the Library and its activities. To get to the card catalog, click on LOCIS located under LC Online Systems on the Library's home page. When you click on LOCIS—voilá!—the Web just fires up a Telnet client and the same Telnet session (`locis.loc.gov`) you could have opened yourself, off the Web.

Whether it's easier to get to this site by clicking through the Web or entering an address in your Telnet client is up to you. But because you know something about Telnet, you have options.

- **CARL** (Telnet `pac.carl.org`): Created by a group of Colorado libraries (Colorado Alliance of Research Libraries) and now operated by a company called CARL Systems, Inc., CARL provides a searchable index of magazines and journals—more than 4 million records' worth—and the full transcripts of thousands of hours of television and radio programming, including popular talk shows and news programs.
- **FedWorld** (Telnet `fedworld.gov`): Developed by the National Technical Information Service, FedWorld is an Internet gateway to over 100 separate online bulletin board systems (BBSs) run by Federal government agencies such as NASA, the CIA, and the

Census Bureau. Through a series of menus, FedWorld (see Figure 11.2) enables you to read thousands of government documents, learn about job opportunities, order tax forms, and much more.

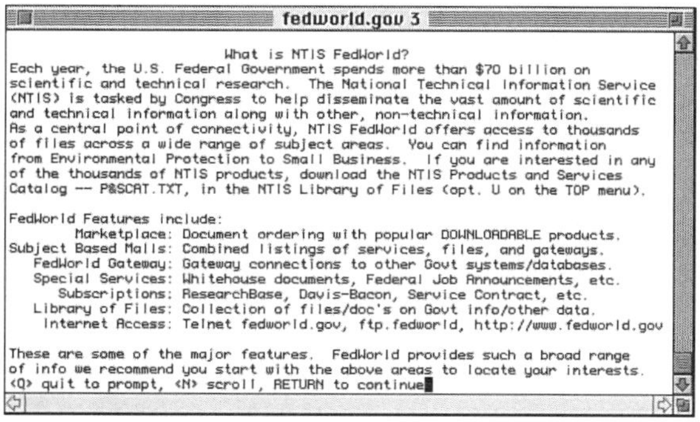

FIGURE 11.2.
FedWorld.

> **Tip**
>
> MUDs—a family of multiuser role-playing programs Internet users play together for fun, education, or scientific inquiry—are accessed two ways: through special client software and through Telnet. Given the dearth of Macintosh MUD client software, Telnet is the main doorway to the land of MUDs for most Mac users. For more about MUDs, see Chapter 14, "Interacting in Real Time: Talk, Chat, and Games."

In addition to important sites like those just listed, there are thousands of lesser-known Telnet sites, particularly local public libraries and small colleges. In fact, it is for these lesser-known sites that Telnet becomes especially valuable. Large, nationally known resources are fast finding a place on the Web. But given the relative trouble and cost of setting up a Web server, many local and college libraries are accessible only through Telnet—or through Gopher and Web links that start a Telnet session.

Logging On To Telnet Automatically

On the Web and in Gopherspace, you can find lists of library links, each of which instructs your client to open a Telnet session to a local, state, college, or other institutional or public library. In most cases, when you select one of these links, the Gopher menu or Web link opens the Telnet session and supplies the required login information. In some cases, the required login information instead appears in a message just before the Telnet session opens. Figure 11.3 shows the message displayed when you select a Web link pointing to the New York Public Library. The message supplies login information; clicking the underlined word `telnet` opens the Telnet client and starts the connection.

You can jot down the login information and use it when you are prompted for it in the Telnet session.

In Gopherspace (for more about Gopher, see Chapter 13), you can find a list of Telnet-accessible libraries at this site:

`libgopher.yale.edu`

On the Web (for more about the World Wide Web, see Chapter 10, "Browsing the World Wide Web"), you can find a list of Telnet-accessible libraries (see Figure 11.4)—as well as libraries accessible in many other ways—at this site:

`http://sjcpl.lib.in.us/homepage/PublicLibraries/PublicLibraryServers.html`

To use the Telnet sessions opened by these links, your Gopher or Web client must be properly configured to open your Telnet client whenever necessary.

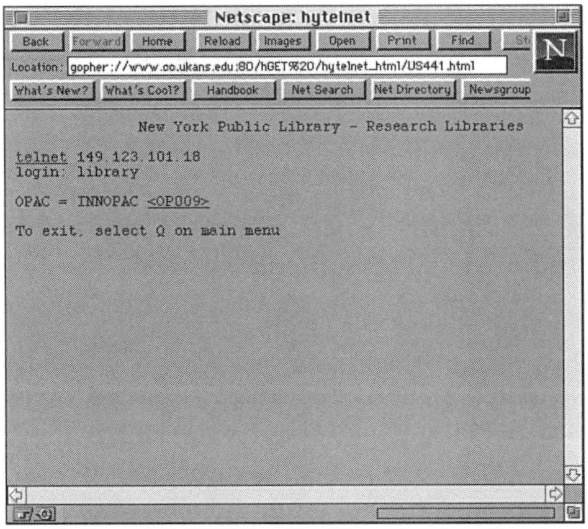

FIGURE 11.3.
A message describing login instructions for a Telnet session accessed through the Web.

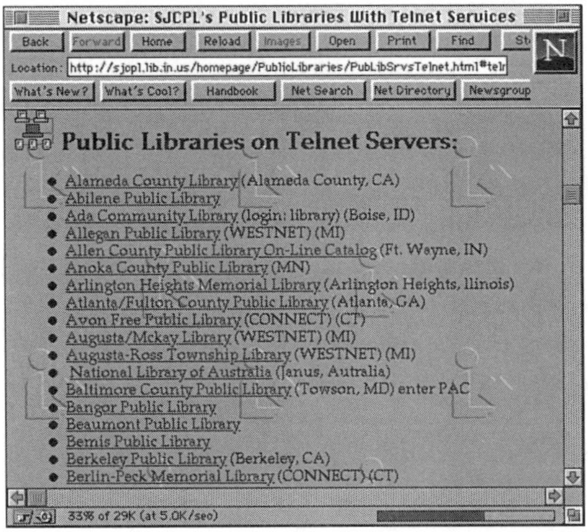

FIGURE 11.4.
A list of Web links to Telnet-accessible public libraries.

About Connecting and Logging In

Again, all you need to use a Telnet site is the following:

- The Telnet host's Internet address, typically a domain name but sometimes a numeric IP address. (For more about Internet addresses, see Chapter 3.)
- A port number (not always required). Some Telnet servers run more than one Telnet activity on the same server. Ports enable people to connect directly to the activity they want. A port is not always required; most of the time, when it is required, the standard Telnet port (23) does the job. Typically, when you come across a description of a Telnet resource, any port requirements are mentioned. Also, when you access Telnet resources through Gopher or the Web, these tools often pass along any required port setting to your Telnet client. Most of the time, you needn't worry about ports.
- Whatever specific login information the given system requires.

You enter the Telnet site's address (and port number, if necessary) in your Telnet client to establish the connection. Figure 11.5 shows the Connect dialog box in the NCSA Telnet client, filled out to connect to the Library of Congress's card catalog database (`locis.loc.gov`).

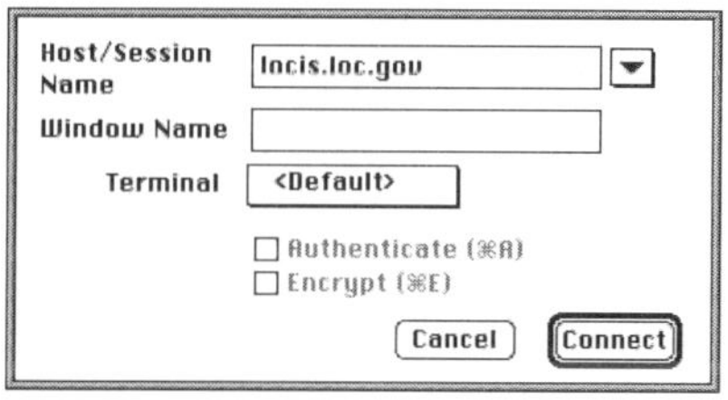

FIGURE 11.5.
Connecting to a Telnet server.

The login steps for a Telnet computer vary based on how happy it is to be visited by the Internet world at large. Friendly systems simply log you in when you connect. Others display messages at connection, telling you the "guest" username and password for the system. (See Figure 11.6.) The most restrictive systems require a username *and* a password, and don't tell you what they are—you have to know them before you log in. (In many cases, Gopher menus or Web pages can supply you with login information if you use them to access the Telnet session.)

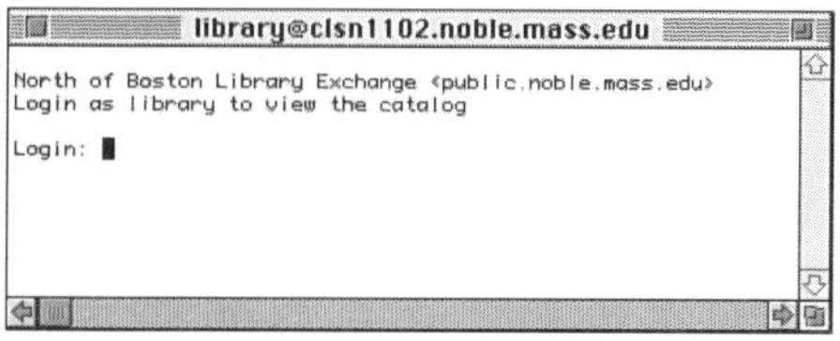

FIGURE 11.6.
Logging in to a Telnet site.

Once you've connected to the remote computer, you must log in. Many systems that supply guest logins require you to move through a procedure after you log in to choose a personal username and password for the next time you log in. For example, FedWorld lets you log in anonymously, but once you're on, it wants you to identify yourself and create a username to be used for all subsequent logins. (The U.S. government is happy to supply you with information—as long as it can keep track of who you are.)

Once you're logged in, every system is different. Most systems available through Telnet are designed and maintained primarily for the benefit of their regular users—typically employees of a company, university, or government agency. Internet users are guests, and although a system may offer visitors a little assistance, the system's administrator feels no great need to retool the system just to make Internet visitors happy.

After you log in, most systems display menus on-screen (refer to Figure 11.1, shown previously). Some tell you right away how to get help; for example, the system may display the message, `For help, press ? at any menu`. Be sure to jot down any such messages—you may need them later. Especially important is the command or procedure for logging off. You must log off the remote computer before quitting Telnet. If you forget to log off before quitting Telnet or disconnecting, don't worry; most Telnet computers are smart enough to terminate your session when they sense the broken connection or after a few minutes of inactivity.

To use most menus you see in Telnet sessions, press the number or letter of the menu item you want and then press Enter to transmit your selection to the remote computer. When you use a remote system, push your mouse aside; you use Telnet systems with your keyboard. Most of the time, your cursor keys are useless as well. Most Telnet systems operate like all computer systems did 20 years ago. Enjoy the nostalgia.

About Terminal Emulation

When a Telnet client negotiates a connection with a Telnet server, one of the first things the two must agree on is the terminal type of the client. Telnet servers are set up to interface with one or more specific types of terminals; your Mac must be able to emulate one of those if it is to use the remote computer. Otherwise, screen information may appear garbled, or the remote may not understand your commands.

Fortunately, most Telnet clients and servers support either of two widely used types: VTx or TTY. Ideally, if the server requires a VTx terminal, your Mac should be able to emulate the specific model: VT52, VT100, VT200, or VT220. If the remote wants a VT100, and your Mac emulates only VT200, try it—it will probably work. Some remotes ask you to specify the type of terminal you use (or, rather, the terminal your Mac is emulating) when setting up the connection. When all else fails, look for choices like `dumb`, `generic`, or `hardcopy` terminal; these emulations sacrifice screen formatting in order to be as universally compatible as possible.

At the client end, terminal emulation is controlled by the Telnet client software you run. The NCSA Telnet client emulates VT100 and VT220 terminals.

Tip

After you begin to work on a remote computer, the window in which you're using Telnet doesn't know it's on a Mac anymore; it thinks it's a display, glowing on a terminal connected to the remote computer.

You can still switch to other Mac programs and perform regular Macintosh activities. But while the Telnet session is the active window, whatever you type is sent to the remote computer (after you press Enter) as a command. You cannot, for example, click with the mouse on a Telnet screen and expect the cursor to move to where you just clicked.

Using the NCSA Telnet Client

The NCSA Telnet client for Macintosh was developed by the National Center for Supercomputing Applications—they're also responsible for the Web browser, NCSA Mosaic (described in Chapter 10). NCSA has tried to make Telnet as friendly as possible for Mac users. Most of the dialog boxes in the NCSA Telnet client are intuitive and simple to use.

Although it isn't flashy, the NCSA Telnet client gets the job done. And to be frank, Telnet is not a flashy occupation. Telnet is merely a link to another program running on a remote computer; it doesn't perform any special operations on its own. The great thing about NCSA's Telnet is that it doesn't require configuration to use it. When you install it on your computer, it's ready to go. The default terminal configuration is pre-set to the most common settings you will encounter in a Telnet session and for the most part you shouldn't have to ever fiddle with them.

The NCSA Telnet client is also handy to have around since other Internet tools, such as Gopher and Web clients, launch it whenever they encounter Telnet-based services.

Sams could not license NCSA Telnet for inclusion with this book, but you can obtain a copy by FTP from:

```
ftp://mirrors.aol.com//pub/mac/util/comm/ncsatelnet2.6.sit.hqx
```

For more details on how to download a file by FTP, see Chapter 12, "Collecting Files with FTP."

Tip

Like any other Mac program, NCSA Telnet can be launched from the Apple menu or from an icon. You can place an alias of the program in your Apple menu folder or even on the desktop.

To create an alias, follow these steps:

1. Locate the original program icon.
2. Select it with the mouse and choose Make Alias from the File menu in the Finder.
3. Drag the new alias to the folder of your choice or the Desktop for easy access.

Starting a Telnet Session

To use the NCSA Telnet client to perform a remote login, follow these steps:

1. Connect to the Internet. (See Chapter 3.)
2. Open the NCSA Telnet client program. An NCSA Telnet screen appears as the program is launching and disappears when the program is open.
3. When NCSA Telnet is launched, select Open Connection from the File menu. The Open Connection dialog box is displayed, as shown in Figure 11.7.

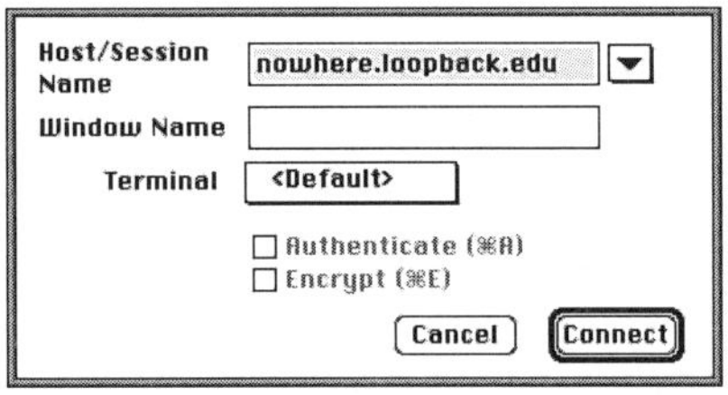

FIGURE 11.7
The Open Connection dialog box.

4. In the Host/Session Name: field of the dialog box, enter a host name. If you must enter a port number, append it to the end of the host name, separated by a space. There is also a pop-up menu from which you can select a predefined host name.
5. You can leave the Window name blank if you are opening a single connection.

> **Tip**
>
> NCSA Telnet allows simultaneous Telnet connections to multiple computers. It's useful to name each window if you plan to have more than one Telnet session window open at a time. It isn't necessary to name a window for a single connection. If you do not specify a window name, the connection's window title is taken from the contents of the Host/Session Name box and a number is appended.

6. You can leave the FTP session checkbox blank unless you want to connect as an FTP client.
7. Leave the Authenticate and Encrypt blank, unless you already have additional software to use with these features.

> **Note**
>
> NCSA has developed a comprehensive User's Guide for NCSA Telnet which is available at the NCSA Web site (`http://www.ncsa.uiuc.edu/SDG/Software/MacTelnet/Docs/MacTelnet.Home.html`). Advanced features of NCSA Telnet such as multiple sessions and the use of encryption are explained in this document.

8. Click the Connect button. NCSA Telnet attempts to connect to the host computer you specified. If the connection is successful, the remote system prompts you for a username or offers other instruction for logging on. (See Figure 11.8.)

FIGURE 11.8.
A sample Telnet login.

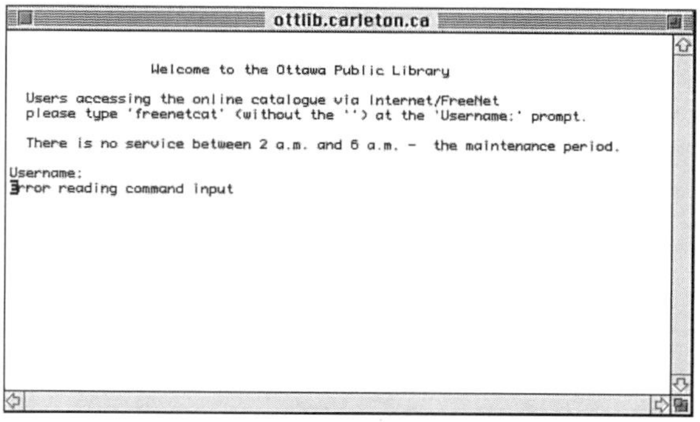

Using Telnet Menu Options

If the characters coming in from the remote system appear garbled or improperly formatted on your screen, your terminal emulation settings are probably incorrect. Choose Preferences under the Edit menu. From the pop-up menu that appears, select Terminals to display the Terminal Preferences dialog box. Click the Change button to display the Terminal Configuration Record dialog box (as shown in Figure 11.9) and switch the Emulation terminal type from either VT100 or VT220 by clicking on the appropriate radio button. When you are finished making changes, click the OK button.

FIGURE 11.9.
The Terminal Configuration Record dialog box.

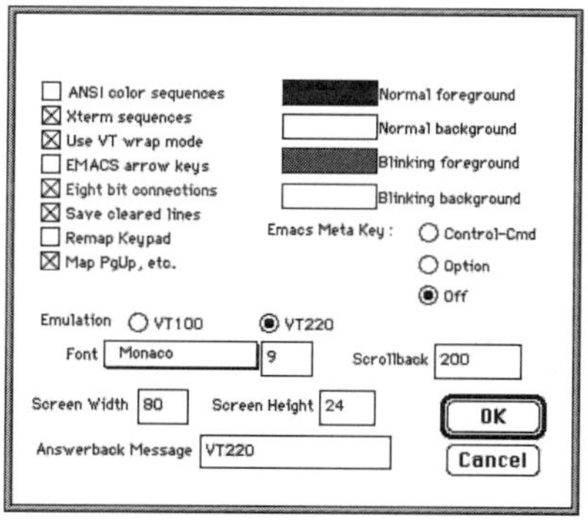

Note that you can also make the following changes in the Terminal Preferences dialog box, shown in Figure 11.9:

- Use VT Wrap mode—When you check this box, NCSA Telnet will stop lines of text from extending past the edge of the screen.
- Map PgUp, etc.—When you check this box, NCSA Telnet uses the PAGE UP, PAGE DOWN, HOME, and END arrow keys to change position in the session window.
- Font—A pop-up menu enables you to change the type of display font used, and the size box next to it enables you to set the font size.

- Screen Colors—The four boxes in the right-hand column (Normal foreground, Normal background, Blinking foreground, and Blinking background) let you set the foreground and background colors for the normal and blinking text modes. Telnet can't blink text so it changes the color instead. When you click any of the four boxes the standard Apple Color Wheel dialog box appears from which you can make your color selection.

Capturing Telnet Text

When in a Telnet session, you may want to capture the text of some or all of what you see. For example, a Telnet menu may lead to an online document; as you read through the document, you may want to save it for later reference. To keep online time to a minimum, you can scroll through entire documents quickly without reading them and save all the text, as described in the next paragraph. You can then read the document later, offline, or print it.

To save text, select Capture Session to File in the Session menu. Capturing stores everything that appears on-screen in a text file, from the moment you start the capture until you log off that session.

Another handy feature in NCSA Telnet is the ability to Copy and Paste the contents of Telnet windows. When you have a word processor program running in addition to Telnet, simply select the text you want to copy (choose Copy from the Edit menu) in the Telnet window and Paste (choose Paste from the Edit menu) it into the word processor file.

Ending a Telnet Session

To end a Telnet session, first log off the remote computer, if possible. If you've forgotten how to log off a given system, try to display its command help. Failing that, good entries to try are `q` (for quit), `x` (for exit), or the commands `logoff`, `logout` or just `log`. Failing that, close the session window. NCSA Telnet displays a dialog box asking if you want to close the connection. Click the OK button to end the session.

If you use a command to log off the remote system, NCSA Telnet automatically disconnects from the remote host. You can then connect to another Telnet host or choose Quit from the File menu to quit NCSA Telnet. Note that disconnecting from or quitting Telnet does not sever your Internet connection. You can start up a different Internet client and perform another activity after quitting Telnet.

Summary

Telnet is a handy tool and is not really too difficult to master. It's not sexy, though, and there's such a huge Internet world available outside Telnet that many users don't use—indeed, may not even be aware of—poor, practical Telnet. *You*, on the other hand, want to understand the whole Internet experience—and you've just uncovered an important part of it.

Another important part of the Internet is file transfer, which you discover in Chapter 12, "Collecting Files with FTP."

CHAPTER 12

COLLECTING FILES WITH FTP

Free stuff. Nothing makes your heart beat faster than the prospect of getting something for nothing. And nothing gets you something for nothing like FTP, the doorway for downloading files from the Internet.

The Internet is a treasure trove of computer files: freeware, shareware, and demo software; binary photos and artwork; sound, video, and animation; books, reference materials, and so much more. Much of this stuff can be downloaded to your Mac through more than one resource. For example, Gopher (described in Chapter 13, "Navigating with Menus: Gopher") and the World Wide Web both function as "front ends" to FTP file transfers so that you can download a file simply by choosing a menu item or clicking a hyperlink.

Sometimes, however, it's easier to go straight to the files through an *FTP client*, the Mac software that enables you to download files from an *FTP server*, the computer on which the files reside. And FTP is not restricted to downloading files—you can send (*upload*) files from your Mac to an FTP server.

Anarchie, a Shareware program designed by Peter Lewis, is one of the most popular Mac FTP clients available today. Another FTP client in widespread use is Fetch. An FTP client program for the Mac, however, would be incomplete without a decoder utility such as Stuffit Expander.

About FTP

FTP (File Transfer Protocol) is the file transfer mechanism of the TCP/IP protocol suite. Nearly all file transfers on the Internet—whether initiated through FTP client software, a Gopher menu, or a Web link—are actually accomplished using the FTP protocol.

FTP servers are prepared to display lists and directories of files available for downloading. These servers often accept "anonymous" FTP logins so that you won't need a password or user ID to download files. Some FTP servers are set up for the exclusive use of a group. For example, some universities set up a private FTP server for exclusive use by a particular department. A special username and password is then needed to gain access to the FTP files.

Using an FTP client to download a file typically involves two steps. The first step is logging in to the FTP server, which involves nothing more than supplying the FTP client with the correct address of the FTP server. In some cases (when anonymous logon isn't supported), you may also have to supply a username and password.

After a successful login, you arrive at the top level of a hierarchical directory or folder structure. For example, in Anarchie, a window listing all the files in the directory is displayed, as shown in Figure 12.1. Double-clicking on a folder takes you into that sub-directory, similar to the way directories are displayed in the Macintosh Finder.

FIGURE 12.1.
A listing of folders containing files on an FTP server.

To download a file, you must know its precise name and directory location. You can find this by browsing through the folders in the listing window or by reading the contents of a *file index* available in the topmost directory of many FTP sites. The index is a text file that usually has a name like `INDEX` or `README` (`README` files may contain other useful tips, as well). When first visiting a particular FTP site, it's a good idea to download and read such files before doing anything else—they can save you time later by preventing mistakes.

After you log in, the second step to using an FTP site is navigating among the directories and file lists and ultimately downloading files. If you know, before you log in, the exact filename and directory location of the file you want to download, you can configure most FTP clients, including Anarchie, to log on, retrieve files, and log off all in one action without your intervention.

Finding FTP Files

You can find instructions all over the Internet and in Internet publications telling you a particularly cool file "is available via anonymous FTP at..." and then reporting the FTP address. The *addresses* reported are pretty reliable but *filenames* or *directory locations* change often. It's good practice to log in to the FTP server and download the `README` or `INDEX` file to make sure of the directory location and filename.

Another way to find files available through FTP is to use Archie. You can use Archie to search through databases of FTP information to locate specific files, or files related to a given subject. For more about Archie, see Chapter 16, "Finding Files and Directories with Archie and Veronica."

Finally, as with all other things, the Web is a great place not only to locate FTP files, but to download them without having to fiddle with FTP. For more about finding FTP files on the Web, see Chapter 18, "Finding It on the Web." For more about the Web itself, see Chapter 10, "Browsing the World Wide Web."

Working with Files

When harvesting files from the Internet, there are a few points you must remember. First, just because you can download a file doesn't mean you can use it. Because there are many different types of computers on the Internet, not every file you see is Macintosh compatible.

Text files are universal—they can be read in any environment. On the other hand, downloading *program files* written for Windows or UNIX systems is a waste of time. Many other binary files, such as graphics and video clips, may or may not work on a Mac.

Fortunately, the better FTP sites are pretty good about keeping software for different platforms in different environments. If you navigate to a directory called `...pub/mac`, you can safely bet that anything stored there runs on a Macintosh. Still, even files written for Macintosh may require special software.

Macintosh-Ready File Types

The file types in the following list include common Macintosh files that can be decoded with Stuffit Expander.

Note

As a Mac user, you take for granted that when you double-click a file icon it will automatically open in the right application. The Macintosh knows which documents go with which programs. As a result, Mac users tend not to pay as much attention to file types as users of Windows or other systems. As you rummage around the Internet, you will discover, however, that most files you encounter have filename extensions, like those in Windows. For example, a compressed file may end in the .SIT extension which indicates a Stuffit file.

There are only a few filename extensions for Macintosh that you need to know. Be aware, however, that these conventions are not universally followed. For example, a file with the extension .DOC may not be a Word for Windows document.

The first part of Table 12.1 lists some of the more common Macintosh filename extensions you will find on the Internet, as well as the tool you will need to decode or decompress them. You will also come across many filename extensions for Windows files like the ones listed in Table 12.2.

Table 12.1. Macintosh filename extensions.

Extension	*File Type*	*Decoder*
.TXT	Any file identified as a text file (sometimes they use the extension .TXT, sometimes they don't)	Any word processor

Extension	*File Type*	*Decoder*
.SIT	Stuffit file	Stuffit Expander
.CPT	Compact Pro file	Stuffit Expander
.HQX	BinHex encoded file	Stuffit Expander
.SEA	Files compressed into self-extracting archives	None (double-click the file)
.MOV	QuickTime movie files	Simple Player
.BIN	MacBinary file	None (automatically decoded by Fetch or Anarchie)
.MPG	MPEG Video clips	Sparkle
.JPG	JPEG compressed graphic	JPEG View
.GIF	Graphics interchange file	JPEG View
.AU	Audio file	Sound Machine
.RAM	RealAudio file	RealAudio Player

Table 12.2. Windows filename extensions.

Extension	*File Type*
.EXE	Windows or DOS application program files
.AVI	Windows video clip
.WAV	Windows sound clip
.MMM	Animation
.BMP, .WMF, .PCX	Windows graphic image files
.ANI	Animated cursor/icon
.TTF	TrueType font
.SCR	Windows screen saver
.DOC	Word for Windows document (opens with WordPad)
.WRI	Windows Write file (opens with WordPad)

Text Files Versus Binary Files

FTP transfers files in either of two modes. The two modes are required because simple text files, also known as ASCII files, use a smaller and less complicated character set than binary files, which include all files except simple text files. Any ASCII file is an unformatted text file of the kind you can edit in SimpleText or other word processor.

When downloading binary files, you must use binary mode. You can also use binary mode for ASCII files, but using ASCII mode for plain text is more efficient. ASCII mode cannot be used to transfer binary files.

Most FTP client software is pretty smart about choosing the right mode for the transfer. However, if you run into mode problems, switching between the modes is usually a simple matter of clicking a button.

> Many of the files you can download from the Internet are *compressed.* Compressed files have been processed by a special program that makes them smaller so that they transfer more quickly. Compressed files are often easy to spot because many of them use the extension .SIT.
>
> Before compressed files can be used, they have to be uncompressed. Sometimes, the files are stored in a *self-extracting archive* (SEA), a program file that automatically decompresses itself and other archived files when you run it. Other times, you must decompress the files yourself, using a program capable of undoing the particular compression method used.
>
> .SIT files are decompressed by a shareware Mac program called Stuffit Expander (see "Working With Stuffit Expander," later in this chapter). To automatically decompress files, System 7.5 users can drag and drop them onto the Stuffit Expander.

Important FTP Sites for Macintosh Users

Table 12.3 provides a small sample of the FTP sites you may want to visit.

Table 12.3. FTP sites.

Site	*Description*
`Info-Mac`	This site has many mirrors available all over the world. Consult the Anarchie Bookmark window to find one near you.
`mac.archive.umich.edu`	Another motherload of Mac shareware at the University of Michigan. Look for `umich` in the Anarchie Bookmark window.
`ftp.support.apple.com`	Software updates from Apple.
`jplinfo.jpl.nasa.gov`	Text and images from the Jet Propulsion Laboratory's NASA missions.

Site	*Description*
`ftp.ncsa.uiuc.edu`	Among many other files, supplies a helpful guide to the Internet.
`ftp.merit.edu`	Supplies PostScript-format maps (for printing on a PostScript printer) of the Internet.
`sunsite.unc.edu`	Among many other files, offers most White House speeches and press releases.
`cdrom.com`	Great source for information on CD-ROM products.

Note: You may encounter the term mirror site when looking for FTP servers. A mirror site is simply a copy of another FTP archive. Mirrors are created when an FTP site becomes too popular for its own good and is constantly overloaded. For example, there are numerous mirrors of the well-liked Info-Mac archive, which is the mecca for Mac shareware.

Using Anarchie

To use Anarchie to make a File Transfer, connect to the Internet (see Chapter 3, "Configuring Your Macintosh for the Internet") and open Anarchie. Before you can use Anarchie you must configure it by choosing Preferences from the Edit menu. (See Figure 12.2.) Enter your e-mail address in the Email Address: field. (Anarchie submits your email address to anonymous FTP servers as your password.) In the Info-Mac Mirror: field, select a site from the pop-up menu that is geographically near to you. Do the same for the UMich Mirror: field. Select the destination folder to which you would like to save files, by clicking the Save Files button. Select the Decode Files checkbox, if you want Anarchie to automatically launch Stuffit Expander when you download a compressed file.

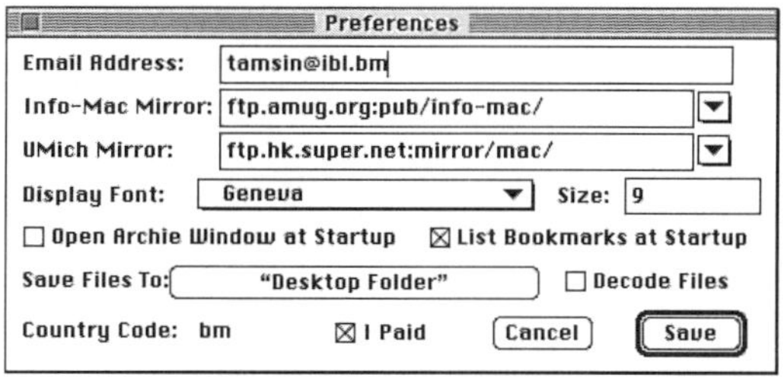

FIGURE 12.2.
The Preferences dialog box.

Retrieving a File with Anarchie

You can use Anarchie to browse an FTP site to see what files are available by connecting to an FTP site and searching through the directories in the Listing Window. (See Figure 12.1, shown previously.) If you spot a particular file you would like to download, double-click the file to retrieve it or if you are a System 7.5 user, click the filename and drag the file out to the Desktop to retrieve it.

If you already know the name of the file you want to retrieve and where the file is located on an FTP site, choose Get from the FTP menu. The Get via FTP window opens, as shown in Figure 12.3. Enter the name of the FTP site in the Machine: field and fill in the pathname of the file in the Path: field. Select the Get File radio button and then click Get button. Anarchie connects to the FTP site and retrieves the file you specified. If you don't know the name of the file you want to retrieve, but you do know the pathname to it, select the Get Listing radio button and then click the List button. Anarchie connects to the FTP site and shows the files and directories in the pathname in a Listing Window. From there, you can scroll through the list and open folders to sub-directories to locate a file.

FIGURE 12.3

The Get via FTP window.

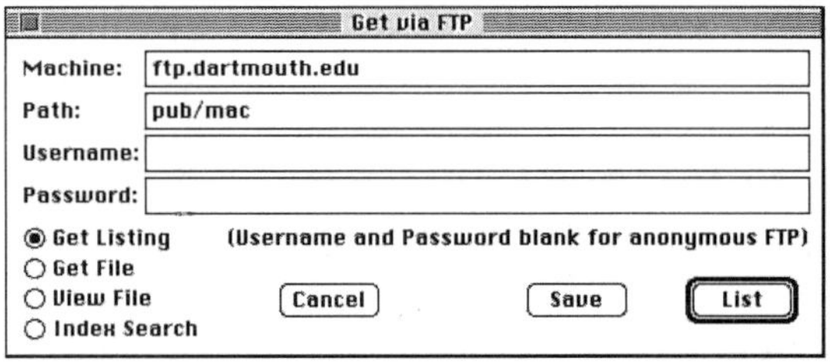

Stuffit Expander

Stuffit Expander is a nifty little utility to decode or decompress many files you'll find on the Internet. Typically, when you download software from the Net you will find it has a filename extension such as .SIT. Your Mac can't use this file until you unpack it or unstuff it with Stuffit Expander. This ingenious program is to the Internet world what can openers are to cooks in the kitchen. Stuffit Expander is easy to use: simply drop an archived file onto the Stuffit Expander icon. By default, it will expand the file into the same location on your computer as the original archived file.

To unstuff files as soon as they're downloaded, many frequent FTPers are in the habit of keeping an alias of Stuffit Expander within easy reach on their Desktop.

Using Other Macintosh FTP Clients

Anarchie is an excellent FTP program for the Mac, but if it doesn't turn you on, consider giving Fetch a try. The layout of Fetch differs from Anarchie, but the two share many common features. (See Figure 12.4.)

Fetch is available for downloading at:

`ftp://ftp.dartmouth.edu/pub/mac/`

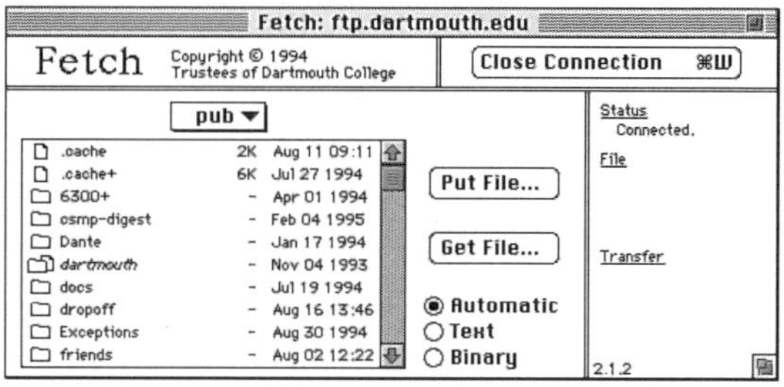

FIGURE 12.4.
FTP client Fetch for the Mac.

Summary

FTP is the smorgasbord of the Internet: dial it up and you get stuff. FTP is also a useful research tool you can use to collect volumes of information stored in electronic files all over the world.

If FTP seems a little tricky, don't worry—Gopher makes many FTP activities, and many other Internet tasks, a snap. You discover Gopher in Chapter 13.

CHAPTER 13

NAVIGATING WITH MENUS: GOPHER

- Who's the Gopher?
- Multimedia Gophers
- Using a Gopher Client
- Cool Gopher Sites for Macintosh Users
- Summary

Ah, the menu. Where would we be without it? What could make a computer easier to use than simple on-screen lists of things to do? (Well, of course, every Macintosh user knows that icons make it even easier.)

Since the beginning, lucky Macintosh users, unlike their poor Windows-using cousins, have enjoyed consistent menu layout throughout all Mac programs. Whatever program you're using on a Mac, you can rest assured you will always find basic commands in the same menu. You don't even have to think about it, you know that from application to application, the Save and Quit commands, for example, are always found in the File menu. Not only do uniform menus make using a computer so much easier, but they also improve productivity since you don't have to waste time scrolling through menus trying to locate the command you want.

The same is true of Gopher, which lays a simple, consistent system of menus on top of a number of Internet sites and activities—no matter the content. Not all the Internet is accessible through Gopher, but everything that is accessible works the same way. Clicking your way through Gopher menus, you can navigate to sites all over the world, read documents, conduct Telnet sessions (as described in Chapter 11, "Tapping into Remote Systems with Telnet"), and even download files. In certain cases, you can even view images and play multimedia through a Gopher connection. Once you connect to a single Gopher server, you can navigate all over the world without ever typing—or even seeing—an Internet address.

Best of all, once you understand the basics of using Gopher menus, you have acquired a skill that works everywhere in Gopherspace, the nickname for all the Internet sites and activities accessible through Gopher menus.

Who's the Gopher?

The University of Minnesota is an enormous state university, located across the Mississippi from downtown Minneapolis (for the protection of Minneapolis's citizens). Isolated from the bustle of the city, U of Minnesota students have lots of free time. Some ride bikes, some write poetry, many drink beer—a few do all three at once.

A surprising number of students and faculty at Minnesota busy themselves building a better Internet. Over the years, the University of Minnesota has made many significant contributions to the evolution of the Net, but its most significant is the Gopher software. Developed in 1991 and originally made available to "nonprofit institutions" (that's academic lingo for other universities), the Gopher server software is now used in more than 300 nonprofit and commercial sites. The site uses the software to configure one or more *Gopher servers*, computers containing menu text linked to real Internet resources such as files, and Telnet, and FTP sessions. In concert with the Gopher client software on your Mac, the servers present Gopher menus for all activities available through the server. Figure 13.1 shows a typical Gopher menu. (Actually, it's the top menu at the University of Minnesota's Gopher (`gopher.micro.umn.edu`), also known variously as *Gopher Home*, *Mother Gopher*, and even *Mama Gopher*, since the University of Minnesota was the original Gopher site.)

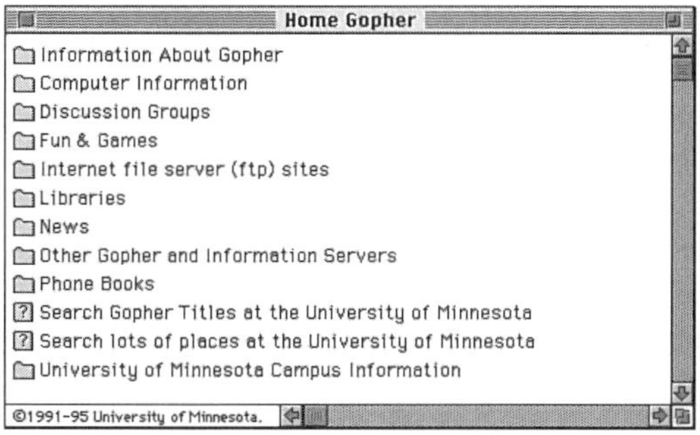

FIGURE 13.1.
A Gopher menu.

Each Gopher server (sometimes simply called a *Gopher*, to keep things friendly) holds only its own menus and linking details. However, all Gopher servers in the world are linked with one another and share information; when you access any Gopher server, you work as if *everything* was on that server—all the thousands of sites and menus of Gopherspace are at your command.

Through a Mac-based Gopher client, you can literally point-and-click your way around the world. Gopher covers up the details and smoothes out the inconsistencies to make resources simpler to use.

Which resources? There are four basic things you can do after you select an item from a typical Gopher menu:

- **Navigate.** A menu item may lead to another Gopher menu or submenu, usually containing more specific choices related to the preceding menu item. This is not always the case—a menu item on one Gopher menu may jump to another server, much as Web links jump from site to site.
- **Retrieve a document.** Millions of text files are available through Gopher servers. Some are informative, some are fun, and all appear on your screen at the touch of a menu item. You will see an "index" file listed as an item in the top menu of many Gopher servers. Check out that file's contents to save yourself a lot of browsing around.
- **Download files.** Binary files (including program files, images, and more) and some text files are available for download through Gopher menus. All you do is click a menu item, and the file transfers to your Mac.
- **Conduct Telnet sessions.** A Gopher menu item may start up a Telnet session for you. Once the Telnet session has begun, however, you work within it as you do in any Telnet session (see Chapter 11), but using Gopher can make finding the right Telnet site—and getting there—more convenient. Most importantly, a Gopher menu item may help you log on by reporting required login instructions—such as the guest username and password—before starting the Telnet session.

Multimedia Gophers

Some Gopher clients, like TurboGopher can also retrieve image, video, and sound. The Gopher automatically opens a viewer program to display or play the file. (See Figure 13.2.)

FIGURE 13.2.
An image in Gopherspace, displayed through JPEG View, an image viewer.

The viewer programs aren't part of the client software itself. A viewer program is any application capable of playing the file. The client software simply interprets the attribute information to choose which viewer program to open.

The result is a Gopher that thinks it's the World Wide Web: You click a menu item, and an image pops open on your screen, or a sound clip plays, or a movie appears.

Hunting Down Gophers

Gopher has a companion search engine, Veronica, that can generate a list of Gopher servers, documents, or other resources based on a search term you supply. The best thing about Veronica is that the list it produces is itself a Gopher menu; you can jump straight from Veronica's report to a Gopher resource. For more about Veronica, see Chapter 16, "Finding Files and Directories with Archie and Veronica."

Also, as with all things, the World Wide Web provides access to all of Gopherspace and to Veronica searches. Other search engines accessible through the Web may produce links that point to Gophers, as well. For more about accessing Gophers through the Web, see Chapter 10, "Browsing the World Wide Web." For more about Web searching, see Chapter 18, "Finding It on the Web."

Using a Gopher Client

By far and away, the most widely used Gopher client for the Macintosh is TurboGopher—developed by the same folks at the University of Minnesota who devised Gopher. But there are alternatives to using TurboGopher including:

- Other Gopher clients for the Mac such as MacGopher. The examples in this chapter use TurboGopher, a popular client included with this book.
- Use your Web browser (see Chapter 10) as your Gopher front-end.

The examples in this chapter use TurboGopher, a popular shareware client included with this book, which is also widely available for download through the Web or from anonymous FTP. Although minor details differ among Mac Gopher clients, navigating among Gopher menus is performed the same way in nearly all of them. Put simply, you double-click an item to go wherever that item takes you; you click a back-pointing arrow icon to move backward to the previous menu.

Setting Up a Gopher Client

As with other client software—like POP3 e-mail and newsreader software—your Gopher client needs the address (IP address or DNS name) of a Gopher server. (See Figure 13.3.) Any Gopher server will do—they all provide access to all other Gopher servers. Unlike e-mail or newsreader clients, however, Gopher clients often don't give you the luxury of configuring the software to access a single, local server so that you can forget about it. Your access provider might not run a Gopher server (if your provider *does* have a Gopher server, by all means use it). Also, Gopher servers are notorious for becoming overloaded and refusing new client connections.

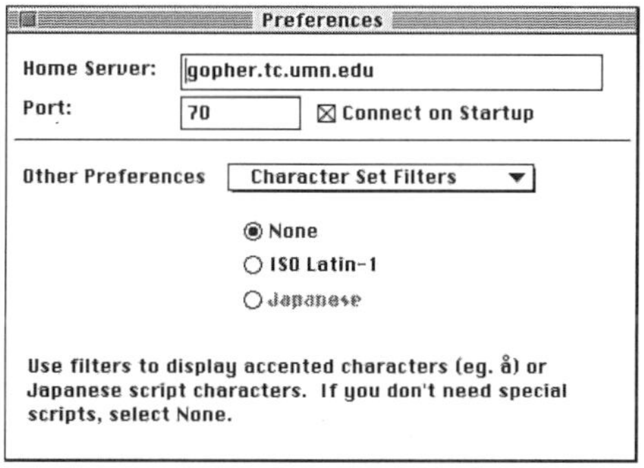

FIGURE 13.3.
Configuring a Gopher client.

To use Gopher successfully, you need the addresses of a small stable of Gopher servers so that you can try each until you find one that works. Fortunately, the following are true:

- Most Macintosh Gopher clients enable you to maintain a Gopher menu of servers so that you can easily jump among them. In Figure 13.1, shown previously, the menu option Other Gopher and Information Servers leads to a list of servers from which you can choose.
- Many Mac clients come preconfigured with a short menu of popular servers to get you started.

Finally, a Gopher client may enable you to specify a "home" server. Whenever you open the client, the client attempts to connect to the startup server. A startup server is not required, however; you can simply connect to the Internet, open your Gopher client, and then choose your server. TurboGopher comes preconfigured to connect to the University of Minnesota—the home of Gopher.

Navigating Gopherspace

To navigate Gopherspace, you select menu items until you get what you want. That's it, in an acorn. After connecting to the Internet (see Chapter 3, "Configuring Your Macintosh for the Internet"), you open your Gopher client, which typically displays the top menu of the Gopher server you have selected as your home server (alternatively, you see a list of Gopher servers to which you can connect). The list that appears does not mean you are connected to a Gopher server (unless you have specified a "startup" server); it's just a list of items. In general, you begin your Gopher session by choosing a Gopher server through which you will access all of Gopherspace. Figure 13.4 shows a typical opening menu listing some bookmarks for Gopher servers and other resources.

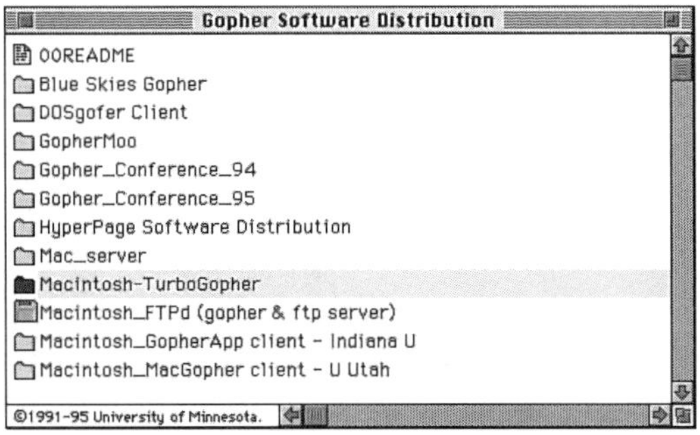

FIGURE 13.4.
A starting point: choose a Gopher server from available bookmarks.

Bookmarks Know All

Bookmarks are locations in Gopherspace that you record in the client software for easy retrieval. A bookmark can lead to a Gopher server or to any menu on that server; bookmarks can also lead to a Telnet or FTP session initiated through a Gopher menu or to files and documents located out in Gopherspace or on the local server of the Gopher to which you are connected. Most Gopher client software comes with a default bookmark file that contains several Gopher servers and often a bookmark for reaching the software supplier. Bookmarks are also used by Web browsers in much the same way.

Note that bookmarks work without regard to your starting point. When you select a bookmark, it takes you to its destination no matter what server you're connected to, and no matter what menu or other Gopher activity you've last performed.

In TurboGopher, you can create a bookmark for any menu that appears on your screen by selecting an item in the Gopher menu window, copying it, and pasting the item into a Bookmark worksheet window. With this feature, you create a shortcut for getting straight back to any Gopher item you find interesting or useful.

If your first server choice results in a new menu, you're on your way. Once you connect to a server, you can branch off to any other part of Gopherspace. The top level menu at any Gopher server typically includes a range of items leading to local resources, plus one or more choices that lead out into Gopherspace.

If, however, choosing a server bookmark results in a `Too many connections` message, the server you selected is too busy to accept another client connection. Try another server. With practice, you'll quickly learn which servers are most accessible and what is the best time of day to use a given server.

In TurboGopher, if you want to connect to a server for which you don't already have a bookmark, choose Another Gopher from the Gopher menu to open a dialog box. Enter the name of the Gopher server in the Domain name: field and click OK.

If you want to create a bookmark for the new Gopher server to which you just connected, deselect all the menu items in the Gopher window (click with the mouse after the last item in the window) and choose Copy from the Edit menu. Then click in your Bookmarks worksheet window and choose Paste from the Edit menu. (See Figure 13.5.) The new Gopher server will be added to the items in your Bookmarks worksheet window.

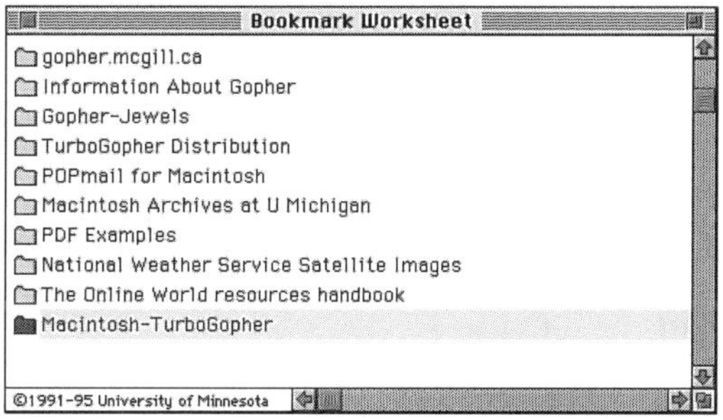

FIGURE 13.5.
Creating a new bookmark to connect to a server.

All the Gophers in the World

You can retrieve the entire worldwide list of Gopher servers by selecting an item called All the Gopher Servers in the World from the University of Minnesota Gopher (among many other places). If you're using TurboGopher, the University of Minnesota's Gopher is the default "home" server. Double-click Other Gopher and Information Servers to open a listing window and then double-click All the Gopher Servers in the World. You'll see a list like the one shown in Figure 13.6. Otherwise, if you're using another Gopher client, access the University of Minnesota's Gopher at `gopher.micro.umn.edu` and double-click Other Gopher and Information Servers; then double-click All the Gopher Servers in the World. A list like the one shown in Figure 13.6 will appear.

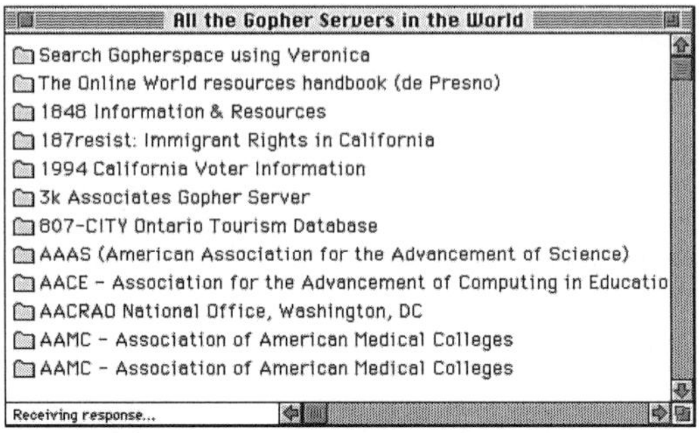

FIGURE 13.6.
The All the Gopher Servers in the World menu.

The list of servers is itself a Gopher menu; you can double-click any item to check out a particular server. To return from that server to the list of servers, click the title bar of the All the Gopher Servers in the World window or use the Recent menu, which lists all the Gopher servers you've visited. By selecting any item in the Recent menu, TurboGopher takes you back to it immediately.

As you discover items that interest you, copy the item and paste them into your Bookmarks worksheet window. This is a quick and easy way to build a list of useful or interesting Gopher starting points.

Remember that, like everything else on the Net, the list of Gopher servers changes constantly. You may want to retrieve the list regularly to get up-to-date addresses. Note that retrieving the list does not update bookmarks; to update the bookmarks you created from the list of all servers (or any other bookmarks, for that matter), you must re-create them.

Moving Through Menus

Truthfully, all you need to know to browse around through Gopherspace are the following notes:

- Double-clicking a folder takes you to a submenu, document, file, or FTP or Telnet session.
- In TurboGopher, clicking once on the title bar of a previous window takes you back to that window, to the previous menu.
- TurboGopher's Recent menu contains a list of all the places you've visited in reverse order—the most recent site is at the bottom of the list. If you select Home Gopher from the Gopher menu, you will return to where you started, your home server.

Although these three points can get you into Gopherspace and safely home again, you needn't rely on guesswork and trial-and-error for the rest of your explorations. Examine the choices in the menu shown in Figure 13.7. Notice that several different types of icons precede items. These icons are used to indicate the type of information the menu item leads to. Some of the more common icons used in TurboGopher are described in Table 13.1.

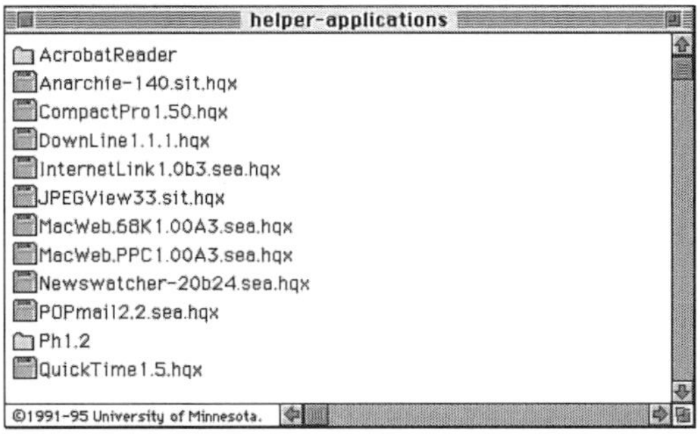

FIGURE 13.7.
Icons next to menu items tag the type of item.

Note

The icons in TurboGopher used to label different types of Gopher items are not necessarily the same as those used in other Gopher clients. Other Mac clients may use a different method of labeling items; text clients have a system of text characters for accomplishing the same thing. Consult the Help file of your client application to determine how it labels items.

Table 13.1. TurboGopher common icons.

Icon	*Function*
	Contains another menu (also called a Gopher directory).
	Denotes archived Mac software or documents that you can save to your hard disk.
	Identifies a text file that will be displayed when you double-click it. These items, like README files, often provide important information about the other items on the menu you're viewing.
	Double-clicking this icon enables you to search a database.
	Identifies a graphics file which requires a helper application such as JPEG to view.
	Denotes sound files.
	Indicates MS-DOS files.
	Double-clicking this icon will launch the Ph application with which you can search electronic phone books.

continues

Table 13.1. continued

Icon	*Function*
	Signifies HTML documents which requires a Helper Application such as Netscape.
	Launches a Telnet session.

Configuring a Gopher Client

TurboGopher is preconfigured (right out of the box, as they say) to launch a group of Helper Applications when it encounters files containing images, sounds, and movies. (See Figure 13.8.) Since TurboGopher makes extensive use of other applications (Helper Applications to fetch items via FTP or to render GIF or HTML items), TurboGopher suggests that you install their recommended group of Helper Applications on your hard disk. The group is available at this URL:

```
GOPHER://boombox.micro.umn.edu:70/11/gopher/Macintosh-TurboGopher/helper-
➥applications%09%09+
```

You can access this URL with a Web browser or through TurboGopher, by choosing Use Uniform Resource Locator from the Gopher menu. Enter the URL in the Uniform Resource Locator dialog box and click OK.

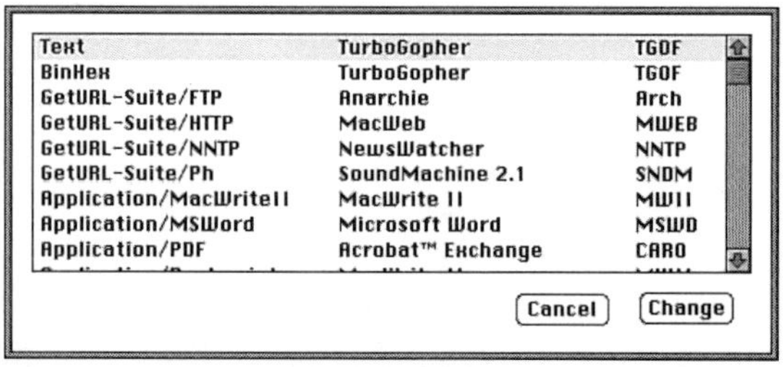

FIGURE 13.8.
Helper Applications in TurboGopher.

To configure a helper application in TurboGopher, choose Preferences from the Gopher menu. Then, choose Helper Applications from the Other Preferences pop-up menu and click the Changer Helper Applications button. Select the application you want to change in the Helper Applications dialog box list and click the Change button. (See Figure 13.9.) The standard Mac Open dialog box is displayed. Find the location of the helper application on your hard disk. Select the application (when you select an application, the file type is automatically selected) and click OK. The new application is automatically added to the Helper Application list.

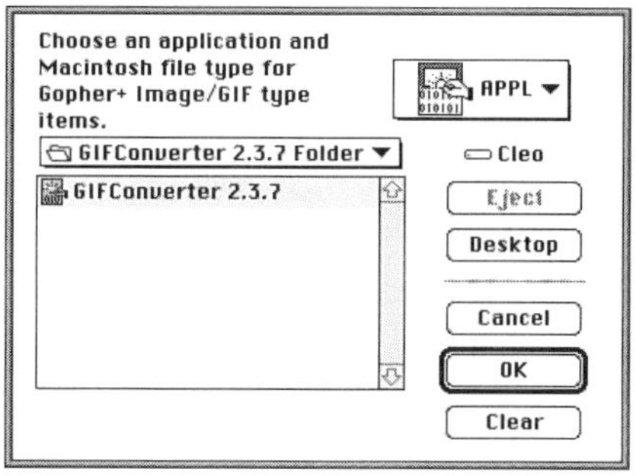

FIGURE 13.9.
Configuring Helper Applications preferences.

Cool Gopher Sites for Mac Users

Table 13.2 lists a few great starting points for Gophering.

Table 13.2. Getting started on Gophering.

Address	*Description*
`gopher.micro.umn.edu`	The "Mother of all Gophers" at theUniversity of Minnesota. A great source for the latest Gopher software and information.
`gopher.usc.edu`	Under Other Gophers and Information Resources is Gopher Jewels, an indispensable subject-sorted guide to the best inGopherspace. (For more about Gopher Jewels, see Chapter 16.)
`infolib.lib.berkeley.edu`	The University of California at Berkeley library.
`gopher.well.sf.ca.us`	The Whole Earth 'Lectronic Library.
`gopher.eff.org`	The Electronic Frontier Foundation, an advocacy group for free speech on the Net.
`yaleinfo.yale.edu`	The Yale library, plus links to many other cool Gophers.
`gopher.msen.com`	A Gopher for looking up the addresses of other Internet users.
`gopher.unc.edu`	Lots and lots of stuff at the University of North Carolina.
`gopher.tc.umn.edu`	A starting point (at the University of Minnesota) for lots of great resources, including a list of news sources (choose `News`)and reference works (choose `Libraries` and then select `Reference Works`). Figure 13.10 shows the news items at this site; Figure 13.11 shows the reference works.

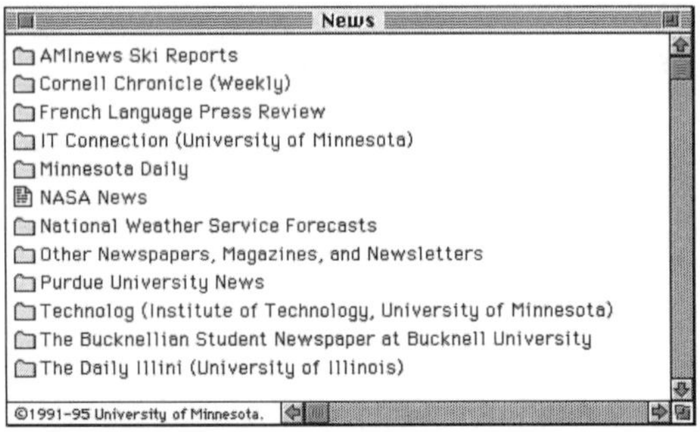

FIGURE 13.10.

Links to news sources from `gopher.tc.umn.edu`.

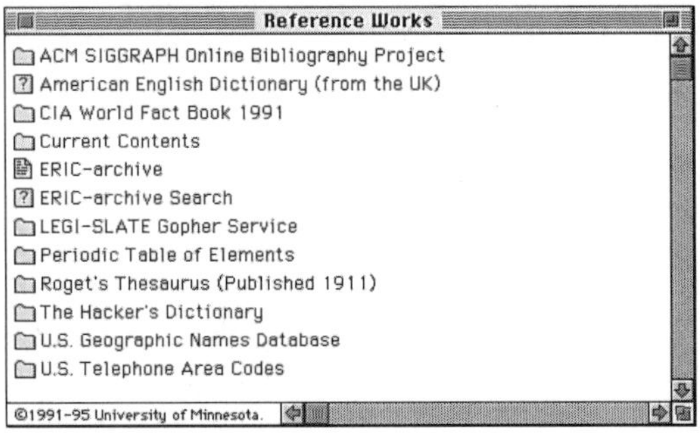

FIGURE 13.11.

Links to reference works from `gopher.tc.umn.edu`.

Summary

When the time came to invite the world of novices onto the Internet, Gopher opened the door—and the Web pulled everybody through it. Despite Gopher's recent overshadowing by the Web, Gopher remains an essential, simple, and incalculably useful part of any Internetter's arsenal. Get to know your little Gopher well, and watch it thrive.

In Chapter 14, "Interacting in Real Time: Talk, Chat, and Games," the final chapter of Part II of this book, you discover the last of the major Internet resources: live, interactive communication with your fellow Internet denizens. Go talk to 'em. You've earned it.

CHAPTER 14

INTERACTING IN REAL TIME: TALK, CHAT, AND GAMES

All the Internet resources discussed in preceding chapters have one problem in common: freshness.

Like the burgers at most fast-food restaurants, the contents of these resources are waiting for you before you get there, sitting under a heat lamp. When you ask a question through these facilities, who knows when you'll get an answer? It's all reminiscent of the days before the telephone, when everybody communicated by letter. People knew how to write in those days, and they were accustomed to being patient. In the speed-dial and microwave 1990s, however, we communicate *live* (on the phone) much more often than we write, and we can't bear to wait longer than two minutes for a complete chicken dinner.

We yearn for some "real time" action, some immediacy, some spontaneity, some *contact.* We want to reach out through the Internet and touch somebody, and to be touched back—not in tomorrow's e-mail but ***now.*** In short, we want to experience live, interactive communication with others on the Internet.

You can scratch that itch in two basic ways: Talk and Internet Relay Chat (IRC). Talk enables live, one-on-one conversations; Chat enables live group discussions (and indeed, the chats get lively). Using Telnet and other core Internet resources as enablers, folks also play a variety of interactive games (some part game, part scientific experiment) on the Net, playing with—or against—opponents spread all over the world.

Talk

Talk sets up a one-to-one, private conversation between you and another Internet user. Talk supports only two-party conversations—three or more participants requires Chat, described later in this chapter.

For Talk to work, both you and your partner in conversation must be running Talk software. Talk software is a standard part of most UNIX systems (which comprise a large part of the Internet); Macintosh Talk programs are available as well. Still, not everybody has Talk, and not all Talk programs are fully compatible with one another. In other words, you can try to establish a Talk session with anybody, but be prepared for failure.

Tip

> If you know that the person you want to talk with is a Mac user, send him or her an e-mail message containing instructions for acquiring the same Mac Talk program you use. If you both use the same Talk program, you can communicate without a problem.

To use a Talk program, you usually arrange the conversation in advance with e-mail, setting a date and time and agreeing on who will initiate the conversation. (It is possible to initiate an unplanned Talk session, but your partner must be online and must have his or her Talk program configured to notify him or her when a Talk session is requested. People generally don't work that way unless they use Talk often.)

At the appointed time, you and your partner both connect to the Internet (see Chapter 3, "Configuring Your Macintosh for the Internet") and open your Talk programs. Using the Talk program, the person responsible for initiating the conversation enters the `talk` command followed by the address of the other party. (A Talk program may offer a dialog box in which you enter the address; the program then issues the talk command automatically.) The other party receives a message in his or her Talk program, informing him or her that you are requesting a conversation. The other party accepts the conversation with a simple menu choice or Answer command. Once the other party responds, the connection is established and the conversation can begin.

Your screen splits into two halves, as does your partner's screen. Everything you type appears in one half (usually the bottom); everything your partner types appears in the other half. To converse, you simply type and read, type and read. You can even "talk over" one another, or interrupt, because you can type at the same time. As each person fills up his or her talking area, that area scrolls up to make room for the talk to continue.

Talk, a simple Macintosh program designed by Peter Lewis (who also developed the FTP application Anarchie), is included on this book's CD-ROM. See Chapter 5, "Choosing Client Software for Internet Services."

Internet Relay Chat (IRC)

Internet Relay Chat, also known as IRC or just Chat, enables any number of users to collectively participate in a discussion.

Instead of splitting the screen as Talk does, Chat simply displays all the comments made by everybody in the discussion in one long scrolling listing. (See Figure 14.1.) Each participant in a Chat session chooses a nickname before entering the session. The nickname of each speaker is displayed next to his or her statements so that everybody knows who's talking. Note that if you use a nickname, some Chat programs will show up on your screen between greater-than and less-than signs (< >); other nicknames show up in brackets (`[ ]`). This notation, which is created by an IRC client and may not appear in other clients, helps you remember who you are.

Also unlike Talk, Chat doesn't display each letter as it's typed—that would result in on-screen chaos. Instead, each statement is not transmitted to the Chat server until the participant presses Return. The statements are displayed in the order received by the computer running the Chat program—which may not be the exact order in which they were created (some folks type slower than others, and some speaker's statements may take longer to reach the server than those of other speakers). It takes a little concentration to follow a Chat session.

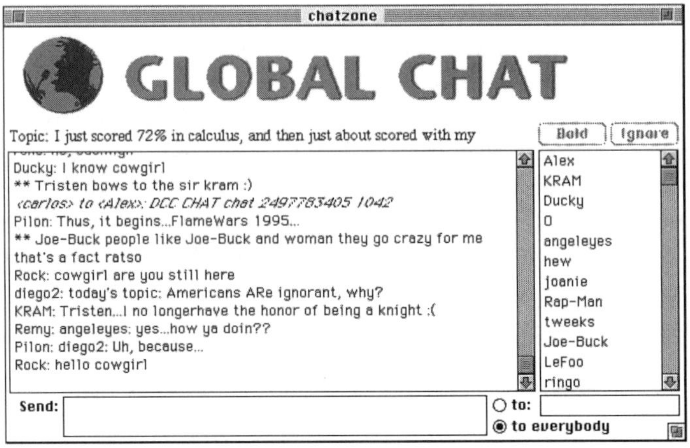

FIGURE 14.1.
An IRC (Chat) session.

A Lag in the Conversation

Although it affects all Internet tools in one way or another, IRC is particularly affected by "Net lag," the varying time it takes for messages to travel from your Mac to another computer, and the time required for the return trip.

In IRC, Net lag prevents the conversation shown on the screen from appearing in a precise, logical order. For example, when you respond to another's comment, your response does not show up on screen directly below the comment you're responding to. By the time you type your response, several other responses are already on their way. When you ask a question, the response may not show up until several exchanges later. Obviously, as in life, the more people on a channel, the more confused the screen output can be. But with a little experience, you'll soon learn to follow the flow.

IRC is a client/server system. The fundamental Chat program runs on a server connected to the IRC network; you must run an IRC client to interact with the server. Several good clients are available for Macintosh. Figure 14.1 shows a session through Global Chat, an excellent little IRC client for Macintosh included with this book (see Chapter 5) among others. After you install a client, you must connect to a server on the IRC network, using the IRC server's domain name and a port number. Following are several IRC servers in operation at this writing:

- `irc.bu.edu`
- `irc.colorado.edu`
- `underdog.org`
- `ug.cs.dal.ca`

To connect to a server through Global Chat, simply launch Global Chat and a Connect dialog box is displayed, as shown in Figure 14.2. Choose a server from the Connect to: pop-up menu, enter your nickname and click the Connect button. You can pick any nickname you want. If you somehow embarrass yourself in an IRC session, you can leave the session, change your nickname, and come back as someone else. (If only we could do this in real life!) Note, if you you choose a nickname that is already in use by someone else, the server will send you a message asking you to come up with another one.

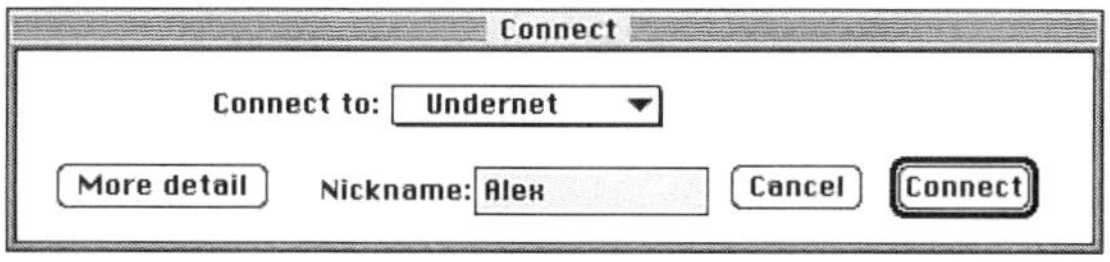

FIGURE 14.2.
Connecting to an IRC server.

Tip

You can locate lists of currently available IRC servers and other useful IRC information in a variety of ways:

- You can locate the IRC frequently asked questions (FAQ) file on the Web at this address:

  `http://www.kei.com/irc.html`

  You can also find the FAQ file using anonymous FTP at this site:

  `ftp.kei.com`

- A number of Web pages are helpful to new IRC users, especially those at this URL:

  `http://www2.undernet.org:8080/~cs93jtl/IRC.html`

- A number of mailing lists offer updates on IRC developments. The subscription address for the most useful one is as follows:

  `irchat-request@cc.tut.fi`

- A whole family of newsgroups covers IRC. Check out groups whose names begin with `alt.irc`.

Unlike most Internet tools, setting up preferences for Global Chat is a breezy, one-step process. The simplicity and clean interface of this program are its greatest assets. To configure Global Chat, click the More Detail button in the Connect dialog, as shown in Figure 14.3, to display an expanded window. Now, you can add a new server by creating a new setting. In addition, you can assign a default Channel to join when you Connect to the server. (Mac IRC clients generally supply a default port number; if you have trouble connecting, change the port number setting in your connect dialog box).

After you connect to a server, you immediately see various messages pertaining to the version of the IRC server software, system maintenance, and so on. This "message of the day" is important because it announces any anticipated problems with the server or current restrictions.

For example, you may see a message prohibiting the use of *bots*. A *bot* is simply a program that performs some actions automatically. Some users create bots that automatically chat in IRC, sending out preprogrammed comments and performing other actions—sometimes benign actions, like chatting, and other times malevolent actions, like kicking people out of channels. Although bots were once considered creative fun, they're lately viewed as menaces that annoy users and tie up system resources to no good end. The administrators of IRC servers, called *IRC operators*, may permanently ban from the IRC server those caught using bots.

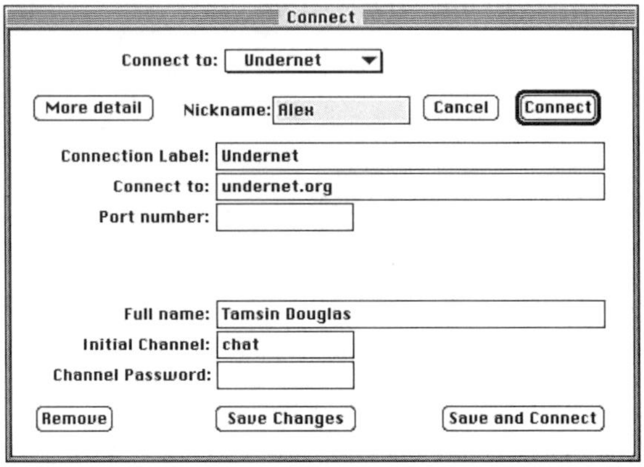

FIGURE 14.3.
Expanded Connect dialog box.

Once you've reviewed the message of the day, you can select a *channel*, or particular Chat session in which to engage.

> **Tip**
>
> When you first connect to an IRC server, look for a channel with a name like `irchelp`. The Help channel is a good place to ask questions and get comfortable because the help channel is a place where no one expects you to know what you're doing.

Choosing a Channel

A *channel* is a particular discussion. To see a list of available channels in Global Chat, choose Display Channel List from the Channels menu. A list of all the channels is displayed in a new window. (See Figure 14.4.) The number of people currently participating in the discussion appears on the left, followed by the actual channel name. To the right of each channel name is a description of the current topic of discussion within that channel, if there is one.

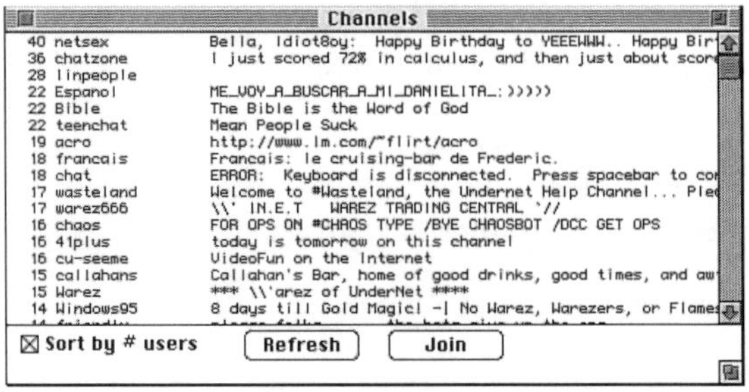

FIGURE 14.4.
A listing of IRC channels.

Tip

Global Chat displays channels in the Channel List window according to the number of participants—from high to low—in a given channel. If you're looking for a particular channel (for example, one for Macintosh users), you can also view the list alphabetically. To view the list of channels alphabetically in the Channel List window, uncheck the Sort by # users box (refer to Figure 14.4).

IRC Commands

IRC is operated by a standard set of commands. User-friendly Macintosh clients issue commands when you select menu items so that the most commonly used commands—`join`, `list`, and so on—are easy to use. But you can enter any IRC command yourself, using the same text window you use for typing your part of the conversation. All IRC commands are preceded by a slash (/). When you type a slash, the IRC server knows that what follows the slash is a command. (Once you join a channel, IRC automatically treats everything you type as a statement to be added to the conversation—unless it is preceded by a slash character.) IRC commands are not case-sensitive.

For example, enter `/help` (or `/HELP`) to display IRC help; enter `/list` to display the channel list.

Note that IRC commands accept optional *arguments.* The `-min` argument, for example, is used with the `list` command to display a list of channels in which a *min*imum number of users are participating. For example, the command `/list -min 10` displays a list of channels in which 10 or more people are chatting.

It's useful to know about these IRC commands in case you want to perform an action for which your client offers no menu choice. You can get more information about commands from IRC help.

The subject of many channels is easy to identify by the channel names. Some channels have no real subject; they're just free-form places to hang out and rap. Other channels have not only a subject, but a given topic for the conversation of the moment.

Although most IRC channels have purely social purposes (for example, `hottub` for casual chatting, or `jeopardy` for trivia exchange), some are set up as forums for serious discussion. IRC gained fame during the 1991 Persian Gulf War, during which it was used to distribute important news to users in areas where news was blacked out. IRC served the same function two years later, when Internet users in Russia and surrounding countries gathered in IRC channels to exchange news about the coup against Boris Yeltsin.

Most channels are created for various styles of purely social fun. Still, you'll see some dedicated to scientific disciplines (`biochemistry`), culture (`bible`), and countries (`belgium`). In most channels, the dominant language is English, but there are channels where the dominant language is another. This is particularly true of channels named after countries and languages (`polska`, `español`), and those that you may see near the top of your channel list in seemingly garbled characters. These are mostly Japanese channels, whose names appear garbled on your Windows screen because the channels require a terminal designed for the Kanji alphabet.

> **Note** Some channels are the Internet equivalent of phone-sex party lines; bored, lonely people chat there for a cheap turn-on. If that's not your bag, steer clear of channels with names like `SEXXXY-CHAT`.

In Global Chat, you join a channel by selecting a channel in the Channel List window and clicking the Join button. (See Figure 14.4, shown previously.) Global Chat does not enable you to join more than one channel simultaneously. When you join a new channel, it automatically drops you from the previous channel you were participating in. Alternatively, if you already know the name of the channel you want to join, choose Join Channel from the Channels menu. In the JoinChannel dialog box, enter the channel name in the Join Channel: field and click OK.

In another client, you might choose a Join menu item or type the command `/join` followed by the channel name (for example, `join #jeopardy`). As soon as you join a channel, a window opens to display the conversation as it progresses. You may not see anything for a few moments because IRC shows you only the statements that come into the channel after you join.

When you join, IRC automatically announces your presence to others in the channel with a message. For example, if I use the nickname Melchior and join a channel called `CHAT`, the message `Melchior is here` or `Melchior has joined` appears to me and everyone else in the channel. Others on the channel may enter *Hello*s, or they may not. One channel may have dozens of participants; if everybody stopped to say *Hello* to each new participant, things would be polite, but dull.

In Global Chat, a rectangular box, one inch high, appears at the bottom of the window. Anything you type appears here, but it does not go out to the discussion until you press Enter. That gives you a chance to fix your spelling and consider your statements carefully before they hit the group. Other clients provide a similar area for entering your statements. This area is also where you type IRC commands, always preceded by a slash (`/`) so that the IRC server knows your entry is a command and not a contribution to the conversation.

To leave a channel in Global Chat, choose Leave Channel from the Channels menu. You leave the channel but retain your IRC connection so that you can immediately join another channel. (When you leave, IRC displays a message informing others in the channel that you're gone.) To quit IRC completely, choose Quit from the File menu.

> **Note** You can join IRC channels directly through Global Chat's page on the Web. First you must configure the Helper Applications in your Web browser to launch Global Chat. To find out how to do this, consult Global Chat's online handbook on the Web at:

`http://www.prospero.com/globalchat/help/mac/`

Once you have configured your Web browser to launch Global Chat, connect to Global Chat's Internet Chat Guide at:

`http://www.prospero.com/globalchat/schedule.html`

The Guide provides Chat information and highlights subject areas. Click on a link to a chat subject area and your Web browser automatically launches Global Chat. It's pretty cool.

Advanced Chatting

Each channel on IRC has a "channel operator," or *chanop*, who is the king or queen of the channel. You can identify chanops easily because their nicknames are preceded by the "at" character (`@`).In general, the chanop is the person who creates or first joins a given channel; that chanop has the power to bestow chanop status on other users (even multiple users at once), so that a chanop remains even if the original chanop leaves.

Chanops have special capabilities in an IRC session. Most importantly, they have the power to declare a topic for the current conversation (they can also delegate this power to others.) The declared topic appears in the channels list (refer back to Figure 14.4, shown previously) as the descriptive text to the right of the number of participants. A chanop declares a topic by entering the command `/topic` followed by a description of the topic.

If a participant in a channel harasses other users, refuses to stick to the topic, or misbehaves in another way, the chanop can kick the offender off the channel by entering the `/kick` command followed by the offender's nickname.

New channels are created with the `/invite` command. You can create a public channel (one that anybody can join) by entering the following command:

`/invite all #channelname`

If you want to invite a specific person to the channel, replace `all` with the person's nickname.

Other useful IRC commands are listed in Table 14.1.

Table 14.1. Useful IRC commands.

IRC Command	*Meaning*
`/away`	Signifies that you have temporarily left your PC and can't respond for a while. IRC displays a message informing others you are away. When you return, type `/away` again to inform others that you're back.

continues

Table 14.1. continued

IRC Command	*Meaning*
`/msg nickname message`	Sends a private message to another user in the channel; only the person named by `nickname` sees the message you send. It's the IRC equivalent of whispering in someone's ear.
`/topic description`	Sets the topic for the current discussion.

Tip

Some frequent IRC chatters post photos of themselves on FTP servers or Web pages so that those with whom they chat can see what they look like. There are a number of different places where these photos can be found; to try one, point your Web browser to the following URL:

`http://www-stud.enst.fr/~tardieu/irc/`

MUDs and other Internet Games

The final group of resources available on the Internet is games, and that's a mixed bag. The first group of games, MUDs (and their cousins, MOOs, MUCKs, and MUSHes), create gaming environments that are increasingly used not simply for fun, but also for serious scientific inquiry. MUDs operate as unique Internet resources; many can be used through Telnet—all depend on Telnet as the basic communications vehicle—but using a MUD effectively often requires special client software.

The other diversions described on the following pages are all available through resources you already know about: the World Wide Web and e-mail. Which simply proves that whenever someone invents something for a serious purpose, some joker comes along and finds a way to play with it—except for MUDs, of course. MUDs were all laughs until some joker came along and made them serious. Go figure.

MUDs, MOOs, and More

MUDs are Internet role-playing scenarios that enable users to interact with one another, and with an imaginary online environment, in real time. Mudding is a lot like using Chat, except that the following are true with MUDs:

- Everybody in the conversation is pretending to be someone else, playing a role or *character.*
- Everybody in the conversation is pretending to be in a particular environment or situation, such as fighting a battle or exploring a castle or recreating some scientific experiment.

- The environment itself plays a part, displaying descriptions of the surroundings and events, responding to the actions and commands of players, and enforcing the rules of the game.

Originally, the MUD acronym stood for *multi-user dungeon*, because the early MUDs resembled *Dungeons and Dragons*, the fantasy role-playing game popular on college campuses when geeks had lots of free time because they weren't on the Internet yet. Because MUDs have long since expanded into many other styles of environments and games, the source of the acronym has been backformed to *multi-user dimensions*, *multi-user domains*, and *multi-user dialogs*. No matter. In the end, it's all just MUD, and players are often known as *mudders*.

Serious Play

Other than for entertainment, how else is MUD technology used? It's used in any discipline in which interaction and collaboration are valued.

For example, a group of college writing teachers learned about MediaMOO, a MOO at the Massachusetts Institute for Technology. MediaMOO was created by and for media researchers, who use it for real-time discussion and collaboration on media research projects. After studying how MediaMOO was used, the teachers wondered how the technology could be applied to their own field. They realized that, through MUDs, students could get instant feedback on their work and ideas from other students in different countries and cultures. They could write collaboratively and play the roles of characters they were writing or reading about as a way of exploring the characters. They could create virtual environments to test ideas about the environment in a story. And they could experience immediately the effects their words had on other people.

As they began working with their students in MUDs, the teachers also discovered that MUDs helped students open up and communicate more freely. The anonymity and virtual equality of the MUD environment enabled students to overcome the fears, inhibitions, and self-consciousness common in traditional classroom settings. Also, the MUD offered everyone the opportunity to speak and be heard because it is impossible to "talk over" others in a MUD—or to silence them.

The experiment continues, but the teachers are already reporting (on the Web, no less) extraordinary results.

For more about the project and other serious MUD/MOO-related initiatives, check out "Sensemedia Surfer: the ChibaMOO Papers" at `http://sensemedia.net/papers`.

Although *MUD* is the accepted generic term, there are variations. Each variation is actually a different program running on a MUD server. You'll see MUSHes (*multi-user shared hallucinations*), MOOs (*multi-user object-oriented*—nobody knows where the *U* went), and MUCKs, so named because designated users have the authority to manipulate the environment, or "muck" around in it. Sometimes, you'll see any of these names preceded by *Tiny* (TinyMUD,

TinyMUCK). Tiny MUDs are run by a server program designed to take up minimal system resources. Tiny types are also usually "social-oriented" scenarios rather than fantasy or combat types of MUDs.

Each MUD is created and controlled by a program running on a MUD server. You can often run these programs through Telnet, and so require no special software. MUDs have become more sophisticated of late, however; some can display graphics and play other tricks that can greatly enhance the role-playing experience. These advanced features require client software—and each special server program requires a different client. Most are for various flavors of the UNIX operating system, common at colleges.

A common Telnet-like MUD client for the Macintosh is MudDweller available via FTP at:

`ftp.tcp.com:/pub/mud/Clients`

To decompress this file, use Stuffit Expander. (For more details on Stuffit Expander, see Chapter 12, "Collecting Files with FTP.")

A MUDdy Web?

With its ability to show graphics and play multimedia, the World Wide Web would appear to be a great place to put MUDs. At this writing, many MUD writers are working feverishly to make MUDs work there, but for now, no one's really pulled it off.

To see the latest on Web-based MUD efforts, search the Web using *MUD* as a search term (Chapter 18, "Finding It on the Web," provides helpful hints on Web searches).

To see a Web-based interactive game that proves MUDs can, and will, find a home on the Web, check out Boston University's Hunt the Wumpus at this address:

`http://www.bu.edu/htbin/wcl`

Your goal is to kill the Wumpus with arrows, without killing (or being killed by) the other players. Figure 14.5 shows one of the Wumpus screens using the Netscape Navigator Web browser.

MUDs look like fun, and they often are. They are also, surprisingly, the Internet resource that requires the most skill and experience to master.

After all, when you make a blunder in a Web, Telnet, or FTP session, you've only done it to a computer (who doesn't care). When you post a stupid question in a list or newsgroup, the others can simply ignore you. If you say something dumb in a Chat session, well, conversations get that way. But when you join a MUD, you're usually entering an elaborate world with precise gaming rules, populated by experienced players who take it *very* seriously (*way too* seriously, at times—but then, it's their game).

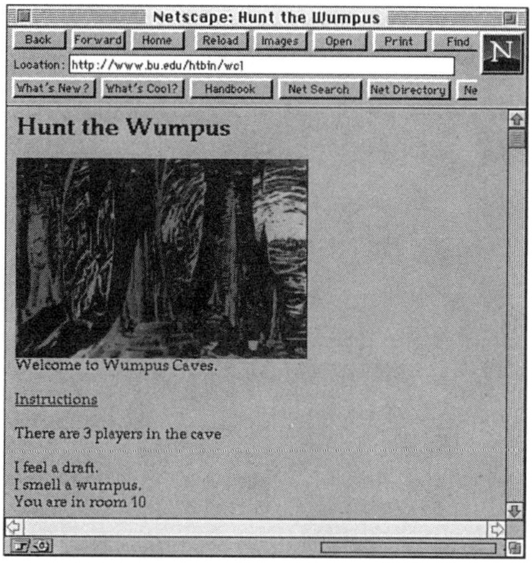

FIGURE 14.5.
Hunt the Wumpus.

Do something dumb and you spoil the game for others—and *boy!* will they let you know it! Experienced mudders are sometimes called *dinos;* new users are *newbies.* Nice dinos help newbies, but other dinos may flame newbies off the MUD for the first dumb move. In other words, if it's the first moment you've set foot on a basketball court, don't grab the ball.

MUD Rules

Every MUD, like any game, has rules. It is your obligation to learn the rules before participating. When you first connect to a MUD server, you almost always receive information about displaying instructions or for acquiring them with FTP. (See Chapter 12.) If you don't see instructions, type `help` after connecting.

Some MUDs enable you to create your own character right away; others require that you send an e-mail message to the MUD God or Wizard (as the leaders of MUDs are known) before playing, and wait for an e-mail response. When it comes, the response includes information about your character and, usually, complete rules and instructions for playing the game.

Even after you know the rules, it's a good idea to lurk in the gaming environment for a while, studying what other players do, before taking any action yourself. If you lurk first, you're much less likely to incur the wrath of dinos, and you'll also find the gaming more enjoyable when you do take the plunge. Of course, if another player or the MUD environment steers you into a corner, pick up a knife....

Finding a MUD

Finding lists of available MUDs is simple. On the World Wide Web, you can find lists of MUDs and other MUD information at the MUD Connector, which also includes direct Telnet links to MUDs that don't require special client software. The MUD Connector's URL is as follows:

`http://www.absi.com/mud/`

Another two useful Web pages about MUDs are the MUD Home Page at this URL:

`http://www.shef.ac.uk/uni/academic/I-M/is/studwork/groupe/home.html`

and the MUD Resource Collection, located at:

`http://www.cis.upenn.edu/~lwl/mudinfo.html`

> **Tip**
>
> On the Web, you can find links to many of the Telnet-accessible MUDs. These links open the Telnet client used by your Web browser (see Chapter 10, "Browsing the World Wide Web"), and supply the proper address, port number, and login information to take you directly into the MUD's opening dialog boxes, from which you choose a character and learn about the rules of the game.
>
> A good place to find links to Telnet MUDs is the MUD Connector page at this URL:
>
> `http://www.absi.com/mud/`

The following newsgroups may be helpful (Chapter 9, "Browsing Newsgroups," has more about newsgroups and how to access them):

- `rec.games.mud.announce`—A complete listing of active MUDs, plus other helpful information.
- `rec.games.mud.tiny`—Information on the TinyMUD family of MUDs.

Joining a MUD

From Telnet, you access a MUD like any other Telnet site: You supply your Telnet client with the address of the host computer running the MUD, and often a port number as well. (The address and port number, if one is required, are listed with the MUD information you find on the Web or in the newsgroup `rec.games.mud.announce`.) You can find more about Telnet in Chapter 11, "Tapping into Remote Systems with Telnet."

Once connected to a MUD server, read carefully any announcements or instructions you see. The server provides you with the procedures for creating a character (which may be done immediately but may instead require that you e-mail the MUD God) and joining the MUD; the server will also provide you with instructions for finding game rules and other important information.

Playing a MUD

When you join a MUD through Telnet, what you see is a lot like what you see on IRC: The statements and actions of other players appear on-screen, preceded by their character names. (See figures 14.6 and 14.7.) You'll also see *descriptions* displayed by the MUD program. Descriptions detail the environment around you as you move through the game; they also itemize the events around you and even facts about you, such as how you are dressed or what you are holding.

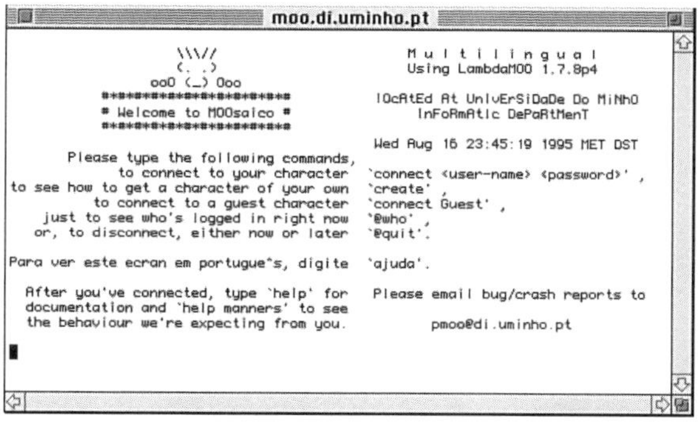

FIGURE 14.6.
Getting started in a MUD through Telnet.

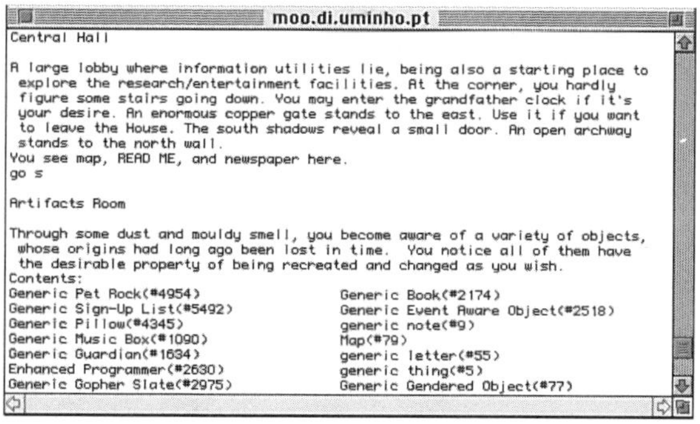

FIGURE 14.7.
Playing a MUD through Telnet.

Because every MUD program is different, the commands used to navigate within MUDs also differ. A few common commands, such as those listed in Table 14.2, are available in many types of MUD environments.

Table 14.2. Common MUD commands.

Command	*Function*
`who`	Displays a list of the character names of the other players.
`look`	Displays a description of the current environment; a "look around," so to speak.
`go`	Moves you in a direction (`go east`), into or out of a room (`go in`), or toward an object or player (`go fredo`).

`say`	Displays whatever you type next as a quote, so that others can see what you're saying. Suppose that my character is Melchior and I enter this command:
	`say Where the hell are we?`
	Every other player sees this message:
	`Melchior says, "Where the hell are we?"`

continues

Table 14.2. continued

Command	Function
	The `say` command can often be replaced with a quotation mark (`"`) for faster typing.

`act`	Displays whatever you type next as an action of your character. If I enter this command:
	`act kicks the ball`
	Every player sees this message:
	`Melchior kicks the ball`
	The `act` command can often be replaced with a colon (`:`) for faster typing.

`get, drop`	Enables you to manipulate objects. Use `get` to pick something up (`get knife`); use `drop` to put something down (`drop money`).

`whisper`	Lets you say something privately to another player; the statement you type following the `whisper` command appears only on his or her screen.
	If I type this command:
	`whisper suzy=Let's get out of here!`
	The player nicknamed Suzy—and only Suzy—sees this message:
	`Melchior whispers, "Let's get out of here!"`

Other Games

MUDs and MOOs are not the only games in town. There is no limit to the resourcefulness of Internet users when it comes to adapting important, serious information resources into a big waste of time. (More power to 'em.)

Through the facilities of Internet resources covered in earlier chapters, you can play a variety of games, including those listed in the following sections.

Board Games

Backgammon, chess, checkers, and so on are available through Telnet. Some support the use of client software that displays a graphical game board on your screen.

You can use the Web to learn about many of the games all over the Internet. You can even hot-link to some of them from this address:

```
http://www.yahoo.com/Entertainment/Games/
```

Play by Mail Games

Play by mail, or PBM games, are the Internet e-mail version of the old practice of playing a long-distance chess game by mailing your move to your opponent and awaiting a counter-move by return mail. It's hardly interactive, but it's faster than the pony express. There are dozens of PBM games, some based on traditional board games, others MUD-type fantasy games. (See Figure 14.8.)

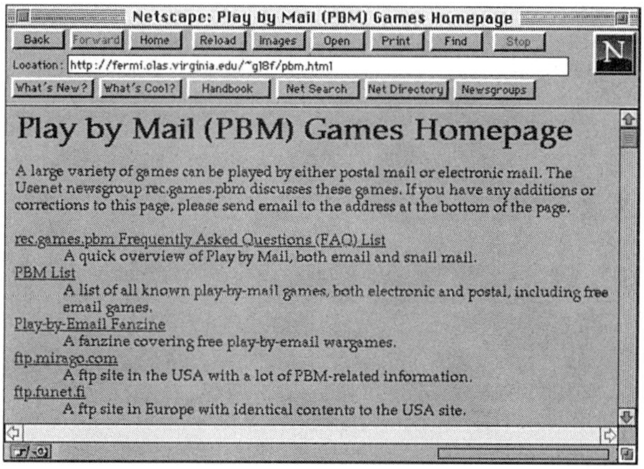

FIGURE 14.8.
A Web page listing PBM games.

On the Web, you can learn about the PBM games available, and how to play them, at this URL:

```
http://fermi.clas.virginia.edu/~gl8f/pbm.html
```

Interactive Web Games

The Web itself supplies a rich variety of games, including fantasy games, puzzles, and board games. You can even do crosswords on the Web. (See Figure 14.9.) Go see for yourself by pointing your browser to the following URL:

```
http://www.linc.or.jp/~hamano/game/crossword.html
```

To get a list of links to interactive games on the Web, go to this site:

```
http://www.yahoo.com/Recreation/Games/Internet_Games/Interactive_Web_Games/
```

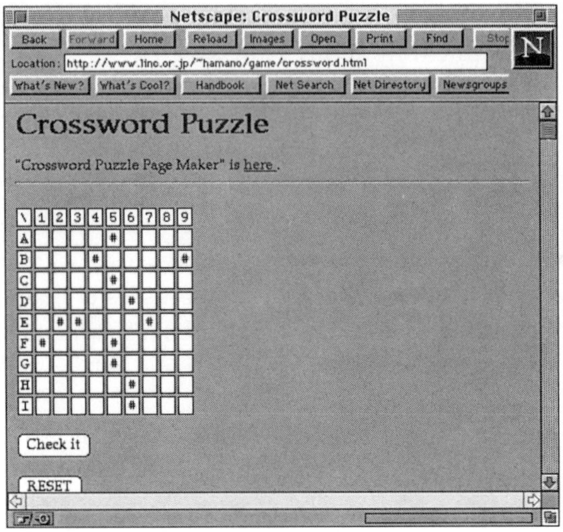

FIGURE 14.9.
Crosswords on the Web.

Summary

The Internet is more than just an e-mail carrier and a big database you can harvest. The Internet is an immediate link to millions of other Internetters, all over the world. *Why* you hook up with them—fun, science, profit, other—is up to you and your cyberspace partners.

This chapter concludes Part II of this book. Now that you know how to use all the major Internet resources, Part III, "Finding People and Places," shows how to *find* the treasures and people within them.

PART III

FINDING PEOPLE, PLACES, AND OTHER RESOURCES

CHAPTER 15

THE TOUGH TRUTH ABOUT INTERNET SEARCHES

Okay, the bottom line: There is no all-in-one, comprehensive card catalog for the Internet. The Internet is just too big and fragmented—and it changes too rapidly—for a comprehensive catalog to be feasible.

Whenever you search the Internet, you actually search only through databases or text files containing references to only *some* of the resources available. Whether you find what you're looking for may depend not just on *how* you search but on where you start.

To put it another way, the first step in successfully searching the Internet is choosing the proper approach—a certain *search engine*, a given index file, and so on. You must also choose to begin in the resource that is most likely to deliver results for the type of information you want. It's no different than using a regular library: to find what you want, you need to know when to try the card catalog, when to try the reference section, when to hit the *Reader's Guide to Periodical Literature*, and when to give up and ask a librarian. You also need to look through catalogs and indices with the right search term in mind—is *cars* really what you want, or is what you want filed under *automobiles*?

Chapter 16, "Finding Files and Directories with Archie and Veronica," through Chapter 19, "Finding Stuff Other Ways," describe the various starting points and specific search techniques. This chapter covers concepts common to many Internet search tools, such as *Boolean logic* and the effective use of *strings*. The most popular, and often most useful, way to search involves *search engines*—programs that look up information based on a given term—but they are not always the best choice. This chapter can also help you work productively with all the searching resources available.

The Ups and Downs of Search Engines

No doubt about it, search engines are cool. Pick an engine, enter a word, words, or even a part of a word for the *search term*, and the engine produces a list of choices it finds that are somehow related to that term. For example, you can enter the word *Africa* as a search term and see a list of references about that continent.

Some of the more popular search engines are listed here:

- **Archie**—For finding files available with FTP
- **Veronica**—For finding menus, directories, documents, and anything else available from Gopher menus
- **Yahoo** and **Lycos**—For finding many different types of references on the World Wide Web

You'll probably choose one of these as your starting point for most of your Internet searching. Amazing as they are, however, keep in mind their limitations. Most importantly, understand that none of these really "searches" the Internet. They search databases of information collected from the Internet on a regular basis.

Limitations of Search Engines

Like all databases, the search databases can contain errors, can be incomplete, or can fall out of date. Update timing differs, but most databases used by search engines are updated no more than weekly. That may sound like it's often enough, but what if an important document or reference related to your search term just hit the Net yesterday? It's more than likely that the search engines won't find it for at least a few days.

Also, information on the Internet is moved or renamed pretty often; the search engines may not catch up with it for weeks. For example, it's not uncommon to navigate to a Web page listed in the results of a Web search, only to get an error message telling you that the page cannot be found. The page has either been removed or has changed its URL since the last time the database was updated.

Searches based on broad search terms can produce so many choices that you can never wade through them all to find what you want. It's not uncommon to find hundreds, or even thousands of matches for a search term, especially in Veronica or on the Web. Most search engines enable you to limit the search to a maximum number of results (say, 100 references, or *hits*, as search engines call them). But only the most sophisticated engines are smart enough to deliver the 100 *best* matches; others may simply show you the first 100 they find or the first 100 alphabetically. If what you're looking for happens to be reference number 101, limiting the number of hits isn't much help.

Finally, remember that search engines are just computer programs—they're not librarians (who are slower but still smarter). They only search the kind of information they're designed to search. For example, an engine may search only the titles of documents. If you're looking for information about Al Gore, and use *gore* as your search term, that engine will overlook a document called "About Our Vice President." The search engine is not smart enough to make the connection.

Much of the stuff on the Internet isn't named very well. Searches on filenames or titles often fail to find important references because the filename or title does not contain the search term. Engines that search the entire text of documents or descriptions may be more successful in this regard, as are engines that look for *keywords* associated with a reference. Unfortunately, descriptive text and keywords are on file for only a small portion of the resources on the Internet; most of the time, search engines depend on the text of filenames and titles to find references.

Helpful Hints for Searching

Given all of these limitations, how can you search productively? The tips that follow may help:

- Phrase your search terms carefully, making them specific enough to keep the results manageable but broad enough to hit most of the possibilities. See "Phrasing Search Terms," later in this chapter.

- Consider what the selected engine is searching for—keywords, titles, filenames, and so on—and phrase your search term accordingly. For example, when using Archie to find a file, don't search for *FTP* unless you think the word *FTP* might actually appear in the filename or directory name. Filenames and directory names are all Archie searches.
- Start with the most specific engine, and move to more general engines only if the first searches fail. For example, if you're looking for a file, try Archie first. If that doesn't work, try Veronica, which may lead to a file or to a Gopher menu that can help you. If that fails, try a Web engine, which may lead anywhere.
- In Gopher, FTP, and the Web, watch for references to index or catalog files. For example, you will often find a file with a name like INDEX.TXT in the top-level directory of an FTP site. By downloading index or catalog files from resources you use often, you can build your own database of searchable references. You can open these text files in a word processing program that boasts a decent search tool. In Microsoft Word, for example, use the Find option in the Edit menu to look for words in the text. Note that you can use this method offline, possibly saving connect-time charges.
- Check out newsgroups that cover the topic you're after. Post a message, asking whether anybody knows where you can find what you're after.
- Apply a little technique I like to call "ballpark and browse." When you do a broad search, you may not find exactly what you want. But you'll more than likely see references that can ultimately lead to what you want. For example, repeated references in search results to the same university indicate that the university is a good source for information related to the search term. A little browsing through that school's Gopher or Web page may get you the answers you need. So you use the search engine to get into the right *ballpark* and then *browse* the likely suspects to find more specific information.

Phrasing Search Terms

All search engines have one thing in common—they're created by programmers. Now, some of my best friends are programmers (honest!). But many programmers have a small problem: They don't realize that things which seem perfectly obvious to them fly straight over everybody else's head.

Search engines require you to apply programming logic in the proper phrasing of the search term. Fortunately, knowing just a few basic methods can greatly improve your chances of phrasing a search term that will return useful results.

Search Terms and Strings

You use a search engine by supplying the engine with a *search term*, sometimes also known as a *search string* (because it is made up of a string of characters).

Most search engines enable you to choose whether to treat the search term as a complete word or as a part of a word, or *substring* (see how the programmers have made this more complicated?). When you designate a term as a complete word, the search engine chooses only the references in which the string appears as a complete word. When you designate the search term as a substring, the search engine chooses all references in which the string appears as a complete word *and* those references in which the search term appears as only part of a word. The difference in results is surprising.

For example, suppose you are looking for information about the Internet role-playing games called MUDs. You might search on the term *mud*. If you designate the term as a complete word, you'll likely get a listing of references to MUDs as well as a few references to real, dirt-and-water-based mud. Designate *mud* as a *substring* (partial word), however, and you get all the same references plus many more about Ber*mud*a, blues great *Mud*dy Waters, the holy book the Tal*mud*, and more.

So when are substrings useful? Well, in the preceding example, the substring choice delivered a lot of useless references. However, designating the search term *mud* as a complete word, or *fixed string*, probably missed important references to MUD*s* (plural), *TinyMUD*, and other MUD-related topics that attach other letters to MUD. A better search term might have been *muds*, designated as a substring. This new search string would have eliminated many of the dead-wrong, Bermuda-type hits, but it would have correctly delivered references to *MUDs*, *TinyMUDs*, and more. (Of course, *muds* as a substring rejects singular references to *MUD*!)

Some search engines also aren't too smart about treating compound terms—single terms made out of multiple words—as discrete items. Consider the following search term:

```
artificial intelligence
```

By default, many engines search for each word separately and produce a list containing every reference that includes the word *artificial* or the word *intelligence*—few of which will meet your needs. To treat a compound term correctly in most engines, you must connect words with dashes, as in this sample search term:

```
artificial-intelligence
```

Boolean Logic

Boolean logic is another holdover from programming languages. It is a way of expressing how you want the search engine to treat multiple words in a search string. The method is named for a 19th century English mathematician and nutcase, George Boole, who developed an algebra for working with sets. Boole's innovations make him admired among programmers and hated among high school students to this day.

Whole books are written about Boolean algebra, but only two of its *operators* are significant in the phrasing of search strings: `AND` and `OR`. You'll find Boolean operators supported in Archie and Veronica searches and in many Web search engines.

Note

> For searching purposes, Boolean logic is irrelevant when your search string contains only a single word or multiple words expressed as a fixed string (see the preceding section, "Search Terms and Strings"). Boolean logic comes into play only when you use more than one search term in the same request.

Put simply, the Boolean operator OR is used to collect all references that contain *any* word in the string; the AND operator is used to collect *only* references that contain *all* words in the string. (Please reread the preceding sentence until it starts to make sense, then read on. Thank you for your cooperation.)

Suppose that you're using a search engine to generate a list of references to Macintosh-based Internet client software. For a search string, you can enter this search term as a fixed string:

```
macintosh-client
```

The list produced will contain only references that contain the precise term *macintosh client*; the list will not include references to Windows-based client software that don't happen to use that term. For example, some useful references may use the words *client software for Macintosh*—these would be ignored by the fixed string in this example.

Instead, you can try this Boolean phrase:

```
macintosh or client
```

The OR tells the search engine to retrieve every reference to *macintosh* (whether or not that reference also contains *client*), and every reference to *client* (whether or not that reference also contains *macintosh*). True, this search term would deliver every reference delivered by *macintosh-client*, plus every reference that had phrases like *client software for Macintosh*. Unfortunately, the *macintosh or client* search term would also deliver hundreds of other references that included one term or the other, but not both. Most of these references, of course, would be useless because they refer to Macintosh topics other than clients and clients other than those for Macintosh.

The most effective choice is the following Boolean phrase:

```
macintosh and client
```

The AND tells the search engine to retrieve only references that contain both the word *macintosh* and the word *client*. (In most cases, the search engine first assembles a list of all the *macintosh* references and then discards any of those that don't also contain *client*.) The search term that uses the AND operator is the one most likely to capture all the likely references without also capturing lots of irrelevant references.

Consider another example. Suppose that you're looking for information about the hobby of beer-making, a practice also known by other terms such as *home-brewing* or even its scientific term, *zymurgy*. To save yourself the trouble of conducting a separate search for each name, you could use this Boolean phrase:

```
beer-making or home-brewing or zymurgy
```

The `OR` operator is especially useful when you're not sure which term will work best and you want to collect all references in a single search. Consider this example:

```
movie or film or cinema or hollywood
```

Observe that you can use multiple `OR` operators (as shown in the preceding two examples). You can also use multiple `AND` operators:

```
macintosh and client and FTP
```

Finally, you may come across support for one more Boolean operator: `NOT`. The `NOT` operator enables you to exclude certain references from the results of a search by ignoring any reference containing the term following `NOT`. Consider this search string:

```
macintosh not power
```

It collects all references containing the term *macintosh* but discards any of those that also contain the term *power* (as in PowerMacintosh). You can use this search term to locate references that cover Macintosh in general and exclude those references that include information about Power Macintosh.

Other Search Parameters

Strings/substrings and Boolean phrasing are the most common ways to tailor a search phrase. Depending on the search engine, however, there may be other ways to narrow your search. Most importantly, some Web engines are case sensitive; they deliver only the references that match the exact way you capitalized your term. For example, searching on *MUD* delivers all the *MUD* references but none of the *mud* references. A search on *Bush* locates references to *George Bush*, *Barbara Bush*, and others by that name but not references to *bush*, the shrub. In most engines that can use it, case sensitivity is optional.

There are still other useful options for tailoring searches, but the rest are specific to the search engines that use them. These other options are described where they apply in the course of the next four chapters.

Summary

Internet searching is immensely powerful, but perfect it ain't. To track down a given item on the Net, you need to do a little detective work—and be smart about how you apply the tools available.

Chapter 16 introduces the first two of these tools: Archie (for finding files) and Veronica (for searching Gopherspace).

CHAPTER 16

FINDING FILES AND DIRECTORIES WITH ARCHIE AND VERONICA

Archie

Veronica

Summary

What do you want? You want a program, a book, an article, a printer driver, a FAQ file? You know it's all out there in text and binary files stored on anonymous FTP servers (if you don't, read Chapter 12, "Collecting Files with FTP"), all yours for the taking. But how do you locate a particular file? Well, you can take one of these routes:

- Call Larry, your psychic friend, at 1-900-BIG-SCAM. Maybe he knows.
- Search FTP servers with Archie.

Not sure you want a file? Just know you want something about something that may be out there in the vastness of Gopherspace—maybe a file, a university library, or a database of helpful information about the Internet? Veronica has all the answers.

Where Are Betty and Reggie?

Let's get the question of the names out of the way up front, so that we can get on with this chapter and have no more foolishness.

As far as I know, Archie was invented at McGill University *before* Veronica was invented at the University of Nevada. More importantly, the name *Archie* is a play on *archives*, which is what Archie searches through to find files. That makes the Veronica people the ones responsible for the fact that the two search tools appear to borrow their names from the same comic book.

Mais non! protest the Veronica people. They say Veronica is an acronym for Very Easy Rodent-Oriented Netwide Index to Computerized Archives. The connection to Archie is an extraordinary, *staggering* coincidence.

This is simply one more example of the wry humor one finds among Net denizens, to say nothing of the wry humor one finds in Nevada.

Archie

Archie is a search engine that finds the names and locations of files stored on anonymous FTP servers. Because Archie finds only files accessible with anonymous FTP, you know that any file you locate through Archie is available without any special password or other restrictions.

A common misconception about Archie is that it, like some Web-based search engines, can search for a file by subject. Archie only searches through the text of file and directory names, so it can find a file only if you can supply the filename—or at least part of the filename. (There is a kind of subject-searching facility on Archie servers, but that facility is not available through Archie clients; anyway, its usefulness is doubtful. (See "Finding a File by Description," later in this chapter.)

Like most search engines, Archie doesn't really go out and search all the FTP servers when you request a search. Instead, each Archie server regularly polls FTP servers to update its database of filenames and locations. When you fire up your Archie client, connect to an Archie server, and search for a file, you're searching the database stored on the Archie server. This approach allows Archie to provide answers quickly, but also allows for the possibility that an Archie server may deliver inaccurate or outdated directions to a file.

Note

> Because the records of Archie servers can fall out of date, you may discover that the results of an Archie search lead to a dead end—that is, the file you want is not where Archie said it would be. Fortunately, most Archie searches turn up directions to a file in several different locations. If one is a bust, you can try another. If all are a bust, you can try your Archie search again on a different server.

An Archie database must keep track of millions of files stored on thousands of FTP servers. Most Archie servers poll a small group of servers each night, working through the entire list of FTP sites in the course of a month or so. That means the information delivered by Archie in response to your search may be weeks old. It's probably still accurate, but there's no guarantee. Also, because each Archie server updates its database on its own schedule, there may be minor differences between the databases stored on different Archie servers.

Tip

> Like many Internet facilities, Archie is a client/server system. Because good Archie clients for Macintosh are readily available on the Internet and elsewhere (see Chapter 5, "Choosing Client Software for Internet Services"), this chapter focuses on using Anarchie, which has Archie built in, to contact an Archie server and search for files.
>
> However, you can also contact Archie servers directly through Telnet. (See Chapter 11, "Tapping into Remote Systems with Telnet.") If you log in as `archie`, you can perform Archie searches using simple commands. To learn more about the commands, connect to an Archie server and enter the command `help` at the `archie>` prompt.
>
> Also, FTP file searches are available through the World Wide Web. (See Chapter 18, "Finding It on the Web.") Although searching for files through the Web has disadvantages, it offers one great advantage over many Archie clients: When you locate a file, you can download it immediately with a click or two.

After installing your Archie client (the examples in this chapter use Anarchie, a popular Macintosh client with a built-in Archie tool), all you need to know are the addresses of Archie servers. Good client software—including Anarchie—is preconfigured with several client addresses that can be selected from a pop-up menu list. Table 16.1 lists some Archie servers active at this writing.

Table 16.1. North American Archie servers.

Server Address	*Location*
`archie.rutgers.edu`	New Jersey
`archie.sura.net`	Maryland
`archie.unl.edu`	Nevada
`archie.ans.net`	New York
`archie.internic.net`	New Jersey
`archie.uqam.ca`	Canada

Why do you need to know more than one Archie server address? *Aha!* You've found Archie's weak spot. Like Veronica servers (described later in this chapter), Archie servers can get overloaded with connections and requests. (Frankly, the number and capacity of Archie servers has not kept pace with the explosive growth of the Internet in recent years—and authors who tell everybody how to use Archie aren't helping the situation.) When trying to initiate an Archie search, you may have to try several different servers before finding one that's available. Traditionally, it's always been easier to get through to servers located where it's nighttime; for example, daytime users in the U.S. often try European Archie servers because it's night in Europe, so those servers may not be tied up. However, given the small number of Archie servers and the burgeoning numbers of Internet users worldwide, this trick is not reliable. Today, any server can be tied up at any time. So keep trying.

Finding a File by Name

To locate a file with Anarchie, connect to the Internet and open Anarchie. Then, choose Archie from Anarchie's File menu. A search window, as shown in Figure 16.1, is displayed.

FIGURE 16.1.
Starting a search in Anarchie.

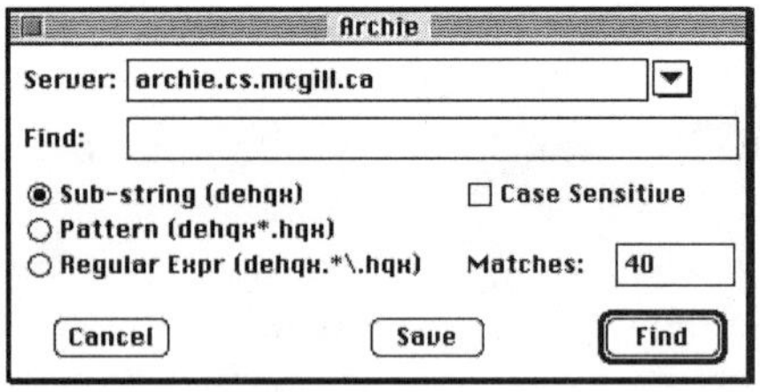

Select a server from the pop-up menu (at the right of the Server: field) and type the name of the file you want to search for in the Find: field.

Tip

> It's a good idea to periodically update the Archie Server list in Anarchie to make your Archie searches as efficient as possible. Using Anarchie, select Update Server List from the Edit menu. Anarchie automatically refreshes the current Archie server list you have running.

Type of Search

There are three methods of conducting a search using Archie in Anarchie: Sub-string, Pattern or Regular Expression.

A Sub-string search is the simplest and will usually do the trick. For example, if you are hunting for a copy of the latest version of StuffIt Expander, enter `stuff` in the Find: field. Archie will turn up many results, but if you find a term like `stuff` is too general, try a Pattern search. A Pattern search enables you to use wildcard characters such as `?` (defined as "any character") or `*` (defined as "any string of characters") to narrow your quest. If you type `stuff*.hqx` in the Find: field, Archie will find any BinHex files that start with `stuff` and end with `.hqx` (the filename extension for BinHex files). A Regular Expression (pattern-matching language) search is a more potent method of searching, but also much more difficult than either Sub-string or Pattern for the average user to handle. In general, most people will never need anything more powerful than Pattern searching.

Choose what type of search you want to conduct and click the appropriate radio button.

> **Note**
>
> Archie works best when you know the exact name of the file you're looking for—or have a pretty good idea what the filename is. You don't have to have the foggiest idea where the file is, but the closer you can get to typing the exact name of the file in your search term, the more likely you are to find it.
>
> You can search for files by description, but that's not a particularly effective approach in Archie. To search by file description, use Telnet (see "Finding Files by Description," later in this chapter). If you have no idea what the filename is, you're better off starting with a Veronica or Web search by subject, which may lead you to the filename.

Other Search Options

Next to the radio buttons that define the type search are two more options to help you refine your Archie search. The Case sensitive checkbox is optional. For the most part, you're best bet is to leave this off since it's impossible to predict how a filename is capitalized on a particular FTP site. In the Matches: field, you can set the number of matches for which Archie asks. A figure less than 100 is recommended; more than this will tie up the server and other users will not be able to access it.

Searching

After filling in the search fields, click the Find button to connect to the Archie server and initiate the search. Be prepared for the server to return a message rejecting your connection because it's too busy. If that happens, elect another server from the Server pop-up menu and click the Find button again.

A progress window is displayed while Archie queries the server. If all goes well, your Archie search should return some matches which show up in a Listing Window. (See Figure 16.2.) To review all of Archie's matches, scroll up or down in the Listing Window. To sort the list, double-click on the appropriate column headers. Double-clicking on the folders you see opens additional Listing Windows—you can have multiple Listing Windows open simultaneously. The size and date for each file appears on the same line as the filename.

FIGURE 16.2.

A Listing Window with search results.

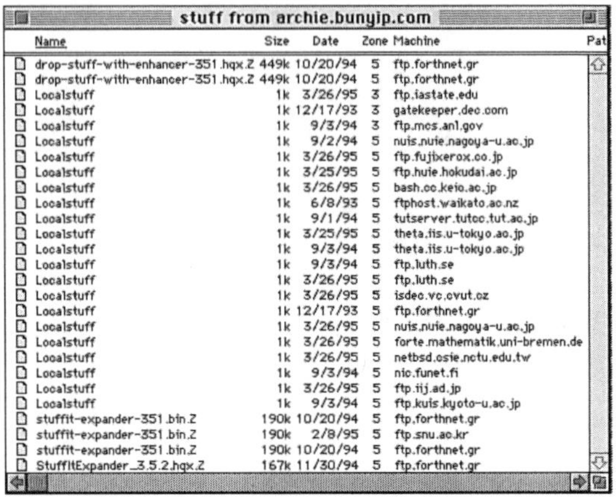

File information:

Field Name	*Meaning*
Size	The size of the file, in bytes.
Date	The date the file was created or last modified.

Both of these are especially useful. The larger the size of the file, the longer it will take to download to your system increasing your connect time. Often, the results of an Archie search show several instances of the same file on the server. This is especially true of popular shareware software programs, which may have gone through several revisions. If you're concerned about downloading the very latest version of a file, select the file Archie reported, which has the most recent date or version number.

Of course, if you don't see the desired file in the results returned by the first Archie search, modify either the server you are querying or your search term and try again. If, after several attempts, you can't find a file, either the file doesn't exist or your best guess about its name or possible substrings are too far off the mark. Try using another search engine (such as a Web search tool).

Retrieving a File

Once you identify the file on the Archie server you want to download, acquiring the file is a snap with Anarchie. Simply double-click on the file or for System 7.5; users drag it out to the Desktop.

Finding a File by Description

Archie servers actually maintain two databases: One contains all the server, file, and directory information used by Archie clients; the other contains descriptions of files cross-referenced to filenames. This second database is called the *Whatis database* because you search it with the `whatis` command.

Unfortunately, Archie clients cannot search the Whatis database; to search the Whatis database, you must Telnet to the Archie server. (For more about Telnet, see Chapter 11.) You can use various `whatis` commands to control the search. In general, however, all you have to do is the following:

1. Connect to an Archie server through Telnet and log on using `archie` as both your username and password.
2. Enter the command `whatis` followed by your search term, as shown in Figure 16.3.

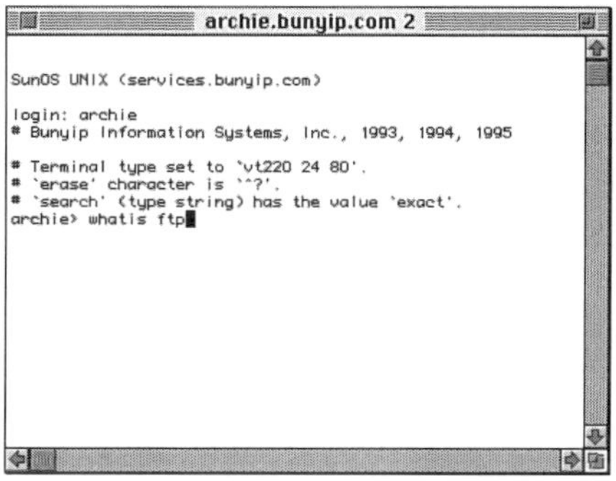

FIGURE 16.3.
Telnetting to an Archie server to use `whatis`.

Any "hits" appear on your screen, as shown in Figure 16.4. It's a good idea to start a log file (see Chapter 11) before starting your search. If a search results in many hits, they may scroll by before you can read them all. The log file records every line that appears on your screen; you can scroll through the log file later to carefully read the results of your search.

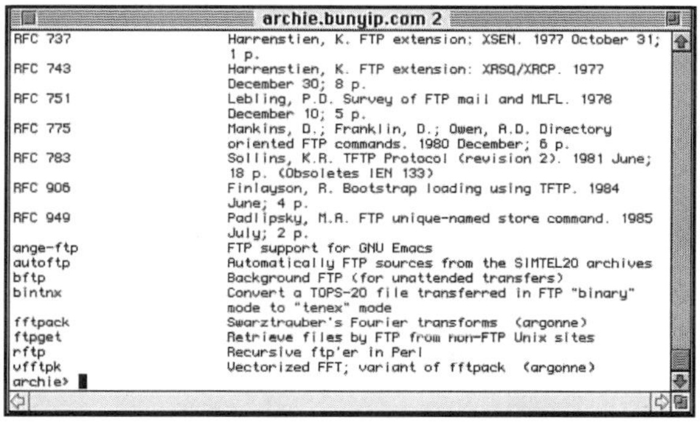

FIGURE 16.4.
Results of the query `whatis ftp`.

Although it may deliver results, `whatis` is an option of last resort. Of the many files available through anonymous FTP, relatively few have any descriptive information stored with them in the Whatis database. If you can't find what you want through Archie, try Veronica or a Web search before resorting to `whatis`.

Veronica

Veronica is an easy-to-use tool for finding anything in Gopherspace. Simply put, Veronica creates a list of anything in Gopher that contains your search term. Best of all, the list created by Veronica is itself a Gopher menu. If you see a menu item that looks promising, you can open it right from the Veronica list. If that item turns out to be a dead end, you can easily navigate back to the Veronica list and make another selection. Veronica is best suited to the "ballpark and browse" method of searching—your Veronica search comes up with a number of choices in the right ballpark, and you browse those choices to zero in on what you want.

Like Archie, Veronica is a search tool that runs on various servers located around the world. These servers poll all Gopher servers (except the few that request not to be included in Gopherspace) on a regular basis (every two weeks or so) to build a database of menus. When you search with Veronica, you search the database—which may not be absolutely up-to-date. Note also that different Veronica servers may deliver different results because they update their databases on different schedules.

As with Archie, Macintosh users don't need a special client to use Veronica. Veronica works through Gopher, so you run it from your Gopher client.

Starting a Veronica Search in TurboGopher

To begin (using TurboGopher as an example), connect to the Internet and open TurboGopher. When TurboGopher is launched, it displays a menu in the Home Gopher Server window. (If the Home Gopher window does not display automatically when you start up TurboGopher, choose Home Gopher from the Gopher menu).

To access Veronica servers, double-click on the folder titled Other Gopher and Information Servers. A new window is displayed, like the one shown in Figure 16.5.

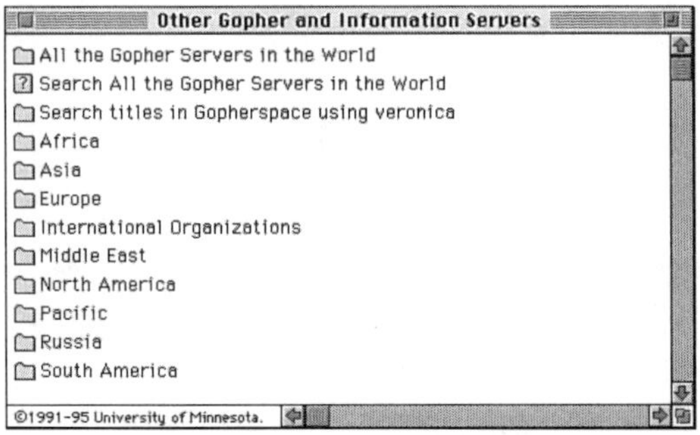

FIGURE 16.5
The Other Gopher and Information Servers window.

Double-click on the folder called Search Titles in Gopherspace using Veronica to display this window. You are presented with a list of different computers for Veronica searches. (See Figure 16.6.) For each, there are two ways listed to search:

- Search for directories—These options search only for Gopher *directories* that contain the search term. Gopher directories are menus of items that lead to other Gopher menus.
- Search all of Gopherspace—These options search the Gopher directories, just like the preceding option, plus anything else stored and indexed on the local Gopher servers (even if it is not a Gopher menu). For example, this type of search locates text files and other files, FTP and Telnet sessions, and other items indexed on Gopher servers.

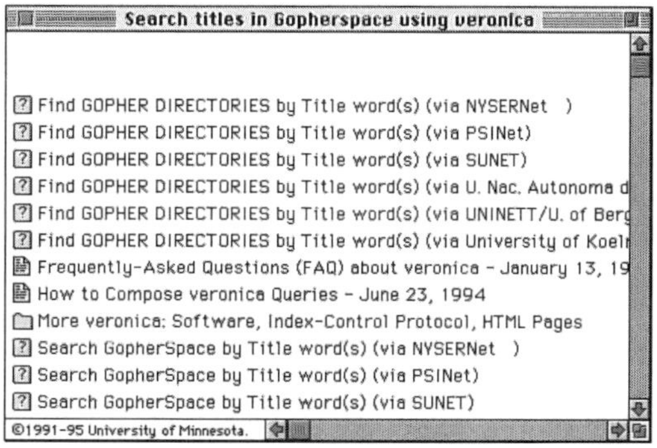

FIGURE 16.6
The Search Titles in Gopherspace using Veronica.

As a rule, when you're really just fishing for information, search for Gopher directories first. Searching for directories is faster and may deliver a list of manageable size. Unless your search term is very specific, searching all of Gopherspace can return a very long list of responses that can be difficult to wade through.

A Veronica Search

Double-click one of the icons marked with a ? called `Find GOPHER DIRECTORIES by title word(s)`.

Note

> One of the great problems with Veronica is that just a few servers have to handle all the Veronica searches in the world. As a result, it's very common to receive a message reading `Too many connections—try again soon` when you try to conduct a search on a particular server. In fact, it's not uncommon to find all the Veronica servers tied up.

Tip

> By default, Veronica shows only the first 200 hits it finds in any search. You can increase or decrease this number by adding the `-m` option to your search term (as described in "Search Term Options," later in this chapter).

When you select a Veronica server that is not overloaded, a dialog box appears like the one shown in Figure 16.7.

FIGURE 16.7.
Entering a search term for Veronica.

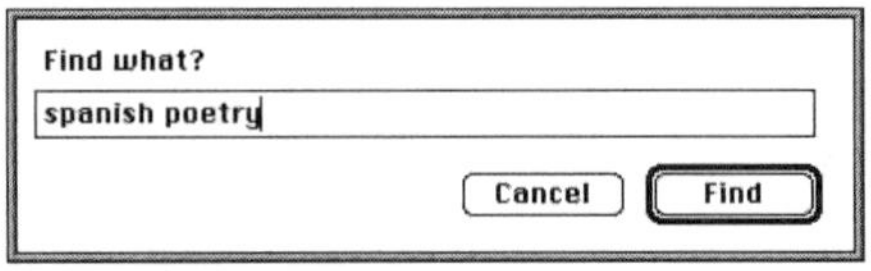

Enter your search term. Keep in mind the tips for phrasing search terms, covered in Chapter 15, "The Tough Truth about Internet Searches." Note also that Veronica is not case sensitive; it makes no difference how your search term is or is not capitalized. When you have entered the search term you want, click Okay.

The search may take a few seconds or even a minute. When the search is finished, a new Gopher menu appears, showing any items located by the search. (See Figure 16.8.) Select any item to follow where it leads, as you do from any Gopher menu. After following any lead, you can return to your list of Veronica hits by clicking on the title bar of that window so that you can try another lead. Remember that an item generated by the search may lead nowhere if the Veronica database on the server you selected is out of date.

FIGURE 16.8.
Results of a search on Gopher directories.

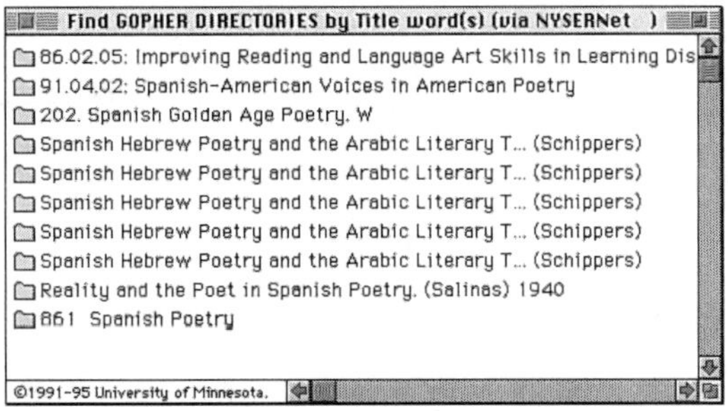

To show the difference between searching all of Gopherspace and searching by Gopher directories, Figure 16.9 shows the results you can expect if you searched all of Gopherspace using the same search term that produced the results in Figure 16.8.

FIGURE 16.9.
Results of a search on all of Gopherspace, using the same search term used to produce Figure 16.8.

Veronica Options

Although Veronica queries are not case sensitive, you can use a number of other options for phrasing your search terms.

Tip

> In addition to the options described in the following sections, you can use an asterisk (`*`) in Veronica to stand in for any character or number of characters. For example, the search term `cl*s` matches *clouds, clowns, classes, clips*, and many more. The asterisk wildcard is especially useful for finding a particular type of file. The search term `w*.txt` matches any text file beginning with *w* and using the common text file extension, .TXT.
>
> The asterisk is also useful to stand in for the letter `s`, to make sure that you pick up both singular and plural references. For example, `gopher*` picks up references to *Gopher* and *Gophers.*

Boolean Phrasing

Veronica supports the Boolean operators `AND`, `OR`, and `NOT` (see Chapter 15) for multiword search terms. When a search term includes multiple words with no operator between them, Veronica assumes the `AND` operator. For example, the search term `history america` is read by Veronica as `history and america`. This search selects only items that contain both the word *history* and the word *america.* To find all items that use either term, but not necessarily both, you use the `OR` operator: `history or america`.

To exclude certain references, use the `NOT` operator. For example, to produce a list that contains all references to *history* but discards any that also include the word *america*, use `history not america`.

Veronica also supports the use of parentheses for phrasing complex queries. Unless your job involves algebra, you haven't used this kind of logic since high school. (Your teachers *said* you'd need to know algebra one day, didn't they?) But if you think back, remember that placing an expression in parentheses means "do what's in the parentheses and use the result in the equation outside the parentheses." Consider this example:

```
trek not (deep or voyager)
```

It might be used to produce a Gopher menu of *Star Trek* references that excludes specific references to the sequel series *Deep Space Nine* or *Voyager*.

Search Term Options

In addition to Boolean phrasing, Veronica enables you to use optional parameters to control the search. These parameters are added after the search term and one blank space. All begin with a hyphen (-). In the phrase `motorboats -ti`, `motorboats` is the search term and `-ti` is the option.

The most important of these parameters is `-t`, which restricts the search to a certain type of information. For example, you can instruct Veronica to search only for files. The `-t` option is always followed by a letter or number. The important options are as follows:

Option	*Meaning*
`-t0`	Files
`-t1`	Gopher directories
`-t2`	Phone Book server (see Chapter 17, "Finding People")
`-t7`	Index-search engines (see "Other Ways To Hunt a Gopher," later in this chapter)
`-t8`	A Telnet session
`-t9`	A binary file
`-ti`	An image
`-ts`	A sound clip

For example, to search only for Telnet sessions related to the search term *Library*, you could enter this phrase:

```
library -t8
```

Note that you can combine the arguments following the `-t`. To search for sound clips *and* images related to John F. Kennedy, try this phrase:

```
kennedy -tis
```

The other useful option is -m, which enables you to specify a maximum number of hits different from Veronica's default of 200. To specify that you want only the first 50 hits from your search for *dogs*, enter this phrase:

```
dogs -m50
```

Other Ways To Hunt a Gopher

Each Gopher server may have its own searchable index and search engine. The index typically contains references to all Gopher resources contained on the local server and may also generate links to other Gophers and servers. You'll know you've come across a link to another server when you see a menu item offering a "search" of something, like the last choice in the screen shown in Figure 16.10.

FIGURE 16.10.
A Gopher menu showing a search engine for indexed Gopher servers.

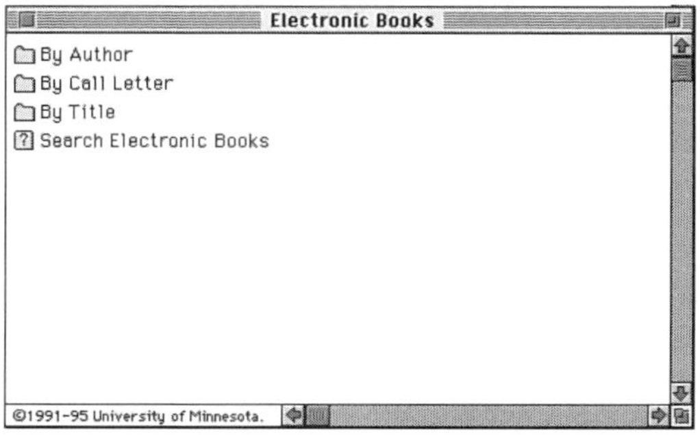

You use these indexes in much the same way you use Veronica. You choose the menu item and enter a search term. Note that you can search for these search engines through Veronica, using the -t7 option (see the preceding section, "Search Term Options.")

Summary

Whatever the true explanation for their names, Archie and Veronica are an essential part of your Internet navigation toolkit. As you gain experience with them, you'll find that you turn quickly and confidently to them when you need an FTP file or a starting place in Gopherspace.

Neither of these tools, however, does much to help you locate and contact other Internet users. As you discover in Chapter 17, nothing does much to help you in that regard—one of the Internet's true weak spots.

CHAPTER 17

FINDING PEOPLE

- Where Are All the Internet Addresses Stored?
- Tools for Finding Addresses Today
- Tools for Finding Addresses Tomorrow
- Finding the Latest Directory Services
- Summary

In only one way do online information services like America Online, CompuServe, and the eWorld beat the Internet: finding people. Because each of the services needs to bill its users, each maintains a complete database of who everybody is, where they are, their favorite color, pets, hobbies....

If you're on CompuServe, for example, and you know the name of a friend who's also on CompuServe, you can search CompuServe's member directory by name and find your friend's exact CompuServe e-mail address. You can use the same tool to find the e-mail addresses of Roger Ebert, Rush Limbaugh, and other famous people who haunt CompuServe.

The Net has no such directory, nor is a such directory technically feasible at the moment. For the most part, it's up to you to keep track of the Internet addresses of those with whom you correspond. It's not that difficult; if you have a single e-mail message or newsgroup posting on file for that person, you can read his or her e-mail address right off the header. You can also pick up the e-mail addresses of helpful people from within Gopher documents or Web pages they've authored. Increasingly, people put their e-mail addresses on their business cards and letterhead. Finally, if all else fails, there's nothing wrong with calling people on the telephone, asking for their e-mail addresses, and communicating electronically thereafter. It's done all the time.

But suppose that you want to contact someone you know (or suspect) has an Internet e-mail address. How do you find it? Whether or not you can find it at all may depend on how much else you know about the person. For example, if you know the organization the person works for, you've got a much better chance of tracking him or her down.

This chapter describes the various methods available today for finding e-mail addresses. You also learn how efforts already underway may lead to a real Internet "white pages" in the future.

Where *Are* All the Internet Addresses Stored?

That's the problem. Names, e-mail addresses, and other information about network users all reside on local servers. The servers on which the information is stored are called *directory servers* (although the same computer is usually also used for other purposes as well). In most cases, the directory server is not responsible for maintaining the required account records a network needs to operate. The *real* address and password information is kept elsewhere, in a database heavily protected from public view. The directory server is just a directory, and like any directory, it can be incomplete, inaccurate, or out of date.

Not all the directory servers on the Internet are publicly accessible. Among those that are, not everybody on the system is necessarily represented in the database. A college at which students have their own e-mail addresses may store only faculty addresses on the directory server; students come and go so frequently that they're not worth keeping track of, apparently.

More importantly, not all directory servers are set up the same way. Client programs that search for information depend on that information to be formatted and arranged the same way every place they look. For example, Archie can build a database of the contents of all anonymous

FTP servers in the world because all FTP servers index their files the same way. Veronica can build its database of Gopher information because every Gopher site stores its records the same way. Directory servers vary widely in what they store about each user and how they store it. That means that different client programs are required to query different types of servers.

The inconsistency among directory servers has so far made it impossible to build a client program that can poll all the Internet directory servers to build a comprehensive Internet "white pages" of e-mail addresses. The other problem is, of course, the sheer number of records. A complete Internet white pages directory would have to keep track of 25 million people, whose information is actually stored and maintained on hundreds of thousands of computers using hundreds of different directory systems. Simply keeping such a database up to date across a global network would be a staggering feat of distributed data management.

As things stand, to look up an address today, you really have to have some idea of where the person works; or rather, the organization through which he or she has an e-mail account.

Tools for Finding Addresses Today

Different directory servers respond to different clients. The most widely supported client, Whois, is easily applied through Gopher, as are several other good sources for addresses. Another client, Finger, is used to query machines running Finger servers.

Gophering for Addresses

Finding different addresses stored in different places requires different methods. The best way to start looking for an address is from within a resource that lets you jump among different approaches easily—namely Gopher or the World Wide Web. Either of these are a good starting point for address searches. In particular, a number of university Gophers offer menus whose items lead to most of the principle address resources available.

For example, Gophering to `k12.ucs.umass.edu` and then choosing the menu item `Whois Services` gets you to a Gopher menu at the University of Massachusetts. (See Figure 17.1.)

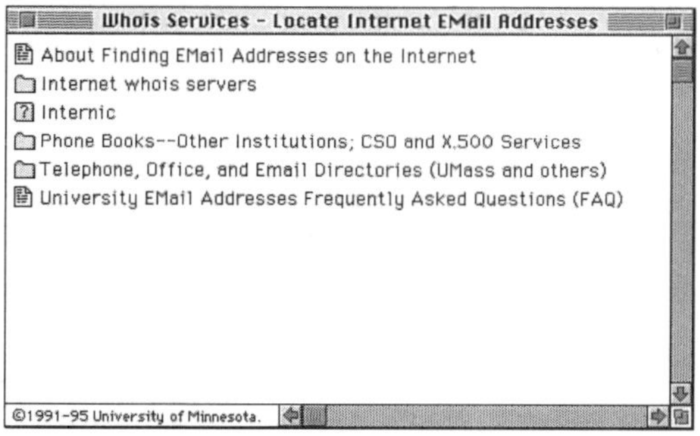

FIGURE 17.1.
A Gopher menu of good address sources.

Note

> The University of Massachusetts's Gopher is used here only as an example. Other university Gophers offer similar menus and services. Another good set of directory services can be found at Notre Dame's Gopher: `gopher.nd.edu`.
>
> Also try the "Mother Gopher" at the University of Minnesota (`gopher.micro.umn.edu`), choose Phone Books, and then select WHOIS Searches.

Of the items shown in Figure 17.1, the most important is Internet Whois Servers. Whois directory servers are the most common type on the Internet. To search them, you need a Whois client, which the Gopher item pointing to "Whois" stands in for. The problem with Whois is that you really can't find anybody unless you have some idea where they are. If you select the Whois item from the menu shown in Figure 17.1, you get a list of Whois servers, shown in Figure 17.2. You can search only one of these at a time, so if you have no idea where your companion has an e-mail account, you have to search each server individually.

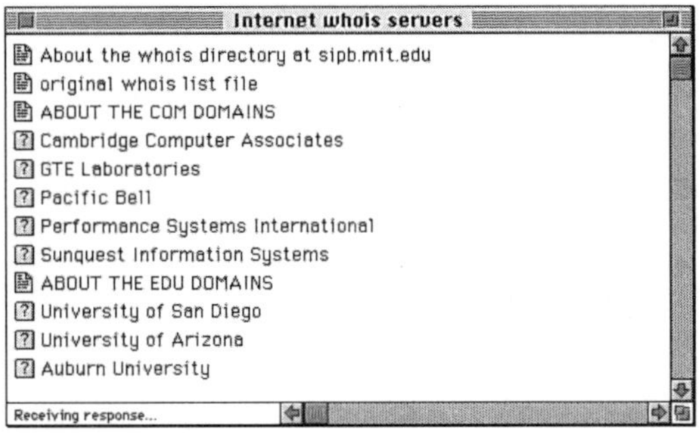

FIGURE 17.2.
The Gopher list of Whois servers.

Assume that you know that your friend is at Indiana University. When you select Indiana University's server from the Whois Gopher menu, a dialog box like the one shown in Figure 17.3 appears.

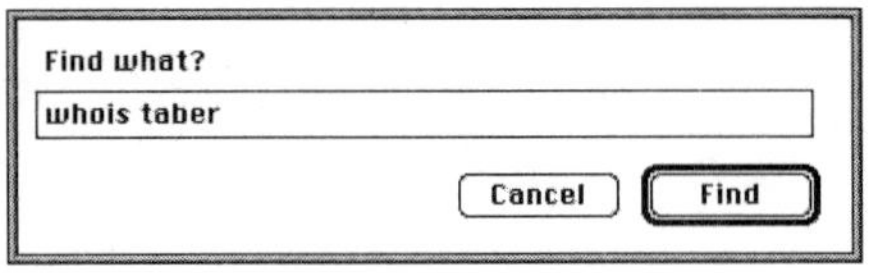

FIGURE 17.3.
Searching a Whois server.

In this box, type a name. Whois can deliver a list of possible matches, so it's best not to be too specific when you're not sure. In other words, if you're not sure whether you want *taber, mark* or *taber, marcus,* type just `taber` as a search term and see what you get. If Whois locates multiple Tabers, a list of choices is returned.

If your Gopher client is configured to display the contents of text files, the results of your search appear on your screen. Otherwise, results are written to a text file on your hard disk. The information delivered varies dramatically. Usually, you receive names and e-mail addresses, plus other information such as department names. Sometimes, you get no e-mail address but a regular mail address, instead. (Write your friend a letter, and ask for his e-mail address!)

In addition to Whois, you can use the Phone Books choice shown in Figure 17.1, shown previously. The Phone Books option points to menus from which you can search three different types of directory servers: Whois servers, computing services offices (CSO) servers, and X.500 directory services. Together, these three types make up the bulk of publicly accessible directory servers.

Tip

> The Internet Network Information Center, or InterNIC, is a good source for all sorts of information, including some names. A menu choice for searching InterNIC also appears on the screen shown in Figure 17.1. You learn about InterNIC in Chapter 19, "Finding Stuff Other Ways."

When you select Phone Books, you see a menu like the one shown in Figure 17.4. Before doing any searching, select the top item (About Phone Books) to display or download a text file containing information about the different types of directory servers and about phrasing searches for each type of server.

FIGURE 17.4.
Options for searching a variety of directory server types.

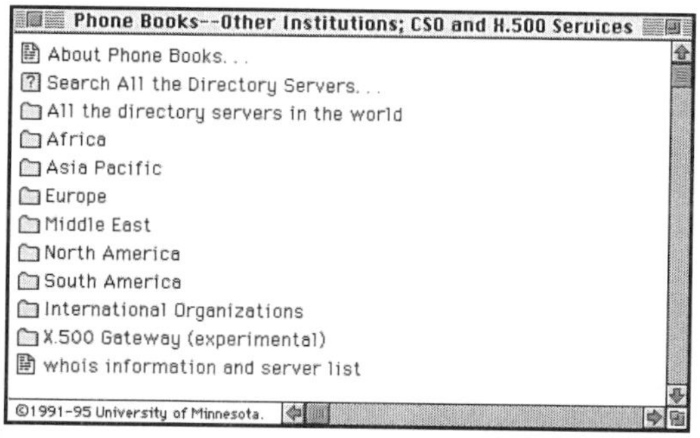

Finger

Finger is used to query a Finger server in a specific host environment. It's not terribly useful because you have to know the actual Internet address of the host you want to search—and most of the time, when you know that, you know the e-mail address for the person you want to contact.

The easiest way to try Finger on your Macintosh is to use Eudora Light. Refer to Chapter 7, "Exchanging E-Mail," for more information about using Eudora Light. To use the Finger tool in Eudora Light, connect to the Internet, open Eudora Light, and choose Ph from the menu. You'll see a screen like the one in Figure 17.5.

FIGURE 17.5.
Using Finger.

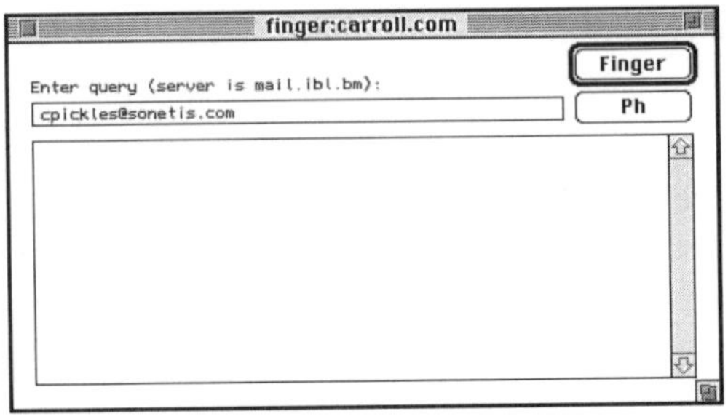

To Finger someone, enter their e-mail address and click the Finger button. The Finger tool will query the host specified in the `@domain` component of the address and ask for information on the name specified. Its findings are displayed in the response field below (see Figure 17.6) and it will ask for information on the name specified. If you get no response or if Eudora Light returns an error message such as `The Connection came up halfway and failed...` it doesn't mean that the e-mail address is invalid. The Host you specified doesn't run a Finger server. If you do get a response, it confirms the e-mail address still exists or if it has been active recently.

FIGURE 17.6.
A Finger response in Eudora Light.

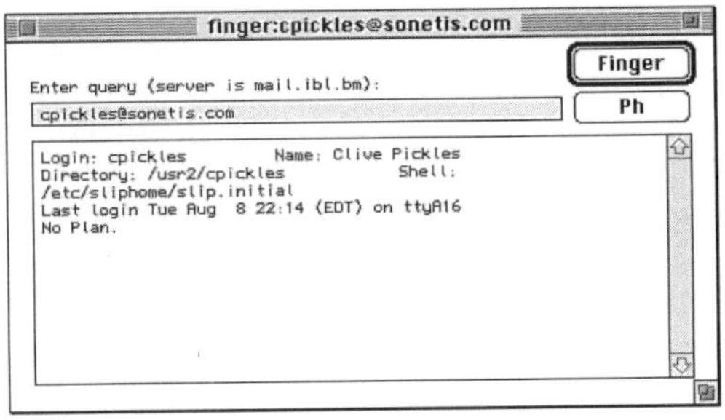

Other Directory Services

Friendly, helpful institutions want people to know who they are and who's a part of them. They've set up their own Web pages or Gophers to help you locate people within the institution. Sometimes, these interfaces are simply pretty faces pasted over Whois clients; other times, they are homemade, easy-to-use interfaces for locating people. The University of Massachusetts Gopher shown previously in Figure 17.1 is a good example. Others, including Stanford University, Columbia and the University of Arizona have set up Web directories for themselves. (See Figure 17.7.) You can expect this trend to continue as use of the Web mushrooms.

Tip

> The Web features a number of powerful search engines, as you discover in Chapter 18, "Finding It on the Web." Coupled with the growing presence on the Web of homemade directory services, Whois gateways, and other directory services, these engines make the Web an excellent starting place for people searches.

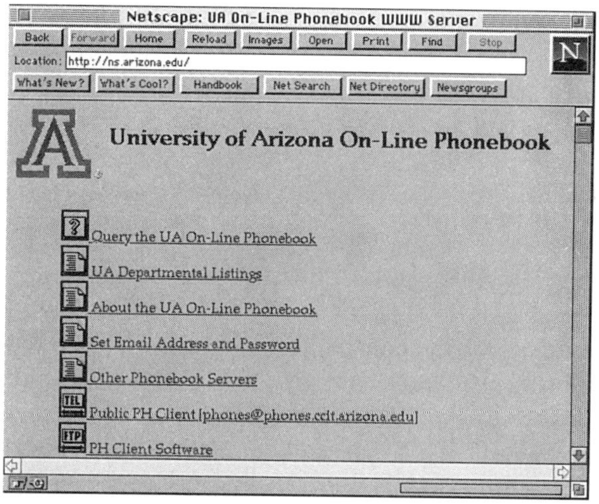

FIGURE 17.7.
The University of Arizona's directory page on the World Wide Web.

Tools for Finding Addresses Tomorrow

Work proceeds apace on better search engines for finding people. A new Whois program, Whois++, is emerging, but its improvements over Whois have more to do with improving searches of Whois servers, not with pulling an Internet white pages together.

Internet White Pages

Despite the obvious challenges, efforts are underway to define the technical underpinnings of an Internet white pages. The most important of these efforts, unfortunately, must work its way through the impressively open, but agonizingly slow, approval process for Internet standards.

New standards for the Internet are created by consensus. People who have a proposal publish on the Net (and, increasingly, on the Web) a *Request for Comment*, or RFC. Others in the community—in particular, the Internet Engineering Task Force (IETF)—evaluate and comment on the proposal. If consensus approves, the proposal moves forward and may eventually be ratified by the Internet Architecture Board (IAB).

Although all this sounds terribly official, nobody on the Internet is forced to follow any new standard. But if the idea is good enough, folks follow new standards to reap the benefits of participation. Obviously, participating in a new white pages standard means people can find you. Businesses, universities, and individuals may flock to such a standard; the CIA and FBI may not.

One RFC now floating through the Net does proposes a standard for creating an Internet white pages. The proposal defines a standard approach to organizing information in directory servers so that all servers can be queried by a single client. The RFC then defines how the client would work to extract address information from the servers.

If the proposal were implemented and the guidelines were followed on all Internet servers, it would be possible to create a program that regularly polls every directory server on the Internet to build a centralized database of Internet addresses—including names, e-mail addresses, host names, organization/department names, and perhaps even telephone numbers, fax numbers, and postal mailing addresses. Any Internet user could run a client program (or use a public client through Gopher or the Web) to search this database for any Internet user in the world.

Although it all sounds great, there are significant roadblocks to this effort. One is the question of privacy and security: Should Internet users be permitted to have "unlisted" addresses, in effect opting out of the white pages? Should whole organizations have the right to be left out, or to select who can look them up and who can't? Working these issues out may take years. Getting a reasonably large proportion of the Net to reformat their directory servers to the white pages standard may take many more years.

A true Internet white pages is a definite possibility. It's also a long-term one, at best.

Tip

> Although there is no true Internet white pages, there *is* a page that pretends to be one by offering links to a variety of directories, including Whois servers and a directory of Web home pages. The page has been set up by Netscape (makers of the Navigator Web browser) and anyone can get to it on the Web. The URL of the Netscape White Pages page (shown in Figure 17.8) is as follows:
>
> `http://home.netscape.com/home/internet-white-pages.html`

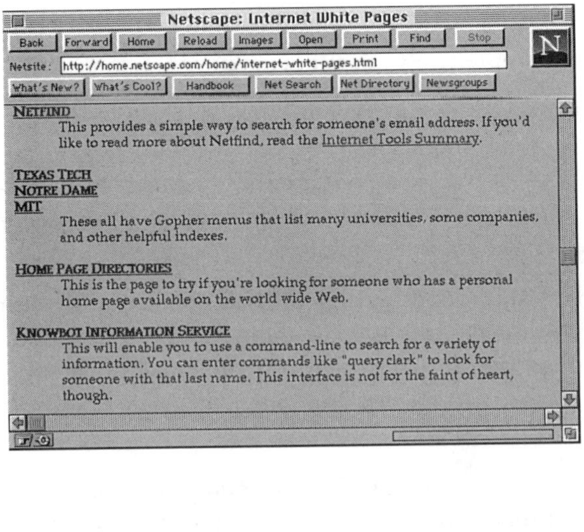

FIGURE 17.8.
Netscape's page of white pages links.

Who's Who Online

In the meantime, unreasonably ambitious folks are attempting to build white pages themselves—at least a part of a white pages. On the Web, you'll find a project called Who's Online at this address:

`http://www.ictp.trieste.it/Canessa/ENTRIES/entries.html`

Who's Online is an attempt to develop a searchable index of Internet users grouped by profession. (See Figure 17.9.) Unfortunately, to be included in the database, a user has to personally sign up for it—the Who's Online folks aren't going out and collecting names. As you might expect, the current database lists only a few hundred names, mostly scientists. But hey, who knows? At this rate, Who's Online—or a similar effort—might build a functional white pages before the specifications for the *official* Internet white pages can even be approved.

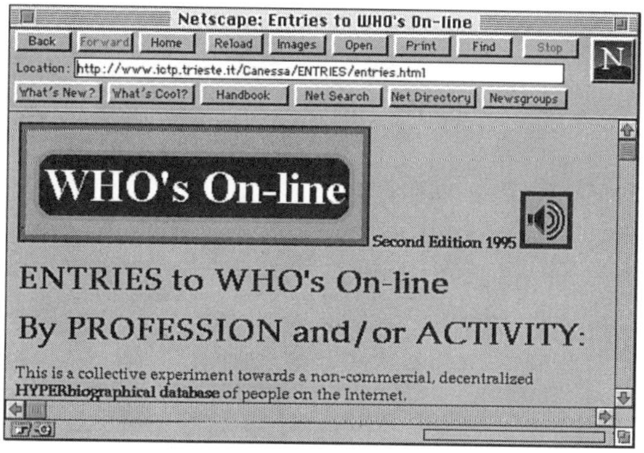

FIGURE 17.9.
The Who's Online home page.

Finding the Latest Directory Services

Because the lack of a white pages is one of the Internet's biggest problems, it's no surprise that solving the problem is one of the most active and volatile Internet activities. New ideas, new facilities, and new programs pop up every month with a new angle on solving an old problem.

From time to time, try a Web search to find out what's new in the world of white pages. A Yahoo search (see Chapter 18) on the term *white pages* will drum up the latest developments. Other searches to try include *whois* and *lookup.*

Summary

The Internet is such a satisfying place when you're looking for information about 15th-century costumes, *Star Trek* trivia, and sports stats. Why can't it look up one lousy user?

In perhaps one out of 10 or 20 cases, it can. Knowing about all the tools that help you with such searches improves your odds of success. This problem will not go away in the next few years—but significant progress *will* be made toward solving it.

In the next chapter, you discover a far more satisfying arena to search: the World Wide Web, home of the coolest search engines in cyberspace. In fact, you may decide that the Web is the first place you go when you don't know where to look.

CHAPTER 18

FINDING IT ON THE WEB

Starting Points

Web Directories

Web Spiders

Summary

When you first surf the Web, it's a free-association blast—point, click, *Wow!*...point, click, *Wow!* Soon, however, the time comes when you want to track down something specific. That's where Web searching comes in.

Web searching is both the most powerful and the least powerful way to track down information. It's the most powerful because it can deliver not only the locations of Web resources related to your search term, but also Gopher menus, FTP files, newsgroup messages, and more. Web searching is also powerful because search results are almost always reported as a directory of links: you can easily jump to any resource the search reveals.

However, it's not as easy, even for an automated database engine, to poll and catalog the Web as it is for Archie, for example, to poll all anonymous FTP sites or for Veronica to poll all of Gopherspace. When you conduct a Web search, you almost always find *something.* But the databases built and searched by Web engines (or even by hardworking Webmasters) simply cannot be comprehensive. Inevitably, there's relevant stuff out there that a Web search misses.

That's why, when choosing from among the available Web searching tools, you must pay close attention to what the search database is built from. Is it built from document titles, URLs, keywords in the text, or all three? Always seek out a search engine whose database is built from information where your search term is likely to be found. You can usually find details about how a search tool's database is maintained through an About... link that appears somewhere on the tool's home page.

Ultimately, however, consider what matters most: what you miss or what you find? I say the latter. With that spirit in mind, this chapter discovers and demonstrates tools and techniques that cast a broad net over the Web (is that a mixed metaphor?).

Starting Points

I have a confession to make. There aren't many Web search tools. There are only a half-dozen of any real consequence—plus a gaggle of lesser tools that can come in handy. There are few enough, in fact, that a "trial and error" approach to searching is not a bad way to go. Pick a tool, try your search term, then try a variation or two. No luck? Try the same terms in another tool.

Yes, I know, high-IQ Web surfers make a carefully calculated, intellectually supportable decision about which search engine provides the highest mathematical probability of a *hit.* But when you think about it, isn't the very idea of the Web to enable disorganized, undisciplined people like me to click around at random until we're happy? Why should I suddenly think rigidly about the Web just because I'm searching?

My approach requires that you know good starting places from which you can access several different tools. You can try one out and if you don't get results, use the Back button to backtrack to the starting point and try another tool.

Perhaps the most convenient starting points are the default home pages of the Web browsers. Like all savvy Web-based businesses, the browser makers have peppered their home pages with handy links to draw you in—so that you can see their ads. It's a fair deal. Netscape's home page is an especially useful starting place for searches because it contains a link to a set of Net Directories and a link to a set of Net Searches. (If you use Netscape Navigator, you can reach these lists anytime, whether you're at the home page or not, by clicking the Net Directory or Net Search button.)

The Search/Directory Schism

Web-based search tools are generally separated into two groups:

- **Directories** are databases containing index trees of Web document titles, URLs, and descriptive information. In general, directories are created and maintained by people and expanded by contributions from others on the Web who want their favorite sites included. Often, a directory has its own search engine for locating information within the directory database by search term. In some cases, however, you are expected to browse through indexed categories and lists to find what you want.
- **Web spiders**, sometimes also called *crawlers, worms,* or simply *search engines,* are typically more detailed databases of Web information that include not only titles and URLs, but often keywords from within documents. Of necessity, these databases are created and updated by automated polling programs whose names suggest the way they squiggle around the Web gathering information. Because they contain such a depth of data, these search tools are accompanied by sophisticated search engines for locating information by keyword.

For example, selecting Net Search from the Netscape home page (`http://home.mcom.com`) brings up a screen like the one shown in Figure 18.1, which includes links to three keyword-searchable spiders. You can type a search term and initiate an Info Seek search directly from the home page or you can select one of the other two search engines.

Similarly, Mosaic's home page features a section called Starting Points, which has links to a variety of Web resources, including a glossary of Web terms and links to Web search facilities. (See Figure 18.2.)

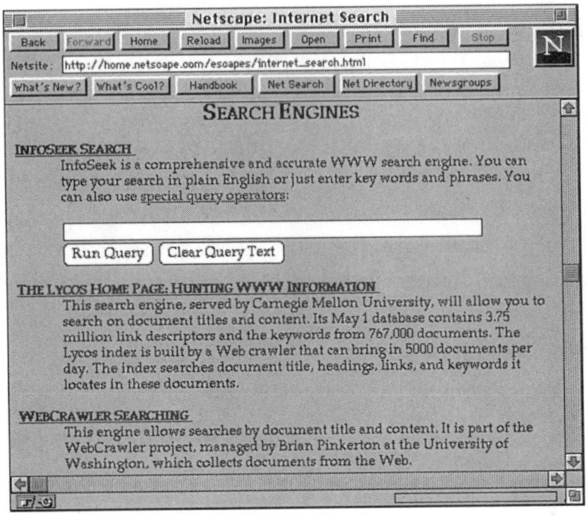

FIGURE 18.1.
Links to search engines are accessed through Netscape's home page, `http://home.mcom.com`.

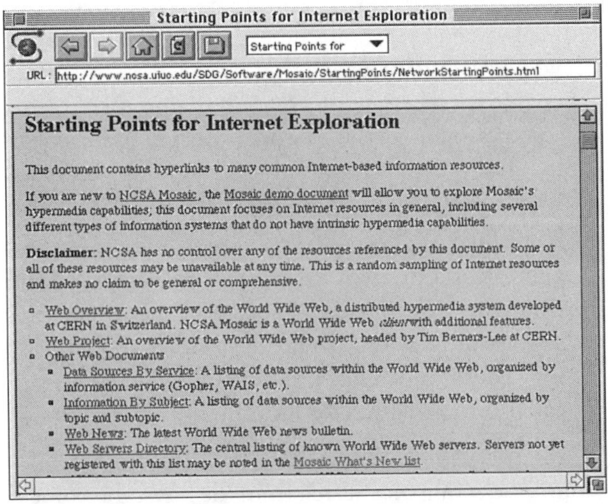

FIGURE 18.2.
Links to directories are accessible through Mosaic's home page, `http://www.ncsa.uiuc.edu/SDG/Software/Mosaic/NCSAMosaicHome.html`.

Another great starting point is the Clearinghouse for Subject-Oriented Internet Resource Guides, a joint effort of the University of Michigan's University Library and the School of Information and Library Studies. Students find and build links to dozens of searchable Internet directories so that the links can all be accessed from a single point, the Clearinghouse. (See Figure 18.3.) Some of the guides are just text, but increasingly, the guides are Web pages containing links to other places on the Internet.

Another valuable "directory of directories," the W3 Search Engines Meta-Index, is a directory of links to dozens of other search engines. What's most useful about the Meta-Index is that it offers some guidelines about which search engines are appropriate for finding certain kinds of information. For example, in Figure 18.4, you'll see that you can access directories of search engines based on whether you're "looking for" servers, software, people, and so on.

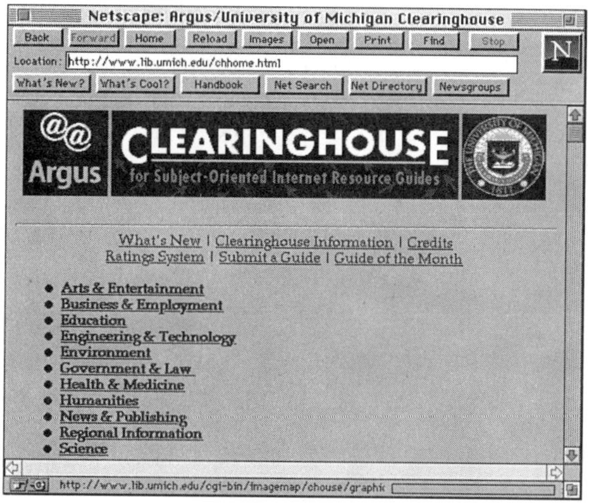

FIGURE 18.3.
The Clearinghouse for Subject-Oriented Internet Resource Guides at http://www.lib.umich.edu/chhome.html.

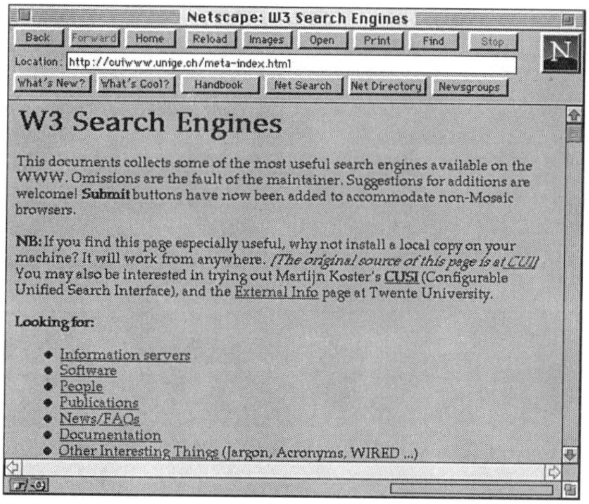

FIGURE 18.4.
The top of the W3 Search Engines Meta-Index, at `http://cuiwww.unige.ch/meta-index.html`.

Finding the addresses of other Internet users is especially tricky on the Internet, as you learned in Chapter 17, "Finding People." Choosing People from the Meta-Index directory shown in Figure 18.4 provides access to five different search engines for finding other Internet users, as shown in Figure 18.5. In Figure 18.5, note also that the Meta-Index enables you to enter search terms and initiate searches without first navigating to the search engine's home page.

Finally, the World Wide Web Virtual Library (described later in this chapter) includes a page of links to other virtual libraries (see Figure 18.6), which are directories of Web information that can be searched by subject.

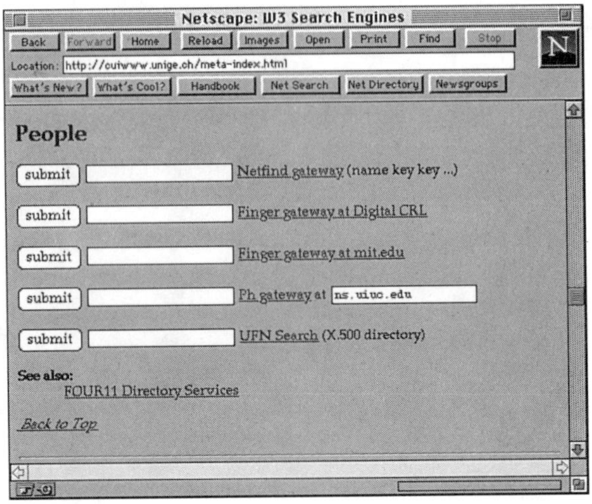

FIGURE 18.5.
People-finding tools can be accessed through the Meta-Index.

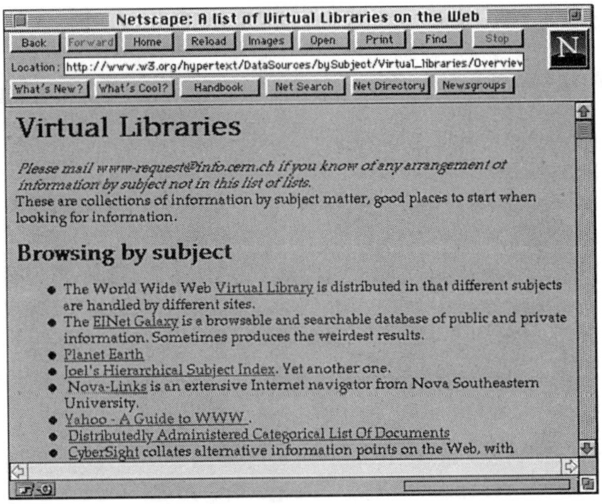

FIGURE 18.6.
The Virtual Libraries page of the WWW Virtual Library at `http://www.w3.org/hypertext/DataSources/bySubject/Virtual_libraries/Overview.html`.

Web Directories

The next several pages describe useful directories of Web-based information. These directories are databases built by people, usually by accepting submissions from Webmasters who want their pages listed. Directories are organized hierarchically and list links representing general categories, each of which leads to more specific subcategories and ultimately to entries describing Web pages, newsgroups, FTP files, and other Web-accessible items. Some directories also have accompanying search tools; others don't.

Yahoo

Yahoo stands for *Yet Another Hierarchical Oracle.* (The developers invite you to fill in whatever you want for the second *O.*) Yahoo is a hierarchical index of the Web. The database is written and maintained by David Filo and Jerry Yang, self-proclaimed yahoos. Anyone else who wants to add to the database is invited to do so; the yahoos themselves verify any additions before making them official.

You can browse Yahoo easily because it's organized hierarchically. As you can probably tell from Figure 18.7, you can click on a link named for a subject (Art, Business, and so on) to display a further set of links related to that topic. Typically, you navigate down several levels before hitting actual links to Web pages and other resources.

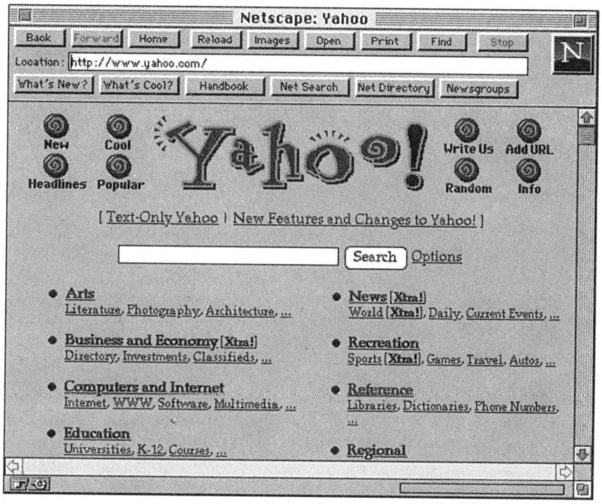

FIGURE 18.7.
Yahoo's home page at `http://www.yahoo.com/`.

> **Tip**
>
> Just under the title in the page shown in Figure 18.7, you'll notice four fun Yahoo links:
>
> - **What's New?** Displays links to the latest URLs added to the Yahoo database.
> - **What's Cool?** Displays links to URLs the yahoos consider fun.
> - **What's Popular?** Displays links to the 50 links most frequently accessed from Yahoo.
> - **A Random Link.** Links you somewhere, completely at random. Close your eyes and see where you end up.

In Figure 18.7, observe the links just above the list of categories. Up is used to navigate up one level in the Yahoo hierarchy; Suggest enables you to make suggestions to the developers; Add enables you to add a URL to the Yahoo database.

The Search link brings up a surprisingly sophisticated search engine. (See Figure 18.8.) The search engine enables you to specify whether to look for your search term in document titles, URLs, or comments (descriptive text). You can also use case-sensitive matching, string/substring matching, and Boolean phrasing. (See Chapter 15, "The Tough Truth about Internet Searches," for more about phrasing search strings.)

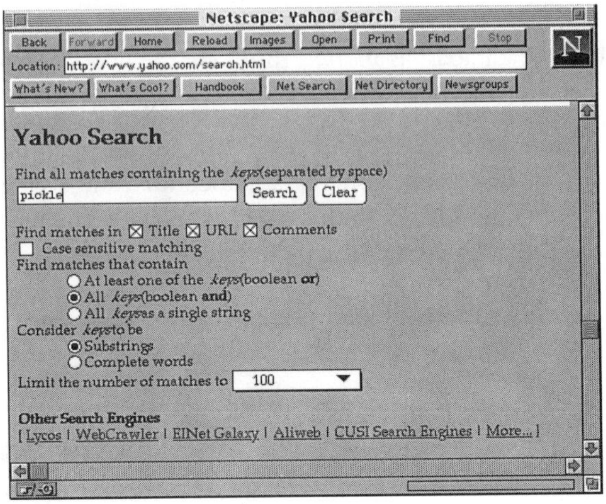

FIGURE 18.8.
Phrasing a Yahoo search.

In the example in Figure 18.8, I'm searching for information about *pickle*. I've decided to search all types of information in the database, turned off case-sensitivity, and designated my search term as a substring so that *pickles*, *picklepuss*, and *pickler* are all considered matches. At the bottom of Figure 18.8, note that I can specify the maximum number of hits to report. I've chosen 100, the default.

The results of my search appear in Figure 18.9. Each result is a link. Note that my search term is highlighted in each result to show the context in which each hit related to my search term. If I am unhappy with the results, I can click the Back button at the top of the screen to return to the Yahoo search page, from which I can rephrase my search.

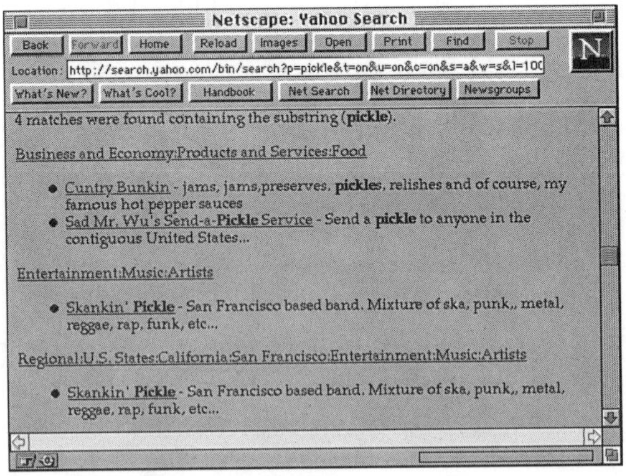

FIGURE 18.9.
Results of the Yahoo search phrased in Figure 18.8.

Tip

> The creators of Web search tools really want you to find what you're looking for—even if you have to use somebody else's search tool to do it. They are very responsible about supplying on their own pages links to other search engines.

When working within any Web search tool, look near the top and near the bottom of pages for links to other search tools. (*Hint:* To see the bottom of a Web page, you may have to use the scroll bar to scroll to the very bottom.) For example, if you scroll to the very bottom of the Yahoo home page (`http://www.yahoo.com`), you see links to the next three directories described—The WWW Virtual Library, EINet Galaxy, and the Whole Internet Catalog. If you scroll to the bottom of the Yahoo search page (`http://www.yahoo.com/search.html`), you see links to Web-based search engines.

EINet Galaxy is another searchable directory, similar in many respects to Yahoo but containing much more data. Like Yahoo, EINet Galaxy has a search engine for finding any entry in the EINet database.

You can try out EINet at `http://www.einet.net/galaxy.html`.

WWW Virtual Library

The WWW Virtual Library (formerly known as the CERN Virtual Library) is maintained by World Wide Web Consortium, the group overseeing the Web as a whole. It is probably the most comprehensive of all Web directories, not just because the Consortium heads it, but because the Consortium relies on others—often leaders in a field—to create and maintain directories of links related to a given subject. The library supplies a link to that directory. Some of the directories covering scientific or social disciplines, for example, are actually managed by university departments in the subject field. The maintainers are in a position to know exactly where the best information can be found—and can supply links to that information.

Figure 18.10 shows the Virtual Library's home page (`http://www.w3.org/hypertext/DataSources/bySubject/Overview.html`), which offers general information about the library and links to useful ancillary information. Scroll down past this introductory information to discover the subject headings shown in Figure 18.11.

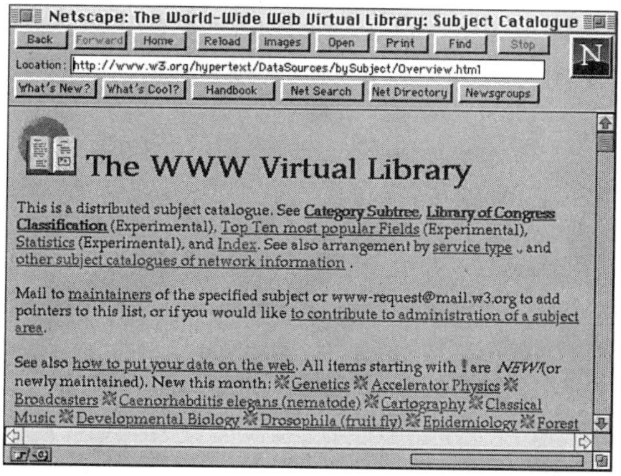

FIGURE 18.10.
The top of the home page of the WWW Virtual Library, at `http://www.w3.org/hypertext/DataSources/bySubject/Overview.html`.

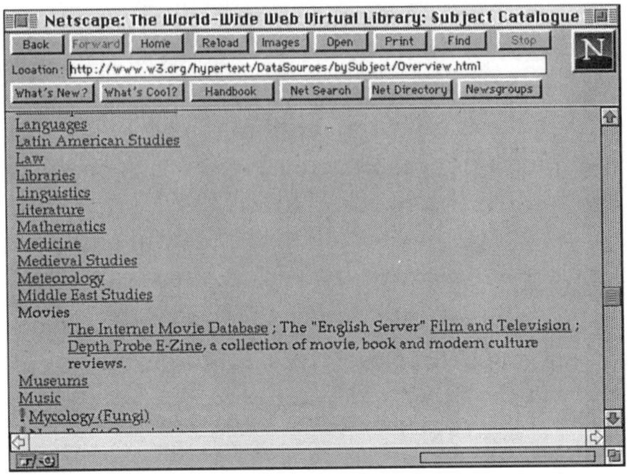

FIGURE 18.11.
Further down on the home page of the WWW Virtual Library, where the subject links live.

When I select the Latin American Studies link in the screen shown in Figure 18.11, I get the directory shown in Figure 18.12. Although it was accessed through the Virtual Library, note that this directory is created and maintained by the Latin American Network Information Center at the University of Texas, a leader in the field of Latin American Studies.

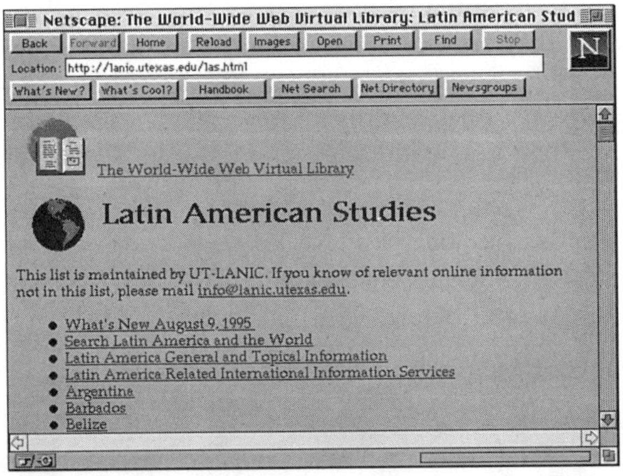

FIGURE 18.12.
A directory of links to Latin American Studies information.

Note

> Although the WWW Virtual Library is a valuable browsing tool, it lacks, at this writing, a search engine. To find something, you must click your way through the categories or consult the Index (accessible from a link in the top paragraph of the home page).

When viewing the subject headings in the WWW Virtual Library, you can choose to see the list in either of two ways. You toggle between the two views by selecting the link following the word *See* in the second sentence at the top of the home page. (See Figure 18.10, shown previously.)

- The Overview view shows just the top-level headings. Figure 18.11 shows headings in Overview view.
- The Category Subtree view shows the subject headings as well as any subcategories. (See Figure 18.13.)

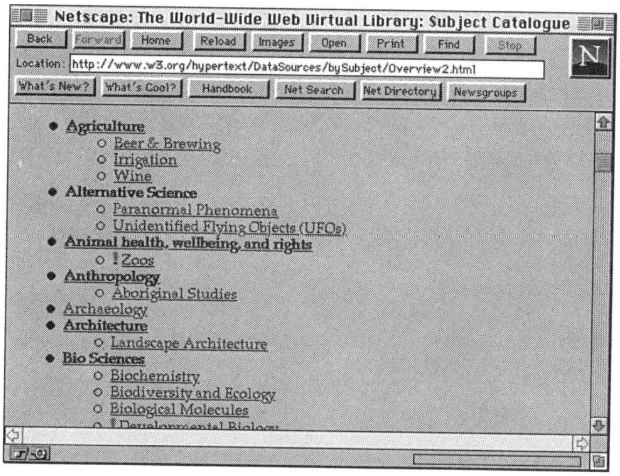

FIGURE 18.13.
The WWW Virtual Library Category Subtree view.

Whole Internet Catalog

The Whole Internet Catalog is a collection of links to more than 1,000 Internet resources, organized by subject and divided into easy-to-surf subject areas. In the screen shown in Figure 18.14, note that the Catalog sells advertising space on its home page.

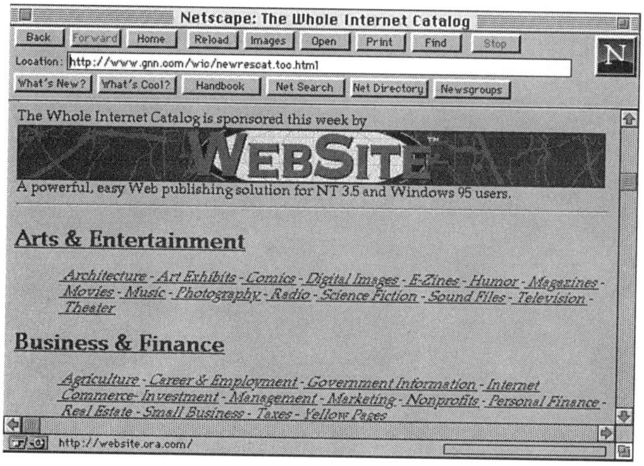

FIGURE 18.14.
The Whole Internet Catalog, at `http://www.gnn.com/wic/newrescat.toc.html`.

Web Spiders

The next several pages describe useful "spider"-based searchable databases of Web-based information. Remember that there are two basic types of Web search tools: *directories*, whose databases are largely built by people, and *spiders* (or *crawlers*, or *worms*, or any other crawly name), which use a program that regularly connects to and checks out areas of the Internet to build its database.

Lycos

Created at Carnegie Mellon University, the Lycos spider employs an unusual approach to crawling around the Web and collecting information. It intelligently exercises preferences about which files to search on a server, and what to search for. It accesses an URL and collects simple, basic information from files—titles, headings, the first 20 lines of documents, and any words determined to be important by their placement or frequency. It also makes intelligent choices about which documents to search first, favoring those that show up as links in many other documents (which proves they're used often).

By crawling around this way, Lycos accomplishes two things:

- It amasses a particularly effective cross-section of data without having to index every word in every file.
- It does its data collection work without causing an unacceptable drain on server resources, which Web spiders can do if they try to analyze many documents in rapid succession.

You can reach the Lycos index in a variety of ways. Links to Lycos appear in most directories of search engines. (See Figure 18.1, shown previously.) Lycos has its own home page at `http://lycos.cs.cmu.edu/`. If you select the Net Search button in Netscape Navigator, you arrive at Netscape's Internet search screen listing several search engines. From there, you can click on the Lycos link to go to the Lycos home page, as shown in Figure 18.15.

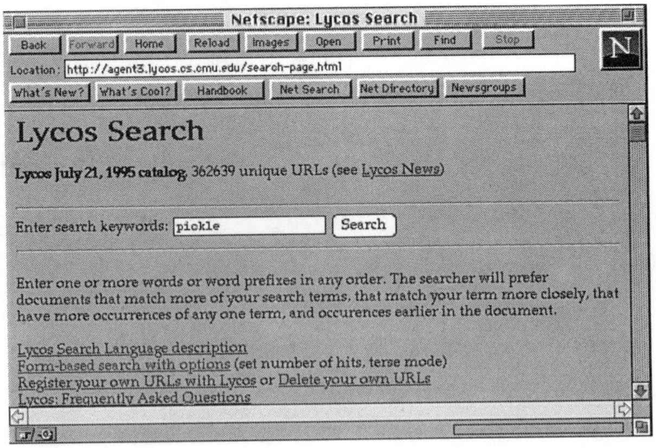

FIGURE 18.15.
A Lycos search.

The basic search from either the big or small Lycos catalogue (see Figure 18.5, shown previously) is made deliberately simple: enter a term and click Start Search. A few more options are available if you click the Lycos Search Form link; a screen like the one in Figure 18.16 appears. From this screen, you can control the number of hits (pages) to report, the number of keywords in your search term, and a "relevance ranking." Lycos uses its records of the number of times a term occurs in a reference, where it occurs, and other criteria to determine whether a reference is highly relevant (1.0), not at all relevant (0.0), or somewhere in between. On the Lycos Search Form screen, you can specify the minimum relevance level for hits.

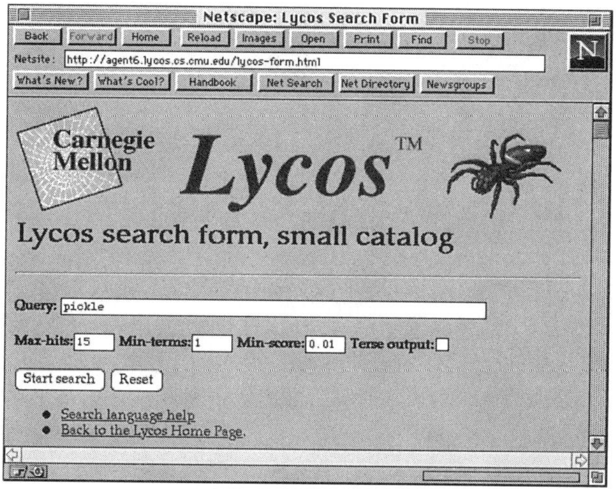

FIGURE 18.16.
An advanced Lycos search using the Lycos Search Form.

WebCrawler

When building its database, WebCrawler not only searches the URLs and links, but also the complete contents of Web documents. That makes WebCrawler's database an excellent choice for finding information buried within documents (the kind of information that may not show up in the URL or a title). WebCrawler searches not only Web URLs (such as `http://`), it also searches Gophers (such as `gopher://`), FTP servers (such as `ftp://`), and other servers off the Web. Its broad search field makes WebCrawler's database a great place to look for things you suspect may not even reside on Web servers. The disadvantage of WebCrawler is that, because it searches so thoroughly, it can't update itself very often.

Searching is simple. A checkbox lets you use the Boolean `AND` when you type more than one word in the search box; otherwise, the search is assumed to be a Boolean `OR` search. You can also control the number of results (hits) to report. Figure 18.17 shows a WebCrawler search. WebCrawler's home page is located at `http://webcrawler.com/`.

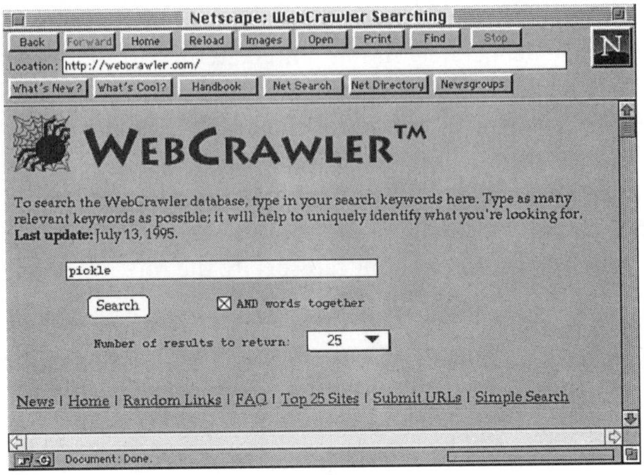

FIGURE 18.17.
A WebCrawler search.

World Wide Web Worm

The World Wide Web Worm—also known as WWWW or just *the Worm*—builds its database by searching the Web for URLs, titles, and links. Its search engine enables you to search either URLs alone or all information in the database. The Worm also supports the use of Boolean phrases through a drop-down list. (See Figure 18.18.) Note that you can also specify the number of matches to report. If you visit the Worm, you'll find several other powerful ways you can tailor your search.

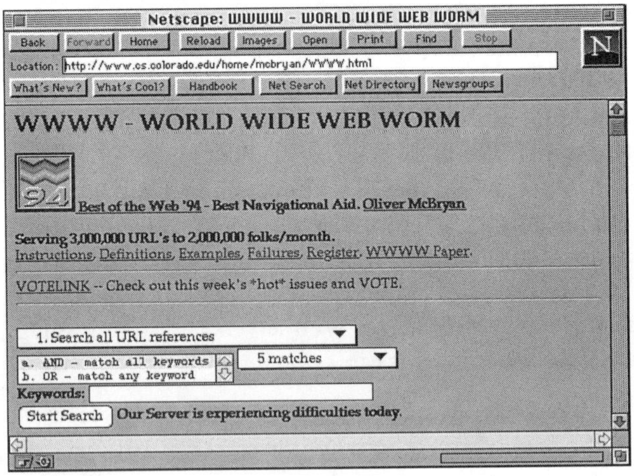

FIGURE 18.18.
The World Wide WebWorm at `http://www.cs.colorado.edu/home/mcbryan/WWWW.html`.

Note

> Although spiders do a great job of building a database from what they find on the Internet, they manage too much information to be updated constantly. And if they were continuously updated, they would cause an unacceptable drain on network resources.
>
> Sometimes, you can tell the age of the database. In Figure 18.17, which shows the WebCrawler, you can see a line that says `Last update:` followed by a calendar date. In Worm, you will see a line that says `Last Run:` followed by a calendar date.
>
> The Worm database was almost two months old when I accessed it. Although the overwhelming majority of the database entries would still be valid, some links would inevitably fail because of resources that were removed, moved, or renamed.

Summary

Like everything else on the Web, searching the Web is both simple and complicated at the same time. But you needn't worry about that. When you want to find something, begin with simple and see where it takes you. The complicated takes care of itself.

In Chapter 19, "Finding Stuff Other Ways," you discover still more ways to find what you want on the Internet.

CHAPTER 19

FINDING STUFF OTHER WAYS

I've always had a little trouble with categories. As soon as I see someone pigeonholing anything—philosophies, people, fruit, socks and underwear, colored blocks—into discrete groups, my mind zeroes in on all the exceptions, the things that don't fit. That's why my apartment looks the way it does (don't ask).

The result of that peculiarity is that I always end up with leftovers after I've categorized what I could. The Internet is such a vast, varied place that you can't simply squeeze it all into nicely defined chapters. So you arrive here at my favorite category in all things: "Miscellaneous." This chapter covers everything I thought up but couldn't manage to reasonably fit elsewhere.

In this chapter, you'll discover other Internet resources—and some offline resources—as well, for making the most of the Internet. The main value of these resources, as they relate to this part of the book, is that they provide directions to Internet sites that may interest you. But they all have other benefits, as well. So don't label them. Take 'em or leave 'em for what they are.

Other Online Resources

The next several pages offer suggestions for finding helpful information about the Internet and the resources within it. The addresses are all entered in Universal Resource Locator (URL) format. Using a Web browser, enter each address exactly as shown. To use a resource through its specific client (that is, a Gopher client, newsreader, and so on), omit the part of the URL up to and including the double slashes (`//`).

For example, to reach the Net-Happenings newsgroup described in this chapter, you use one of the following:

- In a **Web browser**: `news:comp.internet.net-happenings`
- In a **Newsreader client**: `comp.internet.net-happenings`

Newsgroups

```
news:comp.internet.net-happenings
news:alt.best.of.internet
news:news.newusers.questions
```

These three newsgroups are always good resources for general information about the Internet. They are also excellent places to post questions about where to find a particular resource or type of information.

The Net-Happenings Mailing List

The Net-Happenings mailing list keeps you apprised of important (or interesting) developments and events on the Net. It includes the contents of the `comp.internet.net-happenings` newsgroup. Send e-mail to the following address:

```
majordomo@is.internic.net
```

In the message body, include only the words `subscribe net-happenings`.

The Electronic Frontier Foundation

`gopher://gopher.eff.org`

An advocacy group that lobbies for freedom of expression on the Internet, the EFF is an excellent source of information about Internet politics and events. In particular, the EFF is leading the resistance to online censorship. The EFF Gopher also provides links to other civil rights and advocacy groups, such as the America Civil Liberties Union (ACLU).

Apple Computer, Inc.

`http://www.apple.com/`

Information about Apple and easy access to online software files for Macintosh. (See Figure 19.1.)

FIGURE 19.1.
Apple Web site.

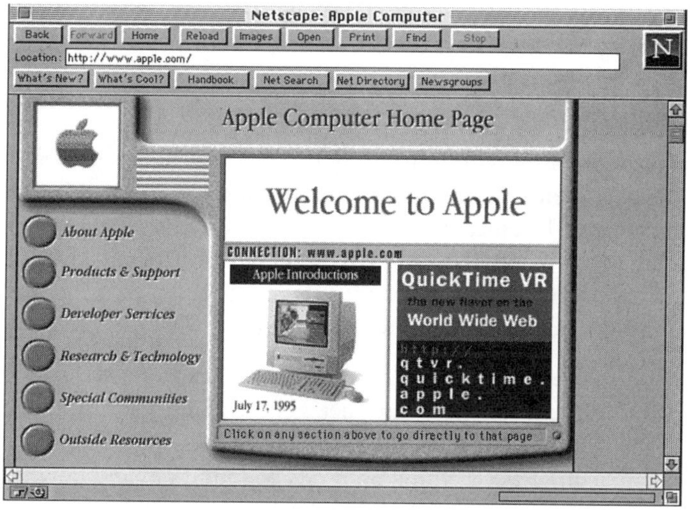

Internet Network Information Center (InterNIC)

`gopher://gopher.internic.net`

InterNIC offers a broad set of Internet reference and information services (once, they even offered a real voice line for answering any Internet question, but no more). Through InterNIC's Gopher, you can see (or download) a "directory of directories" to assist your navigation, read InterNIC's online newsletter, find out about Internet seminars, and much more.

Offline Resources

The following pages describe helpful Internet resources you can use offline.

Seminars

Several companies offer Internet seminars around the country. Local service providers often hold Internet seminars to drum up new customers. InterNIC (see "Internet Network Information Center," earlier in this chapter) holds seminars all over the United States.

In the summer of 1995, Apple toured the United States presenting free Internet Publishing seminars for educators and business people. For the latest on Apple events like this one, check Apple's Web site (mentioned earlier in this chapter).

Tip

> You may also find good Internet courses offered through your nearest community college or adult education center. (After reading this book, you'll be bored by a beginner's course. Look for an intermediate or advanced curriculum.)

Software-Based Internet Guides

Software publishers are putting out CD-ROM-based guides to the Internet, featuring databases of reference information, on-screen instruction, and even technical information, such as the details of Internet standards and specifications. Although these disc-based guides may be useful, their obvious flaw is that they fall out-of-date quickly and don't teach the use of specific client applications—in some ways the hardest part of using the Internet. Yes, I know, books fall out-of-date, too—but books are cheaper.

- **Internet Info** (from Walnut Creek Software). A CD-ROM containing thousands of documents covering Internet technical information, plus archives of thousands of FAQ files. Although the CD pulls all these files together in one handy place, be aware that almost everything on it can be found on, and downloaded from, the Internet for free. Also, if you pick this stuff up online instead of from the CD, you have the assurance that each file you read is the most up-to-date version; inevitably, the CD will fall out of date.
- **Internet for Everybody** (Emerging Technology Applications). A beginner's CD-ROM tutorial for the Internet, with two hours of video clips containing personal instruction from real faces.

Magazines

All the general-interest PC and Windows magazines have begun to cover the Internet regularly, offering software reviews and announcements of new and exciting resources. Several other magazines are exclusively dedicated to coverage of online communication (principally the Internet, but they also include America Online and other commercial services).

- *Wired.* The leader in the field, *Wired* mixes technical articles with thought-provoking analysis of online culture and issues. It may be a little on the techie side for true novices.
- *The Net.* A new magazine, *The Net* is aimed at novices and features how-to articles, analysis, and listings of new and interesting places to visit online.
- *NetGuide.* Another new magazine, *NetGuide* mixes helpful advice columns and commentary with notes about the latest and greatest sites—all in a familiar consumer-style magazine that's less funky than *Wired* or *The Net. NetGuide* is aimed at a reader a little more Internet-literate than a reader of *The Net* but a little less Net-literate than a reader of *Wired.*

> **Note**
>
> *NetGuide* is also available online, at this address:
>
> `http://techweb.cmp.com/net/current`
>
> *The Net* hosts it's own Web site, as well (see Figure 19.2), at this location:
>
> `http://www.thenet-usa.com/`

FIGURE 19.2.
The Net *magazine online.*

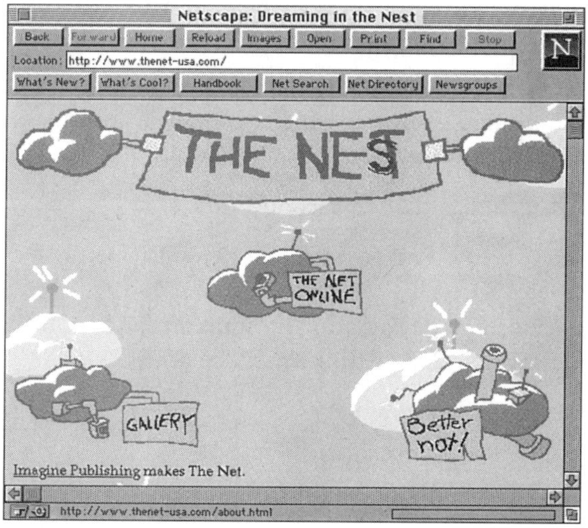

Books

The book you are reading provides a thorough introduction to using the Internet with your Macintosh. From here, you can certainly discover online everything else you need to know. However, you can't take the Internet with you on the subway, or other places you may want to expand your knowledge without tying up a phone line. The Internet and Macintosh titles that follow offer excellent expansion on what you've learned here (of course they do; they are all published by Sams or Sams.net Publishing). All are written at an appropriate level for anyone who has read this book.

The Internet

The Internet Unleashed, Second Edition

Authors: (More than 40 Internet experts)
Pages: 1,384
A best-selling encyclopedia (now in its second edition) of the Internet and everything that's on it, geared to Windows, Mac, and UNIX users as well.

The World Wide Web Unleashed, Second Edition

Authors: John December and Neil Randall
Pages: 1,346
A compendium of all that is the Web, including advanced navigation tips and instructions for creating Web pages and sites.

Your Internet Consultant

Author: Kevin M. Savetz
Pages: 550
A handy Internet reference guide organized in a useful question-and-answer format.

Teach Yourself the Internet in a Week, Second Edition

Author: Neil Randall
Pages: 675
A thorough, all-purpose Internet guide featuring scenarios for applying the Internet in business, education, and scientific tasks.

The Internet Business Guide, Second Edition

Authors: Rosalind Resnick and Dave Taylor
Pages: 450
A detailed guide to setting up shop on the Net. Sample business scenarios include creating an online customer service center.

Education on the Internet

Author: Jill H. Ellsworth
Pages: 591
Insightful, complete information on the many educational applications of the Internet for teachers, professors, and students.

Curious about the Internet?

Author: Ned Snell
Pages: 247
An easy-to-read introduction to the world of the Internet. Some of what this book covers you already know, but this concise, inexpensive book covers many aspects of Internet history and culture not included in the navigation-oriented *Navigating the Internet with Your Macintosh*. A good way to round out your Internet education.

eWorld

eWorld: The Official Guide for Macintosh Users

Authors: Cary Lu and John Milligan
Pages: 403
The authorized handbook to Apple's online service, includes eWorld software package. For beginners to advanced users.

Summary

The principle Internet search tools—Archie, Veronica, and the Web search engines—are often the most reliable starting points to find anything on the Internet. But they are not the only starting points. You can find informative, insightful Internet information in many places, sometimes where you'd least expect.

This chapter concludes Part III of this book. In Part IV, "Putting It Together," you find advice for applying the Internet to three important disciplines—business, education, and fun.

PART IV

PUTTING IT TOGETHER

CHAPTER 20

USING THE INTERNET IN THE OFFICE

How Is the Internet a Business Tool?

The Bottom Line: Getting Started

Internet Professional Resources

Job Hunting

Internet Business Resources

Summary

It doesn't matter how you define yourself—as a seller, as a buyer, or as a disinterested bystander. As you travel the Internet, one way or another, you move through a commercial environment. Once a public square with the occasional street vendor, the Internet is rapidly becoming a mall—a public place where buying and selling are not absolutely required, but are hard to ignore. The Internet has always offered great resources in support of careers and professions, and you're likely to find on the Net plenty of help with your career. But if you're also entrepreneurially inclined, you may want to know how the Internet doesn't just *assist* business but can actually be a *vehicle* for commerce.

As you may know, the commercialization of the Internet has been its central controversy for the last several years. Much of the die-hard Internet community has been resistant to business uses of the Net, hoping to preserve the Internet as an oasis of commercial-free communication in an overly commercial world. Although the corporate world has used the Internet as an international e-mail backbone and research tool for many years, only recently has the potential of the Net as a place to buy and sell been explored.

Grow Up—It Was Always Commercial

Of course, the concept of the Internet as an egalitarian, non-profit, utopian, fat-free society never held water. Its first users were *defense contractors* (name me one *less* utopian enterprise). Despite today's defining presence of think-tanks, universities, and non-profit organizations, commercial users have outnumbered non-commercial users for many years.

The notion of a business-free Internet grew out of the U.S. government's National Science Foundation (NSF), which for a time administered an important portion of the Internet, NSFnet, a network of academic and government computers. Although NSF exerted no control over the Internet at large, its "Acceptable Use Policy" restricted commercial activity on its own network. Even that policy—which was little enforced—allowed some kinds of commercial activity. In 1991, most NSFnet anti-commercial policies began phasing out; by mid-1995, NSFnet was for all intents and purposes nullified by the government's withdrawal of any sanction or control over national internetworks.

The only checks and balances on the Internet today are enforced by the collective will of its participants. See "The Dos and Don'ts of Net Commerce," later in this chapter.

This chapter describes how business is done on the Internet. It also lists some good resources that can help you embark on your own online business venture.

How Is the Internet a Business Tool?

The original and still most common business use of the Internet (other than e-mail) is research. Obviously, the wealth of free information available in newsgroups and through Gopher and the Web can be valuable for marketing, acquisitions, product development, regulations research, and many other business research activities. The Internet also offers a wealth of information in support of many different professional disciplines and is also an important source of detailed economic and financial data, both domestic and international. A number of important financial journals are available on the Internet as well. (See Figure 20.1.)

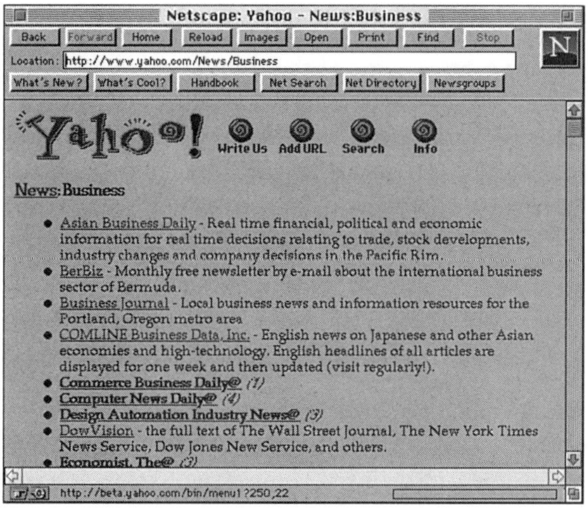

FIGURE 20.1.
A list of Web links to business journals and other business-related news sources (`http://www.yahoo.com/News/Business`).

As the United States and other leading industrial nations move deeper into service-based economies, we are finding that *communication* is business. A huge number of business services can be provided almost completely over the computer. If a service can be performed on a computer, it can be marketed to clients everywhere. The Internet provides a communications medium through which clients can send work to distant service providers, and providers can transmit the results back. Such services include the following:

- Financial management and accounting
- Legal services
- Consulting
- Design
- Electronic publishing and other document services
- Research services
- Custom programming services

Although the Internet provides the point-to-point communications vehicle for supplying these services, it may be more significant as a presentation medium for marketing these and other products. In particular, the World Wide Web is shaping up as the perfect electronic billboard: it can show off splashy graphics and multimedia and can offer hyperlinks to expanded information about a company's products and services. As things stand, there is much more advertising on the Net than there is selling. In particular, companies whose product can't really be sold on the Net are nonetheless advertising there for the sheer visibility value. These advertisers include movie studios, television networks, and auto companies.

It's easy to overstate the importance of the Internet as an advertising medium today. Although there are millions of potential customers on the Net, their activities are fragmented among thousands of different activities. It's impossible to draw to a Web page the kinds of crowds you can get with a national TV commercial. Then again, a Web page is cheaper than a commercial, and it may grab and hold customers for much longer than the 15 or 30 seconds of exposure a commercial provides.

An important characteristic of the Internet as an advertising (and selling) medium is that it's an inherently *narrowcast* environment. The population is spread among resources defined by area of interest; to advertise, you must lead customers to your message based on their area of interest. There's no accepted way today to "blitz" the Net with broad visibility. On the other hand, the small proportion of Net users you can manage to attract to your ad are a preselected, well-targeted group—something advertisers today pay special-interest magazines top dollar to draw.

Leading Customers to an Ad

The Internet isn't like television or billboards. In most cases, customers don't simply "come across" an ad while looking for something else. Advertisers have to find ways to incite customers to deliberately navigate to a Web page where the pitch is waiting.

There are two exceptions: First, as you see later in this chapter, magazines are being published on the Web itself. Many online 'zines publish only articles, depending on their print versions to deliver ad revenue. But a few have recognized that they can sell ad space within the online versions. Just as with print magazines, the articles in online 'zines draw a selected audience; advertisers pay the publisher for ad space (or, more accurately, for a hyperlink from the magazine pages) to sell that audience. This is likely to become one of the principle advertising methods on the Net.

The other exception is offered by local Internet service providers, who sometimes cleverly set up their own Web home pages and then configure those pages as the default home page in the browsing software they supply to subscribers. Whenever subscribers fire up their browsers, the first thing they see is their provider's home page, which may feature advertising, usually from local companies. Although this approach comes dangerously close to forcing ads on people (an Internet no-no—see "The Dos and Don'ts of Net Commerce," later in this chapter), users can easily reconfigure their browsers to use a different default home page and avoid the pitch, if they so choose.

Outside these two exceptions, advertisers must let their potential customers know where their home pages are, and must draw customers in by promising nifty graphics or other carrots-on-sticks. (For example, the major movies studios often post video clips of current hits on their pages—an extremely popular lure.) To inform customers of the page's location, advertisers are increasingly listing the site address in their regular print advertising; they may also post brief, non-assertive notices in newsgroups whose subscribers tend to have an interest in the product.

The logical extension of Internet advertising is Internet selling. After all, if customers can see a picture of your product on the Web, and read about it through a hyperlink to a product description, why shouldn't they be able to order it right then, when the electronic pitch is burning a hole in their pockets? Unfortunately, online sales is a real sticking point of online business.

As it stands, the Internet is simply not a very secure place for people to send others their credit card numbers or bank account information—currently, the only two means of performing online transactions. Similar transactions made today over the telephone are a major source of fraud, which is why businesses are approaching online sales very cautiously—and with good reason. (See the next section, "The Open Question: Security.")

It wouldn't be very difficult for a "cracker" or an unscrupulous system administrator to harvest credit card information from online transactions moving through the Net, make his or her own purchases using stolen credit card information, and then cover his or her tracks before anyone knew what happened. For their parts, VISA and MasterCard each maintain a Web site to show how credit cards can be used today and what's being done to make credit-card transactions more secure. (See Figure 20.2.) These sites also offer consumer services, such as maps of ATM locations.

FIGURE 20.2.
MasterCard's Web page at `http://www.mastercard.com`.

One good way to learn about companies doing business on the Net is through CommerceNet, a consortium of companies dedicated to exploring the Net's commercial potential. These advertisers' Web pages can be reached directly, of course, but CommerceNet maintains a page of links to them to help you find them all. CommerceNet's home page also includes information about the CommerceNet project and good general information about doing business on the Web. (See Figure 20.3.)

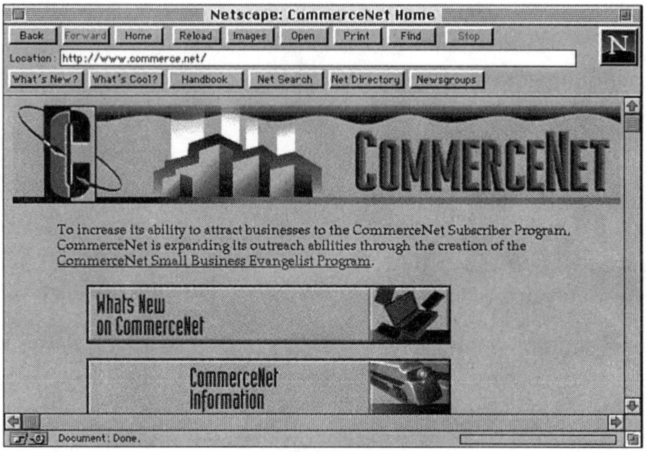

FIGURE 20.3.
CommerceNet's Web page at `http://www.commerce.net`.

> **Note**
>
> CommerceNet is not the only engine to which companies have hitched their cars. Another, the Internet Mall, also maintains a list of links to Internet sellers. Bear in mind, however, that selling can be done anywhere on the Web and in other Internet resources, so long as it is done using accepted practices (see "The Dos and Don'ts of Net Commerce," later in this chapter). A company does not have to be part of CommerceNet or any other shopping center to sell, although it's possible that the companies benefit from their shared presence under one roof (after all, that's where the shoppers are going). Note that CommerceNet, populated by corporations with deep pockets, charges a hefty membership fee to companies that want to be a part of CommerceNet.

The Internet itself is also a publishing medium. There are many newspapers and magazines published on the Web (see Chapter 10, "Browsing the World Wide Web"), many of them online versions of publications that are also printed. Recently, science magazine *Omni* pointed the way by announcing it would retire its print version and move the whole operation onto the Web.

The Open Question: Security

Security is a concern for all uses of the Internet, but online financial transactions are a particular problem. There have been several highly publicized cases of online fraud and computer-based theft and espionage. This problem has done more than discourage the adoption of online sales and ordering.

It has also prevented any widescale adoption of the Internet as a backbone for business-to-business transactions such as electronic funds transfers. Many such transactions are performed electronically today, but nearly all are performed over more secure—and more expensive—private communications networks. The banks don't trust the Internet with their money, and neither do large corporations. Think about that before you type your VISA number on a Web page.

The Security Chip

It's likely that the Internet will never be made crime-free, just as no public place can be. Of the many efforts to make it more secure, the most significant is the development of the Clipper chip, a U.S. government–sponsored project to create a microprocessor that could encrypt every message sent over the Internet (and phone calls, as well) in a way that enables only the intended recipient to decrypt it on receipt. Anyone who illegally intercepts the message will be unable to decrypt and use it, thanks to Clipper's sophisticated encryption routines. Clipper supporters hope that the adoption of the chip will inspire the necessary confidence to bring more business transactions online.

The sticking point in the adoption of Clipper is whether the government should have the right (after securing a court order) to "borrow" the secret code to Clipper and decrypt messages. The government says it needs this capability to catch high-tech drug traffickers by discovering suspicious transactions and messages. Critics say the government's real interest is making sure that the Internal Revenue Service gets its full cut of the dollars that will change hands online if Internet business takes off. The critics want no one to be able to break the code, for any reason.

Although high-level security systems are required for overall Internet security, two initiatives are underway to make credit card transactions on the Web more secure to encourage online sales. The first, already in use, is Secure Sockets Layer (SSL), developed by Netscape Communications, developer of the Netscape Navigator Web browser. SSL has been endorsed by Microsoft, IBM, and other major companies, and is the security system for a Web shopping center called marketplaceMCI (`http://www.marketplace.internetMCI.com/marketplace`), operated by MCI, the same company that keeps calling you to ask whether you're happy with your current long-distance service. (For more about online shopping, see Chapter 22, "Using the Internet for Family Fun.") The other Web-based security system, yet to debut, is called Secure HTTP and is championed by CommerceNet. At this writing, the jury is still out on both systems.

Until an effective security system is developed for protecting credit-card transactions, the Internet will be a dicey place to sell. Whether that's a reason to stay away or jump right in depends on the type of businessperson you are.

The Dos and Don'ts of Net Commerce

The basic rule for Internet business ventures is passivity—let the buyers come to you, don't reach out and grab them. That philosophy runs counter to everything today's aggressive, competitive businesspeople have been weaned on, but for now, it's the best approach. In a famous case a few years ago, a Phoenix law firm cross-posted an ad to thousands of newsgroups, hoping to drum up some customers. Internet users flamed the firm by e-mail so severely that the law firm's Internet provider had to cut off the firm's account.

A Web page is a great place to advertise, not only because of the sexy ways you can use it to show off your product but also because you can't snare users—any user who navigates to your Web page *wants* to be there. You can post gentle announcements about the existence of the Web page in newsgroups and mailing lists whose topics relate directly to your product or service. Don't advertise in your announcement—simply let people know where your Web page is (or your e-mail address if you're not using the Web), and save the pitch for when they arrive. Obviously, if you want them to come, you have to offer a carrot to get them there—cool video or sound clips, an online game, and so on.

Another good technique for passive advertising is to sponsor something non-commercial and build a Web page for your sponsoree that also happens to promote your company. For example, laser disc maker Voyager Co. sponsors a number of cultural events, including the Nuyorican Cafe, a project promoting Latino poetry and concerts by performance artist Laurie Anderson. Folks are drawn to Voyager's Web site to learn about the Cafe, and while there, discover links to information about Voyager products and services.

The Bottom Line: Getting Started

Here's the bottom line: You can advertise, market, and sell anything on the Internet. And if your product or service can be coded into a computer file and sent over a wire, you can even provide it over the Internet. Today, the Internet is unlikely to make you rich. But success depends on being in the right place at the right time; within a few years, the Internet may well be the right place. If you get started today, you'll be there when it happens.

To get started, think about the type of product or service you supply (or want to supply) and how the Internet can play a role. Check out the rest of this chapter for some great sources offering good starting points and other business-related information.

Note

> The addresses in this section are given in Universal Resource Locator (URL) format. Using a Web browser, enter each address exactly as shown. To use a resource through its specific client (such as a Gopher client, newsreader, and so on) omit the part of the URL up to and including the double slashes (`//`).
>
> For example, to reach the Digital Future Gopher described in this chapter, you use one of the following:
>
> - In a **Web browser:** `gopher://marketplace.com`
> - In a **Gopher client:** `marketplace.com`

Internet Professional Resources

The Internet offers journals, job openings, peer networking opportunities, and other resources for every profession imaginable. Perhaps the best way to locate resources about your profession is to do a Web search (see Chapter 18, "Finding It on the Web") using the name of your professional area (medicine, law, design, and so on) as a search term.

It's impossible to adequately show the breadth of professional resources available on the Internet. But the following few examples may give you an idea.

- **The American Institute of Graphic Arts** (`http://www.dol.com/Root/org/AIGA/AIGAlink.html`)

  A great starting place for professional designers and illustrators.
- **The Engineer's Club** (`http://www.engineers.com/tec.html`)

  The place where the slide-rule set hangs out.
- **The Midwifery Page** (`http://www.csv.warwick.ac.uk:8000/midwifery.html`)

  Links and resources for professional midwives and other childbirth professionals. (See Figure 20.4.)

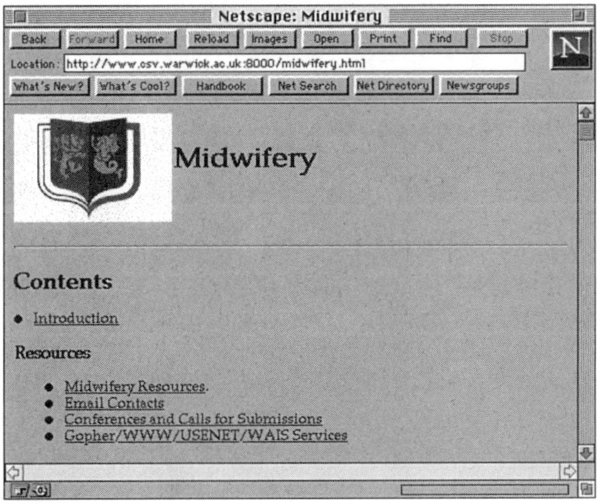

FIGURE 20.4.
The Midwifery page.

Job Hunting

Yes, you can find a job on the Internet—although the jury's out on whether the Internet is really an effective job hunting/recruiting tool. The Internet population is so large and spread out and most recruiters look for a few local people. Still, the want ads are there, and the Internet is as good a place as any to start.

Probably the best way to find a job online is to locate a resource related to that job and then look for job listings. For example, many of the federal government's Web pages feature a link that lists jobs in the department or agency to which the page pertains. You may find job listings at specific companies available from a link on the companies' home pages.

There are also more general job listings available. Figure 20.5 shows the Job Search page, a searchable database of more than 40,000 jobs in Southern California.

FIGURE 20.5.
The Job Search home page at `http://www.adnetsol.com/jsearch/jshome1.html`.

Internet Business Resources

The next several pages describe places to find business information and support services on the Internet.

First, you may want to see a list of links to companies already doing business on the Net. Try the Yahoo directory at `http://www.yahoo.com/Business/Corporations`. (See Figure 20.6.)

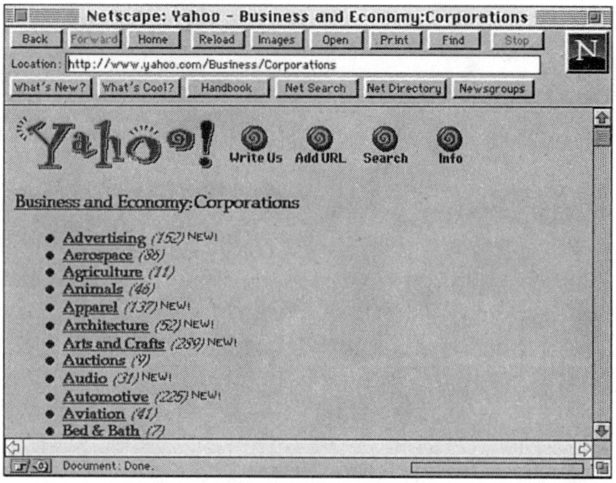

FIGURE 20.6.
A list of links to online business ventures.

Starting an Internet Business

- **Internet Plaza** (`http://plaza.xor.com/plaza/index.html`)

  Internet Plaza offers a range of business services to help companies get started in online business. (See Figure 20.7.)

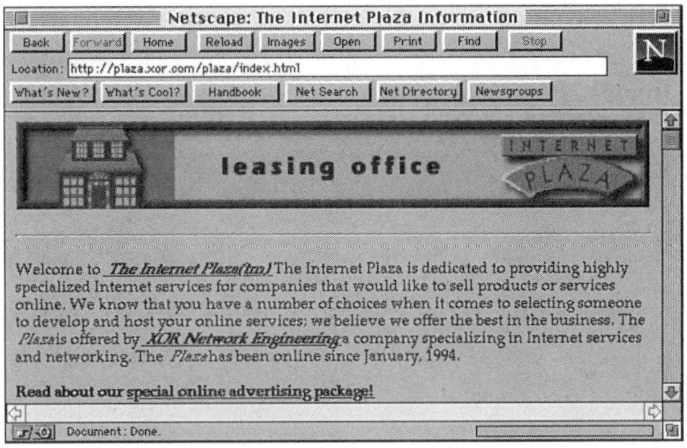

FIGURE 20.7.
Internet Plaza.

- **Digital Future** (`gopher://marketplace.com`)

  An online newsletter about Internet-based commerce.

- **Internet Business Center** (`http://www.tig.com/ibc`)

  A Web server specializing in providing information about business uses of the Internet.

- **Commercial Use Strategies Home Page** (`http://www.netrex.com/business/usage.html`)

  More strategies and tips for online businesses. (See Figure 20.8.)

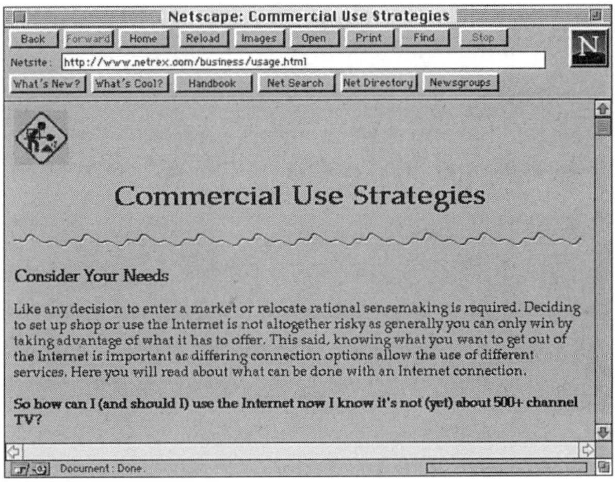

FIGURE 20.8.
Commercial Use Strategies home page.

- **Small Business Administration** (`http://www.sbaonline.sba.gov`)

  A Web page for the U.S. Small Business Administration, created to help new and existing small businesses compete. Includes business development services and links to other resources.

- **Open Market Commercial Sites Index** (`http://www.directory.net`)

  A pile of links to economic information, such as the files of the Financial Services Technology Consortium and the customer support pages of major corporations. (See Figure 20.9.) A great place for ideas.

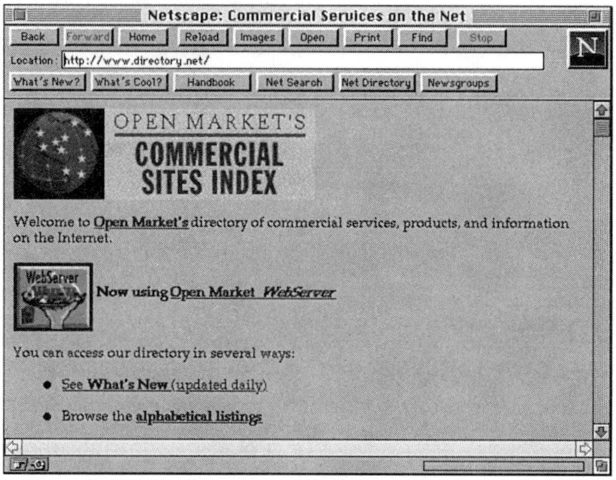

FIGURE 20.9.
The Open Market's Commercial Sites Index.

Economic/Financial Data

- **Financial Economics Network** (`http://www.crimson.com/fen`)

  Created by the editor of the *Journal of Financial Economics*, this home page features abstracts of forthcoming papers and articles and also includes listings of jobs and job-seekers in the field. (See Figure 20.10.)

- **QuoteCom** (`http://www.quote.com`)

  QuoteCom displays stock quotes (delayed 15 minutes), plus a wealth of information from newswires, market data, and more.

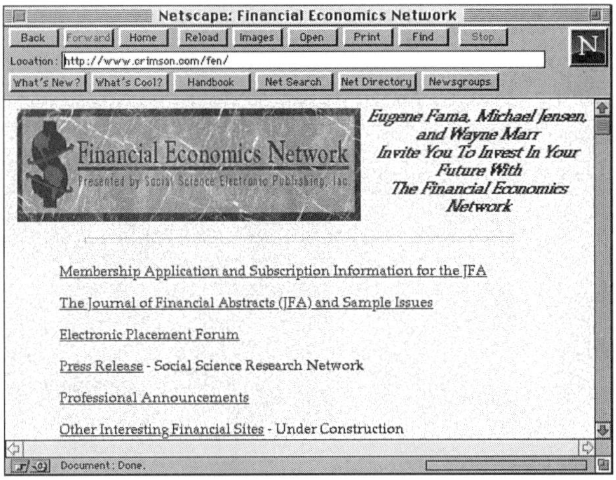

FIGURE 20.10.
The Financial Economics Network.

Advertising

- **Chiat/Day Idea Factory** (`http://www.chiatday.com/factory`)

  Chiat/Day is a former ad agency (now specializing in "brand promotion") whose Web site, a "virtual office," shows off splendidly what a little imagination can do on the Web. (See Figure 20.11.) Whether you do business with Chiat/Day or not, the company's Web pages are a guide to the possibilities.

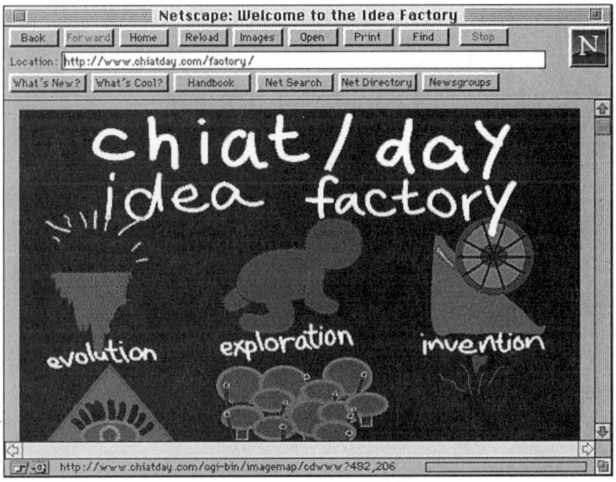

FIGURE 20.11.
Chiat/Day's advertising Web page.

- ***Advertising Age*** (`http://www.adage.com`)

  The venerable advertising magazine and sourcebook, now in an online version. (See Figure 20.12.)

FIGURE 20.12.
Advertising Age *online.*

Summary

Internet business will affect you, whether you buy, sell, or simply try to stay out of the way. You owe it to yourself to check out the ways you can make the most of the emerging business services on the Internet—as a consumer or entrepreneur.

In Chapter 21, "Using the Internet for Education," you'll discover another major discipline for which the Internet offers great support—education.

CHAPTER 21

USING THE INTERNET FOR EDUCATION

Good Starting Points for Teachers

K–12 Resources

Post-Secondary Resources

Summary

After human teachers, the Internet would represent the most important educational resource in the world if every student had a computer. That not being the case, the Internet as it stands is an exercise in the expansion of inequality. By and large, the students who now have access to the Internet already have access to well-supported schools, well-paid teachers, and well-stocked libraries. Students who don't have access to computers or the Internet often don't have much else, either.

Because of that condition, the tremendous educational resources offered by the Internet widen a gap that should not exist in our society. The students most desperately in need of what computers offer are least likely to get it. Educators and politicians have recognized the problem; getting every classroom in America online is a goal championed today by Vice President Al Gore, among others. But in the current climate of taxpayer dissatisfaction and budget cutting, it's unlikely that computers will soon become as commonplace in classrooms as they must be to prepare students for the economic and cultural society they will inhabit.

Note

> I'm transparently partisan on this issue, but I've got company. In the last decade, education experts have been almost unanimous in urging the integration of computers into all levels of education. By extending the computer's reach to distant libraries, instructors, and other resources, an Internet connection only magnifies the computer's value. There's been little disagreement about the need—nearly all the disagreement has been about the cost.

The problem of getting classrooms online is exacerbated by the presence of board members, administrators, and teachers who are ignorant, out of touch, or just plain scared. These people don't recognize that the educational value of computers and online communication far exceed the cost. Scare headlines and misinformation regarding the presence of pornography on the Internet (see Chapter 22, "Using the Internet for Family Fun") provide the anti-computer contingent with the ammunition to keep classrooms offline.

However, by familiarizing themselves with the educational resources the Internet offers, teachers, administrators, and parents may acquire the ammunition they need to sell their schools on the necessity of classroom computing. Also, even if that effort should fail, there are resources on the Internet designed to help teachers become better teachers—even when they cannot offer their students the benefits of an online community. Teachers can use college computer systems or home computers and individual Internet accounts to educate themselves and then bring the benefits of the Internet to their students by proxy.

This chapter identifies Internet resources that can be particularly valuable to teachers, students, and others with an interest in education. As you discover these resources, keep in mind that the *entire* Internet—not just the education-specific resources—offers value to teachers and students. Newsgroups, IRC channels, Gopher menus, and Web pages can offer access to a world of information about, and exchange with, other cultures and communities and experts in every field. It's the best all-around encyclopedia, textbook, and teaching video money can buy.

Good Starting Points for Teachers

The resources listed below are good places to learn about how the Internet is already applied in education.

Note

> Most of the addresses in this chapter are in Universal Resource Locator (URL) format (any exceptions are noted as they come up). Using a Web browser, enter each address exactly as shown to access the resource.
>
> To use a resource through its specific client (a newsreader, Gopher client, and so on), omit the part of the URL up to and including the double slashes (`//`); for newsgroups, omit the characters `news:` at the start of the address.

- **AskERIC** (`http://ericir.syr.edu`)

  AskERIC is a venerable educator's resource of the Educational Resources Information Center (ERIC), long available through Telnet and now available on the Web. (See Figure 21.1.) It features extensive holdings of federally funded education information.

FIGURE 21.1.
The AskERIC Web page.

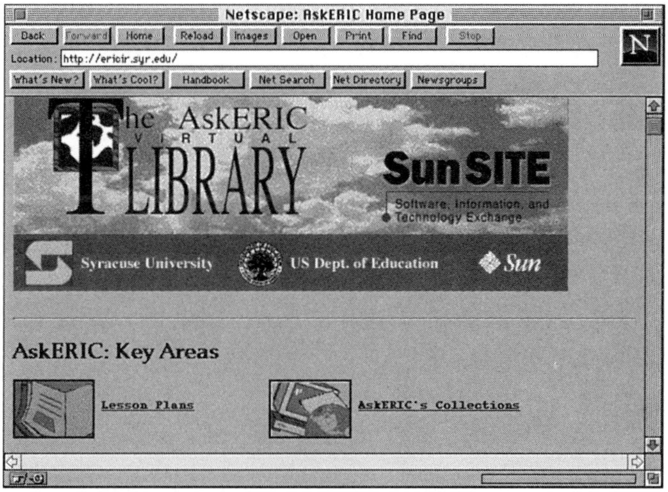

- **Center for Excellence in Education** (`http://rsi.cee.org`)

  Information about programs for keeping U.S. students competitive in science and technology; also has information on other education initiatives.

- **Educational Online Sources** (`http://netspace.students.brown.edu/eos1`)

  Links to all kinds of educational resources all over the Net, courtesy of Brown University.

- **Web Lecture Hall** (`http://www.utexas.edu:80/world/instruction`)

  A collection of materials about using the Web as a teaching tool. (See Figure 21.2.) Resources include course syllabi, notes, textbooks, and more.

FIGURE 21.2.
The Web Lecture Hall.

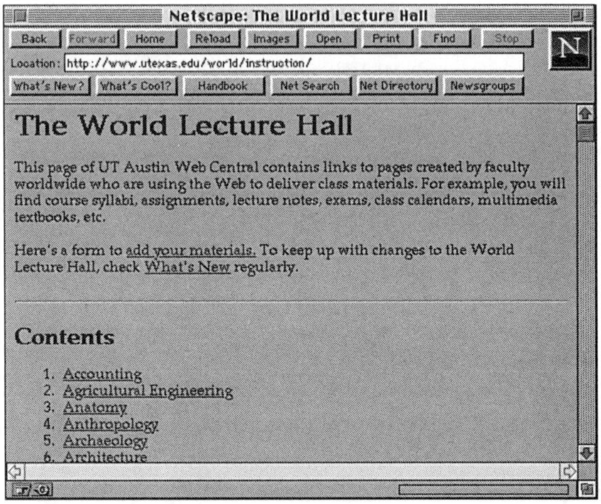

- **Galaxy Education** (`http://galaxy.einet.net/galaxy/Social-Sciences/Education.html`)

  Materials and pointers to educational resources.

- **Educational Technology** (`http://tecfa.unige.ch/info-edu-comp.html`)

  Education-related links in the World Wide Web Virtual Library. (See Chapter 18, "Finding It on the Web.")

- **CoVis: Learning through Collaborative Visualization** (`http://www.covis.nwu.edu`)

  A project at Northwestern University to explore the unique ways the Web can be used in teaching applications. (See Figure 21.3.)

FIGURE 21.3.
The CoVis home page.

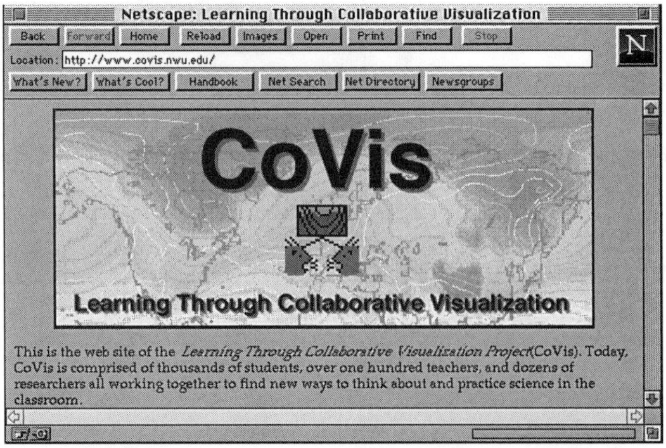

- **Teacher Education** (`http://curry.edschool.virginia.edu/teis`)

  A service of the Society for Technology and Teacher Education, this site contains documents and links to educational resources for teachers.

- **U.S. Department of Education** (`http://www.ed.gov`)

  At this writing, Congress is considering a proposal to abolish the Department of Education. But for as long as it survives, you'll find information about its programs here.

- **Apple Education** (`http://www.apple.com/education/`)

  Information about Apple's educational product discounts and teacher training tools is located here at Apple's corporate Web site. Apple Education is a resource intended for preschool to high school teachers.

K–12 Resources

The resources listed here may be useful in kindergarten through twelfth grade classrooms. They also serve as models for programs teachers can create themselves.

- **Empire Internet Schoolhouse** (`gopher://nysernet.org:3000/11`)

  A rich set of documents and links to K–12 resources, projects and discussion groups.

- **Exploratorium** (`http://www.exploratorium.edu`)

  Hundreds of interactive exhibits about science, art, and human perception. (See Figure 21.4.)

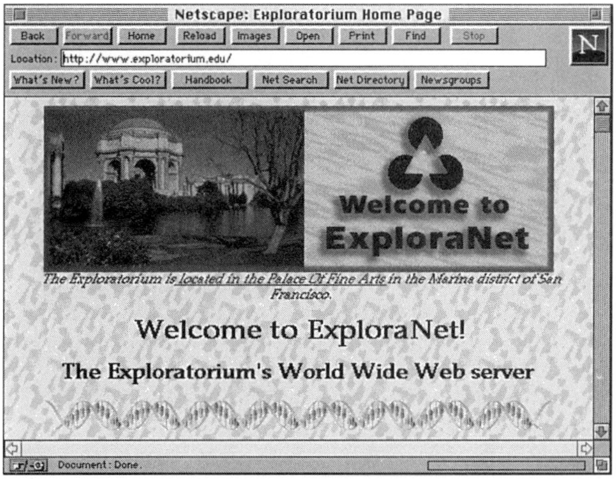

FIGURE 21.4.
The Exploratorium home page.

- **Travels with Samantha** (`http://www-swiss.ai.mit.edu/samantha/travels-with-samantha.html`)

  Travels with Samantha is a travel show on the Internet that takes students to interesting destinations all over North America.

- **The Jason Project** (`http://seawifs.gsfc.nasa.gov/scripts/ JASON.html`)

  A collaborative effort of NASA and scientists to provide an interactive learning environment about science. Jason takes students to the rain forest, outer space, and much more; it's an excellent showcase for the potential of Web-based teaching.

- **NASA** (http://`www.nasa.gov`)

  Documents, graphics, and links to an array of space-related resources, including a K–12 education program.

- **Children's Literature Web Guide** (`http://www.ucalgary.ca/~dkbrown/index.html`)

  Provides abstracts and other information about winners of the Newberry and Caldecott medals for children's literature, plus the *Publishers Weekly* Children's Bestsellers list.

- **The Smithsonian Natural History Gopher** (`gopher://nmnhgoph.si.edu`)

  Offers a treasury of news and information about projects underway at the Smithsonian, divided by natural history disciplines. (See Figure 21.5.) This Gopher also offers links to other natural history Gophers.

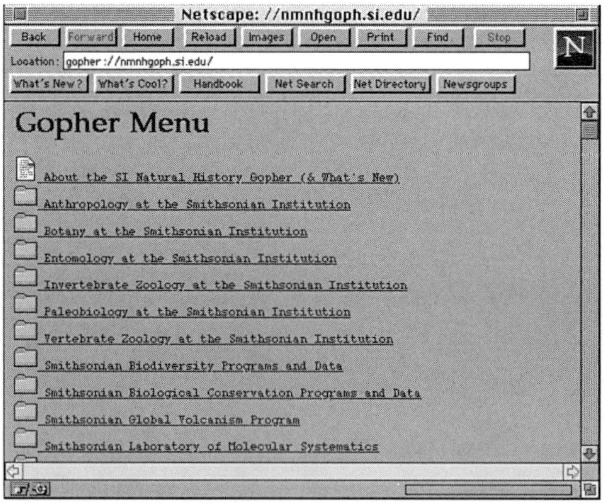

FIGURE 21.5.
The Smithsonian Natural History Gopher.

- **The White House** (`http://www.whitehouse.gov`)

  Pictures of White House interiors, access to speeches, press releases, and other documents, and personal information about the First family, right down to Socks the cat.

- **CapWeb** (`http://policy.net`)

  Unofficial information about events on Capitol Hill, including documents of pending legislation.

- **The Cornell Theory Center Math and Science Gateway** (`http://www.tc.cornell.edu:80/Edu/MathSciGateway`)

  A great clearinghouse of sorts, containing links to dozens of math and science education-related Internet resources for grades K–12. (See Figure 21.6.)

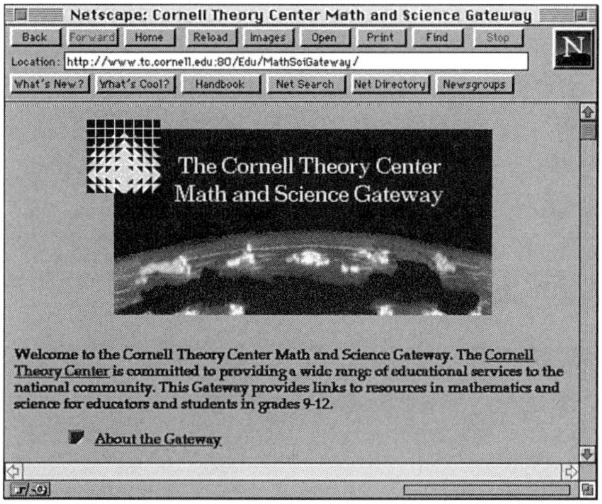

FIGURE 21.6.
The Cornell Theory Center Math and Science Gateway.

Post-Secondary Resources

The resources listed here can be of special interest to college students—or those heading for college.

> **Tip**
>
> Remember that, in addition to what you see listed here, almost every college or university in North America has a Gopher, and more and more also have their own Web pages. You can find a school using the Web or simply by scrolling through the list of All the Gopher Servers in the World. (See Chapter 13, "Navigating with Menus: Gopher.") These Gophers are great places to learn more about schools.

- **Money for College Directory** (`http://www.studentservices.com/mfc`)

  This page offers a searchable database of thousands of scholarships, grants, and special loans to help students locate all the financial resources for which they may be eligible. (See Figure 21.7.)

◆ **IRC Language Channels**

On Internet Relay Chat (IRC) servers, a number of Chat channels conduct conversations in a language other than English. These channels are great places for college students (and teachers) to practice their foreign language conversation skills. Chat channels named after a country (channel `#spain` or `#france`, for example) generally conduct the chat in the native language of that country. Channels named after a language (`#espanol` or `#francais`, for example) also converse in the native tongue.

Note that there are no URLs for IRC channels. The channels described here are accessed through an IRC client, as described in Chapter 14, "Interacting in Real Time: Talk, Chat, and Games."

FIGURE 21.7.
The Money for College Directory.

◆ **CNU Online** (`http://cnuonline.cnu.edu`)

A project of Christopher Newport University (CNU), CNU Online offers credit-bearing courses from CNU—plus links to credit-bearing online courses at other universities—to enable students to acquire a bachelor's degree online. CNU Online is still under construction, but you can check it out to see what courses and degrees are currently offered, or will be offered. (See Figure 21.8.)

FIGURE 21.8.
CNU Online.

Summary

Although it only scratches the surface of the resources available, this chapter shows that the Internet is shaping up as the richest education library in the world. As a user, you can mine that library for the most current, most interactive education tools and research available. As an education professional, you can learn how the Internet plays a role in the classroom and provides the proper instructional support.

Chapter 22 wraps up the book with an overview of wild, free, fun (and sometimes useless), miscellaneous Internet sites.

CHAPTER 22

USING THE INTERNET FOR FAMILY FUN

Is the Internet Fit for Family Consumption?

Internet Pastimes

Summary

A personal note: I have a son, who is two-and-a-half years old at this writing. He doesn't particularly care for the Internet, because while I'm writing about it, we're not at the park chasing ducks.

But as I explore the Internet, I keep thinking about what it will offer him in a few years. He'll be able to use it to play games, research homework, correspond with pen-pals, learn about his favorite star or team or adventure character, order from catalogs (comic books, perhaps, or X-ray specs—with my permission, of course), publish his own magazine, listen to music, and much, much more. Then I realize that I can't think of a single thing he can do on the Internet that I didn't do myself as a boy. I simply did it using other media.

The Internet was not created as a playground, but it's certainly made up for lost time in recent years. The amount of sheer, pointless fun that can be had on the Net has grown more quickly than any other type of activity. That's likely to continue as the Internet completes its transition from research tool to all-purpose information service.

In this chapter, you discover some of the many pointless (or semi-pointless) diversions the Internet has to offer. But first, a serious note about a cultural controversy.

Is the Internet Fit for Family Consumption?

It's impossible to discuss the Internet as a playground without first addressing the very real concerns people have about whether the Net is a safe, appropriate place for children—or for adults, for that matter. Stories about online pornography, Net-cruising pedophiles, hate groups, and addictions to being online have aroused concerns among those wondering whether they or their children are really safe in cyberspace.

The fair and simple answer is *no.* It's important to remember that the Internet is not a product controlled by its owner, as other online services may be. It's simply a vehicle through which millions communicate freely and openly. The overwhelming majority of those who go online do so for wholesome reasons; it's almost impossible to come across pornography, hate speeches, or other unsavory ideas unless you go looking for them. But such ideas are indeed expressed on the Internet, as are erotic (or pornographic) writing, pictures, and discussions; hateful tirades against every imaginable group; kinky chat channels; and more. Also, as recent cautionary books have observed, people can get hooked on the Internet—*so* hooked that they hang out online to the exclusion of other, more important pursuits.

Note

> It's important to observe that, to various extents, eWorld, CompuServe, and America Online all impose some censorship on their services. Yet both CompuServe and America Online have been plagued by the same kind of material that also afflicts the entirely unmanaged Internet. A newer service with a smaller membership, eWorld has not yet suffered from these same kinds of problems.

Some have proposed censoring the Internet, something that's: a) technically impossible and b) almost inarguably unconstitutional (at least in the United States). As I write, a bill to censor cyberspace is wending its way through Congress. But its passage or defeat will have no immediate effect on the Internet or the controversy. If the bill is defeated, concerned citizens and politicians currying conservative favor will continue to lobby for censorship. If it passes, the bill will almost certainly face any number of constitutional challenges and an eventual date with the Supreme Court. So regardless of what happens in Congress, this controversy is going to be with us for a few years, and maybe forever.

With deep respect for the concerns of those who are more cautious, I'll offer my own position, for what it's worth. I think that those who spend any time online quickly discover that the controversial material is a tiny fraction of what's there. I also think one person's pornography is another's adult fiction, and that the censoring of hateful expression—abhorrent though the hatefulness is—opens the door to the censorship of other, worthy ideas and forms of expression. As for addiction, anything useful or enjoyable carries the potential for excess and abuse. The source of any obsession is not the object of that obsession, it is the emptiness elsewhere in the addict's life.

Ultimately, every parent—and every person—must decide for himself or herself whether the benefits of the Internet are worth its risks. I think the risks are small and the rewards great, so it's an easy question for me. I also recognize that, even if I were to prevent my children from using the Internet, my wife and I would still have to supervise their activities, teach them to be appropriately wary of strangers, and help them develop good judgment about ideas to which they are exposed. These life skills are as necessary on the street as they are on the Internet—probably more so.

The Internet does not expose me or my family to any new dangers. It merely reflects the dangers of society at large. Because my kids will have to learn how to live with those dangers anyway, I'll choose to let them enjoy—and learn from—the world online, with their parents' guidance to protect them.

Tip

> If you doubt the potential value of cyberspace to families, check out Helping Your Children Learn To Read, a Web facility set up by the U.S. Department of Education to provide parents with online tools for teaching reading. The page takes parents from exercises designed to get infants off to the right start all the way to fun reading exercises children can perform themselves. You'll find Helping Your Children Learn To Read at the following URL:
>
> `http://www.ed.gov/pubs/parents/Reading/index.html`

Internet Pastimes

Tip

The following pages offer a selection of Internet diversions. However, the resources listed can only scratch the surface of what's available. One good way to hunt down new, fun resources is through the Yahoo directory at `http://www.yahoo.com`. (See Chapter 18, "Finding It on the Web.")

Yahoo offers directories of links arranged by categories, including separate directories for Arts, Entertainment, Sports, and other fun groupings. You can browse through these directories, or choose Yahoo's What's Cool, What's New, or What's Popular link to find many of the best sites on and off the Web. If you're feeling truly adventurous (or are incapable of making your own decisions), you can choose Yahoo's Random Link, which sends you to a random page on the Web.

The following pages describe starting points and specific sites you or your family may want to visit for the heck of it. I won't categorically call these sites "fun" places on the Internet because "fun" rests unequivocally in the eye of the beholder (some people think roller coasters are fun, others throw up on them). Suffice it to say that what you find, here at the close of this tome, is a random collection of Internet stuff that's fun to know about. (At least *I* think it's fun.)

Note

Most of the addresses in this chapter are in Universal Resource Locator (URL) format (any exceptions are noted as they come up). Using a Web browser, enter each address exactly as shown to access the resource.

To use a resource through its specific client (a newsreader, Gopher client, and so on), omit the part of the URL up to and including the double slashes (`//`); for newsgroups, omit the characters `news:` at the start of the address.

Shopping

- **Internet Shopping Network** (`http://shop.internet.net`)

  Owned by TV's Home Shopping Network, the ISN is one of the first Web-based marketplaces. You can shop the catalogs of major mail-order houses and place orders online. Note that the opening page of the Shopping Network requires a registration procedure for new users. The registration process is part of the shopping club's security system, designed to prevent unauthorized users from accessing the credit card information you supply to make purchases online. Note also that the URL shown in Figure 22.1 doesn't match the preceding URL listing for the Internet Shopping Network—but that's OK. When you point your browser to `http://shop.internet.com`, you're automatically bounced to this sign-up procedure at a different URL.

FIGURE 22.1.
The Internet Shopping Network (ISN) home page.

> **Note**
>
> Efforts are under way to make credit-card orders over the Internet safe, but those efforts are incomplete. (See Chapter 20, "Using the Internet in the Office.") As things stand, your credit information can be stolen and misused. Exercise extreme caution when using a credit card online. It's safest to restrict your ordering to big operations such as ISN who have an interest in keeping your credit information secure to encourage confidence in their services.

- **Deep Space Mall** (`http://www.deepspace.com/deepspace.html`)

  An odd combination of shopping sites and links to space pictures. To each his own.
- **One World Plaza** (`http://www.digimark.net/windata`)

  More than 100 shops to browse. Bring lunch. (See Figure 22.2.)

FIGURE 22.2.
The One World Plaza home page.

- **Burlington Coat Factory** (`http://www.coat.com`)

  Order anything from the bargain outlet clothing shop. (Remember: *Not* affiliated with Burlington Industries!)

- **Download Bookstore** (`http://dab.psi.net/downloadbookstore`)

  An innovative online bookstore that lets you "try before you buy" by downloading excerpts or tables of contents from books before ordering. (See Figure 22.3.)

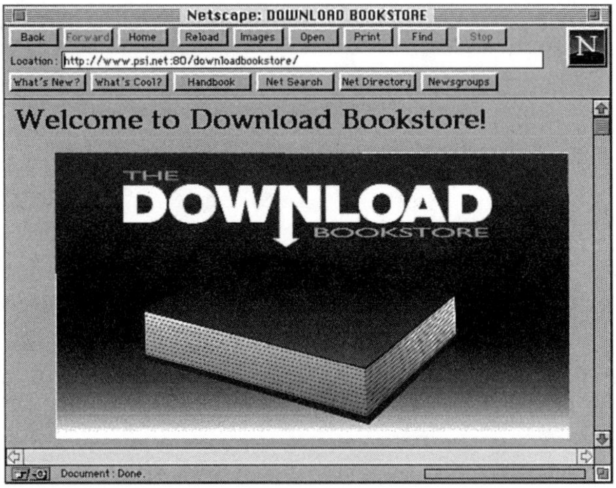

FIGURE 22.3.
The Download Bookstore home page.

- **CDnow!** (`http://cdnow.com`)

  An online CD store offering 140,000 recordings plus online copies of articles and reviews from music industry magazines.

Entertainment

- **Top Ten Lists from *The Late Show with David Letterman*** (`http://www.cbs.com/lateshow/ttlist.html`)

  The latest lists, plus archives of *all* the lists—even the ones that weren't funny. (See Figure 22.4.)

- **Cardiff Movie Database** (`http://www.cm.cf.ac.uk/movies`)

  An elaborate database of *professional* film reviews ("Keanu Reeves can't talk"), film writing, graphics, and much more.

- **Amateur Movie Reviews** (`newsgroup rec.art.movies.reviews`)

  The opinions of your fellow movie fans plus the counterpoints of their colleagues. ("Keanu Reeves *can so* talk!")

- ***Batman Forever*** (`http://batmanforever.com/cinema/cinema.html`)

  A site promoting the summer blockbuster, with cool photos, video clips, and interesting facts about the stars. (See Figure 22.5.)

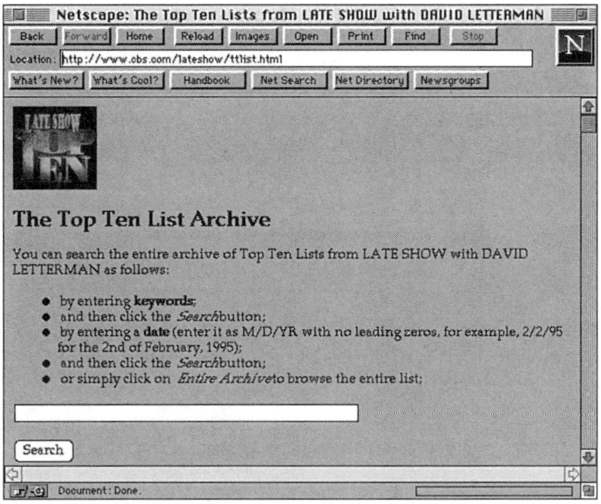

FIGURE 22.4.
David Letterman's Top Ten Lists on the Web, where the lasers can't hurt you.

FIGURE 22.5.
The Batman Forever *home page.*

- **Buena Vista** (`http://bvp.wdp.com`)

  Information, graphics, clips, and more about the Disney empire: Disney Pictures, Touchstone Pictures, and Hollywood Pictures.

- **Fox Broadcasting** (`http://www.eden.com/users/my-html/fox.html`)

  Everything about the rebel fourth network, including the latest about *The Simpsons* and *Melrose Place*. The site is not created and maintained by Fox but by *fans*—which can be for the better or worse, depending on how you look at it.

- **Warner Brothers Records** (`http://www.iuma.com/warner`)

  Complete information on the Warner's label, including tour dates of its artists, new CD releases, and even video clips of stars such as Madonna.

- **The Rolling Stones** (`http://www.stones.com`)

  Yes, the world's oldest working rock band has its own Web site to keep you informed about tour dates and to sell you licensed Stones merchandise. (See Figure 22.6.)

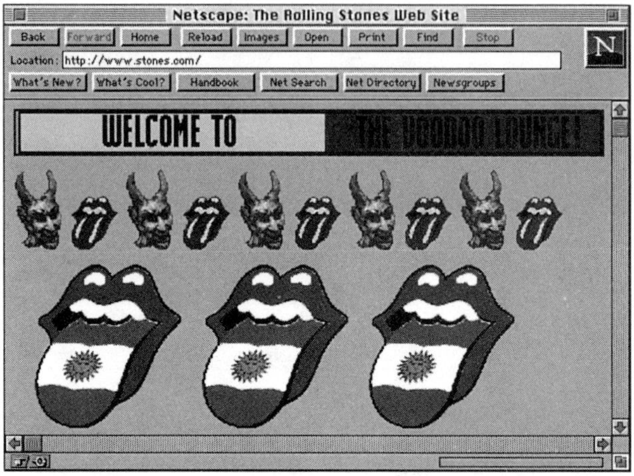

FIGURE 22.6.
The Rolling Stones home page.

- **Ultimate TV List** (`http://tvnet.com/TVnet.html`)

  A listing of links to much of the TV-related stuff all over the Net, including Web sites, Gophers, FTP files, and newsgroups. A great starting place for finding information about your favorite show.

Sports

- **WWW/Sports** (`http://tns-www.lcs.mit.edu/cgi-bin/sports`)

  Links and updates about sporting events all over the world.

- **Sports Server** (`http://www.nando.net/sptsserv.html`)

  Complete coverage of scores, stats, standings, and injuries for professional and college basketball, football, and baseball teams. (See Figure 22.7.)

- **Americas Cup** (`http://www.ac95.org`)

  Everything about the world's biggest sailboat race and national pride surrogate, including photos, history, and more.

- **Tour De France** (`http://www.velonews.com/VeloNews`)

  Everything about the world's biggest bike race and national pride surrogate, including results, course maps, and more.

- **Water Skiing** (`http://www.primenet.com:80/~jodell`)

  Tournament schedules and results, pictures, and more about a sport I tried once and won't try again unless I become suicidally depressed.

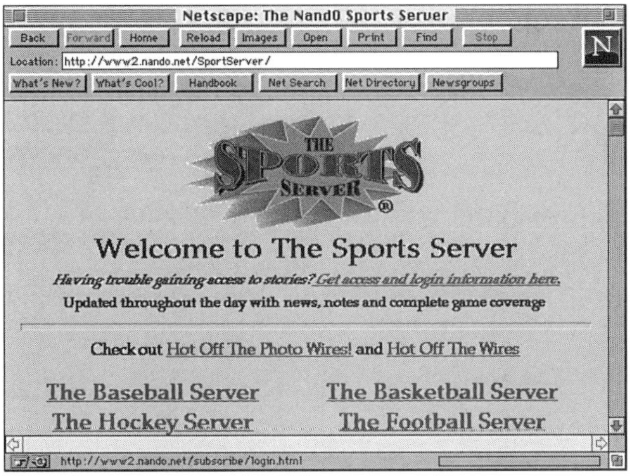

FIGURE 22.7.
The Sports Server home page.

Miscellaneous Weird and Interesting Stuff

◆ **Vegetarian Pages** (`http://catless.ncl.ac.uk/Vegetarian`)

A great place to learn about veggie techniques, recipes, nutritional information, and events. Bring celery. (See Figure 22.8.)

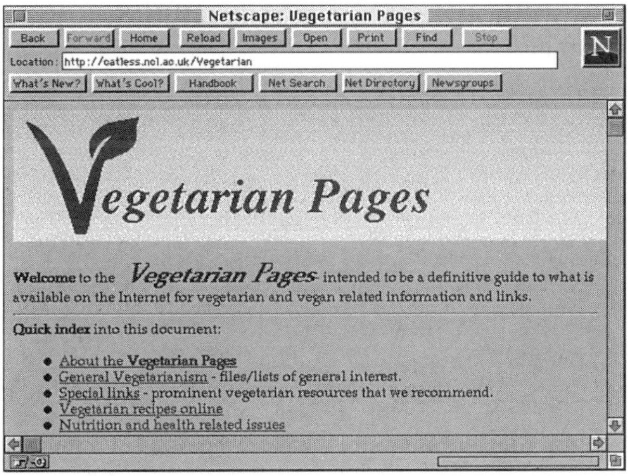

FIGURE 22.8.
The Vegetarian Pages Web site.

◆ **BookWire** (`http://www.bookwire.com`)

The first stop for information about books, BookWire features *Publishers Weekly* bestseller lists, a title database, and hundreds of links to book-related resources elsewhere on the Internet. (See Figure 22.9.)

FIGURE 22.9.
The BookWire home page.

- **Westin Travel Guide** (`http://www.westin.com`)

  An international travel guide with advisories, destination attractions, business and family travel planning, and, of course, Westin hotel reservations.

- **The First Church of Cyberspace** (`http://execpc.com/~chender`)

  Founded by a Presbyterian pastor in New Jersey, the First Church of Cyberspace features a sanctuary, a library, a gallery, a gathering place, and a multimedia Bible. (See Figure 22.10.) Other features include Sunday school classes and files of sermons from ministers across the country. Visitors are encouraged to practice "active worship" by responding to sermons and other material offered through the church. Obviously, the materials and activities are heavily Presbyterian—but everyone's welcome.

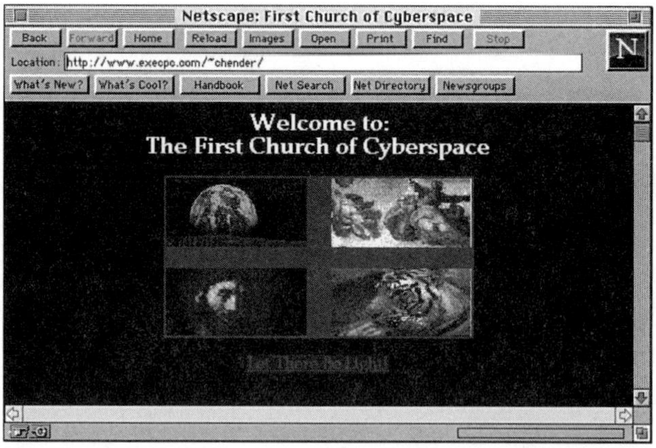

FIGURE 22.10.
The First Church of Cyberspace.

- **Internal Revenue Service** (`http://www.ustreas.gov/treasury/bureaus/irs/irs.html`)

  Yes, the IRS. You can get forms, look up rules, and communicate with the tax commissioner. (My dog ate the receipts. I swear.)

◆ **Genealogy Home Page** (`http://ftp.cac.psu.edu/~saw/genealogy.html`)

Look up your family tree.

◆ **The Wine Page** (`http://augustus.csscr.washington.edu/personal/bigstar-mosaic/wine.html`)

Everything about wine, including tasting notes and "virtual tasting" of online wine.

◆ **Consumer Information Center** (`http://www.gsa.gov/staff/pa/cic/cic.htm`)

The U.S. government's incredible database of consumer information, including guides to personal finance. (See Figure 22.11.)

FIGURE 22.11.
The Consumer Information Center home page.

◆ **Self-Help Psychology Magazine** (`http://www.well.com/user/selfhelp`)

A Web page featuring helpful articles written by mental-health experts for laypeople who have problems (or think they have problems).

Summary

Nice going, Magellan—you have learned not only to navigate the Internet, but to circumnavigate it. I hope you've found the experience a rewarding one. Glad you survived the entire trip—which is more than Magellan did.

Thanks for joining me. See you in cyberspace.

APPENDIXES

APPENDIX A

INTERNET ACCESS PROVIDERS

This appendix lists companies and organizations that provide dial-up Internet accounts for individuals and organizations. The list includes providers in the United States, Canada, and other countries.

If you are already connected to the Internet but are searching for alternatives, check online at `ftp://nis.nsf.net/internet/providers/` or `http://www.internic.net/internic/provider.html`. The National Science Foundataion (NSF) and InterNIC maintain lists of providers that are updated very frequently. Note, however, that because Web addresses are subject to change, it's possible that either or both of these addresses have changed by the time you read this. If you're not already connected, other good sources are your local newspaper and Yellow Pages.

For more information on different types of Internet access and what to look for in a provider, see Chapter 1, "The Basics: What's Involved in Setting Up and Going Online?"

Geographical and Area-Code Summary of Providers in the United States and Canada

This section presents North American Internet provider names grouped by the state or province the provider services, by area code, and then alphabetically by provider name. Details and contact information for each provider follow in the next section. The first (and largest) portion of this list presents providers that supply *standard access* (Internet access through a local telephone connection). At the end of this list are the providers that supply *packet/network* or *toll-free access* (connections that require the use of special data networks or long-distance phone service, usually at a higher cost than standard access). Always look for a standard carrier in your local calling area first.

Standard Access

Alabama—205

InterQuest Inc.
Nuance Network Service
Planet Access Networks

Alaska—907

Internet Alaska

Alberta—403

Alberta SuperNet Inc.
CCI Networks

Arizona—602

ACES Research
CRL Network Services
Evergreen Internet
Internet Direct, Inc.
Internet Express
Network 99, Inc.
New Mexico Technet, Inc.
Primenet

Arkansas—501

Sibylline, Inc.

British Columbia—604

Cyberstore Systems Inc.
DataFlux Systems Limited
Wimsey Information Services

California—209

Sacramento Network Access
West Coast Online

California—213

CRL Network Services
CSUnet (California State University)
DHM Information Management, Inc.
DigiLink Network Services
Earthlink Network, Inc.
KAIWAN Corporation
Primenet

California—310

CERFnet
CRL Network Services
CSUnet (California State University)
DHM Information Management, Inc.
DigiLink Network Services
Earthlink Network, Inc.
KAIWAN Corporation
Lightside, Inc.
Netcom On-Line Communication Services

California—408

Aimnet Information Services
Best Internet Communications, Inc. (BEST)
CSUnet (California State University)
ElectriCiti Incorporated
Internet Connection
InterNex Information Services, Inc.
Netcom On-Line Communication Services
Portal Communications Company
Scruz-Net
South Valley Internet
West Coast Online
zNET

California—415

Aimnet Information Services
APlatform
Best Internet Communications, Inc. (BEST)
CERFnet
CRL Network Services
CSUnet (California State University)
ElectriCiti Incorporated
Institute for Global Communications (IGC)
InterNex Information Services, Inc.
LineX Communications
Netcom On-Line Communication Services
QuakeNet
Scruz-Net
The Well
West Coast Online

California—510

Access InfoSystems
Aimnet Information Services
Best Internet Communications, Inc. (BEST)
CCnet Communications
CERFnet
Community ConneXion
CRL Network Services
CSUnet (California State University)
ElectriCiti Incorporated
HoloNet
InterNex Information Services, Inc.
Netcom On-Line Communication Services
Sacramento Network Access, Inc.
West Coast Online

California—619

CERFnet
CSUnet (California State University)
CTS Network Services (CTSNet)
ElectriCiti Incorporated
ESNET Communications
Netcom On-Line Communication Services
Network Link, Inc.

California—707
Access InfoSystems
CRL Network Services
CSUnet (California State University)
Northcoast Internet
Pacific Internet
West Coast Online

California—714
CERFnet
CSUnet (California State University)
DHM Information Management, Inc.
DigiLink Network Services
Digital Express Group (Digex)
KAIWAN Corporation
Lightside, Inc.
Netcom On-Line Communication Services
Network Intensive

California—805
Dataware Network Services
KAIWAN Corporation

California—818
CERFnet
CSUnet (California State University)
DHM Information Management, Inc.
DigiLink Network Services
Earthlink Network, Inc.
KAIWAN Corporation
Lightside, Inc.
Netcom On-Line Communication Services
Primenet

California—909
CSUnet (California State University)
Digital Express Group (Digex)
KAIWAN Corporation
Lightside, Inc.

California—916
CSUnet (California State University)
Netcom On-Line Communication Services
Sacramento Network Access, Inc.
Sierra-Net
West Coast Online

Colorado—303
CNS
Colorado Internet Cooperative Association
Colorado SuperNet
DASH—Denver Area Super Highway
Internet Express
Netcom On-Line Communication Services
New Mexico Technet, Inc.
Nyx
Rocky Mountain Internet, Inc.

Colorado—719
CNS
Colorado SuperNet
Internet Express
Old Colorado City Communications
Rocky Mountain Internet, Inc.

Connecticut—203
Connix: The Connecticut Internet Exchange
The Dorsai Embassy
I-2000
New York Net
PCNet

Delaware—302
SSNet, Inc.

District of Columbia—202
CAPCON LibrARY Network
Capitol Area Internet Service (CAIS)
ClarkNet (Clark Internet Services, Inc.)
NovaNet, Inc.
US Net, Inc.

Florida—305
Acquired Knowledge Systems, Inc.
CyberGate
Florida Online
Gateway to the World, Inc.
IDS World Network
SatelNET Communications

Florida—407
Florida Online
IDS World Network

Florida—813
CENTURION Technology, Inc.
Florida Online
PacketWorks, Inc.

Florida—904
Florida Online
SymNet

Georgia—404
CRL Network Services
Internet Atlanta
MindSpring Enterprises, Inc.
Netcom On-Line Communication Services
Ping

Georgia—706
MindSpring Enterprises, Inc.

Hawaii—808
Hawaii OnLine

Idaho—208
WLN

Illinois—217
FGInet, Inc.

Illinois—312
American Information Systems, Inc. (AIS)
InterAccess Co.
MCSNet
Netcom On-Line Communication Services
Ripco Communications, Inc.
Tezcatlipoca, Inc.
WorldWide Access

Illinois—708
American Information Systems, Inc. (AIS)
CICNet
InterAccess Co.
MCSNet
Ripco Communications, Inc.
Tezcatlipoca, Inc.
WorldWide Access
XNet Information Systems

Illinois—815
American Information Systems, Inc. (AIS)
InterAccess Co.
MCSNet
WorldWide Access

Indiana—317
IQuest Network Services
Network Link, Inc.

Indiana—812
IgLou Internet Services

Iowa—319
INS Info Services
Planet Access Networks

Iowa—515
Cyberlink Communications
INS Info Services

Iowa—712
INS Info Services

Kansas—316
Southwind Internet Access, Inc.
Tyrell Corp.

Kansas—913
Tyrell Corp.
SkyNET Corp.

Kentucky—502
IgLou Internet Services

Kentucky—606
IgLou Internet Services

Louisiana—504
Neosoft, Inc.
Tyrell Corp.

Maine—207
maine.net, Inc.

Manitoba—204
MBnet
Traveller Information Services

Maryland—301
CAPCON LibrARY Network
Capitol Area Internet Service (CAIS)
ClarkNet (Clark Internet Services, Inc.)
Digital Express Group (Digex)
FredNet
NovaNet, Inc.
US Net, Inc.

Maryland—410
CAPCON LibrARY Network
Capitol Area Internet Service (CAIS)
ClarkNet (Clark Internet Services, Inc.)
Digital Express Group (Digex)

Massachusetts—508
Inter Access Company
intuitive information, inc.
Schunix
UltraNet Communications, Inc.
The World

Massachusetts—617
BIX (Delphi Internet Services)
Inter Access Company
Internet Access Company
Netcom On-Line Communication Services
North Shore Access
Pioneer Global
Wilder Systems, Inc.
The World
Xensei Corporation

Michigan—313
CICNet
ICNet/Innovative Concepts
Innovative Data (ID-Net)
MichNet
Msen, Inc.

Michigan—517
ICNet/Innovative Concepts
MichNet
Msen, Inc.

Michigan—616
ICNet/Innovative Concepts
MichNet
Msen, Inc.

Michigan—810
ICNet/Innovative Concepts
Innovative Data (ID-Net)
MichNet
Msen, Inc.
Rabbit Network, Inc.

Michigan—906
ICNet/Innovative Concepts
MichNet
Msen, Inc.

Minnesota—218
Minnesota Regional Network (MRNet)
Red River Net

Minnesota—507
Millenium Communications
Minnesota Regional Network (MRNet)

Minnesota—612
Cloudnet
Millenium Communications
Minnesota MicroNet
Minnesota Regional Network (MRNet)
StarNet Communications, Inc. (Winternet)

Missouri—314
Neosoft, Inc.

Missouri—816
SkyNET Corp.
Tyrell Corp.

Montana—406
WLN

Nebraska—402
INS Info Services
Internet Nebraska Corp.

Nevada—702
Evergreen Internet
Great Basin Internet Services
Network 99, Inc.
Sacramento Network Access, Inc.
Sierra-Net

New Hampshire—603
MV Communications, Inc.

New Jersey—201
The Dorsai Embassy
Internet Online Services
Neighborhood Internet Connection
New York Net
Planet Access Networks
Zone One Network Exchange (ZONE)

New Jersey—609
Digital Express Group (Digex)
New Jersey Computer Connection
New York Net

New Jersey—908
Digital Express Group (Digex)
I-2000
New York Net
Planet Access Networks
Zone One Network Exchange (ZONE)

New Mexico—505
Internet Express
New Mexico Technet, Inc.

New York—212
Blythe Systems
Creative Data Consultants
CRL Network Services
The Dorsai Embassy
Echo
Escape (Kazan Corp.)
Ingress Communications, Inc.
Internet Online Services
Interport Communications Corp.
Maestro Technologies, Inc.
Netcom On-Line Communication Services
Network 23, Inc.
New York Net
NYSERNet
Panix
Phantom Access Technologies, Inc.
Pipeline Network
Zone One Network Exchange (ZONE)

New York—315
NYSERNet

New York—516
Creative Data Consultants
The Dorsai Embassy
I-2000
LI Net, Inc.
Long Island Information, Inc.
Maestro Technologies, Inc.
Network Internet Services
New York Net
NYSERNet
Panix
Phantom Access Technologies, Inc.
Zone One Network Exchange (ZONE)

New York—518
Internet Online Services
NYSERNet
Wizvax Communications

New York—607
NYSERNet

New York—716
NYSERNet

New York—718
Blythe Systems
Creative Data Consultants
The Dorsai Embassy
Echo
Escape (Kazan Corp.)
I-2000
Ingress Communications, Inc.
Interport Communications Corp.
Maestro Technologies, Inc.
New York Net
NYSERNet
Phantom Access Technologies, Inc.
Zone One Network Exchange (ZONE)

New York—914
Cloud 9 Internet
The Dorsai Embassy
I-2000
New York Net
NYSERNet
Phantom Access Technologies, Inc.
TZ-Link
WestNet
Zone One Network Exchange (ZONE)

New York—917
Network 23, Inc.
New York Net
Zone One Network Exchange (ZONE)

North Carolina—704
FXnet
Interpath
Northcoast Internet
VNet Internet Access, Inc.

North Carolina—910
Interpath

North Carolina—919
Interpath

North Dakota—701
Red River Net

Ohio—216
APK Public Access UNI*
Exchange Network Services, Inc.

Ohio—513
EriNet Online Communications
Freelance Systems Programming
IgLou Internet Services

Ohio—614
OARNet

Oklahoma—405
GSS Internet

Oklahoma—918
GSS Internet
South Coast Computing Services, Inc.

Ontario—416
UUNorth Incorporated

Ontario—519
Hookup Communication Corporation

Oregon—503
Agora
Hevanet Communications
Internetworks
Netcom On-Line Communication Services
Teleport
Teleport, Inc.
WLN

Pennsylvania—215
FishNet (Prometheus Information Corp.)
VoiceNet/DCS
You Tools Corporation (FAST.NET)

Pennsylvania—412
Telerama

Pennsylvania—610
FishNet (Prometheus Information Corp.)
SSNet, Inc.
You Tools Corporation (FAST.NET)

Pennsylvania—717
You Tools Corporation (FAST.NET)

Rhode Island—401
IDS World Network

Quebec—514
Communications Accessibles
Montreal, Inc.

South Carolina—803
FXnet
Global Vision, Inc.
SIMS, Inc.
South Carolina SuperNet, Inc.
A World of Difference, Inc.

Tennessee—615
Edge

Texas—210
Freeside Communications

Texas—214
DFW Internet Services, Inc.
Metronet, Inc.
Neosoft, Inc.
Netcom On-Line Communication Services
Texas Metronet

Texas—409
Info-Highway International, Inc.
Internet Connect Services, Inc.
Neosoft, Inc.

Texas—512
Eden Matrix
Freeside Communications
Illuminati Online
Internet Connect Services, Inc.
Netcom On-Line Communication Services
Onramp Access, Inc.
Real/Time Communications
Zilker Internet Park

Texas—713
Black Box
Info-Highway International, Inc.
Internet Connect Services, Inc.
Neosoft, Inc.
South Coast Computing Services, Inc.

Texas—817
ACM Network Services
DFW Internet Services, Inc.
Metronet, Inc.
Texas Metronet

Texas—915
New Mexico Technet, Inc.

Utah—801
Evergreen Internet
Internet Direct of Utah
XMission

Virginia—703
CAPCON LibrARY Network
Capitol Area Internet Service (CAIS)
ClarkNet (Clark Internet Services, Inc.)
Digital Express Group (Digex)
Netcom On-Line Communication Services
NovaNet, Inc.
PSI
US Net, Inc.

Virginia—804
Global Connect Inc.
Widomaker Communications

Washington—206
Cyberlink Communications
Eskimo North
Netcom On-Line Communication Services
NorthWest CommLink
Northwest Nexus, Inc.
Pacific Rim Network, Inc.
Pacifier Computers
Skagit On-Line Services
Teleport
Teleport, Inc.
Townsend Communications, Inc.
WLN

Washington—509
Internet On-Ramp, Inc.
WLN

Wisconsin—414
BINCnet
Exec-PC BBS
FullFeed Communications
Internet Connect, Inc.
MIX Communications
WorldWide Access

Wisconsin—608
BINCnet
FullFeed Communications

Wisconsin—715
BINCnet
FullFeed Communications

Packet Network/Toll-Free Access

CompuServe Packet Network
IDS World Network

PSINet
HoloNet

SprintNet
Neosoft, Inc.
Portal Communications Company

Toll-Free/800 Access

AlterNet (UUNET Technologies)
American Information Systems, Inc. (AIS)
BIX (Delphi Internet Services)
CENTURION Technology, Inc.
CERFnet
CICNet
CNS
CRL
DASH—Denver Area Super Highway
Digital Express Group (Digex)
Exec-PC BBS
Freeside Communications
FXnet
Hookup Communication Corporation
IgLou Internet Services
Info-Highway International, Inc.
INS Info Services
InterAccess Co.
Internet Express
Internet Online Services
Interpath
IQuest Network Services
Msen, Inc.
Neosoft, Inc.
Netcom On-Line Communications Services
Network Intensive
New Mexico Technet, Inc.
OARNet
Pacific Rim Network, Inc.
PCNet
Ping
Primenet
Rabbit Network, Inc.
Rocky Mountain Internet, Inc.
Sacramento Network Access, Inc.
Scruz-Net
South Coast Computing Services, Inc.
Traveller Information Services
Tyrell Corp.
UltraNet Communications, Inc.
VNet Internet Access, Inc.
VoiceNet/DCS
West Coast Online
WLN
Zone One Network Exchange (ZONE)

Tymnet

Holonet

Alphabetical List of Providers

This section presents an alphabetical list of providers grouped by country and then by provider name. Countries included are the United States, Canada, Australia, Germany, the Netherlands, New Zealand, Switzerland, and the United Kingdom.

United States and Canada

The following is a list of North American Internet provider names in alphabetical order by provider name.

Access InfoSystems

Area code(s):	707, 510
Voice phone:	707-422-1034
E-mail address:	`info@community.net`
Services provided:	Shell, SLIP, PPP

ACES Research

Area code(s):	602
Voice phone:	602-322-6500
E-mail address:	`sales@aces.com`
Services provided:	SLIP, 56-T1

ACM Network Services

Area code(s): National/International
Voice phone: 817-776-6876
E-mail address: account-info@acm.org
Services provided: Shell, SLIP, PPP, T1

Acquired Knowledge Systems, Inc.

Area code(s): 305
Voice phone: 305-525-2574
E-mail address: samek@aksi.net
Services provided: Shell, SLIP, PPP

Agora

Area code(s): 503
E-mail address: info@agora.rain.com
Dial-up number: 503-293-1772
Services provided: Shell, Usenet, FTP, Telnet, Gopher, Lynx, IRC, mail, SLIP/PPP coming

Aimnet Information Services

Area code(s): 408, 415, 510
Voice phone: 408-257-0900
E-mail address: info@aimnet.com
Services provided: Shell, SLIP, PPP, DNS

Alberta SuperNet Inc.

Area code(s): 403
Voice phone: 403-441-3663
E-mail address: info@supernet.ab.ca
Services provided: Shell, e-mail, Usenet, FTP, Telnet, Gopher, SLIP/PPP

AlterNet (UUNET Technologies)

Area code(s): All
Voice phone: 800-4UUNET4
E-mail address: info@uunet.uu.net
Services provided: Telnet only, SLIP, PPP, 56, 128 T1, 10Mps

American Information Systems, Inc. (AIS)

Area code(s): 312, 708, 800, 815
Voice phone: 708-413-8400
E-mail address: schneid@ais.net
Services provided: Shell, SLIP, PPP, leased lines

APK Public Access UNI*

Area code(s): 216
Voice phone: 216-481-9428
E-mail address: support@wariat.org
Services provided: Shell, SLIP, PPP

APlatform

Area code(s): 415
Voice phone: 415-941-2641
E-mail address: support@aplatform.com
Services provided: Shell, SLIP, PPP

Best Internet Communications, Inc. (BEST)

Area code(s): 408, 415, 510
Voice phone: 415-964-2378
E-mail address: info@best.com
Services provided: Shell, SLIP, PPP, leased lines

BINCnet

Area code(s): 608, 414, 715
Voice phone: 608-233-5222
E-mail address: ward@binc.net
Services provided: SLIP, PPP, 56-T1

BIX (Delphi Internet Services)

Area code(s): National/International
Voice phone: 800-695-4775, 617-354-4137
E-mail address: info@bix.com
Services provided: Shell

Black Box

Area code(s):	713
Voice phone:	713-480-2684
E-mail address:	`info@blkbox.com`
Services provided:	Shell, SLIP, PPP, ISDN

Blythe Systems

Area code(s):	212, 718
Voice phone:	212-348-2875
E-mail address:	`accounts@blythe.org`
Services provided:	Shell

CAPCON LibrARY Network

Area code(s):	202, 301, 410, 703
Voice phone:	202-331-5771
E-mail address:	`info@capcon.net`
Services provided:	Shell, SLIP, PPP

Capitol Area Internet Service (CAIS)

Area code(s):	202, 301, 410, 703
Voice phone:	703-448-4470
E-mail address:	`dalston@cais.com`
Services provided:	Shell, SLIP, PPP, ISDN, 56-T1

CCI Networks

Area code(s):	403
Voice phone:	403-450-6787
E-mail address:	`info@ccinet.ab.ca`
Services provided:	Shell, e-mail, Usenet, FTP, Telnet, Gopher, WAIS, WWW, IRC, Hytelnet, SLIP/PPP

CCnet Communications

Area code(s):	510
Voice phone:	510-988-0680
E-mail address:	`info@ccnet.com`
Dial-up number:	510-988-7140, log in as `guest`
Services provided:	Shell, SLIP/PPP, Telnet, e-mail, FTP, Usenet, IRC, WWW

CENTURION Technology, Inc.

Area code(s):	800, 813
Voice phone:	813-572-5556
E-mail address:	`jablow@cent.com`
Services provided:	Shell, PPP, 56, 128, T1

CERFnet

Area code(s):	619, 510, 415, 818, 714, 310, 800
Voice phone:	800-876-2373
E-mail address:	`sales@cerf.net`
Services provided:	Full range of Internet services

CICNet

Area code(s):	313, 708, 800
Voice phone:	800-947-4754 or 313-998-6703
E-mail address:	`info@cic.net`
Services provided:	SLIP, FTP, Telnet, Gopher, e-mail, Usenet

ClarkNet (Clark Internet Services, Inc.)

Area code(s):	410, 301, 202, 703
Voice phone:	800-735-2258, ask for extension 410-730-9764
E-mail address:	`info@clark.net`
Dial-up number:	301-596-1626, log in as `guest`, no password
Services provided:	Shell/optional menu, FTP, Gopher, Telnet, IRC, news, Mosaic, Lynx, MUD, SLIP/PPP/CSLIP, and much more

Cloud 9 Internet

Area code(s):	914
Voice phone:	914-682-0626
E-mail address:	`scottd@cloud9.net`
Services provided:	Shell, SLIP, PPP, ISDN, 56 and up

Cloudnet

Area code(s):	612
Voice phone:	612-240-8243
E-mail address:	`info@cloudnet.com`
Services provided:	Shell

CNS

Area code(s):	303, 719, 800
Voice phone:	800-748-1200
E-mail address:	`service@cscns.com`
Dial-up number:	719-520-1700, 303-758-2656
Services provided:	Shell/menu, e-mail, FTP, Telnet, all newsgroups, IRC, 4m, Gopher, WAIS, SLIP, and more

Colorado Internet Cooperative Association

Area code(s):	303
Voice phone:	303-443-3786
E-mail address:	`contact@coop.net`
Services provided:	SLIP, PPP, 56, T1, ISDN

Colorado SuperNet

Area code(s):	303, 719
Voice phone:	303-273-3471
E-mail address:	`info@csn.org` or `help@csn.org`
Services provided:	Shell, e-mail, Usenet news, Telnet, FTP, SLIP/PPP, and other Internet tools

Communications Accessibles Montreal, Inc.

Area code(s):	514
Voice phone:	514-931-0749
E-mail address:	`info@cam.org`
Dial-up number:	514-596-2255
Services provided:	Shell, FTP, Telnet, Gopher, WAIS, WWW, IRC, Hytelnet, SLIP/CSLIP/PPP, news

Community ConneXion

Area code(s):	510
Voice phone:	510-841-2014
E-mail address:	`info@c2.org`
Services provided:	Shell, SLIP/PPP

Connix: The Connecticut Internet Exchange

Area code(s):	203
Voice phone:	203-349-7059
E-mail address:	`office@connix.com`
Services provided:	Shell, SLIP, PPP, leased lines

Creative Data Consultants

Area code(s):	718, 212, 516
Voice phone:	718-229-0489 x23
E-mail address:	`info@silly.com`
Services provided:	Shell

CRL

Area code(s):	213, 310, 404, 415, 510, 602, 707, 800
Voice phone:	415-837-5300
E-mail address:	`support@crl.com`
Dial-up number:	415-705-6060, log in as `newuser`, no password

Services provided:	Shell, e-mail, Usenet, UUCP, FTP, Telnet, SLIP/PPP, and more

CSUnet (California State Unversity)

Area code(s):	All in California
Voice phone:	310-985-9445
E-mail address:	maryjane@csu.net
Services provided:	56, 128, 384, T1

CTS Network Services (CTSNet)

Area code(s):	619
Voice phone:	619-637-3737
E-mail address:	support@cts.com
Dial-up number:	619-637-3660
Services provided:	Shell, e-mail, Usenet, FTP, Telnet, Gopher, IRC, MUD, SLIP/PPP, and more

CyberGate

Area code(s):	305
Voice phone:	305-428-4283
E-mail address:	sales@gate.net
Services provided:	Shell, e-mail, Usenet, FTP, Telnet, Gopher, Lynx, IRC, SLIP/PPP

Cyberlink Communications

Area code(s):	206
Voice phone:	206-281-5397, 515-945-7000
E-mail address:	sales@cyberspace.com
Services provided:	Shell, SLIP, PPP

Cyberstore Systems Inc.

Area code(s):	604
Voice phone:	604-526-3373
E-mail address:	info@cyberstore.ca
Dial-up number:	604-526-3676, log in as guest
Services provided:	E-mail, Usenet, FTP, Telnet, Gopher, WAIS, WWW, IRC, SLIP/PPP

DASH - Denver Area Super Highway

Area code(s):	303
Voice phone:	800-624-8597, 303-674-9784
E-mail address:	info@dash.com, custserv@dash.com
Services provided:	Shell, SLIP, PPP, leased lines

DataFlux Systems Limited

Area code(s):	604
Voice phone:	604-744-4553
E-mail address:	info@dataflux.bc.ca
Services provided:	Shell, e-mail, Usenet, FTP, Telnet, Gopher, WAIS, WWW, IRC, SLIP/PPP

Datawave Network Services

Area code(s):	805
Voice phone:	805-730-7775
E-mail address:	sales@datawave.net
Services provided:	56

DFW Internet Services, Inc.

Area code(s):	214, 817
Voice phone:	817-332-5116
E-mail address:	sales@dfw.net
Services provided:	Shell, SLIP, PPP, 56-T1

DHM Information Management, Inc.

Area code(s): 213, 310, 714, 818
Voice phone: 310-214-3349
E-mail address: dharms@dhm.com
Services provided: LAN, PPP, SLIP, T1-56, Shell

DigiLink Network Services

Area code(s): 213, 310, 714, 818
Voice phone: 310-542-7421
E-mail address: info@digilink.net, bob@digilink.net
Services provided: ISDN, PPP

Digital Express Group (Digex)

Area code(s): 301, 410, 609, 703, 714, 908, 909
Voice phone: 800-969-9090
E-mail address: info@digex.net
Dial-up number: 301-220-0258, 410-605-2700, 609-348-6203, 703-281-7997, 714-261-5201, 908-937-9481, 909-222-2204, log in as new
Services provided: Shell, SLIP/PPP, e-mail, newsgroups, Telnet, FTP, IRC, Gopher, WAIS, and more

The Dorsai Embassy

Area code(s): 718, 212, 201, 203, 914, 516
Voice phone: 718-392-3667
E-mail address: system@dorsai.dorsai.org
Services provided: Shell, SLIP, PPP

Earthlink Network, Inc.

Area code(s): 213, 310, 818
Voice phone: 213-644-9500
E-mail address: info@earthlink.net
Services provided: Shell, SLIP, PPP, ISDN, 56, T1, DNS

Echo

Area code(s): 212, 718
Voice phone: 212-255-3839
E-mail address: info@echonyc.com
Dial-up number: 212-989-3382
Services provided: Conferencing, e-mail, shell, complete Internet access including Telnet, FTP, SLIP/PPP

Eden Matrix

Area code(s): 512
Voice phone: 512-478-9900
E-mail address: jch@eden.com
Services provided: Shell, SLIP, PPP, T1

Edge

Area code(s): 615
Voice phone: 615-455-9915 (Tullahoma), 615-726-8700 (Nashville)
E-mail address: info@edge.net
Services provided: Shell, SLIP, PPP, ISDN, 56

ElectriCiti Incorporated

Area code(s): 619, 408, 415, 510
Voice phone: 619-338-9000
E-mail address: info@electriciti.com
Services provided: SLIP, CSLIP, PPP

EriNet Online Communications

Area code(s): 513
Voice phone: 513-436-1700
E-mail address: info@erinet.com
Services provided: Shell, SLIP, PPP

Escape (Kazan Corp.)

Area code(s): 212, 718
Voice phone: 212-888-8780
E-mail address: info@escape.com
Services provided: Shell, SLIP, PPP, 56

Eskimo North

Area code(s): 206
Voice phone: 206-367-7457
E-mail address: nanook@eskimo.com
Services provided: Shell

ESNET Communications

Area code(s): 619
Voice phone: 619-287-5943
E-mail address: steve@cg57.esnet.com
Services provided: Shell

Evergreen Internet

Area code(s): 602, 702, 801
Voice phone: 602-230-9339
E-mail address: evergreen@libre.com
Services provided: Shell, FTP, Telnet, SLIP, PPP, others

Exchange Network Services, Inc.

Area code(s): 216
Voice phone: 216-261-4593
E-mail address: info@en.com
Services provided: Shell

Exec-PC BBS

Area code(s): 414
Voice phone: 800-EXECPC-1, 414-789-4200
E-mail address: info@earth.execpc.com
Services provided: Shell

FGInet, Inc.

Area code(s): 217
Voice phone: 217-544-2775
E-mail address: newuser@mail.fgi.net
Services provided: Shell, SLIP, PPP

FishNet (Prometheus Information Corp.)

Area code(s): 215, 610
Voice phone: 610-337-9994
E-mail address: info@pond.com
Services provided: Shell, SLIP, PPP

Florida Online

Area code(s): 407, 305, 904, 813
Voice phone: 407-635-8888
E-mail address: jerry@digital.net
Services provided: Shell, SLIP, PPP, ISDN, 56-T1

FredNet

Area code(s): 301
Voice phone: 301-698-2386
E-mail address: info@fred.net
Services provided: Shell, SLIP

Freelance Systems Programming

Area code(s): 513
Voice phone: 513-254-7246
E-mail address: fsp@dayton.fsp.com
Services provided: Shell, SLIP

Freeside Communications

Area code(s): 210, 512
Voice phone: 800-968-8750
E-mail address: sales@fc.net
Services provided: Shell, SLIP, PPP, ISDN, 56-T1

FullFeed Communications

Area code(s): 608, 414, 715
Voice phone: 608-246-4239
E-mail address: info@fullfeed.com
Services provided: Shell, PPP, 28.8, 56, 384, T1

FXnet

Area code(s): 800, 704, 803
Voice phone: 704-338-4670
E-mail address: info@fx.net
Services provided: Shell, SLIP, PPP, ISDN, 56, T1

Gateway to the World, Inc.

Area code(s): National/International
Voice phone: 305-670-2930
E-mail address: mjansen@gate.com
Services provided: Shell

Global Connect Inc.

Area code(s): National/International
Voice phone: 804-229-4484
E-mail address: info@gc.net
Services provided: SLIP, CSLIP, PPP, DNS

Global Vision, Inc.

Area code(s): 803
Voice phone: 803-241-0901
E-mail address: derdziak@globalvision.net
Services provided: Shell, SLIP, PPP, ISDN, 56-T1

Great Basin Internet Services

Area code(s): 702
Voice phone: 702-829-2244
E-mail address: info@greatbasin.com
Services provided: UUCP, SLIP, PPP

GSS Internet

Area code(s): 405, 918
Voice phone: 918-835-3655
E-mail address: info@galstar.com
Services provided: Shell, SLIP, PPP

Hawaii OnLine

Area code(s): 808
Voice phone: 808-246-1880, 808-533-6981
E-mail address: info@aloha.net
Services provided: Shell, SLIP, PPP, 56-T1, DNS, ISDN

Hevanet Communications

Area code(s): 503
Voice phone: 503-228-3520
E-mail address: info@hevanet.com
Services provided: Shell, SLIP, PPP, Telnet

HoloNet

Area code(s): 510, PSINet, Tymnet
Voice phone: 510-704-0160
E-mail address: support@holonet.net
Dial-up number: 510-704-1058
Services provided: Complete Internet access

Hookup Communication Corporation

Area code(s): 519, Canada-wide
Voice phone: 800-363-0400
E-mail address: info@hookup.net
Services provided: Shell, e-mail, Usenet, FTP, Telnet, Gopher, WAIS, WWW, IRC, Hytelnet, Archie, SLIP/PPP

I-2000

Area code(s): 203, 516, 718, 908, 914
Voice phone: 516-867-6379
E-mail address: mikef@i-2000.com
Services provided: SLIP, PPP

ICNet/Innovative Concepts

Area code(s): 313, 810, 616, 517, 906
Voice phone: 313-998-0090
E-mail address: info@ic.net
Services provided: Shell, SLIP, PPP, DNS, ISDN, 56K, T1

IDS World Network

Area code(s): 401, 305, 407, CompuServe Network
Voice phone: 401-885-6855
E-mail address: info@ids.net
Dial-up number: 401-884-9002
Services provided: Shell, FTP, Gopher, Telnet, Talk, Usenet news, SLIP

IgLou Internet Services

Area code(s): 502, 812, 606, 513
Voice phone: 800-436-IGLOU
E-mail address: info@iglou.com
Services provided: Shell, SLIP, PPP, ISDN

Illuminati Online

Area code(s): 512
Voice phone: 512-462-0999, 512-447-7866
E-mail address: admin@io.com
Services provided: Shell, SLIP, PPP, ISDN

Info-Highway International, Inc.

Area code(s): 409, 713
Voice phone: 713-447-7025, 800-256-1370
E-mail address: smcneely@infohwy.com
Services provided: Shell, SLIP, PPP

Ingress Communications, Inc.

Area code(s): 212, 718
Voice phone: 212-679-8592
E-mail address: info@ingress.com
Services provided: Shell, SLIP, PPP, 56-T1

Innovative Data (ID-Net)

Area code(s): 313, 810
Voice phone: 810-478-3554
E-mail address: info@id.net
Services provided: Shell, SLIP/CSLIP, PPP, 56-T1

INS Info Services

Area code(s): 800, 319, 402, 515, 712
Voice phone: 800-546-6587
E-mail address: service@ins.infonet.net
Services provided: Shell, SLIP, 56-T1

Institute for Global Communications (IGC)

Area code(s): 415
Voice phone: 415-442-0220
E-mail address: support@igc.apc.org
Dial-up number: 415-322-0284
Services provided: E-mail, Telnet, FTP, Gopher, Archie, Veronica, WAIS, SLIP/PPP

InterAccess Co.

Area code(s): 312, 708, 815
Voice phone: 800-967-1580
E-mail address: info@interaccess.com
Dial-up number: 708-671-0237
Services provided: Shell, FTP, Telnet, SLIP, PPP, and so on

Internet Access Company

Area code(s):	617, 508
Voice phone:	617-276-7200
E-mail address:	`info@tiac.net`
Services provided:	Shell, SLIP, PPP, ISDN, 56

Internet Alaska

Area code(s):	907
Voice phone:	907-562-4638
E-mail address:	`info@alaska.net`
Services provided:	Shell, 56-T1

Internet Atlanta

Area code:	National/International
Voice phone:	404-410-9000
E-mail address:	`info@atlanta.com`
Services provided:	UUCP, SLIP, PPP, ISDN, 56, T1

Internet Connect Services, Inc.

Area code(s):	409, 512, 713
Voice phone:	512-572-9987, 713-439-0949
E-mail address:	`staff@icsi.net`
Services provided:	Shell, SLIP, PPP, ISDN, 56-T1

Internet Connect, Inc.

Area code(s):	414
Voice phone:	414-476-ICON (4266)
E-mail address:	`info@inc.net`
Services provided:	Shell, SLIP, PPP, ISDN, 56-T1

Internet Connection

Area code(s):	408
Voice phone:	408-461-INET
E-mail address:	`sales@ico.net`
Services provided:	SLIP, PPP, ISDN, 56-T1

Internet Direct of Utah

Area code(s):	801
Voice phone:	801-578-0300
E-mail address:	`johnh@indirect.com`
Services provided:	Shell, SLIP, PPP, 56-T1

Internet Direct, Inc.

Area code(s):	602
Voice phone:	602-274-0100, 602-324-0100
E-mail address:	`sales@indirect.com`
Services provided:	Shell, SLIP, PPP

Internet Express

Area code(s):	719, 303, 505, 602, 800
Voice phone:	800-592-1240
E-mail address:	`service@usa.net`
Services provided:	Shell, SLIP, PPP, dedicated lines

Internet Nebraska Corp.

Area code(s):	402
Voice phone:	402-434-8680
E-mail address:	`info@inetnebr.com`
Services provided:	Shell, SLIP, PPP

Internet On-Ramp, Inc.

Area code(s):	509
Voice phone:	509-927-RAMP (7267), 509-927-7267
E-mail address:	`info@on-ramp.ior.com`
Services provided:	Shell, SLIP, CSLIP, PPP, leased lines

Internet Online Services

Area code(s):	201, 212, 518, 800
Voice phone:	800-221-3756
E-mail address:	`accounts@ios.com`
Services provided:	Shell, SLIP, PPP, leased lines, DNS

Internetworks

Area code(s): National/International
Voice phone: 503-233-4774
E-mail address: `info@i.net`
Services provided: SLIP, PPP, ISDN, leased lines

InterNex Information Services, Inc.

Area code(s): 415, 408, 510
Voice phone: 415-473-3060
E-mail address: `sales@internex.net`
Services provided: ISDN

Interpath

Area code(s): 919, 910, 704
Voice phone: 800-849-6305
E-mail address: `info@infopath.net`
Services provided: Full shell for UNIX, and SLIP and PPP

Interport Communications Corp.

Area code(s): 212, 718
Voice phone: 212-989-1128
E-mail address: `sales@interport.net`, `info@interport.net` (autoreply)
Services provided: Shell, SLIP, PPP, dedicated lines

interQuest inc.

Area code(s): 205
Voice phone: 205-464-8280
E-mail address: `paul@iquest.com`
Services provided: Shell, SLIP, PPP

intuitive information, inc.

Area code(s): 508
Voice phone: 508-342-1100
E-mail address: `info@iii.net`
Services provided: Shell, SLIP/CSLIP, PPP, 56

IQuest Network Services

Area code(s): 317
Voice phone: 317-259-5050, 800-844-UNIX
E-mail address: `info@iquest.net`
Services provided: Shell, SLIP, PPP, ISDN, 56, T1

KAIWAN Corporation

Area code(s): 714, 213, 310, 818, 909, 805
Voice phone: 714-638-2139
E-mail address: `sales@kaiwan.com`
Services provided: Shell, SLIP, PPP, 56, 256, 512, 768, T1

LI Net, Inc.

Area code(s): 516
Voice phone: 516-476-1168
E-mail address: `questions@li.net`
Services provided: Shell, SLIP, 56, T1

Lightside, Inc.

Area code(s): 818, 310, 714, 909
Voice phone: 818-858-9261
E-mail address: `lightside@lightside.com`
Services provided: Shell, SLIP, PPP, 56-T1

LineX Communications

Area code(s): 415
Voice phone: 415-455-1650
E-mail address: `info@linex.com`
Services provided: Shell

Long Island Information, Inc.

Area code(s): 516
Voice phone: 516-248-5381
E-mail address: `info@liii.com`
Services provided: Shell, SLIP

Maestro Technologies, Inc.

Area code(s): 212, 718, 516
Voice phone: 212-240-9600
E-mail address: staff@maestro.com, rlekhi@maestro.com
Services provided: Shell, SLIP, PPP

maine.net, Inc.

Area code(s): 207
Voice phone: 207-780-6381
E-mail address: atr@maine.net
Services provided: SLIP, PPP, 56, T1

MBnet

Area code(s): 204
Voice phone: 204-474-9590
E-mail address: info@mbnet.mb.ca
Dial-up number: 204-275-6132, log in as mbnet with password guest
Services provided: Shell, e-mail, Usenet, FTP, Telnet, Gopher, WAIS, WWW, IRC, Archie, Hytelnet, SLIP/PPP

MCSNet

Area code(s): 312, 708, 815
Voice phone: 312-248-8649
E-mail address: info@mcs.net
Services provided: Shell, SLIP, PPP, dedicated lines, ISDN

Metronet, Inc.

Area code(s): 214, 817
Voice phone: 214-705-2900, 817-543-8756
E-mail address: info@metronet.com
Services provided: Shell, SLIP, PPP

MichNet

Area code(s): 313, 616, 517, 810, 906
Voice phone: 313-764-9430
E-mail address: recruiting@merit.edu
Services provided: SLIP, PPP, host services, 56, T1

Millennium Communications

Area code(s): 507, 612
Voice phone: 507-282-8943, 612-338-5509
E-mail address: info@millcom.com
Services provided: Shell, SLIP, PPP

MindSpring Enterprises, Inc.

Area code(s): 404, 706
Voice phone: 404-888-0725
E-mail address: sales@mindspring.com
Services provided: Shell, SLIP, PPP

Minnesota MicroNet

Area code(s): 612
Voice phone: 612-681-8018
E-mail address: info@mm.com
Services provided: SLIP, SLIP, PPP

Minnesota Regional Network (MRNet)

Area code(s): 612, 507, 218
Voice phone: 612-342-2570
E-mail address: sales@mr.net
Services provided: SLIP, 56, T1

MIX Communications

Area code(s): 414
Voice phone: 414-228-0739
E-mail address: sales@mixcom.com
Services provided: BBS, SLIP, PPP

Msen, Inc.

Area code(s): 800, 313, 517, 616, 906
Voice phone: 313-998-4562
E-mail address: `info@msen.com`
Services provided: Shell, SLIP, PPP, ISDN, 56 to T1

MV Communications

Area code(s): 603
Voice phone: 603-429-2223
E-mail address: `info@mv.mv.com`
Services provided: Shell, SLIP, PPP, 56

Neighborhood Internet Connection

Area code(s): 201
Voice phone: 201-934-1445
E-mail address: `info@nic.com`, `combes@nic.com`
Services provided: Shell

NeoSoft, Inc.

Area code(s): 800, 713, 409, 214, 504, 314
Voice phone: 713-684-5969
E-mail address: `jmw3@neosoft.com`
Services provided: Shell, SLIP, PPP, ISDN, 56, T1

Netcom On-Line Communications Services

Area code(s): 206, 212, 214, 303, 310, 312, 404, 408, 415, 503, 510, 512, 617, 619, 703, 714, 818, 916
Voice phone: 800-501-8649
E-mail address: `info@netcom.com`
Dial-up number: 206-547-5992, 212-354-3870, 214-753-0045, 303-758-0101, 310-842-8835, 312-380-0340, 404-303-9765, 408-261-4700, 408-459-9851, 415-328-9940, 415-985-5650, 503-626-6833, 510-274-2900, 510-426-6610, 510-865-9004, 512-206-4950, 617-237-8600, 619-234-0524, 703-255-5951, 714-708-3800, 818-585-3400, 916-965-1371; log in as `guest`
Services provided: Shell, e-mail, Usenet, FTP, Telnet, Gopher, IRC, WAIS, SLIP/PPP

Network 23, Inc.

Area code(s): 212, 917
Voice phone: 212-786-4810
E-mail address: `info@net23.com`
Services provided: Shell

Network 99, Inc.

Area code(s): National/International
Voice phone: 702-442-7353, 602-780-7533, 800-NET-99IP
E-mail address: `net99@cluster.mcs.net`
Services provided: 56K-T3

Network Intensive

Area code(s): 714
Voice phone: 800-273-5600
E-mail address: `info@ni.net`
Services provided: Shell, SLIP, PPP, 56, ISDN, T1

Network Internet Services

Area code(s): 516
Voice phone: 516-543-0234
E-mail address: `info@netusa.net`
Services provided: Shell, SLIP, PPP

Network Link, Inc.

Area code(s): 619, 317
Voice phone: 619-278-5943
E-mail address: `stevef@tnl1.tnwl.com`
Services provided: Shell, NNTP, IDSN, 56, T1

New Jersey Computer Connection

Area code(s): 609
Voice phone: 609-896-2799
E-mail address: `info@pluto.njcc.com`
Services provided: Shell, SLIP, PPP

New Mexico Technet, Inc.

Area code(s): 505, 602, 303, 915, 800
Voice phone: 505-345-6555
E-mail address: `granoff@technet.nm.org`
Services provided: Shell, SLIP, PPP, leased lines

New York Net

Area code(s): 201, 203, 212, 516, 609, 718, 908, 914, 917
Voice phone: 718-776-6811
E-mail address: `sales@new-york.net`
Services provided: SLIP, PPP, 56, 64, 128 to T1

North Shore Access

Area code(s): 617
Voice phone: 617-593-3110
E-mail address: `info@shore.net`
Dial-up number: 617-593-4557, log in as `new`
Services provided: Shell, FTP, Telnet, Gopher, Archie, SLIP/PPP

Northcoast Internet

Area code(s): 707
Voice phone: 707-444-1913
Services provided: Shell, FTP, Telnet, Gopher, SLIP/PPP

NorthWest CommLink

Area code: 206
Voice phone: 206-336-0103
E-mail address: `gtyacke@nwcl.net`
Services provided: Shell, SLIP, PPP, 56-T1

Northwest Nexus, Inc.

Area code: 206
Voice phone: 206-455-3505
E-mail address: `info@nwnexus.wa.com`
Services provided: Shell, SLIP, PPP, 56, T1

NovaNet, Inc.

Area code(s): 703, 202, 301
Voice phone: 703-524-4800
E-mail address: `sales@novanet.com`
Services provided: Shell, SLIP, PPP, 56-T1

Nuance Network Services

Area code(s): 205
Voice phone: 205-533-4296
E-mail address: `info@nuance.com`
Services provided: Shell, Usenet, FTP, Telnet, Gopher, SLIP/PPP

NYSERNet

Area code(s): 212, 315, 516, 518, 607, 716, 718, 914

Voice phone:	315-453-2912
E-mail address:	`info@nysernet.org`
Services provided:	Shell, 56-T3

Nyx

Area code(s):	303
Voice phone:	303-871-3308
E-mail address:	`info@nyx.cs.du.edu`
Services provided:	Shell, semi-anonymous accounts

OARNet

Area code(s):	614
Voice phone:	800-627-8101
E-mail address:	`info@oar.net`
Services provided:	Shell, SLIP/PPP

Old Colorado City Communications

Area code(s):	719
Voice phone:	719-528-5849
E-mail address:	`thefox@oldcolo.com`
Services provided:	Shell, 56

Onramp Access, Inc.

Area code(s):	512
Voice phone:	512-322-9200
E-mail address:	`info@onr.com`
Services provided:	SLIP, PPP

Pacific Internet

Area code(s):	707
Voice phone:	707-468-1005
E-mail address:	`info@pacific.net`
Services provided:	Shell, SLIP, PPP, 56-T1

Pacific Rim Network, Inc.

Area code(s):	800, 206
Voice phone:	206-650-0442
E-mail address:	`sales@pacificrim.com`
Services provided:	Shell, SLIP, PPP, ISDN, 56-T1

Pacifier Computers

Area code(s):	206
Voice phone:	206-693-2116
E-mail address:	`sales@pacifier.com`
Services provided:	Shell, SLIP, PPP

PacketWorks, Inc.

Area code(s):	813
Voice phone:	813-446-8826
E-mail address:	`info@packet.net`
Services provided:	PPP, ISDN

Panix Public Access UNIX and Internet

Area code(s):	212, 516
Voice phone:	212-787-6160
E-mail address:	`info@panix.com`
Dial-up number:	212-787-3100, 516-626-7863, log in as `newuser`
Services provided:	Shell, Usenet, FTP, Telnet, Gopher, Archie, WWW, WAIS, SLIP/PPP

PCNet

Area code(s):	203
Voice phone:	800-66-4INET
E-mail address:	`sales@pcnet.com`
Services provided:	Shell, SLIP, PPP, ISDN, 56, T1

Phantom Access Technologies, Inc.

Area code(s):	212, 718, 516, 914
Voice phone:	212-989-2418
E-mail address:	`info@phantom.com`
Services provided:	Shell, SLIP, PPP, 56-T1

Ping

Area code(s): 404, 800 (includes Hawaii and Alaska)
Voice phone: 800-746-4835, 404-399-1670
E-mail address: `bdk@ping.com`
Services provided: Shell, SLIP, PPP, 56

Pioneer Global

Area code(s): 617
Voice phone: 617-375-0200
E-mail address: `sales@pn.com`
Services provided: Shell, 28.8, 56, T1

Pipeline Network

Area code(s): National/International
Voice phone: 212-267-3636
E-mail address: `staff@pipeline.com`
Services provided: Shell

Planet Access Networks

Area code(s): 201, 908, 319, 205
Voice phone: 201-691-4704
E-mail address: `fred@planet.net`
Services provided: Shell, SLIP, PPP, dedicated lines

Portal Communications Company

Area code(s): 408, SprintNet
Voice phone: 408-973-9111
E-mail address: `info@portal.com`
Services provided: Shell, e-mail, Usenet, FTP, Telnet, Gopher, IRC, SLIP/PPP

Primenet

Area code(s): 602, 213, 818
Voice phone: 602-870-1010, 800-4 NET FUN
E-mail address: `info@primenet.com`
Services provided: Shell, SLIP, PPP, 56, 128, T1

PSI

Area code(s): North America, Europe, and Pacific Basin; send e-mail to `numbers-info@psi.com` for list
Voice phone: 703-709-0300
E-mail address: `all-info@psi.com`
Services provided: Complete Internet services

QuakeNet

Area code(s): 415
Voice phone: 415-655-6607
E-mail address: `info@quake.net` (autoreply), `admin@quake.net` (human)
Services provided: SLIP, PPP, DNS, 56-T1

Rabbit Network, Inc.

Area code(s): 810, 800 (entire U.S. and Canada)
Voice phone: 800-456-0094
E-mail address: `info@rabbit.net`
Services provided: Shell, SLIP, PPP, leased lines

Real/Time Communications

Area code(s): 512
Voice phone: 512-451-0046
E-mail address: `info@realtime.net`
Services provided: Shell, SLIP, PPP, IDSN, custom services

Red River Net

Area code(s): 701, 218
Voice phone: 701-232-2227
E-mail address: `lien@rrnet.com`
Services provided: Shell, SLIP, 56, T1

Ripco Communications, Inc.

Area code(s): 312, 708
Voice phone: 312-665-0065
E-mail address: `info@ripco.com`
Services provided: Shell

Rocky Mountain Internet, Inc.

Area code(s): 303, 719
Voice phone: 800-900-RMII
E-mail address: `mountr@rmii.com`, `jimw@rmii.com`
Services provided: Shell, SLIP, PPP, 56, T1

Sacramento Network Access, Inc.

Area code(s): 800, 916, 209, 510, 702
Voice phone: 916-565-4500
E-mail address: `sales@sna.com`
Services provided: Shell, SLIP, PPP

SatelNET Communications

Area code(s): 305
Voice phone: 305-434-8738
E-mail address: `martinson@saTelnet.org`
Services provided: Shell, SLIP, PPP

Schunix

Area code(s): 508
Voice phone: 508-853-0258
E-mail address: `info@schunix.com`
Services provided: Shell, SLIP, PPP, ISDN, 56, 128, T1

Scruz-Net

Area code(s): 408, 415
Voice phone: 800-319-5555, 408-457-5050
E-mail address: `info@scruz.net`
Services provided: SLIP, PPP, ISDN, 56, T1

Sibylline, Inc.

Area code(s): 501
Voice phone: 501-521-4660
E-mail address: `info@sibylline.com`
Services provided: Shell, SLIP, PPP, 56, 128, T1, DNS, advertising

Sierra-Net

Area code(s): 702, 916
Voice phone: 702-832-6911
E-mail address: `info@sierra.net`
Services provided: Shell, SLIP, PPP, 56-T1

SIMS, Inc.

Area code(s): 803
Voice phone: 803-762-4956
E-mail address: `info@sims.net`
Services provided: Shell, SLIP, PPP, ISDN, 56, 128, 256

Skagit On-Line Services

Area code(s): 206
Voice phone: 206-755-0190
E-mail address: `info@sos.net`
Services provided: Shell, SLIP, PPP

SkyNET Corp.

Area code(s): 816, 913
Voice phone: 816-483-0002
E-mail address: `info@sky.net`
Services provided: Shell, SLIP, PPP, 56-T1

South Carolina SuperNet, Inc.

Area code(s): 803
Voice phone: 803-748-1207
E-mail address: `info@scsn.net`
Services provided: SLIP, PPP, 56, T1

South Coast Computing Services, Inc.

Area code(s): 800, 713, 918
Voice phone: 800-221-6478
E-mail address: `sales@sccsi.com`
Services provided: Shell, SLIP, PPP, 56, T1

South Valley Internet

Area code(s): 408
Voice phone: 408-683-4533
E-mail address: `info@garlic.com`
Services provided: Shell, SLIP, PPP, dedicated and leased lines

SouthWind Internet Access, Inc.

Area code(s): 316
Voice phone: 316-263-7963
E-mail address: `staff@southwind.net`
Services provided: Shell, TIA-SLIP

SSNet, Inc.

Area code(s): 610, 302
Voice phone: 302-378-1386
E-mail address: `info@ssnet.com`, `sharris@ssnet.com`
Services provided: Shell, SLIP, PPP UUCP

StarNet Communications, Inc. (Winternet)

Area code(s): 612
Voice phone: 612-941-9177
E-mail address: `info@winternet.com`
Services provided: Shell, SLIP, PPP

SymNet

Area code(s): 904
Voice phone: 904-385-1061
E-mail address: `info@symnet.net`
Services provided: Shell, SLIP, PPP

Teleport

Area code(s): 503, 206
Voice phone: 503-223-4245
E-mail address: `info@teleport.com`
Dial-up number: 503-220-1016
Services provided: Shell, e-mail, Usenet, FTP, Telnet, Gopher, SLIP/PPP

Teleport, Inc.

Area code(s): 503, 206
Voice phone: 503-223-0076
E-mail address: `sales@teleport.com`
Services provided: Shell, SLIP, PPP, ISDN

Telerama

Area code(s): 412
Voice phone: 412-481-3505
E-mail address: `sysop@telerama.lm.com`
Dial-up number: 412-481-4644
Services provided: Shell, e-mail, Telnet, Usenet, FTP, Gopher, IRC, SLIP/PPP

Texas Metronet

Area code: 214, 817
Voice phone: 214-705-2900
E-mail address: `info@metronet.com`
Dial-up number: 214-705-2901, 817-261-1127; log in as `info`, with password `info`
Services provided: Shell, e-mail, Usenet, FTP, Telnet, Gopher, IRC, SLIP/PPP

Tezcatlipoca, Inc.

Area code(s): 312, 708
Voice phone: 312-850-0181
E-mail address: `ilixi@tezcat.com`
Services provided: Shell, TIA

Townsend Communications, Inc.

Area code(s): 206
Voice phone: 206-385-0464
E-mail address: `inquiries@olympus.net`
Services provided: PPP, 56

Traveller Information Services

Area code(s): 204
Voice phone: 800-840-TNET, 204-883-2686
E-mail address: `info@traveller.com`
Services provided: Shell, CSLIP, PPP, ISDN

Tyrell Corp.

Area code(s): 816, 913, 504, 316
Voice phone: 800-TYRELL-1
E-mail address: `support@tyrell.net`
Services provided: Shell, SLIP/CSLIP, PPP

TZ-Link

Area code(s): 914
Voice phone: 914-353-5443
E-mail address: `drew@j51.com`
Services provided: Shell

UltraNet Communications, Inc.

Area code(s): 508
Voice phone: 508-229-8400, 800-763-8111
E-mail address: `info@ultranet.com`
Services provided: SLIP, PPP, ISDN, 56, 128, 384

US Net, Inc.

Area code(s): 301, 202, 703
Voice phone: 301-572-5926
E-mail address: `info@us.net`
Services provided: Shell, SLIP, PPP, DNS, 56-T1

UUNorth Incorporated

Area code(s): 416
Voice phone: 416-225-8649
E-mail address: `uunorth@north.net`
Dial-up number: 416-221-0200, log in as `new`
Services provided: E-mail, Usenet, FTP, Telnet, Gopher, WAIS, WWW, IRC, Archie, SLIP/PPP

VNet Internet Access, Inc.

Area code(s): 704, public data network
Voice phone: 800-377-3282
E-mail address: `info@vnet.net`
Dial-up number: 704-347-8839, log in as `new`
Services provided: Shell, e-mail, Usenet, FTP, Telnet, Gopher, IRC, SLIP/PPP, UUCP

VoiceNet/DCS

Area code(s): 800, 215
Voice phone: 215-674-9290
E-mail address: `info@voicenet.com`
Services provided: Shell, SLIP, PPP, ISDN

The Well

Area code(s): 415
Voice phone: 415-332-4335
E-mail address: `info@well.com`
Services provided: Shell

West Coast Online

Area code(s): 415, 510, 707, 408, 916, 209
Voice phone: 800-WCO INTERNET
E-mail address: info@calon.com
Services provided: Shell, SLIP, PPP, ISDN, 56-T1

WestNet

Area code(s): 914
Voice phone: 914-967-7816
E-mail address: staff@westnet.com
Services provided: Shell

Widomaker Communications

Area code(s): 804
Voice phone: 804-253-7621
E-mail address: bloyall@widomaker.com
Services provided: Shell, SLIP, PPP

Wilder Systems, Inc.

Area code(s): 617
Voice phone: 617-933-8810
E-mail address: info@id.wing.net
Services provided: Shell, pipeline, PPP, SLIP, ISDN, 56-T1

Wimsey Information Services

Area code(s): 604
Voice phone: 604-936-8649
E-mail address: admin@wimsey.com
Services provided: Shell, e-mail, Usenet, FTP, Telnet, Gopher, WAIS, WWW, IRC, Archie, SLIP/PPP

Wizvax Communications

Area code(s): 518
Voice phone: 518-271-6005
E-mail address: root@wizvax.com
Services provided: Shell, SLIP, CSLIP, PPP

WLN

Area code(s): 800, 206, 509, 503, 208, 406, 360
Voice phone: 800-DIAL-WLN, 800-342-5956, 206-923-4000
E-mail address: info@wln.com
Services provided: Shell, SLIP, PPP, 56-T1

The World

Area code(s): 617, 508
Voice phone: 617-739-0202
E-mail address: staff@world.std.com
Services provided: Shell, DNS

A World of Difference, Inc.

Area code(s): 803
Voice phone: 803-769-4488
E-mail address: info@awod.com
Services provided: Shell, PPP

WorldWide Access

Area code(s): 312, 708, 815, 414
Voice phone: 708-367-1870
E-mail address: support@wwa.com
Services provided: Shell, SLIP, PPP, ISDN, leased lines

Xensei Corporation

Area code(s): 617
Voice phone: 617-773-4785
E-mail address: sales@xensei.com, terri@xensei.com
Services provided: SLIP, PPP, ISDN, 56K

XMission

Area code(s):	801
Voice phone:	801-539-0852
E-mail address:	support@xmission.com
Services provided:	Shell, SLIP, PPP, leased lines

XNet Information Systems

Area code(s):	708
Voice phone:	708-983-6064
E-mail address:	info@xnet.com
Dial-up number:	708-983-6435, 708-882-1101
Services provided:	Shell, e-mail, Usenet, FTP, Telnet, Gopher, Archie, IRC, SLIP/PPP, UUCP

You Tools Corporation (FAST.NET)

Area code(s):	610, 215, 717
Voice phone:	610-954-5910
E-mail address:	internet@youtools.com
Services provided:	SLIP, PPP, ISDN, 56-T1

Zilker Internet Park

Area code(s):	512
Voice phone:	512-206-3850
E-mail address:	info@zilker.net
Services provided:	Shell, SLIP, PPP, ISDN

zNET

Area code(s):	408
Voice phone:	408-477-9638
E-mail address:	info@znet.com
Services provided:	SLIP, PPP, ISDN, DNS

Zone One Network Exchange (ZONE)

Area code(s):	800, 718, 212, 914, 516, 917, 201, 908
Voice phone:	718-549-8078
E-mail address:	info@zone.net
Services provided:	UUCP, SLIP, PPP, 56-T1

Australia

Following is a list of Australian Internet providers in alphabetical order by provider name.

Aarnet

Voice phone:	+61 6-249-3385
E-mail address:	aarnet@aarnet.edu.au

Connect.com.au P/L

Areas serviced:	Major Australian capital cities (2, 3, 6, 7, 8, 9)
Voice phone:	1 800 818 262 or +61 3 528 2239
E-mail address:	connect@connect.com.au
Services provided:	Shell, SLIP/PPP, UUCP

Bermuda

Following is the only known Internet provider in Bermuda.

Internet (Bermuda) Limited

Areas serviced:	Bermuda
Voice phone:	819-296-1800
E-mail address:	info@ibl.bm
Services provided:	Shell, SLIP/PPP, UUCP

Germany

Following is a list of German Internet providers in alphabetical order by provider name.

Contributed Software

Voice phone: +49 30-694-69-07
E-mail address: info@contrib.de
Dial-up number: +49 30-694-60-55, log in as guest or gast

Individual Network e.V.

Area serviced: All of Germany
Voice phone: +49 0441 9808556
E-mail address: info@individual.net
Dial-up number: 02238 15071, log in as info
Services provided: UUCP throughout Germany; FTP, SLIP, Telnet and other services in some major cities

Inter Networking System (INS)

Voice phone: +49 2305 356505
E-mail address: info@ins.net

Netherlands

Following is a list of Internet providers in the Netherlands, in alphabetical order by provider name.

Knoware

E-mail address: info@knoware.nl
Dial-up number: 030 896775

NetLand

Voice phone: 020 6943664
E-mail address: Info@netland.nl
Dial-up number: 020 6940350, log in as new or info

Simplex

E-mail address: simplex@simplex.nl
Dial-up number: 020 6653388, log in as new or info

New Zealand

Following is the only Internet provider in New Zealand.

Actrix

Voice phone: 04-389-6316
E-mail address: john@actrix.gen.nz

Switzerland

Following is the only known Swiss Internet provider.

SWITCH—Swiss Academic and Research Network

Voice phone: +41 1 268 1515
E-mail address: postmaster@switch.ch

United Kingdom

Following is a list of English, Scots, and Irish Internet providers in alphabetical order by provider name.

Almac

Voice phone: +44 0324-665371
E-mail address: alastair.mcintyre@almac.co.uk

Cix

Voice phone: +44 49 2641 961
E-mail address: cixadmin@cix.compulink.co.uk

Demon Internet Limited

Voice phone:	081-349-0063 (London) 031-552-0344 (Edinburgh)
E-mail address:	`internet@demon.net`
Services provided:	SLIP/PPP accounts

The Direct Connection (UK)

Voice phone:	+44 (0)81 317 0100
E-mail address:	`helpdesk@dircon.cu.uk`
Dial-up number:	+44 (0)81 317 2222

Note to Providers

If you would like to be included in future versions of this list, for use in subsequent editions of this book as well as other Sams.net books, send an e-mail message to Mark Taber at `mtaber@netcom.com`.

APPENDIX B

THE INTERNET FOR SYSTEM 6 USERS

If you're a System 6 user, the software included in this book—with the exception of NCSA Telnet and Fetch—will not work on your computer. It's no big deal; you just need to get hold of older software versions. The only bad news is that as a System 6 user you are denied the wonders of the World Wide Web. Macintosh Web browsers aren't compatible with System 6. If you really want Web access than you should check with your computer dealer about upgrading to System 7 or even better, System 7.5.

To retrieve the software listed here, use Fetch, included with this book to perform an FTP file transfer. (For an explanation of how to use FTP, see Chapter 12, "Collecting Files with FTP.") Make sure you get a copy of Stuffit Expander first so that you can decompress the other Internet client applications noted here.

Decompressor utility: Stuffit Expander 3.0.7
host: `ftp.une.edu.au`
directory: `/pub/NCSA/Mac/Utilities/`
file: StuffItExpander.3.0.7.hqx

Gopher client: TurboGopher 1.0.8
host: `boombox.micro.umn.edu`
directory: `/pub/gopher/Macintosh-TurboGopher/TurboGopher_1.0.8/`
file: TurboGopher1.0.8b4.hqx

Newsreader program: InterNews 1.0.8
host: `ftp.dartmouth.edu`
directory: `/pub/mac/`
file: InterNews_1.0.8.sea.hqx

Chat Program: Talk 1.1.1
host: `ftp.amug.org`
directory: `/pub/peterlewis`
file: talk-111.sit.bin

E-mail program: Eudora 1.3.1
host: `ftp.qualcomm.com`
directory: `/quest/eudora/mac/1.3`
file: eudora131.hqx

INDEX

Symbols

A

B

C

L

M

N

O–P

Q–R

T

Book ISBN 1-57521-04

WHAT'S ON THE DISC

The companion CD-ROM contains most of the various software programs and utilities referred to by the authors.

Software discussed by the authors, which is on the CD-ROM, includes:

- Anarchie
- Fetch
- MacPPP
- Stuffit Expander
- TurboGopher
- Eudora
- GlobalChat
- MacTCP
- Telnet

Bonus software on the CD-ROM includes:

- Finger
- FTPd
- InternetConfig
- Talk
- ObiWan
- Internews

Macintosh Installation Instructions:

1. Insert the CD-ROM disc into your CD-ROM drive.
2. When an icon for the CD appears on your desktop, access the disc by double-clicking on its icon.
3. Double-click on the icon named Guide to the CD-ROM and follow the directions that appear.

   Note: Some of the programs are self-installing and some may be installed by dragging their icons to your desktop.

sams net